WHY EUROPE?
PROBLEMS OF CULTURE AND IDENTITY

VOLUME 2: Media, Film, Gender, Youth and Education

From the same publishers

Joe Andrew, Malcolm Crook and Michael Waller (*editors*)
WHY EUROPE? PROBLEMS OF CULTURE AND IDENTITY
Volume 1: Political and Historical Dimensions

Why Europe? Problems of Culture and Identity

Volume 2: Media, Film, Gender, Youth and Education

Edited by

Joe Andrew
Professor of Russian
Keele University

Malcolm Crook
Professor of History
Keele University

Diana Holmes
Professor of French
Leeds University

and

Eva Kolinsky
Professor of Modern German Studies
Keele University

First published in Great Britain 2000 by
MACMILLAN PRESS LTD
Houndmills, Basingstoke, Hampshire RG21 6XS and London
Companies and representatives throughout the world

A catalogue record for this book is available from the British Library.

ISBN 0–333–72444–5

First published in the United States of America 2000 by
ST. MARTIN'S PRESS, INC.,
Scholarly and Reference Division,
175 Fifth Avenue, New York, N.Y. 10010

ISBN 0–312–22794–9

Library of Congress Cataloging-in-Publication Data
Why Europe? : problems of culture and identity / edited by Joe Andrew,
Malcolm Crook and Michael Waller.
p.   cm.
Based on papers presented at a conference held at Keele
University, Sept. 6–9, 1996.
Includes bibliographical references and index.
Contents: v. 1. Political and historical dimensions — v.
2. Media, film, gender, youth and education.
ISBN 0–312–22793–0 (v. 1 : cloth). — ISBN 0–312–22794–9 (v. 2 :
cloth).
1. Europe—Politics and government Congresses.   2. Nationalism–
–Europe Congresses.   3. Ethnicity—Europe Congresses.   I. Andrew,
Joe.   II. Crook, Malcolm, 1948–   .   III. Waller, Michael, 1934–   .
D217.W49   1999
940 — dc21   99–36945
                                                        CIP

This book is printed on paper suitable for recycling and made from fully managed and
sustained forest sources.

10   9   8   7   6   5   4   3   2   1
09   08   07   06   05   04   03   02   01   00

Printed and bound in Great Britain by Antony Rowe Ltd, Chippenham, Wiltshire

Contents

List of Tables

List of Figures

Acknowledgements

The chapters in this volume, like those in the companion volume, *Political and Historical Dimensions*, arise from a conference, 'Why Europe? Problems of Culture and Identity', which was held at Keele University, UK, from 6 to 9 September 1996. A number of individuals and organizations were instrumental in making that event a success, and I would like to take this opportunity to thank both them and those who have helped me with the preparations of this volume.

In particular, I wish to thank La Délégation Culturelle Française, the ESRC and the Goethe Institut; my fellow organizers and editors, Malcolm Crook, Diana Holmes, Eva Kolinsky and Michael Waller, as well as Pat Borsky, Joan Hope, Shirley Stubbs; and Angela Merryweather who has provided invaluable assistance in preparing this volume for publication.

JOE ANDREW

Notes on the Contributors

Gill Allwood is Senior Lecturer in French at Nottingham Trent University. Her publications include *French Feminisms: Gender and Violence in Contemporary Theory* (1998) and articles on masculinity and parity. She is currently working on women and politics in France.

Joe Andrew is Professor of Russian at Keele University, where he has worked since 1972. He has published four monographs with Macmillan on Russian literature and society, and women in Russian literature. He has also edited a number of works devoted to structural analysis and formalism. He is co-Chair of 'The Neo-Formalist Circle' as well as co-editor of its journal *Essays in Poetics*.

Susan Bassnett is Pro-Vice-Chancellor at the University of Warwick and Professor in the Centre for British and Comparative Cultural Studies. She has published over 20 books on comparative literature, translation studies, women's theatre history and British cultural studies. Her most recent books are *Constructing Cultures*, co-authored with André Lefevere (1998) and *Postcolonial Translation: Theory and Practice*, co-edited with Harish Trivedi (1999). She has translated novels, plays and poetry from several languages and is a regular contributor to the *Independent*.

Anna Bull is Professor in Italian Studies at the University of Bath. She has published widely on nineteenth- and twentieth-century history and politics and has just completed a forthcoming book, *Social Identities and Political Culture in Italy*. A jointly authored book on the Italian Northern League is currently in preparation for Macmillan. Also for Macmillan, she is jointly editing a volume on European feminisms and women's movements.

David Coulby is Dean of Faculty of Education and Human Sciences and Professor of Education Sciences at Bath Spa University College. He is joint series editor of *The World Year Book of Education*. He is co-author, with Crispin Jones, of *Postmodernity and European Education Systems* (1995). He is currently working on *Knowledge and Europe: Centralist Curricula and Cultural Diversity* to be published in 1999.

Malcolm Crook is Professor of History at Keele University. He has published *Toulon in War and Revolution, from the Ancien Régime to the Restoration, 1750–1820* (1991), *Elections in the French Revolution: an Apprenticeship in Democracy, 1789–1799* (1996) and *Napoleon Comes to*

Power: Democracy and Dictatorship in Revolutionary France, 1795–1804 (1998). He continues to work on the history of revolutionary and Napoleonic France, while preparing a study of electoral culture in nineteenth-century France.

Diana Holmes is Professor of French at Leeds University and teaches both French Studies and European Studies. Her publications on French women writers include *Colette* (1990) and *French Women's Writing 1848–1994* (1996), as well as articles and chapters on Colette, Rachilde and others. She is co-author of a study of the films of François Truffaut (1998) and is currently working on a study of Brigitte Bardot for a book on stardom, written in collaboration with French studies colleagues at Keele. She is also writing a book on the only woman writer of the French decadent movement, Rachilde.

Peter Humphreys is Reader in Government at Manchester University, where he has taught comparative West European politics since 1986. His principal research interest is comparative media policy. He is co-author of *New Media Policies in Western Europe* (1988), author of *Media and Media Policy in Germany* (1994) and author of *Mass Media and Media Policy in Western Europe* (1996). At the end of 1998 he completed a three-year ESRC-funded research project investigating the control of media concentration in Britain and Germany. Since 1988 he has been a Fellow of the European Institute for the Media (based in Düsseldorf, Germany).

Eva Kolinsky, D Phil, FRSA, is Professor of Modern German Studies at Keele University. She directs an international research group on post-communist social transformation and is currently undertaking a comparative study of minority cultures in Germany. Recent books include *Women in Contemporary Germany* (1993); *Women in Twentieth-Century Germany* (1995); *Between Hope and Fear: Everyday Life in Post-Unification East Germany* (ed., 1995); *Turkish Culture in German Society Today* (ed. with D. Horrocks, 1996); *Social Transformation and the Family in Post-Communist Germany* (ed., 1998) and *Companion to Modern German Culture* (ed. with W. Van der Will, 1999). She is editor of the *Culture and Society in Germany* book series for Berghahn and co-editor of *German Politics*.

Rosalind Marsh is Professor of Russian Studies at Bath University, and former Director of the Centre of Women's Studies at Bath. She is author of *Soviet Fiction since Stalin: Science, Politics and Literature* (1986), *Images of Dictatorship: Stalin in Literature* (1989), and *History and Literature in Contemporary Russia* (1995); the editor of *Women in Russia and Ukraine*

(1996), *Gender and Russian Literature: New Perspectives* (1996), and *Women in Russian Culture: Projections and Self-Perceptions* (1998); and has published articles on post-Stalin culture, Russian women and women writers. In 1997 she became President of the British Association for Slavonic and East European Studies.

Pamela Moores is Senior Lecturer in French and Director of Under-graduate Programmes in the School of Languages and European Studies at Aston University. She has researched on the nineteenth-century novelist, journalist and Communard, Jules Vallès, and on the contemporary French media. Her recent research and publications focus on regional and national newspapers, press agencies, media personalities in politics, media coverage of elections, and the street press.

Murray Pratt teaches in the Department of French Studies at Warwick University. He has published widely on AIDS writing in France, particularly on the works of Hervé Guibert, as well as articles on Roland Barthes and masculinity in Hollywood cinema. Together with Jean-Pierre Boulé, he edited a special issue of *French Cultural Studies* on AIDS in France (October 1998).

Keith Reader is Professor of French at the University of Newcastle. He is co-editor, with Alex Hughes, of the *Encyclopedia of Contemporary French Culture* (1998). He is currently working on Renoir and the French cinema set-designer Alexandre Trauner.

Graham Roberts graduated from Manchester University with a degree in French and Russian, and then completed a D Phil at New College, Oxford, on the Soviet literary avant-garde. He is currently Lecturer in Russian Studies at the University of Surrey, where he teaches a variety of courses on topics ranging from contemporary Russian cinema to post-communist Russian business culture. His current research interests include Russian and East European film, and French popular culture.

Alison Smith is Lecturer in French at Keele University. She has published a monograph on Agnès Varda, as well as several articles on French cinema of the 1960s and 1970s, in journals including *French Cultural Studies* and *Modern and Contemporary France*.

Chris Warne is Lecturer in French Studies at Sussex University. His research interests are broadly concerned with the evolution of popular culture in twentieth-century France, with a particular focus on generational conflict and social change. He has published various pieces on contemporary French youth culture, the most recent on the impact of world music in France in *Post-Colonial Cultures in France* (ed. Alec Hargreaves and Mark McKinney, 1997) and is working on a book on youth and society in post-war France.

Stephen Webber is Lecturer in International Security at the Centre for Russian and East European Studies, University of Birmingham. He was previously Research Associate at the University of Birmingham (Modern Languages Unit) and a teacher of English in a Birmingham secondary school. He is author of *School, Reform and Society in the New Russia* (1999), and a number of other publications on Russian education. He has also published *Trade Talks? Language Lessons for Commerce and Industry* (1997). He is also the Secretary of the Study Group on Education in Russia, the Independent States and Eastern Europe.

Introduction
Joe Andrew, Malcom Crook,
Diana Holmes and Eva Kolinsky

The chapters in this volume, like those in the companion volume, *Political and Historical Dimensions*, arise from a conference, 'Why Europe? Problems of Culture and Identity', which was held at Keele University, on 6–9 September 1996. While the scope of the conference, and of both volumes, was by no means limited by or to the European Union, it had as its impulse the Inter-Governmental Conference which took place in that year. Following on from Maastricht this event was envisaged as helping to determine the future direction, shape and size of Europe as a whole, and the European Union in particular.

The conference which was held at Keele adopted a distinctive approach to these issues. Concentrating on questions of history, origins, culture and citizenship, it sought to evaluate the extent to which a specifically European identity had begun to emerge, and what profile this identity was beginning to take. The conference, and this volume alongside its 'twin', addressed a range of issues which underlie the notions of European identity. Among them are: What does it mean to be a European? What ideologies have shaped the political debate over the last two centuries? What place will minorities find in the Europe of the twenty-first century? What roles will women play in the future communities? Will Europe become more open to diversity, or become increasingly introspective, a 'fortress Europe'?

The orientation of the conference was organized by the work of the Department of Modern Languages and the Keele European Research Centre, and focused primarily, but not exclusively, on cultural issues. So too does this volume, as the following sections will illustrate.

1 EUROPEAN FILM

In his discussion of the films of Kieślowski, Graham Roberts quotes the words of the radical British film-director Ken Loach who finds in Kieślowski's films a 'fluency and grace' that place him within 'the great European tradition of cinema'. The invocation of a 'European tradition' comes to seem strategically desirable at a period when European nations feel themselves to be increasingly invaded and colonized by the language, culture, cuisine and values of the USA, for the notion of a shared European identity, and of indigenous, discrete cultural traditions founded in a long, shared history, provide a legitimate basis for European cultural collaboration, hence for a more effective resistance to the perceived threat. One of the underlying reasons for the foundation of the European Union was the recognition that small nations stood little chance against the economic and political might of the great blocs, and the same argument can be applied to European cultural survival. In terms of cinema there is currently a strong sense of the need for European collaboration to resist the imperialist expansionism of Hollywood, as the 1993 GATT talks, and the EU Commission's Green Paper (April 1993) made clear.[1] But what does 'European cinema' mean? To what extent is it simply a collection of national cinemas, linked only by the broad geographical proximity of the nations in question, or alternatively (the boundaries of 'Europe' are notoriously fluid) by their shared membership of the European Union? Is the concept of European film useful at anything other than a strategic level? To what extent does contemporary European film draw upon a 'great tradition' that is specific to Europe, and what might that tradition be? And since European spectators, on the whole, show a marked preference at the box office for American-made films, is the European industry doomed to remain in the high culture but low popularity sector of art-house cinema?

The three essays in Part I address this cluster of questions, from different perspectives and with different emphases. Two of them (Keith Reader on Belgian cinema of the early 1990s, Alison Smith on French cinema in the wake of the 1993/4 GATT talks) deal with the issues from the perspective of a particular national cinema, the third (Graham Roberts on the 1990s films of Krzystof Kieślowski) through discussion of a single director working between different cultures.

1.1 National Identity and the Question of Audience

The primary audience envisaged by film-makers and producers is still in most cases a national audience, though increasingly an international market may also be intended, and hence need to be addressed by the film. Films directed at a national or domestic audience can play on a nation's self-perceptions, and on structures of feeling, habitual associations, assumptions and reference points that form part of what might be termed a national consciousness. Surprise at the recent international success of the English film *The Full Monty* (1997) arose in part from the fact that the film's humour appeared to depend on particular, localized conventions of male behaviour and identity and the complex negotiation of these in a post-industrial Northern English town: the ease with which these seem to have been recognized and identified across national cultures had not been foreseen (though account should perhaps also be taken of the pleasure of exoticism, of observing the unfamiliar). More commonly, films appeal in slightly different ways to primary and secondary audiences, negotiating in their representations of the national culture external preconceptions and stereotypes, and cultural differences that may limit comprehension. If European films are to transcend national market frontiers these have to be taken into account.

The Belgian French-speaking film industry commands a small national audience and almost of necessity looks towards a wider European – particularly French – market, also benefiting from the availability of both EU and French financial aid at the production stage. Belgium also presents an extreme case of that negative national stereotyping to which all countries are to some extent subject, for Belgium – the privileged target of French humour for centuries – is popularly associated with boredom, small-mindedness, chips, chocolate, and not a great deal else, and this despite the central role it has played in the whole post-war European project. Keith Reader analyses three generically very different films of the 1990s, all of which have had an impact outside as well as inside Belgium, and shows how each of the directors has worked 'with the grain' of the stereotype, deliberately drawing attention to perceptions of Belgium as a country with a cultural deficit. Strategies vary from the inflation of stereotypes through the use of Surrealist techniques (Surrealism is also part of the country's artistic heritage), to lampooning the perceived national qualities of cosiness, provincialism and thrift, to juxtaposing these with the portrayal of an antithetical but equally 'Belgian' counter-culture. Directed towards domestic spectators, self-ridicule works as a way of positing a shared lucidity, creating a separation between the implied audience of self-aware, cosmopolitan and Europeanized Belgians, and the narrow-minded, culturally challenged people of myth, joke and (some of the films imply) the director and spectator's own experience. Directed outwards, the very act of evoking and playing with the stereotypes bespeaks their transcendence: by putting the most negative perceptions of Belgian culture on the screen, these films demonstrate that such perceptions are partial and inadequate (though a rich source of comedy and satire). Recent Belgian cinema is thus a cinema about national identity, about the interplay between national self-perceptions and international constructions of the other. While films such as these do not achieve high levels of commercial success, they have proved financially viable and have found an audience that extends well beyond Belgium – all three of the films discussed, for example, are quite readily available in video form in the UK.

The French film industry is – or certainly believes itself to be – the most powerful of European national cinemas. Since the GATT negotiations, France has shown itself determined to rival the Americans, and Alison Smith examines the strategies adopted to maximize cinema audiences both at home and abroad. Pre-existing perceptions of national identity also play their part here, for France can capitalize on a well-established identification with high culture – a sort of desirable 'classiness' – and with beautiful landscapes: the heritage costume drama, drawing on both of these, has played an important role in the campaign. Alison Smith draws attention to the different selection of source text and of type of adaptation depending on whether the primary audience is perceived to be inside or outside France. The heritage films directed primarily at foreign markets have tended to be based on nineteenth-century versions of earlier history, thus on texts which have themselves mythified the past, and to favour free adaptation rather than respectful fidelity to the original. The films that have addressed the domestic market as a priority – for example, Claude Berri's 1993 version of Zola's *Germinal* – have been adaptations of (mainly nineteenth-century) novels set at the time of their writing, and have made a virtue of reproducing the original closely, on the assumption that spectators will be familiar with (and perhaps also loyal to) the text. The – somehow pleasing, if only partial – unpredictability of audiences is demonstrated by the successful exporting of the non-standard costume drama *La Reine Margot* (Chéreau, 1994), a disturbingly violent, aesthetically complex version of the Dumas novel set in sixteenth-century France, the self-reflexive sophistication of which might have seemed to make it an unlikely popular success.

National audiences also upset expectations in their selection, through the box office, of the French film that was to outsell the Hollywood block-busters of the 1990s. Although *Germinal* had been carefully tailored and marketed for the French market, it was a historical film of a very different kind that competed best with the Americans: a comedy with a large element of slapstick, the staple genre of domestic national markets. Box office returns showed that *Les Visiteurs* struck an immensely popular chord for the French, but its charm was far less apparent to other national audiences. With few exceptions, the huge popular successes of Europe (unlike those of the USA) seem to depend on particular national reference points and sensibilities, so that their popularity is non-exportable. Mean-while France also tried other strategies to win world markets, including the cross-over model whereby a French director shoots a film within the

Hollywood system, in a classic American genre, but retains elements of 'Frenchness' or 'Europeanness'. The obvious example here is Luc Besson, whose *Léon* (1994) and *The Fifth Element* (1997) were produced or co-produced by major American companies, but connote their French identity through choice of actors, through the maintenance of an outsider's perspective on American culture, and through the selective application to a popular genre of what one critic has called 'modernism lite' (see Nasta and Aubenas in Keith Reader's chapter), connoting the knowingness and artistic experimentalism associated with art-house film (itself often identified with Europe).

Kieślowski's representation of national identities is a very different one, focusing less on the specifics of the nation than on the broader relationship between Eastern and Western Europe, between the nations of the ex-Soviet bloc and those of the largely liberal and democratic West. Graham Roberts demonstrates the importance in his films of the theme of mutual perceptions: the East's investment of hope and idealism in the West, its construction of the West as the desired 'other', the antithesis of all the ex-Soviet societies feel they lack, then the disappointment with the imperfect reality. Because of the director's own biography the characters tend to be mainly Polish or French, but the emphasis remains a broader one. Polish characters living in France suffer from the ignorance or indifference of the French about their own language and culture, a sense of exclusion which is reversed when the Western (French) characters in turn visit Eastern Europe (Poland). Roberts argues that Kieślowski's most optimistic portrayal of human relations occurs in the film *Red*, where the significance of national and East/West identities is minimized by the film's predominant use of a 'neutral' location in Switzerland – outside the European Union, politically and economically non-aligned, and multilingual.

1.2 Language as European Theme

In Kieślowski's *White*, one of the *Three Colours* trilogy, the Polish hero's multi-layered sense of impotence during his residence in Paris focuses particularly on language and the disempowering, in this instance emasculating, effect of his inability to speak French. The question of language is crucial to European cinema, both in the very practical sense of gaining access to international markets, and in the political sense that the absence of a shared language is a distinct impediment to intercultural understanding, co-operation and tolerance.

The two levels of the problem shade into one another in a number of ways. The practical linguistic issue when a film is exported is the choice between dubbing or sub-titling: the former runs the risk of changing and distorting the original, reducing its capacity to reproduce a particular place and milieu, whereas the latter carries art-house connotations for most audiences (or at least Anglophone audiences) and may provide a disincentive to viewing that reduces commercial success. Both modes of translation involve a degree of adaptation of the original for the new target audience, but as Alison Smith points out in relation to the American sub-titling of the French film *La Haine*, excessive adaptation for the new audience can occult the cultural specificity of the world evoked and thus significantly alter meaning. A film dealing with the lives of second/third generation immigrant youth in the French *banlieues*, with its important sub-theme of the importance of Black American youth culture as one (but only one) point of reference, loses its precision when the English sub-titles virtually turn the characters into black rappers.

The dominance of Hollywood has produced the widespread belief that films made in any language other than English are 'foreign-language films', inherently limited in audience and non-commercial. Yet the acceptability of dubbed and sub-titled films to audiences is proved every day as US films gain 70–80 per cent of European audiences.[2] The relative commercial success in the UK of the French *Cyrano de Bergerac* (1991), a film for which the quality of sub-titling was taken seriously and entrusted to the English author Anthony Burgess, suggests that investment in high quality linguistic adaptations can work, economically as well as artistically. A 1992 British Screen Advisory Council report on 'The Challenge of Language in European Film' argued strongly for the viability of non-English language films in the international market-place, provided that the technical and artistic aspects of dubbing and sub-titling were addressed imaginatively:

> although in certain cases the *handling* of language can almost certainly damage a film's chances of commercial success, the choice of language alone need not be a barrier to reaching mass audiences.[3]

The problem of translation between languages and between cultures is addressed by each of these chapters, and is central to the future of European cinema.

1.3   Europe as Tradition, Europe as Ideal

European cinema still functions primarily as a set of national cinemas, though a preoccupation with national identities, with intercultural perceptions of identity and with linguistic difference connects many of the films discussed here and might in itself be characteristic of a 'European tradition'. The three chapters also suggest other ways in which some sense of or aspiration towards a shared European identity recurs across very different films of the 1990s. Intertextual references in Belgian, French and Polish/French films evoke what has become the canon of European cinema, the most widely used reference being to the French *Nouvelle Vague*, which signifies metonymically a whole European heritage of self-reflexive, politically literate and formally experimental cinema.

The danger of consistent allusion to the virtues of such a heritage lies in its possible complacency, in the promotion of a tradition founded in 'High', white (and largely male) culture to the exclusion of new, different and apparently less sophisticated cinematic voices. A 'fortress Europe' sense of shared tradition would risk excluding more recent Europeans, notably those from Europe's ex-colonies, and in some cases women directors: on the other hand, valuing that tradition for its inventiveness and contestatory credentials would work against exclusion and complacency. Several of the films discussed evoke the values of freedom, equality, fraternity associated with Europe's revolutionary tradition, most explicitly Kieślowski's trilogy *Three Colours* but also, through their condemnation of intolerance and social exclusion, films like *La Reine Margot* and *La Haine*. Given the qualities of his own films, Ken Loach's 'great European tradition' might also refer to films that engage and give pleasure to an audience without sacrificing political and moral responsibility.

2 MEDIA ISSUES

There is general agreement that the media play a vital role in shaping outlook and attitudes, not least as regards those 'imagined communities' with which identity is associated. Their precise impact is, of course, a matter of considerable debate. The effects of the recent explosion of international communications, from extra-terrestrial television to the world wide web, are especially problematic. Generally speaking, there has been 'less interest in the underlying organisational structures, patterns of ownership and control, and the institutional and political-cultural framework of media systems', than in their influence.[4] Yet as these fall increasingly under the sway of powerful technological and commercial forces, there is an urgent need to reappraise the key regulatory issues. Drawing upon British and German experience, Peter Humphreys begins to redress the balance in his chapter, which presents preliminary findings from a larger project on which he is currently engaged.

The old technology once justified public broadcasting monopolies, but recent developments in cable and satellite have expanded the frequencies and arguably removed the rationale for this type of control. Technological change fused with the free-market ideology that prevailed in the 1980s, and deregulation became the norm all over Europe. As a consequence, commercial objectives began to outweigh the cultural and social criteria that once predominated in this area; the media are now regarded as an industry like any other. The economic advantages to be derived from attracting footloose international broadcasters to locate their operations in Europe have acted as an additional inducement to the dismantling of regulatory powers.

According to neo-liberal theory, the hidden hand of the market will guarantee pluralism in the broadcasting media, thus diminishing any role for the state. In practice, however, there has been an increasing concentration of ownership and control, not least because of the vast costs that are involved and the ready access which the 'moguls' have to government circles. Moreover, in order to extract the maximum financial reward, the exploitation of these opportunities extends to other media, to produce a combination of press and broadcasting ownership which the authorities have hitherto resisted. A potential political and cultural threat has materialized as a result.[5] The visual media are central to the formation of public opinion which, in a democratic society, needs diversity to flourish in a healthy fashion. At the same time, narrow international audiences are being created, as opposed to the wider communities reached by national broadcasting.

The problem has been recognized and measures are now being taken to tackle it, but Humphreys is sceptical about the attempts to impose greater regulation in the 1990s, which he regards as more symbolic than real.[6] Nor is he over-sanguine when it comes to the European Union as a source of regulation to protect media pluralism. There remains an unwillingness to accept that the media require different treatment from other industries and the adoption of different criteria to govern competition. The power of the new technologies may be awesome, but the uses to which it is put can be controlled. While economic objectives remain at the top of the agenda in this field, however, it is hard to see how the process can be more effectively managed.

A similar threat of concentration is posed to the press by the empires of Murdoch or Kirch/Springer, which also embrace the broadcasting media. While newspapers have always attracted a good deal of academic research, comparative studies that range across national boundaries are few and far between. Pam Moores fills this gap with her analysis of the coverage in British and French dailies of two contentious issues that blew up in the summer of 1996 and have retained a high degree of topicality ever since: food and football. Press treatment of the BSE (Bovine Spongiform Encephalopathy) crisis, which prompted measures against the export of British beef to the continent, and *Euro 96*, the European Football Championship, which was held in England, offers an opportunity to compare and contrast attitudes towards Europe on either side of the Channel.

Since the European press is less homogeneous than television broadcasting, Moores' comparison of Britain and France is far from straightforward. The best selling newspapers in France are provincial rather than national (an interesting comment on the survival of regional sentiment in France).[7] The paper with the largest circulation is in fact *Ouest-France*, which sells twice as many copies as *Le Figaro* or *Le Monde*. The French do not have a popular press which replicates the British *Sun*, *Mirror* or *Daily Star*, the nearest equivalent being *Le Parisien*. Moreover, followers of sport in France have a dedicated daily paper, *L'Equipe*, so sports coverage does not feature as prominently in French national newspapers as it does in their British counterparts.

EU measures to counteract the spread of BSE (popularly known as 'mad cow disease') roused a good deal of British hostility towards the 'Brussels bureaucrats'. It also revived allegations that farming lobbies in Europe, especially in France, were seeking to inhibit competition from superior British products. The issue of beef touches a popular chord in both countries. In Britain it has long been a symbol of national strength and prosperity, while the French are apt to refer to the British as 'les Rosbifs' and are renowned for their culinary concerns. French farmers did take direct action to deter British imports, but press coverage in France showed considerable restraint. If there was alarmism in the French press, it lay in linking the scandal to the dubious methods of 'agribusiness' in general, rather than to the British in particular.

Nor did the French succumb unduly to what might be called 'mad fan disease' when it came to the finals of the European Football Championship. In the event England did not play France, which was also participating, and it was against Spanish and above all German opponents that British tabloid ire was directed. After losing to Germany in a penalty shoot-out, some English supporters attacked German-made cars in a display of mindless chauvinism reminiscent of the First World War. Popular journalists had completely missed the European 'goal' and ended up with an embarrassing 'own goal'. It was interesting to note the appearance of the flag of Saint George alongside the Union Jack in the stadiums where England played and this has now become commonplace. English nationalism is the real issue here and a comparison with the Scottish press, as well as the behaviour of Scottish fans, would surely prove instructive.

Two years later the BSE crisis had become rather less acute as a result of remedial action, but the incidence of 'mad fan disease' was inevitably stimulated by another international football competition, the 1998 World Cup held in France, with English (and Scottish) participation. English supporters were not unique in their bad behaviour, but the culpability of the popular press in the genesis of football-related disturbances was again raised. According to *The Guardian* (one of the British broadsheets), it was the arrival of a publicity bus for the *Sun*, dispensing plastic bowler hats bearing the cross of Saint George that sparked the doleful events off the field before England's match against Tunisia in Marseille.

However, during the World Cup competition of 1998 British newspapers showed much greater restraint than in 1996. Many footballers from the continent now appear regularly in English league sides, while North African or South American opposition is less conducive than that of Germany or Spain to stereotyping; proximity usually breeds greater contempt. The tabloids have always defended their distasteful coverage as harmless fun, but they do seem to tap a deeper vein of xenophobia, perhaps even a sense of insecurity that England's honour is at risk. It has been said that the English fight wars as if they were sporting fixtures, but the reverse is patently true. Perhaps, as one colleague facetiously suggested, the way to foster European rather than national sentiment is to have a continental football team playing in an intercontinental competition.

The chapters included in Part II offer complementary as well as contrasting perspectives on the press and broadcasting. They demonstrate that these major instruments of the mass media have a crucial role to play in the future development of Europe. Much of the British press, for example, is owned or edited by anti-Europeans and the question of adopting the Euro has already attracted a great deal of hostile publicity. The development of similar monopolies in broadcasting could make an even greater political impact, not to mention the social and cultural implications. Media pluralism has its drawbacks, and may work against the creation of a European identity, but it is surely preferable to an increasing concentration of power without responsibility.

3   GENDER AND IDENTITY

It was in the early 1970s that the women's and gay liberation movements erupted on to the public stage, across and beyond Europe, to challenge deeply rooted and powerfully defended definitions of both gender and sexuality. At this point, both movements tended to rest their arguments on a politics of identity: to be a woman, to be gay was the basis for solidarity, shared pride and militancy across classes, generations, nations and continents, just as previously women and gays of all classes and nationalities had suffered oppression and humiliation. Later came the gradual and sometimes painful recognition that within the categories 'woman' and gay' there was as much difference as there was sameness of identity, and that the notion of shared oppression was far from unproblematic. More recent gender theory has attempted to address differences of ethnicity, cultural origin, material situation and history, and to recognize the diverse ways in which masculinity/femininity and hetero/ homosexuality are lived and conceptualized within these parameters. Queer theory in particular has questioned any notion of essential identity and suggested that all gender and sexual positionings need to be read as constructed, performative and mobile rather than fixed. Politically, however, it remains important not to lose sight of the fact that whatever other factors affect their lives, however fluid and constructed their identities, women have long been and still are subjected to discrimination *as women*, and gay men and women *as gays*.

All three of the chapters in Part III deal with the specific ways in which gender and sexuality have been formed and envisioned within different societies. Gill Allwood shows how the effectiveness of French feminism as a political movement and a force for social change has been diminished through misrepresentation: misrepresentation from outside France, since Anglo-American feminists in particular have consistently limited their attention to a small group of writers whose highly theoretical, elegantly discursive work fits neatly with stereotypes of 'Frenchness', even though this work is scarcely even seen as feminist by French women themselves; misrepresented within France by being rapidly relegated to a 'movement of the 1970s', whose goals are assumed to be already won, so that the French can maintain the convenient fiction that problems between the sexes occur only in other countries. Susan Bassnett demonstrates that the demands and priorities of women's movements are shaped by specific as well as by shared histories, so that because under state Communism the women of Eastern Europe suffered very different forms of discrimination from those of their Western sisters, in the post-communist era they display an interest in those very manifestations of 'femininity' deemed oppressive by Western feminists. Murray Pratt's chapter examines the failure of the French state to respond effectively to the AIDS epidemic against the context of specifically French forms of homophobia. All three chapters point towards the conclusion that if productive dialogue is to take place, and political energies are to be mobilized across

Europe for the achievement of feminist and gay liberationist goals, then such differences and specificities will need to be acknowledged and explored.

From the outset, feminism has challenged and rethought traditional concepts of femininity, theorizing gender identity as social construction ('One is not born but *made* a woman' to paraphrase Simone de Beauvoir) and/or as an alternative way of being human that has been suppressed and silenced by masculine hegemony. In recent years attention has also begun to be focused on masculinity, a move that can at one level seem retrograde, since (feminists might feel) almost as soon as women carved out a small space for themselves in political and cultural thought, and in the academy, it was reinvaded by men claiming their right to share women's hard-won theoretical insights and 'room of their own'. Indeed Gill Allwood shows that in France the recent emphasis on men's dilemmas has been largely reactionary, as it belongs within a discourse of 'post-feminism' that claims women were too successful in their reversal of inequalities and that men are now suffering from a dis-enabling identity crisis. This sense of a need for women to compensate men for their loss of privilege fits well with the tendency of French culture to pride itself on its harmonious, though highly differentiated gender roles. However, the critical examination of masculine gender identity can also be seen as the logical outcome of feminist thinking: Susan Bassnett argues for the importance of reading masculinity too as constructed, historically and culturally relative and thus open to change. The achievement of a socially recognized 'masculine' identity has often been tightly imbricated with aggressive nationalism, emotional illiteracy and (in the case of France, as Murray Pratt demonstrates) a level of homophobia that makes gay men the repository for all that must be repressed and hated in oneself and that can (in the case of the AIDS virus and the inadequacy of state responses) be lethal. If one of the aims of feminism is to dissolve the rigid binary divisions that have cramped the lives of so many women, this has to involve the careful exploration of how masculinity is currently constituted in different cultural contexts, and of how it might be redefined.

The three chapters converge in their recognition of the importance of maintaining, together, a sense of the common interests and goals of feminism and of the gay movement, and close attention to specific national and cultural differences. A sense of identity rooted in an essentialist concept of nation, ethnicity, gender or sexuality is perhaps always dangerous; awareness of the complex ways in which our identities are formed does not preclude a strategic and emotional solidarity based on shared experience or situation. In seeking a positive answer to the question 'Why Europe?' for feminists or for gay activists, we will surely have to find what these authors variously designate as 'interconnectedness' and as 'holding on simultaneously to sameness and difference'.

4   WOMEN IN CONTEMPORARY EUROPEAN SOCIETIES

When Luise Otto-Peters founded the first women's journal in the German state of Saxony half-way through the nineteenth century, she challenged the social consensus of her time that women could and should be excluded from political participation and restricted in their rights of education or occupational choice.[8] Like Mary Wollstonecraft before her, she demanded citizenship rights for women and argued that their treatment as intellectually and socially inferior amounted to a denial of such rights.[9] As European societies were transformed by industrialization, women's movements emerged to challenge agendas of political and social exclusion. In the twentieth century, university education, the medical and legal professions, teaching and clerical employment gradually became accessible, although women's wages were lower than those paid to men and they were less likely to rise to senior or managerial positions. In most European countries, the First World War boosted women's access to an unprecedented range of employment opportunities, although many were dismissed as soon as men were again available for employment.

Yet, the mould had been broken. Women in Europe gained active and passive voting rights, rights of secondary and higher education, while the growth of office jobs and tertiarization generally broadened employment opportunities. After the Second World War, most European societies entered the post-war era with a commitment to treating women as equal citizens with unrestricted rights of social and political participation. It took much longer to recast the laws governing marriages, to grant women material and personal equity with their husbands inside a marriage and after divorce.

On the eve of the twenty-first century, European societies have been transformed from the situation in which legal and conventional barriers were still in place and the discourse on women's rights and equality first impacted on views and public policy. Today, women in European societies are equal before the law and social exclusion based on prejudice and gender stereotypes has been de-legitimized, although many social institutions embrace these strictures reluctantly and attitudes have been slow to adapt. At the micro-level of everyday practice, European societies continue to differ in their treatment of women as 'social citizens' and discrimination has by no means disappeared. At the macro-level of constitutional frameworks and policy intent, women's rights have, however, been endorsed and codified. Indeed, the Treaty of Rome, the founding document of the European Economic Community, linked equal rights for women to its overall aim of securing democracy in member countries. Enlargement of the European project to the European Union has not impinged on this commitment although as a theme, women's rights to equal treatment has been overshadowed by the agenda to create a single currency and extend economic integration to its political equivalent. Yet, since 1957, European Community and European Union directives on equal opportunities have advanced women's place in societies throughout Europe by cajoling national legislatures to curtail discriminatory practices and enable and permit women to benefit from the choices and opportunities modern society has to offer.

As post-war societies offered improved living standards to their citizenry, individuals benefited from improved access to educational and occupational mobility. Women were among those beneficiaries. As their life-course choices opened out, women developed a more astute sense of self than their mothers or grandmothers had, as well as the confidence to voice their expectations in public. Since the mid-1960s, the generations of the post-war era have transformed the discourse on women and their place in society. These young women had grown up to expect that their attainment could be translated into quality employment and career advancement only to find their expectations thwarted by glass ceilings, anti-female stereotypes or patterns of work organization which disadvantaged women generally and virtually excluded women with children.

The discrepancies between women's rights of participation in educational, occupational or personal avenues of their choice and access to these rights at an everyday level resulted in a feminist critique of established social and political processes. Women no longer evaluated their self-worth in terms of measurable advances and career gains but developed a sense of self-worth as women. The *New Women's Movement* recast the public discourse in contemporary European democracies as increasing numbers of qualified, confident and articulate women broke well-worn gender barriers in political and economic life. In a European setting, the strong representation of women in the *European Parliament* for instance encouraged women in member states to demand better access to their legislatures and force their party organizations to review their processes of candidate selection.[10] In the Federal Republic, most post-war governments included a token woman in ministerial office; since the early 1980s, however, the political discourse has shifted to women's equal representation at all levels of parliamentary and political life. Some political parties adopted special quotas to promote women, some regional governments consisted even solely or predominantly of women while anti-discrimination legislation has been discussed across the political spectrum and passed in some regions for public service and political appointments.

Women's motivations to fulfil their own potential and their expectations to succeed with their chosen life course frequently conflict with hidden obstacles such as prejudice, family obligations or traditional perceptions of women's role in society. While the legislative shift towards women's equality does not remove gender bias, it has served to ferment women's discontent with the open and clandestine agendas of exclusion. At the time of Luise Otto-Peters or Mary Wollstonecraft, social conventions and stigmatization coerced women from all social classes to limit their choices or risk ostracism. On the threshold of the twenty-first century, the strictures of social norms and the punitive force of convention may not have been eliminated but they have lost much of their sting. Society itself lacks the cohesion of settled social milieux and value systems emanating from them.[11] More than ever, individuals are in charge and free to choose their preferences and behaviour. Thus, the post-industrial democracies of today no longer offer predictable employment tracks for life as individuals are increasingly challenged to upgrade their skills, recast their employment biographies and move in and out of employment while earlier generations had taken life-time employment in the same job as everyday 'normality'. Today's society has become a risk society, demanding flexibility and adaptability from individuals. In return, however, risk society offers an unprecedented range of choices from working opportunities to personal lifestyles. Risk society links freedom with uncertainty. More than ever, it facilitates freedom of decision-making, of exercising choices and following personal agendas. The flip-side of individualization has been uncertainty as frameworks of accepted values and conventions have faded and no longer offer effective guidance. In this risk society, women are more at liberty than in the past to castigate the mismatch between codified women's rights and their actual opportunities, but face the new and all-pervading uncertainties that everyone's agenda may be dogged with uncertainty and experiences of individual exclusion. Since women had not closed the gender gap of socio-economic disadvantage and political under-representation before the transformation to a risk society had taken effect, they have remained particularly vulnerable to exclusion through low incomes, poverty, under-representation, harassment or violence.

The decline of traditional milieux and conventions also had a liberating effect for women. It enabled them to find their new and public voice. In this volume, Anna Bull's case study of electoral choices in Italy offers an incisive account of how women have been more ready than men to break away from established socio-political environments such as Christian Democracy or Communism. As main political parties fail to address issues that are perceived as salient by women, female voters look to other, smaller parties in order to effect change. Since expert opinion has tended to belittle the differences between male and female voting behaviour, the individuation of women's electoral preferences and their active use of the scope for choice have been underestimated. Women have found a voice of their own: not in the sense that they now vote for the same parties as men and gender differences cease to matter, but in the sense that increasing numbers opt for a political party because they expect it to address certain policy issues. Moreover, they perceive smaller parties as more responsive, innovative and citizen-friendly by comparison with larger ones with their unwieldy organizations and established power-brokers.

This new independence of women from established milieux and their political affiliations is a momentous change in European societies. Traditionally, women have tended to be more conservative, more closely bound by religious observance or more prone to abstain from voting than men. None of these assumptions still applies today. While there has been no common pace of change in European societies, women's electoral behaviour has changed in all of them. The Federal Republic of Germany is a good example of this change and its impact on policy-making generally. Until the mid-1960s, the conservative Christian Democratic Party secured a majority of women's vote in all age groups; indeed its dominance as the party of government between 1949 and 1965 was based on this 'women's bonus' and the inability of the rival Social Democratic Party to attract female voters in large enough numbers.[12] Once the post-war generation of women reached voting age, conventional party preferences or allegiances to established milieux no longer applied. These younger women expected that the equal rights promised in the constitution would be matched by equal opportunities in society. In the 1960s and 1970s, they perceived the SPD as the party most likely to advance this agenda of equality. While a majority of older women continued to prefer the Christian Democrats, women who were born after 1940 turned to the Social Democrats as the party that could improve women's place in society. Ten years on and after a decade in government, the SPD lost out to the Greens as the electoral choice of younger women. Although the SPD had introduced a 40 per cent women's quota for all political and party posts, it had done so only after prolonged pressures from its women's associations and without changing its organization or party culture. By contrast, the Greens had enabled women from the outset to hold prominent positions at the top levels of their parliamentary and political activity while its close links to the new women's movement recast the role and perception of women. While the SPD, and established politics generally, consented to include women in an essentially male hierarchy, the Greens developed new styles of organization and participation designed to allow social movements and individuals to retain their own priorities and policy styles. The association between the Greens and the women's movement and the party's commitment to 'basic democracy' appealed to women intent on setting their own agenda. Among younger female voters, support for the Greens has grown particularly rapidly.[13] None of the larger parties can be assured of the female vote. This uncertainty about the female vote has two important consequences. First, political parties ignore women's expectations of equal participation in society at their peril; second, smaller parties enjoy improved chances of gaining enough electoral support to matter politically and force a new diversity on the party system, on decision-making and ultimately on the polity.

Women's readiness to change electoral preferences in line with their changing priorities and perception of party competency is a powerful agent in today's Europe in making politics more responsive to the people. Since most women shun neo-fascist or similar parties, women's search for an effective political voice is not boosting the anti-democratic forces that have gained credence in some European countries in the wake of economic uncertainties, unemployment and disaffection with established politics. While women's new electoral choices also emanate from disaffection with established politics, they have tended to shift the overall policy agenda towards more democracy and in the direction of increased plurality and diversity. In the long term, women's new confidence in their political voice underpins the democratic project that is at the heart of Europe.

4.1 Women in the Other Europe

Before the collapse of Communism east of the Iron Curtain, women in this 'other Europe' lived in a different world. That world included constitutional pledges of equal right to work, equal pay and equal representation in politics. On paper at least, inequality was eliminated and women were treated as fully equal political and social citizens. Was this what August Bebel had predicted more than a century ago in his *Die Frau und der Sozialismus* (1878) when he argued that the destruction of capitalism and its replacement by a socialist order would abolish inequality and with it the 'women's question'?[14]

Reality took a different turn. Despite official pronouncements about equal treatment, women remained disadvantaged compared with men. Although compelled to work – the right to work was in reality a duty – few women rose to leadership positions, most were directed into inferior career tracks and pay averaged one-third less that of men at all levels of seniority and in all occupational categories. In politics, quotas assured that women were represented at the levels deemed relevant by the state. Since political representation did not entail political decision-making but was restricted to an acclamation of state policy, the function of such representation does not compare with that in Western democracy. The virtual exclusion of women from leadership positions extended into politics and was evident in the governments and party leaderships of socialist Europe.

While the promise of equality remained unmet behind the Iron Curtain, in some key areas of daily living women seemed to enjoy a 'modernity bonus' compared with their Western peers.[15] Most obtained educational and vocational qualifications and engaged in full-time employment for the duration of their adult lives between leaving school and retirement. Despite their employment integration, nine out of ten women in all age cohorts had children. For women in Eastern Europe, combining employment and family commitments constituted a normal dimension of their life. Drawing on state-funded institutions to assist with child-care and a plethora of child-related benefits, women saw themselves as working mothers while women's policy was essentially mothers' policy without the focus on equal opportunities that has underpinned agendas for action in the West. Thus, Eastern European states had removed the conflict between employment and family commitments for women by removing the element of choice: women were not free to opt for an existence as a housewife, partly because citizenship was defined through employment and partly because wages were too low to sustain a family on one income alone. Despite the pay discrimination mentioned earlier, women contributed about 40 per cent to household incomes in Eastern European societies; in Western European societies, women's contributions to household incomes amount to 20 per cent on average.

The collapse of Communism removed the state-directed employment integration for all and the state-funded provisions and benefits for mothers. The privatization of the economy privatized the labour market and made unemployment the flip-side of system transformation. In the new economic climate, women were more vulnerable than men. Many were employed in technically outdated and globally uncompetitive industries and found their chances blocked. Women with children faced immediate disadvantages since combining employment with family duties had been privatized alongside the economy. In particular, the demise of state controls revealed that decades of socialist administration had not erased gender stereotypes and discrimination.

Before the collapse of Communism women's inequality had been hidden; now it came out in the open and women were treated as second class citizens. They were the first to lose their jobs and found it more difficult than men to re-enter the labour market. In Eastern Germany, where the system transfer from Western Germany instituted a generous scheme of labour market measures to ease unemployment, women tried to respond to the new challenges by retraining and recasting their employment biography but could only postpone, not escape from, labour market exclusion. Elsewhere in Eastern Europe, women have been exposed more directly to the harsh realities of post-communist life. Deprived of their employment and without the material shelter provided by the German welfare state, women in the former Soviet Union, for instance, have been driven back into the domestic sphere and forced to care for their families in conditions of extreme financial hardship.

The threat of social exclusion through unemployment entails a threat of poverty for women generally in post-Communist societies. This threat has been particularly poignant for women with children, i.e. the majority of women who reached adulthood before the Iron Curtain fell. It had women recast their biography. A massive drop in the birth rate since the collapse of Communism points to women's determination to respond to the new uncertainties by postponing childbirth and reducing family commitments. In Eastern Germany, women hope to secure their careers before having children; in the former Soviet Union, the links between employment prospects and family size are less clear and women respond to the scale of material deprivation they have encountered in an era which should have opened choices and created new opportunities.

One of the surprise discoveries after the end of state socialism has been the perseverance of traditional gender roles and perceptions of women's roles. In the GDR, the discrepancy between women's full employment integration and perceptions about their place in everyday life had manifested itself in the uneven distribution of domestic chores and the delegation of household and child-care tasks to women. Increasingly, however, East German women expected a fairer and more equitable distribution of duties in their daily lives; many even opted for divorce to extend the personal and material independence they had found through employment into their private lives. Living alone seemed to open more choices than living in a partnership constrained by role models which were out of step with women's expectations and sense of self.

In the former Soviet Union, the mismatch between women's state-administered employment integration and their treatment in the private sphere has been even more compelling. The chapter by Rosalind Marsh in this volume reveals the extent to which husbands or partners inflicted violence on women, while rape was widespread enough to constitute a major threat. The demise of socialist state doctrines and controls allowed anti-feminist traits to come into public view. Although they had existed before, public discourse had ignored them and made it appear as if all was well. The emergence of a public sphere with more freedom and less state dominance has revealed a depressing picture for women as excluded from employment, exposed to coping with material deprivation and poverty in their efforts to care for their families and children and subject in addition to discriminatory and even violent behaviour towards them on the part of men.

The advent of risk society has brought former socialist societies closer to the Western model. Here, risk has entailed uncertainties and dislocation but also held the promise of choice and personal avenues of mobility and advancement. As conventional milieux and established patterns of daily living become frayed, individuals have gained a new centrality in shaping their lives. In the risk societies of the Western type, however, the advent of individualization has been supported by a welfare safety net. While at least one in five adults in these societies has experienced unemployment in the last five years, most have been able to re-enter the labour market after an interim period of uncertainty and were cushioned from poverty by unemployment pay and other benefits. In the post-Communist environments, the advent of risk society empowered the individual but destroyed the cushion of welfare socialism. While the transformation towards a risk society should have replaced state dominance by choice, it resulted for many, and for women with children in particular, in unemployment and a mere struggle for physical survival. Without a shield against social exclusion, choices become meaningless while the negative impact of risk becomes all-pervading.

If the European project of democracy, rights of equal treatment and scope for personal choices succeeds, civil societies in Europe West and East should converge, obliterate gender barriers and advance the case of women. Freedom of choice will be one of the core tenets of such a society. Anna Bull's study of Italy documents how women have used their freedom of choice in the political arena. The special case of Eastern Germany with its protective mantle of welfare state and system provisions from the West, shows a blend of exclusion and personal determination among women to master the challenges of the risk society. No European society is free from the injustices suffered by women in the former Soviet Union which Rosalind Marsh describes in her chapter but in the European Union and its member countries, legislative frameworks and public discourse have at least moved on to de-legitimize sexist and discriminatory practices. Although social conditions in the former Soviet Union and other post-Communist countries are still dominated by economic dislocation and the fear of unemployment, the regime collapse created at least the formal pre-conditions for a more humane civil society where women's rights could translate without infringement into social opportunities, lifestyle choices and personal agendas.

5   YOUTH AND EDUCATION

The transnational diffusion of images, music, advertising and stories, the ubiquity of English as the language of popular culture, the ease and low cost of international travel, the increase in exchanges between educational institutions – these phenomena of the late twentieth century have produced, at least superficially, considerable homogenization of youth style and culture across Europe. The chapters in Part V in some senses confirm and in others contest the sense that European young people have enough in common to be viewed – and to view themselves – as a group. The most striking common feature of their experience is perhaps the instability of what were once stable reference points in the construction of a sense of identity. Contemporary Europe has suddenly become something of the kaleidoscope: frontiers shift, nations break apart (the USSR, Yugoslavia, Czechoslovakia) and merge or form close attachments (Germany, the EU itself); meanwhile traditional social configurations lose their contours, as the cultural signifiers and boundaries of class identity weaken, and in many countries the relationship between nationality and ethnicity is shaken up to form more varied and complex patterns. Most young people in Europe find themselves negotiating a sense of who they are within this protean setting, and many of them do so in nations undergoing radical political change, and a consequent crisis of identity that inevitably affects the educational system. It is not so much that young Europeans share a sense of European identity, as that they share the – at best exciting, at worst desolating – complexity of developing viable identities in societies that are themselves confused, in transition, uncertain of their values and allegiances.

David Coulby emphasizes the real – if sometimes overstated – importance of the educational process in the formation of the sense of identity of each generation, and finds that the opposing trends towards, on the one hand, unity and, on the other, fracture characterize both recent European history and the educational process within European states. Attempts

by the European Union to foster a sense of European identity through
a convergence of school curricula may be positively viewed as a counter-
influence to the divisive nationalism implicit in most national curricula.
However, Coulby finds that the EU's initiatives tend to conflate 'Europe'
with the EU itself, and hence to reproduce a 'Western European triumphalism' that has its roots in the Enlightenment and fails to take proper
account of the complexities of a post-imperialist, post-Cold War age.
'Europeanism' can be seen as a new form of nationalism – complacent,
protectionist and exclusionary – and for this reason resistance to the push
for a common European curriculum is to be welcomed. For example, the
apparent tendency for English to become the second language for the
entire continent is resisted within many countries (for example Finland)
who find it more important to maintain local languages alongside the official state language (or languages). Despite widespread state control of
school curricula, Coulby locates some tendency towards local control
of the curriculum (Spain, Russia), and sees in this a healthy counter-force
to the centralized control of education at national or European level. Here
the tendency towards fracture constitutes a corrective to the dangers of
imposed unity, and serves to protect cultural diversity.

Chris Warne shares David Coulby's suspicion of attempts to construct a
sense of pan-European identity that would support economic and political
integration, finding that they tend to be based on a nostalgically imagined
community of 'old Europe' and to occult the whole experience of colonialism and its consequences. At the same time, opposition to European integration can be based on the most reactionary of premises namely, in the
case of the *Front national*, the belief that the nation must assert its traditional, mono-cultural identity against both the external threat of federalism
and the internal threat posed by ethnic and cultural diversity. This chapter
identifies a possible way forward, out of the deadlock of a choice between
nationalism or a narrowly defined Europeanism, in certain elements of
contemporary youth culture which have developed largely outside the
main commercial circuits. Here the cases explored are French, but the
implication is that comparable instances may well be discovered elsewhere.
Three music 'scenes', based in different French cities, are discussed and
shown to share significant features: they draw on, mix and 'sample' the
most diverse cultural traditions, from the music of the black diaspora to
ancient regional cultures (such as that of Catalonia), developing new
'transnational mythologies'; they ally these with new musical technologies
which can be relatively easily learnt, thus creating an egalitarian and par-
ticipatory rather than 'star and audience' mode of performance; they
attract both young people of the ethnic majority who are alienated from

traditional forms of political, class and national allegiance, and those whose ethnic origins produce a sense of double exclusion. These new cultural forms, localized and relatively small scale as they are, acknowledge and deploy the multi-cultural, post-colonial reality of contemporary Europe. They celebrate rather than resist the fact that European frontiers – those of geography, politics and the imagination – are neither fixed nor closed, and that European identity is subject to influences and affinities that extend well beyond continental borders.

Both Coulby and Warne identify deficits in the model of national identity presented to young people through the political and educational systems, and see the development of local or generational counter-cultures as important correctives. Stephen Webber's essay deals with the problem of a society in crisis as it attempts to radically overhaul its educational system, without (as yet) a clear sense of its own collective values. The educational priorities of the Russian government have been to banish as much as possible of the Soviet past and to move towards a more Western, liberal and pluralist model, but Webber shows that this will to radical change has tended to increase inequality, and to exclude many children from school altogether. Here again, the inadequacies of state policy and vision have been to some extent counteracted at local level, in this case by the pragmatism and commitment of teachers' organizations. Webber's conclusion, that there is an urgent need for a wide-ranging, open debate on the goals and methods of the educational process, and its relation to society's values, is applicable not only to Russia but also to Europe as a whole.

NOTES

1. See Finney, A., *The State of European Cinema: a New Dose of Reality* (London and New York, Cassell, 1996), pp. 1–15.
2. Finney, p. 2.
3. Quoted in Finney, p. 105.
4. Humphreys, P., *Media and Media Policy in Germany: the Press and Broadcasting since 1945* (2nd edn, Oxford, Oxford University Press, 1994), p. xii.
5. Curran, J. and Seaton, J., *Power Without Responsibility: the Press and Broadcasting in Britain* (4th edn, London, Routledge, 1991), pp. 234–46.
6. Tunstall, J. and Palmer, M., *Media Moguls* (London, Routledge, 1991), p. 206.
7. Kuhn, R., *The Media in France* (London, Routledge, 1995), pp. 25–32.
8. Luise Otto-Peters published her 'Frauenzeitung' in Leipzig, 1849–50 until a regional law banned women from editing journals. For details

see Gerhard, U., 'Über die Anfänge der Frauenbewegung um 1848', in Hausen, K. (ed.), *Frauen suchen ihre Geschichte* (Munich, Beck), pp. 200–24 and Frevert, U., *Women in German History* (Oxford, Berg, 1990).

9. Coltman Brown, I., 'Mary Wollstonecraft and the French Revolution or Feminism and the Rights of Men', in Reynolds, S. (ed.), *Women, State and Revolution* (Brighton, Harvester Wheatsheaf, 1986), pp. 1–22.

10. See Vallance, E. and Davies, E., *Women of Europe. Women MEPs and Equality Policy* (Cambridge, Cambridge University Press, 1986) and Lovenduski, J. and Norris, P., *Gender and Party Politics* (London, Sage, 1993).

11. Beck, U., *Risiko Gesellschaft. Auf dem Weg in eine andere Moderne* (Frankfurt/ Main, Suhrkamp, 1986); published in English translation as *Risk Society* (Basingstoke, Macmillan, 1990); see also Hradil, S., *Sozialstrukturanalyse* (Opladen, Leske and Budrich, 1987).

12. See Kolinsky, E., *Women in Contemporary Germany* (Oxford, Berg, 1993).

13. See Kolinsky, E., 'Women and the 1994 Federal Election', in Dalton, R. (ed.), *Germans Divided: the 1994 Bundestag Elections and the Evolution of the German Party System* (Oxford, Berg, 1996), pp. 265–92.

14. August Bebel's *Die Frau und der Sozialismus* was first published in 1878; reprinted Berlin, Colloquium, 1969.

15. Geissler, R., *Die Sozialstruktur Deutschlands. Ein Studienbuch zur Entwicklung im geteilten und vereinten Deutschland* (Opladen, Westdeutscher Verlag, 1996: 2nd edn).

Part I
Film

1 Belgian Film Comedy and National Identity

Keith Reader

The *Observer*, one of Britain's most highly regarded Sunday newspapers, recently published (12 May 1996, p. 3) a profile of the Belgian neo-Situationist writer and film-maker Jan Bucquoy, who was referred to in the table of contents as 'that rare thing: an interesting Belgian'. Not only that: appended to the profile was a short piece beginning 'Belgium's contribution to European culture? Chocolate and beer, of course', and challenging its readers to name five famous Belgians (ibid., p. 34). I can think of no other European nation – Switzerland being too seriously rich to constitute an exception – whose identity could be thought, even jocosely, to be so rooted in the tedious and the trivial. The *Observer*'s list of celebrated Belgians seems to reinforce this view. The artists – Rubens, Van Eyck, Breughel – are generally described as 'Flemish', since Belgium did not exist as an independent nation in their time, and the more recent figures would tend to be regarded as insufficiently serious (Georges Simenon, Jean-Claude van Damme), not 'really' Belgian (Django Reinhardt whose Gypsy ethnicity dominates perceptions of him, César Franck whose musical career was based in Paris) or both (Audrey Hepburn who was born in Brussels of Irish and Dutch parents and worked first in Britain, then in Hollywood). Perhaps the most obvious exception – unmistakably Belgian (one of the largest collections of his work is situated in Brussels), and more and more widely classed as a major artist – is the painter René Magritte, whose dry brand of surrealism has won attention from figures as different as Michel Foucault and George Melly.

Surrealism, in a loose and not particularly dry sense of the term, is an important common denominator in the three French-language Belgian comedies I shall be considering in this chapter. These are, in the chronological order in which I shall treat them, *Toto le héros*, by Jaco van Dormael (1991); *C'est arrivé près de chez vous* (titled in English, for reasons I shall explain, *Man Bites Dog*), co-directed by Remy Belvaux, André Bonzel and Benoît Poelvoorde (1992); and *La Vie sexuelle des Belges* (1994), by the aforementioned Jan Bucquoy. The rapid arrival in British cinemas of these three films, after a long period during which Belgian cinema had been represented only by sporadic works from such directors as Chantal Akerman, Gérard Corbiau and André Delvaux, stimulated my curiosity about what might constitute a 'Belgian national cinema', and how that might interact with the social and cultural determinants of 'Belgian national identity'. Overwhelmingly dominant among these latter, of course, is the country's linguistic, and until 1830 political, division. For Philippe Dubois (Dubois and Arnoldy, 1995, p. 91), Belgium is 'a country divided to the point of hysteria' – a cleavage rooted in and exacerbated by the linguistic divide between Flemish and Walloons. Since 1963 this division has been institutionalized in the form of separate culture ministries for the two languages and separate, though supposedly equal, subsidy structures for their film industries (set up in 1964 for 'Flanders', in 1967 for Wallonia). The Flemish industry's visibility, domestic and international, has obviously suffered from its small size and linguistic isolation, as well as from the frequent antagonism between the two communities, to such an extent that Jan Vanderheyden's highly successful Flemish comedies of the 1930s were never screened in French-speaking Belgium. The similarly small size of the Walloon industry caused it, certainly before the system of subsidies was introduced, to lose numerous film-makers and performers to France, as well as engendering a parochialism that led one unnamed critic to berate it for 'giving a grotesque image of the Belgian, through burlesque farces for the mentally retarded', and to lament that 'we must give foreigners the impression of being the most imbecilic race on earth' (Dubois and Arnoldy, 1995, p. 29).

Belgium's small size has posed problems for the reception as well as the production of its culture(s). Francophone courses and options are becoming increasingly common on French degrees in Britain, but these mostly deal with French-speaking Africa or Quebec. To lump Belgium in with countries so far removed from it, under the general rubric of 'Francophonie', would clearly be inappropriate, yet it is too small to have been felt hitherto to merit courses of its own, so that its literature and cinema have been all but ignored by British students of French. The recent establishment of a Centre for Belgian Studies at the University of Edinburgh may represent the beginnings of a change in this neglected status, but at the moment, in academic terms at least, Belgium's independence might well appear a cultural curse as well as a blessing.

There exists, however, a contrary view to this – one that espouses a variant of the 'small is beautiful' thesis and praises Walloon cinema for its quirkiness and independence as manifested in the work of such as Henri Storck or Charles Dekeukelaire. Dubois and Arnoldy (1995, p. 28) say that the Walloon industry 'is at its best and most authentic not in rivalry with large-scale foreign productions, but in unusual, one-off experimentation'.

My lack of first-hand knowledge of this cinema means that I am not well placed to comment on this observation. The phrase 'unusual, one-off experimentation' seems to me, however, to apply with particular force to *C'est arrivé près de chez vous* and *La Vie sexuelle des Belges*, much as it does to the home-grown surrealism of Magritte or the unmistakable guitar style of Django Reinhardt. Something like a Walloon cultural specificity might seem to be figured here.

Toto le héros is in a sense the odd film out, more easily identifiable within a recent art-house cinematic tendency described by David Bordwell (1994, p. 33) as '*modernisme léger/modernism lite*', and including the work of such as Jane Campion and Léos Carax. This, for Bordwell (1994, p. 39), is situated 'half-way between Hollywood and Europe'; Toto's entirely Belgian setting and use of French stars Michel Bouquet and Mireille Perrier might seem to place it firmly as a European film (*Cahiers du cinéma* [1992, p. 92] refers to 'Toto l'Euro'), as might its funding not only from the French Centre National de Cinématographie, but also from the European Script Fund and the EC's MEDIA initiative. Yet Bucquoy's view (*Observer*, 1996, p. 34) is that 'it doesn't really say anything about Belgium', and Bordwell points out that it has the classic Hollywood three-act structure and (albeit posthumous) happy ending. Its intertextual references are also divided between Europe and America. Toto's cremation and the scattering of his ashes at the end echo Catherine/Jeanne Moreau's frustrated ambition at the end of Truffaut's *Jules et Jim* – a film about, among other things, national identities and the role they play, for better and for worse, in the complex and conflictual destiny of Europe. Hollywood asserts itself in the posthumous voice-over that accompanies this sequence – a clear homage to Billy Wilder's *Sunset Boulevard* – and the shot of the white rose and the shattered glass dome in Albert's Xanadu-like mansion shortly before, evoking Welles's *Citizen Kane*. The film's family romance structure (Thomas/Toto believes that he was inadvertently exchanged for Albert soon after birth) calls to mind not only Freud, but Etienne Chatiliez's *La Vie est un long fleuve tranquille*, an enormous popular success in France three years before *Toto*.

In what ways, given this multiplicity of European and American influences, can *Toto* be regarded as a specifically Belgian film? One answer is suggested in van Dormael's own statement (1994, p. 72) that 'Belgium is such a normal country that it is impossible not to be subject to bouts of madness' – Bouquet's mousy, moustachioed little man with his grandiose dreams of revenge might then stand for underrated and culturally colonized Belgium itself, the more so as he vaguely suggests Michel Blanc's eponymous *Monsieur Hire* (Patrice Leconte, 1989), a French film based on a

Belgian novel by Simenon. The family romance of the film would then take on a broader dimension, the nationality of its star implicitly usurping that of its central character in a scenario of wish-fulfilment whereby the neglected Belgian protagonist can imagine himself to have been 'really' French all along. Bordwell (1994, p. 33) nicely positions van Dormael's film where I think it belongs, between the transnational European art cinema represented by such as Leconte and something more specifically Belgian, in saying that:

> It would be equally possible to interpret the film as a distillation of the clichés of Belgian culture ('This is the story of a fellow to whom nothing ever happened ...'), or as the portrait of a Europe of the future, anonymous and antiseptic.

Belgium, on this reading, acts as a synecdoche for a sceptic's-eye view of Europe, an assemblage of cultures which seemingly do little but reinforce one another's insipidity. Van Dormael's second feature, *Le Huitième Jour/The Eighth Day* of 1996, has Daniel Auteuil, one of France's leading stars, as the stressed-out salesman Harry who gives a lift to a young man with Downs Syndrome. The young man (Georges) is played by Pascal Duquenne, a Bruxellois who has the condition himself. That, and the fact that in the film's final sequence he commits suicide – as Chris Darke (1996, p. 49) puts it in *Sight and Sound*, 'dying so that Harry may live an emotionally richer life' – suggest an almost vampiric relationship between French and Walloon culture which the film's determinedly sugary tone, alas, works to undercut. Whether seen as 'free-standing' or as one ingredient among others in the impending fin-de-siècle Europudding, French-speaking Belgium at any rate seems for Van Dormael to lead a sadly constricted existence.

C'est arrivé près de chez vous – winner of three Cannes prizes – is a much more unambiguously 'Belgian' work, made with EC financial help by three recent film-school graduates who also act in it. The film's title – literally, 'it happened near where you live' – is borrowed from the section of the Belgian newspaper *Le Soir* that deals with minor local items of news – in French parlance the '*rubrique des chiens écrasés*' or 'column with news of dogs run over' (*Cahiers du cinéma*, 1992, p. 63). That suggests one possible explanation for the English-language title *Man Bites Dog*, an allusion to the journalistic adage that if a dog bites a man that is not news but if a man bites a dog it is. There is also an intertextual echo of Tarantino's then recently released *Reservoir Dogs* (referred to in *The Guardian* review quoted on the British video cover), and much of the attention the film attracted on its release focused on the extreme violence of its subject matter. It tells of a camera crew who follow a serial killer about his grisly business in a small Belgian town, becoming increasingly implicated in his activities. The murders (there is also a rape) involve shooting, garrotting, battering and in one case literally frightening to death, and there are running gags concerning the amount of ballast that is required to make a body sink and the notorious, and never resolved, *'petit Gregory'* case of a small boy's murder in Eastern France. Ben, the killer, and his documentary accomplices are all themselves killed in a shooting at the end, but any sense of belated justice is likely to be undermined by the apparently undeserved murder of Ben's mother and his girl-friend Valerie, posthumously sodomized respectively with the handle of her broom and the flute she loved to play. Neither domestic nor artistic virtue is respected here. *C'est arrivé près de chez vous* now seems gruesomely premonitory of the paedophile killings whose revelation has recently rocked the Belgian state.

The film is shot in monochrome, which reduces the impact of the literal bloodshed; but its enthusiastic tastelessness and the evident complicity of the camera in Ben's misdeeds were often perceived, notably by *Le Monde*, as shocking and unjustifiable. The camera crew's role is well summed up by B. Ruby Rich (McNeil, 1993, p. 29) when she describes *C'est arrivé près de chez vous* as 'the ultimate film-school revenge film: you thought I was bad, well, take *this*' – a remark one can imagine being made by the derided Belgian film and culture industries to their more aristocratic detractors in France and elsewhere. Debate around the film's violence somewhat overshadowed its specifically Belgian qualities, but it seems to me in many ways difficult to separate the two. Benoît Poelvoorde indeed says as much in a mocking interview with Jean-Claude van Damme in the French film magazine *Première* (1996, p. 104), in which van Damme speaks of himself as being more readily accepted in France than in his native country and describes (the) Belgians as 'wonderful but self-destructive people. For a country of nine million people to have one fellow like me who is a worldwide success is abnormal.'

The sheer absurdity of the narrative premise is perhaps thrown into relief by this remark; is Ben Mr Hyde to van Damme's Dr Jekyll, the international superstar's nightmarishly provincial monochrome underside? This view may be intensified by the film's setting in a small provincial town – doubtless a synecdoche for Belgium – in which Ben's parents (the parents too of the real-life actor) keep a grocery shop. The anachronistic cosiness of Belgian provincial life is the obverse or counterpart of Ben's savagery, his warm relationship with his parents a grotesque parody of the vicious killer who, from James Cagney in Raoul Walsh's *White Heat* through to the Kray twins in real life and in Peter Medak's *The Krays*, has always been a good son to his mother. The film was read by Frédéric Strauss as a parody of an early Belgian television reality show (*Strip Tease*), but its antecedents in Belgian popular culture go back much further than that, to the film comedies of Gaston Schoukens and Jan Vanderheyden. These I have had no opportunity to see, but Schoukens's work has been likened (Michelem, 1990, p. 143) to that oxymoronic-sounding entity a Brussels Pagnol, and in a career that spanned more than twenty years he was the acknowledged master of the *zwanze* or Belgian joke, evidenced in his often-quoted remark that 'I don't sell art, I sell sausages'. Clashes of accents and culture, as in *Mon père et mon papa* of 1937, starring Jules Berry and Gaston Libeau whose benign tubbiness made of him 'the exemplary figure of the "Brusselaire" in the cinema' (Dubois and Arnoldy, 1995, p. 51) are important in Schoukens's work, and echoed in the broad accent of *C'est arrivé près de chez vous*'s Ben contrasted with the more refined tones of the camera crew. Schoukens, like Belvaux, Poelvoorde and Bonzel, also worked on a low budget and produced humorous – even facetious – treatments of serious subjects, as with the Brussels Resistance in *Un soir de joie* of 1954. Patrick Leboutte (1990, p. 18), in *Une Encyclopédie des cinémas de Belgique*, speaks, in reference to the populist tradition to which Schoukens belongs, of how:

> much dancing goes on in the Belgian cinema... as well as much drinking, eating, gambling and marching to the sound of a brass band... Belgium is basically nothing but a bizarre assembly of groups and tribes. Territory is cause at once for dispute and for celebration. Is conviviality perhaps its only kind of citizenship?

Such conviviality, in *C'est arrivé près de chez vous*, is hideously lampooned, notably in the scene where Ben prevails upon the camera crew to join him at the seaside for the Belgian national dish par excellence, *moules-frites* (mussels and chips). So much alcohol is consumed at this meal that Ben, like Barry Humphries's Australian innocent abroad Barry McKenzie, finishes by vomiting into his plate, overindulgence in a national stereotype leading to its quite literal rejection. If Oliver Stone in *Natural Born Killers* reworks the iconography of the chase or road movie to interrogate the role of the media in the propagation of violence, the three co-directors of *C'est arrivé près de chez vous* seem to me to do much the same with a far less central and well-known tradition, and to infinitely more telling effect. The film is studded with allusions to the demise of the old 'people's Brussels', as when Ben comments scathingly on the 'unaesthetic' new social housing that is being built for elderly people or a friend of his complains that she has been forced out of the Sablon area (a rough Brussels equivalent of Montmartre) by property developers. Belgian surrealism, as in the poems Ben periodically declaims or the references to Magritte, is also an important sub-text, so that I would take issue with Camille Nevers (1992, p. 88) when she asserts that the film's 'public space' is that of the 'world of images' rather than that of any particular society. *C'est arrivé près de chez vous* draws, precisely, on a world of images that are indissociable from the national iconographies and identities it puts into play.

Jan Bucquoy, director of *La Vie sexuelle des Belges*, came to filmmaking with an already considerable reputation as a national counter-cultural icon. Founder of the now, alas, defunct Museum of Underpants and author of *La Vie secrète d'Hergé*, an exposé of the far-Right past of the country's doyen of the strip cartoon, Bucquoy was also once sentenced to serve a prison term for decapitating a bust of King Baudoin in Brussels' Grand Place. Given the length of Baudoin's reign and his importance as a symbol of national, and profoundly Catholic, unity, this seemingly mild act of subversion was much more seditious for a Belgian public than it might appear – certainly far more so than any conceivable British act of *lèse-majesté*. We shall see that Baudoin is treated irreverently in Bucquoy's film too.

The title of *La Vie sexuelle des Belges* might well be understood – certainly by a French audience, for whom the Belgians have been the butt of coarse jokes from time immemorial – as an oxymoron. To be sure, the central character's experiences are anything but titillating, including as they do mutual masturbation with a slightly older boy whilst watching Laurel and Hardy films in a seaside caravan, a would-be copulation on a bathroom floor interrupted by the girl's indignant mother, fellation with a prostitute whose ill-fitting false teeth inadvertently draw blood and the morose blowing up of a rubber inflatable woman. Yet he is able, through the diegesis of the film, to fulfil the primal scene fantasy in its purest form by watching, and indeed staging, the moment of his own conception. This takes place under the sign of Gambrinus, the deity of beer, of which both mother and father consume copious amounts before the duly distended and wind-punctuated act.

The other archetypal Belgian foodstuff, chips, make an appearance shortly before the rubber inflatable scene, when Jan is seen buying a cornet of them from one of the vans seemingly omnipresent in Belgian towns and villages. One of Schoukens's early comedies, dating from 1935 and starring Gaston Libeau, was indeed entitled *Le Roi des pommes de terre frites/The King of Fried Potatoes*. Beer, chips, grotesquely joyless sex – the film seems dangerously complicit with the lumbering national stereotypes so beloved of the French. These, however, feature mainly in the provincial episodes, set in Jan's home town of Harelbeek and in the windy seaside resort of Blankenberghe. When Jan migrates to Brussels, the tone and milieu become much more sophisticated; he frequents Marxist-Leninists, has a lover who reads Guy Debord's Situationist classic *La Société du spectacle/The Society of the Spectacle* in bed, fleetingly becomes a vegetarian, and still more fleetingly cohabits with a Lacanian met through a lonely hearts advertisement. I would argue that Brussels in this film – the only one of the three under discussion in which it figures – is constructed as an amalgam of Paris and Amsterdam. Paris is evoked by the allusions to Godard with which the Brussels sections are replete – a wall-poster of *Tout va bien*, scenes shot in the style of *La Chinoise* which is the film he watches on the first date with his soon-to-be ex-wife, a monologue at his typewriter reminiscent of Raymond Devos in *Pierrot le fou* – and more generally by the immense cultural gap between the capital city and the provinces. The 'Dolle Mol' pub Jan assiduously frequents, on the other hand, is reminiscent of an Amsterdam 'brown bar' rather than of a Latin Quarter café, and the anarcho-libertarian lifestyle of its denizens suggests the Amsterdam of the Provos rather than the more ideologically tense Paris of Maoist-Trotskyist rivalries.

This is an attractive Brussels indeed, nourished by the hedonism and iconographic slapstick of the spirit of 1968 yet not riven with its sectarian dialectical conflicts – a worthy capital of a counter-cultural rather than of an 'official' or bureaucratic Europe. The pompous utterances of the writer Pierre Mertens, interviewed on the radio by a former flame of Jan's whom Mertens subsequently marries, suggest by contrast the vapidity of established Belgian culture. Here again, Bucquoy's references are multiple, for Mertens is played by the notorious Belgian practical joker Noël Godin, nicknamed *l'entarteur* because of his fondness for assaulting with custard pies those whose pretentiousness offends him. One recent victim, at the Cannes Film Festival, was Godard, whose first feature, *A bout de souffle*, contains a press conference sequence in which the young American journalist Patricia Franchini (Jean Seberg) interviews the novelist Parvulesco (played by Jean-Pierre Melville, often regarded as the founding father of the French New Wave). Parvulesco's attitudinizing verbosity clearly foreshadows that of Mertens, so that the later film's interview sequence and inclusion of an actor well known in his own right outside the world of the film can be seen as at once a tribute to Godard and a debunking of him along with the high culture of which he is now seen as forming part.

Ambivalent but on the whole appealing Brussels may be: the provinces, on the other hand, represented metonymically by Harelbeek, are seen as uniformly benighted and stultifying. Royalty is worshipped, as we see when Jan's would-be girl-friend Christine gives him a picture book of the Baudoin/Fabiola wedding after showing him her genitals. The implied conjugal transaction does not, alas, take place, for shortly afterwards she leaves for the Congo with her parents – a reminder that Belgium, notwithstanding its small size, was once an African colonial power. The dance to which Jan goes features a combo if possible worse than Kaurismåki's 'Leningrad Cowboys' murdering Buddy Holly songs – in May 1968! – and his family is obsessed with economy. '*Pas cher*'/'inexpensive' are the infant Jan's first words, the cheapest possible headstone is chosen for his father's burial, and when he introduces his fiancée to his mother her words of welcome are: '*Se marier, ça coûte cher*'/'Getting married costs money'. I find it difficult to think of a recent French film, with the possible exception of *La Vie est un long fleuve tranquille*, that depicts provincial life in so consistently a vicious a light.

Bucquoy has made a follow-up feature to *La Vie sexuelle des Belges*, entitled *Camping Cosmos*, which at the time of writing I have not had the opportunity to see. It seems unlikely that the *C'est arrivé près de chez vous* triumvirate will work together again, though Rémy Belvaux's brother, Lucas, has directed an extremely funny comedy film, *Pour rire*, whose structure, modelled on boulevard theatre farce, and use of non-Belgian stars (Jean-Pierre Léaud and Ornella Muti) largely undercut its specifically Belgian dimension. To proffer any kind of conclusion would thus be premature, except to say that the three films between them seem to me to have challenged the widespread derisory image of Belgian life and culture by working with the grain of that derision, and thus in some degree turning it against itself. Belvaux/Poelvoorde/Bonzel and Bucquoy in particular have shown themselves capable of producing the best, most sustained and most vitriolic 'Belgian jokes' on the market, lampooning the shortcomings of Walloon culture by drawing on a populist and surrealist heritage – from Schoekens to Magritte – inherent to it. This is a space I for one shall watch with great interest.

REFERENCES

Bordwell, D., 'Toto le moderne: la narration du cinéma européen d'après 1970', in Nasta, D. and Aubenas, J. (eds), *Toto le héros: itinéraires d'une première oeuvre* (*Revue Belge du Cinéma*, Special Number, 36–7, April 1994), pp. 33–9.
Cahiers du cinéma, No. 455–6, May 1992.
Cahiers du cinéma, No. 457, June 1992.

Darke, C., 'The Eighth Day/Le huitième jour', *Sight and Sound*, November 1996, pp. 49–50.

van Dormael, J., 'L'essentiel de la vie d'un artiste est le stade de l'incompétence', in Nasta, D. and Aubenas, J. (eds), *Toto le héros: itinéraires d'une première oeuvre* (*Revue Belge du Cinéma*, Special Number, April 1994), pp. 69–73.

Dubois, P. and Arnoldy, E., *Ça tourne depuis cent ans – une histoire du cinéma francophone de Belgique* (Brussels, Communauté française de Belgique-Wallonie, 1995).

Jungblut, G., Leboutte, P. and Païm, D. (eds), *Une Encylopédie des cinémas de Belgique* (Paris, Musée d'Art Moderne de la Ville de Paris/Yellow Now, 1990).

Leboutte, P., 'Convivialité', in Jungblut, G., Leboutte, P. and Païm, D. (eds), *Une Encylopédie des cinémas de Belgique* (Paris, Musée d'Art Moderne de la Ville de Paris/Yellow Now, 1990), pp. 75–7.

McNeil, S., 'Mocu(Docu)mentary: Man Bites Dog, Documentary Theory and Other Andalusian Ethics', *Cinema Papers*, October 1993, pp. 28–31.

Michelem, R., 'Kermesse', in Jungblut, G., Leboutte, P. and Païm, D. (eds), *Une Encylopédie des cinémas de Belgique* (Paris, Musée d'Art Moderne de la Ville de Paris/Yellow Now, 1990), pp. 141–7.

Nasta, D. and Aubenas, J. (eds), *Toto le héros: itinéraires d'une première oeuvre* (*Revue Belge du Cinéma*, Special Number, April 1994).

Nevers, C., 'A l'ombre des serial killers', *Cahiers du cinéma*, November 1992 (No. 461), pp. 83–9.

Observer ('Life' section), 12 May 1996.

Poelvoorde, B., 'Histoires belges' in *Première*, No. 154, May 1996, pp. 102–5.

2 Double Lives: Europe and Identity in the Later Films of Krzysztof Kieślowski

Graham Roberts

The collapse of Communism in the late 1980s and early 1990s led to a gradual political and cultural rapprochement between Eastern and Western Europe which continues to gather pace. In May 1991, Václav Havel declared that Europe might at last be able to realize 'the age-old hope of becoming an area of friendship and co-operation for all its inhabitants' and that East Europeans were seeking to return to a civilization that they had helped to develop. 'This is not just a question of ... being fascinated by another world', continued Havel. 'It is just the opposite. After decades of unnaturally following the wrong track, we are yearning to rejoin the road which was once ours too.'[1] Statements such as this, while aimed at reasserting the dream of a common European home stretching from the Atlantic to the Urals, have instead served to give the political debate concerning Europe and European identity an even greater urgency than previously. This issue is a particularly pressing one since, at the time of writing (Autumn 1996), the European Union looks set to expand eastwards over the next twenty years, to embrace a whole swathe of former Communist states, from Estonia in the Baltic to Bulgaria in the Balkans. As many commentators have pointed out, such expansion will bring with it a whole range of political, legal, economic and social problems.[2]

Kieślowski constantly denied that his films contained any 'European' sub-text. Yet his later work (specifically *The Double Life of Véronique* [1991] and the *Three Colours* trilogy [1993–4]), can be seen as making an important contribution to the debate about Europe. In particular, they have much to say about the political, cultural and social relationship between Eastern and Western Europe, and about the thorny issue of European identity. On a more personal note, they constitute statements concerning Kieślowski's own identity as a European film-maker. In the final analysis, as we shall see, they reveal Kieślowski's disillusionment with the West, an experience repeated thousands of times over by East Europeans – intellectuals, artists or manual workers – who settled in the West after the fall of the Berlin Wall. In doing so, these films show how far the idea of

37

a common European home – so vaunted by Havel – still has to go to be achieved in any genuine, lasting sense.

Although Kieślowski achieved much recognition, both at home and abroad, for his series of ten short films based on the lives of the inhabitants of an apartment block in contemporary Warsaw, entitled *The Decalogue (Dekalog*, 1988), it was only with *The Double Life of Véronique (Podwojne Życie Weroniki)* that he began to reach an international audience on a large scale (this was perhaps helped by the fact that the film's Western distributors chose deliberately to retain the familiar French name Véronique in the English-language title, rather than the original Polish Weronika). In his films and his statements prior to the appearance of *The Double Life of Véronique* (hereafter *Véronique*), Kieślowski had been careful to eschew any apparent concern with politics (at least at the 'macro' level of states and state control), preferring instead to focus on the personal and the individual. As he once claimed in a television interview: 'I've realized that basically I don't give a shit about society, which in the case of Poland is forty million people. What I really care about is the individual human being.' Critics have faithfully reproduced this notion of the man as a 'pure' artist, untainted by any trace of politics or ideology. For example, in a recent article on the *Three Colours* trilogy, Dave Kehr (1994) goes so far as to claim that Kieślowski's deeply humanitarian vision can 'save the world'. A similarly apolitical image of Kieślowski was presented by Pascal Mérigeau (1996, p. 25) who claimed, in his obituary in *Le Monde*, that the man's films were underpinned by '*une architecture mathématique au service d'une rêverie sans fin*'.[3]

To a certain extent, the views of critics such as Kehr and Mérigeau are justified. Matters of politics and ideology are, after all, conspicuous by their absence in Kieślowski's early documentaries, including *Hospital (Szpital*, 1976), or *First Love (Pierwsza Miłość*, 1974), and works such as *A Short Film about Love (Krótki Film o Miłości*, 1989; an extended version of *Decalogue VI*). Films such as these rely for their effect on the way in which Kieślowski explores the constantly shifting emotional and existential relationships between individuals. Other early pieces, including *Blind Chance (Przypadek*, 1981),[4] and *A Short Film about Killing (Krótki Film o Zabijaniu*, 1988; an extended version of *Decalogue V*), belong in some respects to the European tradition of the Absurd, with their emphasis on the fortuitous and arbitrary nature of existence, and on human alienation. Even *No End (Bez końca*, 1984), in which the ghost of a young lawyer observes Poland after martial law while his erstwhile colleague defends a Solidarity activist, is more concerned with metaphysics than with politics. Moreover, the subject matter of these films is entirely domestic (a fact not too surprising, given the travelling restrictions on Polish citizens before 1989). 'European' moments in all of Kieślowski's pre-*Véronique* period are few and far between. In *No End*, the lawyer's widow, trying desperately to come to terms with her husband's untimely death, sleeps with a young Englishman who propositions her in a bar and pays her 50 dollars for the favour. And in *A Short Film about Killing* the eventual murderer, wandering aimlessly around Warsaw, is asked by a passing English motorist for directions to the Europa hotel (a request which, since it is made in English, the young man fails to understand).

But what of *Véronique* itself? The film is a slow-moving and emotionally highly charged work (like so much of Kieślowski's *oeuvre*), about two physically identical women: Weronika, a young Polish woman from Kraków who eventually succumbs to a fatal heart condition, and her French namesake, Véronique, a school teacher from the (equally) provincial city of Clermont-Ferrand, who falls in love with an enigmatic puppeteer, only to realize that he has used her for his own ends. From Kieślowski's statements on *Véronique*, one would be forgiven for believing that this film is as unconcerned with the politics of Europe – indeed, with politics in any sense – as his earlier work (and this despite the inevitably political overtones of the notion of a 'double life' in the context of Communist Eastern Europe). 'The film is about sensibility, presentiments and relationships which are difficult to name, which are irrational', the director maintained (1993, p. 173). Claiming that the film was about the 'mystery' of such matters, Kieślowski continued: '*Véronique* is a typical example of a film about a woman because women feel things more acutely, have more presentiments, greater sensitivity, greater intuition and attribute more importance to all these things' (ibid.). In another interview, Kieślowski even went so far as to dismiss the film's European dimension:

> the film didn't need to be a co-production between Poland and France. You could imagine it done with one girl living in Kraków and the other in Gdansk. I didn't frame the story of *Véronique* that way because of the financial background to the production: the subject itself was something close to my heart

(thereby contradicting his claim that women are more sensitive than men).[5]

Kieślowski's apparent unwillingness to explore the specific geographical and political polarity of the film's plot may even have motivated his choice of a relatively unknown actress, Irène Jacob, to play both lead roles (once his first choice, the American Andie MacDowell of *Four Weddings and a Funeral* fame, proved unavailable).[6] Jacob is not French, but a native of Switzerland, a politically and economically non-aligned state at the heart of Europe (perhaps this was why Kieślowski [1993, p. 175] felt that her nationality was 'a good sign').

Of course, there is much to support Kieślowski's claim that the film is concerned with sensibility and could therefore have been set anywhere; Weronika sings in a choir (the film's soundtrack is especially moving), while her French namesake is a music teacher and does, after all, fall in love with a puppeteer, whose gossamer-like creations captivate all the schoolchildren who witness his show. The fact that the film's cinematographer was Sławomir Idziak, who had worked on *A Short Film about Killing*, provided a visual link with Kieślowski's earlier, domestic productions. Yet to take such a view would be to ignore the film's political – and more importantly European – sub-text.

This is in fact a negative sub-text, since *Véronique* is underscored from start to finish not so much by presentiment as by the sentiment, echoing that expressed by Václav Havel in this chapter's opening quotation, that after decades of following the 'wrong path', Eastern Europe is now on the right road. Via its double heroine Weronika / Véronique, the film suggests that the human subject is naturally as 'untainted' by ideology and politics as the new, greater Europe. This is first implied in the opening moments of the film; after the prologue, in which a Polish mother shows her little girl the stars and then a French mother explains the concept of spring (a political 'spring'?) to her own child, we see Weronika singing in the rain. As she and her fellow chorists rush for cover, a lorry is seen carting off a huge statue of Lenin, literally to the rubbish heap of history. Significantly, the girls remain entirely oblivious to the statue. Immediately afterwards, Weronika shares a moment of intimacy with her boyfriend. This refusal to accord politics any significance in the life of the human subject is echoed in a later, much more crucial scene, when Weronika crosses the town square in Kraków during a political demonstration. Weronika does not notice the demonstrators, however (even though one of them accidentally knocks her music sheets out of her hand); what she finds herself staring at instead is her double, the Frenchwoman Véronique, sitting on a coach full of French tourists. Both afflicted by a potentially fatal heart condition (to which one succumbs),[7] Weronika and Véronique stand metonymically for the peoples of Eastern and Western Europe respectively, who, it would appear, share the same biological characteristics, regardless of ideological differences.

Encouraged by the success of *Véronique*, Kieślowski went on to make the *Three Colours* trilogy. Rather like *Véronique*, so the trilogy also establishes a parallel between Eastern and Western Europe, with its tripartite theme of Liberty, Equality and Fraternity echoing the French Revolution just a few years after a revolution of perhaps equal significance had occurred in the Communist bloc. The first film in the trilogy, *Blue* (sup-posed to represent Liberty), refuses to gesture towards any such parallel, however, set as it is exclusively in France (where Kieślowski spent an increasing amount of his time). *Blue* is the story of a woman named Julie (played by Juliette Binoche), who loses here husband Patrice, a renowned composer, and her daughter Anna in a car accident. Selling the family home and moving to a flat in the centre of Paris, she tries desperately to forget the past and start her life again, but finds this impossible to do. Unable to find the freedom she craves, she eventually completes the com-position of a piece of music which had been erroneously attributed to her late husband. Not insignificantly, this piece is a concerto in honour of the Unification of Europe ('cette grande fête de l'Europe' as it is called in the film), commissioned by the Council of Europe no less (a body which part-funded the *Three Colours* trilogy itself), to be played simultaneously by 12 symphony orchestras in each of the member states of the European Union.

Whatever the truth of Kieślowski's (1993, p. 223) claim that '*Blue* could take place anywhere in Europe', the film can be said to offer an interesting view on Western Europe from an Eastern European's perspective. On a superficial level, the image of the West which Kieślowski offers in *Blue* is a heterogeneous one. There are those who are rich, such as the composer Patrice de Courcy and his family who live in a sumptuous villa complete with retinue of servants and domestics, or the busker who is driven to his street corner every day by a well-dressed woman in an expensive car. As Dave Kehr astutely notes (1994, p. 16), '*Blue* takes place in a Paris that could only be imagined by an Eastern outsider (Julie lives an improbably chic life for the widow of a contemporary composer of serious music)'. Others are far less fortunate, however; these include the women who work as prostitutes in Pigalle, or the man who is savagely beaten up one night outside Julie's apartment block.

There is much more to Kieślowski's vision of Europe than snapshots of contemporary Paris, however. Whereas *Véronique* had offered a vision of the human subject untrammeled by politics, *Blue* appears to deny the pos-sibility of such freedom, not just for the individual, but specifically for the kind of creative individual that Julie is. The absence of freedom is empha-sized almost from the outset, as we see Julie breaking a window in the hospital where she is recovering after the accident, as if trying to break out of a prison. Julie does not even experience the freedom of being able to decide whether to live or die; she pops a bottle of pills into her mouth in an attempt to kill herself, only to spit them out again, unable to go through with the deed. Once released from the hospital, Julie tries to live life as a blank page, but finds herself increasingly unable to do so. She is reminded of the harsh truth that absolute freedom is impossible when forced to make a moral choice concerning the petition to get rid of her neighbour who is a prostitute (she in fact refuses to sign). Most important of all, she is constantly haunted by the music which she had begun to compose before the accident, but which she would like to forget, since it stands metonymically for her past life (she is unable to free herself of this part of her self and her past, not even by throwing the manuscript into a passing rubbish truck). This last detail can be interpreted as reaffirming the old myth of Romanticism (which survived much longer in Eastern Europe than in the West), namely 'manuscripts don't burn', that the creative artist is not free to choose not to follow her destiny as an artist.

The true artist, then, must obey her destiny. Yet to read *Blue* in this way would be to ignore the fact that the music Julie composes is not something personal but a piece which has been commissioned from her – by the European Superstate, no less, and for kitschy propagandistic reasons into the bargain. It is equally for this reason, it would seem, that she is not free. The lesson of *Blue*, a lesson which Kieślowski may already have learnt by the time he came to make this film, is that freedom in any meaningful sense is as illusory in the West as it is in the East – hence the image of the bungee-jumpers on the TV screen which Julie finds her mother staring at when she goes to visit her. As they fall toward Earth they have the sensation of total freedom, only to be reminded, just as they are about to hit the ground, of the elastic rope restraining them. (Such tension between freedom and restraint is also present in the image of the tightrope walker, featured in another programme which Julie's mother watches.) Reading *Blue* somewhat against the grain in this way, it is clear how Kieślowski's views on the possibility of personal freedom have changed radically since *Véronique*.

Living and working largely in the West, he now creates a character who is not free to live and work as she chooses – in contrast to Weronika and her French namesake, who had no external pressure when choosing whether or not to pursue a potentially fatal singing career, and therefore no problem making their choice. It is as if after the success of his first Polish–French co-production, Kieślowski now found that the pressures of working in the West – the supposedly apolitical and 'free' West which had previously proved so tempting to him as to so many other East Europeans – curtailed his freedom as an artist and as an individual.[8] Such a realization may lie at the root of an ironic comment made after Kieślowski had completed the trilogy, to the effect that he found no difference between making films in the West and in the East (1993, p. 199). Julie's lack of freedom, according to this interpretation, would then serve as a comment on

Kieślowski's own lack of freedom as an artist in the West – and this despite, or perhaps because of, the film's apparent Romanticism.

As the trilogy continues, the theme of Europe as a whole becomes even more important. At the same time, it would seem, Kieślowski's pessimism about Europe – West *and* East – deepens. If *Blue* suggests that freedom – genuine freedom – is as elusive in the West as it is in the East, the next film, *White* (representing 'Equality'), seems in fact to underline the absolute lack of equality between West and East (and this despite certain superficial socio-economic similarities, as we shall see). Indeed, in crucial respects *White* (1993) is the mirror image of *Blue*. Where the earlier film suggests that individual freedom is an illusion (Kieślowski said in fact that it dealt with 'the imperfections of human liberty' [1993, p. 212]), its sequel implies that personal liberty is in fact attainable. And while *Blue* presents an image of Europe as harmony (figuratively *and* literally), *White* suggests that the East / West divide in Europe is as alive and irresolvable as ever it was before the Berlin Wall came down.

The film begins in Paris, where a Polish hairdresser, Karol, is divorced by his French wife Dominique because, she claims, Karol has been unable to consummate their marriage.[9] Karol tries desperately to win Dominique back, but she remains unmoved, burning down his Paris hairdressing salon into the bargain. Loveless and penniless when his credit card is confiscated, Karol eventually makes it back to Poland clandestinely, crammed inside a fellow Pole's suitcase. Although Karol soon makes his fortune in his homeland as a successful businessman, he still loves Dominique, and in a fantastic scheme to get her back lures her to Poland by faking his death (he buys a Russian corpse and has it buried under his name) and bequeathing her his entire wealth. Dominique arrives from France, only to discover that Karol is still alive. After a night of passion, Karol disappears and Dominique is arrested on a charge of colluding in Karol's death. The film ends with Dominique in prison, visited by Karol who gazes up wistfully at her languishing in her cell.

On one level, *White* can be read as a pessimistic statement concerning post-Communist Poland and its chaotic social fabric. Indeed of all his late films, it is in *White* that Kieślowski most explicitly maps out the multifaceted, heteroglot space of his native culture. For example, there is the stark contrast between on the one hand the streetwise chatter of Poland's *nouveaux riches* and on the other the pre-Second World War folk song which Karol and his compatriot Mikołaj sing together nostalgically in the Paris underground.

This film has a much broader focus, however; it shows a Europe divided between West and East, between those on the inside and those on the outside. Kieślowski dramatizes the conflict between the two opposing cultures metonymically, as a battle for supremacy between two national languages. Right from the film's opening scene, in which Karol, whose French is somewhat limited, is forced to rely on an interpreter to defend himself against his wife's accusations in a French law court,[10] Kieślowski makes us aware of the vulnerability of the East European, marginalized in an alien society which fails totally to understand him. Karol exclaims (and this is also heard in the corresponding scene in *Blue*): 'But where is equality? It's because I do not speak French that you refuse to hear my arguments.' (Karol's vulnerability is given symbolic representation even before he enters the courthouse, when a pigeon dropping lands on his shoulder.) The relationship between language and power is further underscored when Karol reveals that his impotence – the very reason Dominique files for divorce – manifested itself almost immediately he came to live with her in France. Indeed, the language barrier which he faces in his new home would appear to be the direct cause of Karol's 'powerlessness' not just sexually ('impotence', or in French, 'impuissance'), but also legally (he is completely unable to prevent the divorce going through) and economically (after the divorce, it is Dominique who has his credit card stopped).

It is surely significant that the first time we see Karol achieve anything approaching power is also the first time we hear him speak in Polish *to another Pole*, when his compatriot Mikołaj offers him a reward for killing someone who wants to die (this subsequently turns out to be Mikołaj himself). Only when he returns to Poland, to the place where he can speak the language and therefore is not marginalized, does Karol eventually enjoy genuine power, however: first, absolute power to decide whether he kills Mikołaj or not; second 'sexual' power of sorts, since on his return to his salon – which in his absence his brother has decorated with a neon sign, since as he explains 'we're part of the West, now' – all his former female clients beg for him to cut their hair; and third, the economic power which comes with his successful business. The film's dénouement reinforces the relationship between language and power even further, except that this time the tables are turned; when Dominique goes to Poland for what she thinks is Karol's funeral, it is now *she* who cannot speak the language, and *she* who is rendered legally powerless (conversely, the power which Karol now has over his ex-wife is buttressed by/reflected in the fact that he now speaks much better French). The lesson here would appear to be that there can never be genuine equality between lover and loved one, man and woman, East and West, only what Kieślowski referred to as 'equality understood as a contradiction' (1993, p. 217).[11] In *White*, the new, post-Communist European reality resembles a Wittgensteinian language game – a game, furthermore, that the East can only hope to win if *it* determines the rules.[12]

After the unrelenting pessimism of *White* (mitigated only very slightly by the film's closing shot), *Red*, the final part of the *Three Colours* trilogy, is a good deal more optimistic. It is perhaps no coincidence that the most positive of the trilogy's films is the one where the theme of Europe is least evoked. Disillusioned with both Western and Eastern Europe, Kieślowski seeks a 'neutral' space, a place which might be neither West nor East, centre nor margin, but whose location would still make his film attractive to French audiences and French financiers. Kieślowski found (what he believed to be) just the place – politically neutral, economically non-aligned, multilingual Switzerland. *Red* concerns the friendship between a young Swiss model living in Geneva, Valentine Dussaut (played by Irène Jacob, who starred as Véronique) and a retired judge, who feeds his bitterness about people by eavesdropping on his neighbours' telephone conversations (finding out that they all lead 'double lives' in a far more sinister sense than Weronika/Véronique). Initially shocked by the judge's behaviour, Valentine grows fond of the man, who eventually reveals the cause of his bitterness; in his student days he was betrayed by the woman he loved. As their friendship develops, so Valentine's relationship with her boyfriend, Michel, begins to falter. It is in an attempt to repair that relationship that Valentine decides to go to England, where Michel is working. The cross-Channel ferry which she takes capsizes, however, leaving only seven survivors; Valentine herself, a young law student who is a neighbour of Valentine's, Julie and her friend Oliver (from *Blue*), Karol and Dominique (from *White*) and an English barman. As the survivors come ashore, united by Fate, *Red* comes to an end, thereby closing the *Three Colours* trilogy as a whole.

Like the two films which precede it, *Red* is ostensibly concerned with one of the three values espoused by the French Revolution, this time 'Fraternity'. Indeed, the seven survivors of the ferry disaster are 'brothers' in Fate, with their interwoven destinies, as are the retired judge and one of the seven, the young student lawyer whose life story closely mirrors the judge's. *Red* is a very different film from its two predecessors, however. First, its Revolutionary theme is realized in a way in which neither 'Liberty' nor 'Equality' is. Second, the dominant notes of *Red* – Unity, Harmony and Order – set it apart from *Blue* and *White* (the film's opening image of telephone cables under the English Channel presents international communication as harmoniously polyglot). Third, the film is far more optimistic than the other two (here surveillance and the organs of justice are benign rather than malevolent, unlike in either *A Short Film about Killing*, or *White*, and fate is much kinder also). Fourth, its action (apart from the closing shipwreck) takes place entirely outside the European Union. How might one account for the general lack of tension and conflict in *Red*, coming as it does after *White*? The answer to this question would appear to lie in the choice of location, and is fundamentally linked to Kieślowski's attitude towards Europe.

It may of course be sheer coincidence that Kieślowski chose to set the film in Switzerland. It can be argued, however, that this is no coincidence at all, and that Kieślowski was attracted to this neutral state, this marginal country at the heart of Europe, precisely because it offered him the chance to overcome the East/West dichotomy which had characterized his earlier films, and which was now part of him and his own 'double life' as an East European artist working in Western Europe. Switzerland is simultaneously within Europe (geographically) and outside Europe (politically and economically). It becomes in this, what turned out to be Kieślowski's last ever film, a mythical space where the connections between everything and everybody can finally be not just appreciated, but actually realized (in the trilogy's dénouement).[13] Switzerland in *Red* is a fairy-tale land where it is those who eavesdrop who are good, and those who are spied upon who are in fact guilty, with their sordid 'double lives'. This, it would seem, is a place where everyone can live happily ever after – or at least go on living in endlessly cyclical time, as the judge will clearly do in the figure of the young law student who is Valentine's neighbour. It also offers Kieślowski himself a politically neutral way out as an East European artist living and working in a post-Communist Superstate – a 'happy ending' aptly reflected in the dénouement of the *Three Colours* trilogy itself. Switzerland no doubt appealed to Kieślowski as an apolitical state (at least in the context of the European Union which Poland was and still is rushing towards); speaking about his earlier film career, he commented, 'I realized too late that I had to move as far away from the world of politics as possible' (1993, p. 209). Perhaps in this way Kieślowski was actually able to find the freedom which his trilogy seemed to suggest was unattainable – at the editing stage of *Three Colours*, he claimed to have 'freedom' within the production (1993, p. 227).

In conclusion, one may say that with *Véronique*, Kieślowski appears to dream of a Europe free of ideology, where individuals would be free to make choices affecting their lives based on far more personal criteria. His next film, *Blue*, is concerned with the realization that such freedom is as unattainable in the West as it is in the East. *White* then reveals the depths of Kieślowski's disillusionment, both with the West, where people are discriminated against on the basis of the language they speak, and with

Europe as a whole, where equality is a sham, and where survival is a matter of how one plays the game. *Red*, finally, represents Kieślowski's own attempt to determine the rules of the game, not so much by 'shifting the goal posts' as by transporting the whole playing field away from apparently post-political Europe to apolitical Switzerland.

Despite this desire to flee politics, there can be no doubt that all of Kieślowski's films, from his early documentaries to his later 'art' films, are political through and through. As another very different political filmmaker, Ken Loach, so eloquently put it, introducing the *Three Colours* trilogy on British Channel Four television recently, 'while he claimed to despise politics, his [Kieślowski's] films are about the relationship between how people live, who they are, and the world they inhabit, which is the essence of politics'.

His later films are not just concerned with politics in this maximalist sense, however. They also deal with the politics of Europe, the issue of European identity and the vexed question of the relationship between Eastern and Western Europe in particular. At the same time, a constant thread is the question of identity, both personal *and* political – from the 'double lives' of Polish Weronika and French Véronique to Switzerland, a country where every citizen leads a double life, in a political sense as a citizen of what is both a European and non-European state at the same time, and in another, more personal sense, with the judge's neighbours who have homosexual affairs or who engage in drug-trafficking.

Indeed, turning to Switzerland appears to have been the only way that Kieślowski could overcome the dilemma of working in the West, supposedly the land of the freedom, equality and fraternity which he, like most other thinking East Europeans before the Wall came down, had so admired, but which turned out to be a huge deception (or to be realizable only in a profoundly ironic sense). Kieślowski, then, may be said to have begun the final episode in his relatively short but distinguished career by articulating in *Véronique* the kind of optimism shared by Havel about Eastern Europe's place in Europe as a whole, only to realize by the time he made the *Three Colours* trilogy that such optimism was misplaced (this awareness must have been reached fairly quickly, since he completed the trilogy in eight months, from September 1992 to May 1993).

On the basis of the films examined here, what does it mean for Kieślowski to be a European? At the beginning of *Véronique*, it means to enjoy freedom (from politics and ideology), equality (with the West) and fraternity with those who share your fate. By the end of *Red*, it has come to mean the opposite. Europeans, it would appear, experience neither freedom (from one's social and economic context), nor equality (with the West or even with the opposite sex), nor even fraternity (in anything other than a tragic sense). Kieślowski, then, was in many respects a typical East European who sought to make films not about politics but who could not avoid politics, who thought, mistakenly, that life and art could be free of politics, who believed that in the West he would find complete artistic freedom, and equality, and fraternity, but who found none of these things, who thought that in the West he could find his true identity as an artist and stop leading a double life, but who found that this was not possible for him or indeed for anybody else.[14]

Ironically, Kieślowski, by expressing such disappointment and seeking refuge in a marginal European mini-state, may well have confirmed his place as a central, major European film-maker, as central, perhaps, as Swiss-born Jean-Luc Godard – hence the visual allusion in *White* to Godard's film *Contempt* (*Le Mépris*, also a European co-production), as the camera pans across a poster advertising it. To quote Ken Loach once again, 'the fluency and grace of his best work is a reminder, if we need one, of the great European tradition of cinema'. The fact that Kieślowski's untimely death meant that he was unable to see how his native land would fare in the 'grande fête de l'Europe' is as ironic as it is tragic.

NOTES

1.   *Financial Times*, 10 May 1992; quoted in Bideleux, 1996, pp. 283–4.
2.   See, for example, Anon., 'Even more complicated Union', The *Economist*, 7959 (30 March 1996), pp. 41–3.
3.   For a slightly more 'political' reading of the *Three Colours* trilogy, see Paul Coates (1996–7).
4.   The theme of politics does appear in *Blind Chance*, in the guise of the Communist Party and an opposition group, both of which the hero Witek joins in separate possible lives. The political theme is subsumed, however, within the exploration of fate, which is the film's central concern.
5.   See Rains, 1994, p. 9.
6.   Jacob had previously starred in Louis Malle's *Au Revoir, les Enfants* (1987).
7.   In the figure of a young woman who yearns to exploit her talent for singing despite her potentially fatal heart condition, *Véronique* echoes the ninth film of *The Decalogue*.
8.   Interestingly, Kieślowski claimed that it was much harder for him to obtain finance in Poland than in France. As he put it (1993, p. 192), 'it's not even right for me to try to find money there because the Poles quite rightly believe that I can get money elsewhere'. It should be pointed out, however, that Kieślowski's success in obtaining finance in the West was ultimately

dependent on his making a certain kind of movie, the kind which its financiers believed would sell. It was in this crucial respect that his freedom as an artist was limited.

9. *White* is so unlike *Blue* or *Red* that one critic has gone so far as to dismiss it as a 'comical interlude' in Kieślowski's career: see Sobolewski, 1995, p. 135. (I am grateful to Dr John Bates of Glasgow University's Department of Slavonic Languages and Literatures, for this reference.)

10. Lawyers and law courts also appear in *No End* and *A Short Film about Killing*.

11. In *White* Kieślowski uses Karol and Dominique to stand metonymically for East and West respectively precisely because he thought in terms of individuals rather than nations: 'I don't believe societies exist, I don't believe nations exist. I think that there simply are, I don't know, 60 million individual French or 40 million individual Poles or 65 million individual British. That's what counts. They're individual people' (1993, p. 193).

12. The link between power, the state and Wittgenstein's concept of 'language games' is explored in Jean-François Lyotard, *The Postmodern Condition: a Report on Knowledge*, trans. by Geoff Bennington and Brian Massumi (Manchester, Manchester University Press, 1984).

13. Such connections include the figure of the anonymous old woman who is featured in each of the trilogy's films trying to insert a bottle into a bottle bank, and the mythical nineteenth-century Dutch composer Van der Budenmayer, alluded to in each film (Van der Budenmayer is also mentioned in the ninth film of *The Decalogue*).

14. This is not to say that all East European artists have been unhappy in the West. In contrast to Kieślowski, the Czech writer Milan Kundera, who has lived in Paris since the mid-1970s, has embraced Western culture to such an extent that he now writes in French, rather than Czech. His first French-language novel, *La Lenteur* (*Slowness*), was published in 1995 (Paris, Gallimard). Referred to on French television in December 1996 as 'a French writer of Czech origin', Kundera rarely visits his homeland and tends to do so incognito. A number of important writers left Russia for the West in the so-called 'Third Wave' of emigration, between 1973 and 1981. A fascinating collection of articles outlining their mixed reactions to the West can be found in Mcmillin, 1991.

REFERENCES

Anon. (1996), 'Ever more complicated Union', The *Economist*, 7959, 30 March, pp. 41–3.

Bideleux, R., 'In Lieu of a Conclusion: East meets West?', in Bideleux, R. and Taylor, R. (eds), *European Integration and Disintegration: East and West* (London and New York, Routledge, 1996), pp. 281–95.

Coates, P., 'The Sense of an Ending: Reflections on Kieślowski's Trilogy', *Film Quarterly*, 1996–7, Vol. 50, No. 2, Winter, pp. 19–26.

Kehr, D., 'To Save the World: Kieślowski's THREE COLORS Trilogy', *Film Comment*, 1994, Nov.–Dec., pp. 10–20.

Kieślowski, K., *Kieślowski on Kieślowski*, ed. by Stok, D. (London, Faber and Faber, 1993).

Kundera, M., *La Lenteur* (Paris, Gallimard, 1995).

Lyotard, J-F., *The Postmodern Condition: a Report on Knowledge*, trans. by Bennington, G. and Massumi, B. (Manchester, Manchester University Press, 1984).

Mcmillin, A., (ed.), *Under Eastern Eyes: the West as Reflected in Recent Russian Émigré Writing* (London, Macmillan, 1991).

Mérigeau, P., 'Krzysztof Kieślowski, cinéaste du hasard et du mystère', *Le Monde*, 15 March 1996, p. 25.

Rains, T., 'Glowing in the Dark', *Sight and Sound*, 1994, Vol. 4, No. 6, June, pp. 8–10.

Sobolewski, T., 'Peace and Rebellion: some Remarks on the Creative Output of Krzysztof Kieślowski', *Bulletin de la Société des Sciences et des Lettres de Łódź*, Vol. 45 (1995) (*Recherche sur les Arts*, No. 6, 'Polish Films in Ten Takes'), pp. 123–37.

3 Hitmen, Hate and *Grosse Fatigue*: the Search for the French Blockbuster
Alison Smith

The object of this chapter is to look at the various ways in which the French cinema has responded to its perceived position, after the GATT talks of 1993–4, as the 'representative' European film industry and, as a result of this position, 'responsible' for the diffusion of European culture in a medium which is still clearly perceived as having cultural influence. The challenge of GATT was received not only by the film industry proper but by all connected with audio-visual media (which is a large constituency), and also by the government, which has found itself implicated in what sometimes seems to be an affair of national pride – to prove that French films can hold their own against the American invader and even that the French industry can respond to Hollywood in Hollywood's terms and gain access to the enormous American market. The search for the French blockbuster – the film that will impose the French industry on the mass of the national, and international, audience – has certainly taken up much time, and money and newsprint since GATT (and, to a lesser extent, previously).

It has not been an uncontroversial search. There is a vocal and influential constituency (especially among critics and film-students) who want nothing to do with this way of regarding the cinema. *Cahiers du cinéma*, *Libération* and even *Le Monde* have carried articles questioning and/or condemning this attitude to new French production. In the name largely of the *Nouvelle Vague* tradition of the *cinéma d'auteur*, they claim that funding and state encouragement, not to mention all-important distribution deals, are being monopolized by a new version of the stultifying so-called '*qualité française*' tradition, supported by the government in the 1950s (see, for example, Hodgson, 1995). This opposition sometimes seems to be directly aimed at attempts to market French films outside France. However, it must be admitted that arguments tend to polarize, and so long as the government is perceived to be interested above all in selling films to American (and French) audiences without taking an interest in the content, those who oppose this will tend to portray all efforts to sell the films as automatically a compromise with Mammon, forgetting, as Pierre Hodgson points out, that the *Nouvelle Vague* directors organized production as well as the making of the films, and generally took an interest in the 'industry' as well as in the 'art' of making and showing films.

I do not intend to explore this polemic in detail in this context, but it cannot be ignored in any discussion of the possible global place of the French cinema, largely because both sides tend to claim the mantle of French cinema tradition and a certain representative value. For the big spenders, it is the French cinema's high profile, international reputation and production of star actors and celebrated films which counts; on the other, its tradition of directorial independence and its skill in producing highly regarded films for a small but appreciative audience. Both sides regard themselves as representing to some extent a European (not just French) tradition, faced with the Hollywood 'machine' as the main opposing force (I'm not, quite, going to say enemy, although sometimes the rhetoric would lead one to think that this would be no great exaggeration).

However, while the 'art and auteur' writers and film-makers refuse the terms of the GATT debate – saying, broadly, that the quality of a film cannot be judged by its audience figures, and the creative process should come before the search to meet the taste of a possible public – the films with which I am now concerned are those which have, largely, accepted the GATT challenge and set out to capture as large an audience as possible, both at home and abroad (especially in the USA). That this challenge is recognized can be judged by the way in which *Le Monde*, and occasionally *Libération*, reports the weekly figures of tickets sold in Paris. The progress of the French 'champions' and their American rivals are monitored and rejoiced, or lamented, over very much in the manner of sports scores.

These films have, generally, been strongly supported by the industry and by the government, both in terms of direct funding (a major polemic was caused by the attribution to *Le Hussard sur le toit*, 'the most expensive French film ever produced', of the *avance sur recettes*, a government loan-funding intended at its conception in 1960 to encourage independent film-making) and through export drives and publicity. They have, indeed, in some cases, functioned as the Public Face of France.

The questions I now intend to ask concern the way in which France goes about its ambitions, the choice of films which it finances for success, the films which actually *are* successful, and the reasons for their victory.

So, how does France go about its ambitions? Here there arises, inevitably, the issue of the big-budget film. In relation to budgets, the French industry is faced with a vicious circle. On the one hand, there is a growing perception (not always accurate, but with some foundation) that

Hollywood's success comes in proportion to its budgets. Hollywood spends a lot, and behold its money returns to it tenfold (or more). A big budget well spent allows for spectacular effects, and these are more and more at least perceived to be a draw for audiences. It also allows a large amount (both absolutely and proportionately) to be spent on the all-important promotion. If the French industry is to compete, it has to be able to produce spectacle and finance large-scale marketing drives and therefore it needs big budgets.

On the other hand a big-budget film *has* to attract its audience in order to pay for itself. This is even more urgent in the French industry, which has less money all-told, and a home audience which, even if faithful, does not compare in size with the US one. This last point is one reason, apart from pure rivalry, for the intense efforts to penetrate the US market.

Despite the potential problems, the tendency in the French cinema since GATT has been towards bigger budgets. In 1994, for example, the first post-GATT year, the average investment in a film rose to 5.9 mF, as against 3.6 mF in 1993, and six films over 60 mF were put into production as compared with one in 1993 (Frodon, 1995a*)*. *Le Hussard sur le toit,* budgeted at 176 mF, was the most expensive film ever produced in France, a fact which *in itself* loomed large in the press releases for the film in America.

What does France spend these big budgets on, and have they on the whole recouped their cost?

The titles of the very biggest budget French films in recent years may seem to speak for themselves: *Cyrano de Bergerac, Germinal, La Fille de d'Artagnan, La Reine Margot, Les Misérables, Le Colonel Chabert, Le Hussard sur le toit.* The search for the big French blockbuster has passed by way of the costume drama.

These films have in common a scenario adapted from classic literature; magnificent settings and costumes, which provide spectacle; large numbers of extras in big set-piece sequences, and international French stars. It is the last three factors which account for the big budgets (rather than technical effects). The use of classic literature for spectacular films is not confined to France; indeed this particular route to the European blockbuster was actually pioneered by Merchant-Ivory in Britain (and as a route to the blockbuster in general, its greatest role model is probably *Gone with the Wind*). Its potential for spectacle is undoubtedly a major factor in its success, although it may, as *Cahiers du cinéma* suggested in regard to *Le Hussard sur le toit,* have a didactic purpose too (Jousse and Toubiana, 1995). Certainly most of the books involved received a boost in sales as a result of the films. Certainly, also, the GATT polemic was couched by the political players in terms of *cultural preservation*, in which context successtul export of monuments of French culture would seem a desirable end germane to the argument.

However, it is interesting that – to a greater extent than in Britain – the costume drama since GATT in France has shown a distinct tendency to divide. There are two traceable strands: on the one hand (and most frequent among the big exports) are lavish adaptations of nineteenth- and twentieth-century reconstructions of history – *Cyrano*, *d'Artagnan*, *Le Hussard*, *Margot*. On the other hand there is the treatment of novels which at the time of writing genuinely dealt with their own era or one at least in general living memory (*Germinal*, *Les Misérables*, *Chabert* or Chabrol's *Mme Bovary*). Interestingly, the first of these strands is *specifically* French – the British heritage movie has not, to date, turned this way. This is certainly not for want of potential material, so the question why romantic history has been so popular in France, while in Britain the likes of Scott and Blackmore are largely left for TV, remains to be asked.

The division, however, reflects a genuine difference in the apparent aims and the careers of the films involved. The didactic intention which *Cahiers* suggested existed in *Le Hussard* seems very evident in the adaptations of 'contemporary' novels. *Germinal* is a sober, and by-and-large faithful, account of the story, which certainly excises aspects – particularly the political drama – but recounts the novel respectfully with the appropriate and expected set-pieces. Chabrol's *Mme Bovary* was faithful to the novel to the extent of aiming to be an actual *transcription* without additions or deletions (although, unlike *Germinal*, the production values and publicity attached to it don't indicate it as a candidate for the blockbuster). *Les Misérables* takes a rather different course, interspersing the story of the novel proper with its reading in a different era (although still carefully removed from the actual present). Lelouch thus establishes the relevance of 'great literature' to readers outside its strictly contemporary sphere, a complex and interesting approach which, although certainly not a faithful *transcription*, still centres attention on the text.

On the whole, the historical epics have taken a more cavalier approach to the source text, apart, interestingly, from the first – the reference point for the genre in France – *Cyrano*. *La Fille de d'Artagnan* owes nothing to Dumas but the character of d'Artagnan. *Margot* and *Le Hussard*, for different reasons, selected in their source texts only what they wanted. These 'historical' texts (including *Cyrano*, but perhaps not *Margot* which I think is an exceptional case in the whole genre) have largely been used as a source of the scenario for a swashbuckling action film (an approach which in the case of *Le Hussard* at least is a more than questionable *cultural* procedure!).

The two strands do seem to correspond to different intentions – or at least to different results. Take, for contrast, the different careers of *Cyrano* and *Germinal*, each the biggest budget, highest profile production of its year, and each considered to be a success on its own terms. In all, 4.5 million people went to see *Cyrano* in France, but exports accounted for another six million. Its major success was therefore outside France; it made over 15 million dollars in the US (so far a record equalled only by *Léon* and *L'Ours*, which exemplify a very different strategy and will be considered later[1]). *Germinal* achieved a higher score in France than *Cyrano* (5.7 million people). By contrast, its gross in the United States was under $400 000, which is minuscule; later films accounted relative failures have still scored over a million. Since the producers of both films were relatively satisfied with their performance one is led to conclude that the apparent didacticism of *Germinal* corresponded to its anticipated audience among those who were studying it, had studied it, or have some feeling that this is a part of the national culture which they *ought* to be familiar with; in other words, that *Germinal* was never intended for major export success, but expected to justify its budget on the home market. In fact, according to *Sight and Sound* (Forbes, 1994, p. 24) it was intended by the French industry to be the champion which would allow the home team to out-perform *Jurassic Park* in France (in fact, of course, the honour for this went to a very different film).

Le Hussard and, to some extent, *Margot* were certainly made with an international audience in mind. *Le Hussard*'s producer, René Cleitman (in Buob, 1995), called it 'purely French, but with an international vocation'. In the interests of marketing it in the USA, he fought long and hard for production of a dubbed version (this is a constant argument among exporters – no French film to my knowledge has yet been released dubbed, and yet every major export seems to run up against the problem – subtitles confine to an 'art circuit' films which have been geared to a mass audience. The issue will recur later in this chapter). Cleitman claimed that '*Cyrano* subtitled made 6 million dollars' (it made a lot more than that, according to the Internet figures). 'With *Le Hussard* dubbed, we're guaranteed to double, even triple, the profits.' This incidentally was the kind of language which predominated in discussions of *Le Hussard*. The film was submitted to the sneak preview system, which Cleitman has been instrumental in trying to introduce to France against fierce opposition from the auteurist element who see this as the final surrender of creative values to the demand for 'an audience'. Even Rappeneau, the director, in discussing the creative process, appears to be looking first at a foreign audience;

he was quoted by a Canadian critic (admittedly, this may have been taken out of context) as saying:

> I had a great fear that *Le Hussard* was too linked to the sociological history of France to travel well. It wasn't the same kind of fear I had when adapting *Cyrano de Bergerac*, because that was a universal story that everyone could understand; the only thing I had to worry about was how to reproduce the poetry in the right type of English. But *Le Hussard* is all atmosphere: to make it move, I had to reinvent whole sections of the story, and hope I could make them look as though they flowed naturally from the rest of the book.[2]

Clearly (if we are to believe this, which of course was spoken to an American public) the adaptation of reflective novel to action movie, and of 'specifically French' to 'universal' proceeded simultaneously. Rappeneau's approach to the setting is also significant; he spoke (for the French audience) of the importance of reproducing Giono's sensitivity to the land and yet he admitted that before shooting the film he had never been to Provence – 'it was a mythical place...I dreamed about it', he said to the Canadian interviewer – and that he avoided going for as long as possible so as not to 'spoil' his 'mythical' impression. His admittedly sumptuous filming of the place when he finally got there is thus *defined* as being with the eye of a dazzled outsider, one who, what's more, defines himself (to a North American audience) as having an attitude to Provence not unlike that which he might hope a romantically minded North American might have. Anything further from Giono's approach would be hard to imagine. Like *Jean de Florette* and the Pagnol films before it, *Le Hussard* presents scenery so magnificent that one American reviewer commented: 'the setting is so scenic one may think that *Le Hussard* was made in conjunction with the French tourist board'. Paradoxically, *Cyrano*, *Le Hussard's* role model, is as faithful to the original text, both in words and in rhythm, as any of the more 'didactic' films – but then, *Cyrano* was already a spectacle, already in many ways a mass audience text.

How successful were these films? Well, by and large, not up to expectations, with the exception of *Cyrano* and *Germinal*. None of *Cyrano's* successors has approached its export success. *La Fille d'Artagnan* and *Les Misérables* have been major disappointments, especially in France; indeed *all* these films except *Germinal* have trailed away somewhat in their native country, and especially in Paris. (Another interesting fact about them is that the ratio of Parisian to provincial audiences is much lower than for the 'average' French film; for *Germinal* one in eight as opposed to an average of one in three or four [Frodon, 1994]. I don't know the figures for

Le Hussard but the pattern was reported here too.) Neither *Le Hussard* nor *Margot* have yet (September 1996) recouped their budgets; although in the case of *Margot* this is maybe not so surprising or so contrary to expectations. All the later films (including *Les Misérables*) took over one million dollars in the United States – a fleabite by American standards but perhaps reflecting a genuine entry into the market. *Margot* has just topped two million – I have not been able to come by definitive figures for *Le Hussard*, but it had already topped one million by July 1996 without reaching two million, and by this time the major part of its box office career was probably behind it. Given the immense resources ploughed into the genre, it has to be admitted that post-GATT returns have been meagre, especially since the films' market share in France is frequently lower than much smaller budget work.

I would like to say a little, as an aside, about *La Reine Margot*, which seems to me to stand out among these productions, first, as a 'heritage' movie (budget, source novel, settings, costumes and stars are all there) made – and accepted as such from the outset – by a director with an 'auteurist/creative' attitude to the content. Chéreau's interviews, in contrast to Rappeneau's, are exclusively concerned with the creative process, style and content of the film; he seems to have left the marketing to Berri, who, in return, was minimally intrusive in the film's making. Chéreau's background as a theatre director and as a film-maker is largely in 'difficult' production, politically challenging (for example, his collaborations with Koltès and Guibert) and aesthetically adventurous. Despite his ventures into the grand scale of opera production, he has no proven record in big box office, nor much interest in it.

Much of Chéreau's concern in making *Margot* was to *avoid* the conventions of the genre. He gives as his models films from a very different tradition (*The Godfather*, *Goodfellas* and Visconti's *The Damned*). He told *Cahiers*, for example (Chéreau, 1994a, p. 13):

> At Bordeaux, we reconstructed whole streets and one hardly sees them, like one would film a contemporary street. That took the Sets department 15 days, it annoyed the locals, we had to take down lampposts, blacken the houses, lay down earth: if you start thinking about it you do pan shots of the streets just to make the most of the set. And, because it was a historical film, I particularly didn't want to distract the audience's attention from the main point – the power relations, the violence of the story.

The second reason for *Margot*'s singularity is that, made with this attitude, the film can appear in some ways as a commentary on the historical genre (though I don't think it was intended as such; it works that way because it's a strong film *despite* its genre and in unexpected ways). Despite Chéreau's comments on the use of the set, *Margot* flaunts its budget and thus its genre (especially in the use of extras), while – as Chéreau says – avoiding the scenic reconstruction mode. Instead it concentrates on the actors' physical presence. To quote Chéreau again (ibid.):

> If I make films it's to approach the body, and that physical density which the theatre can't give me ... if *La Reine Margot* is filmed from very close, it's because I don't want to distance myself from the actors.

It is indeed filmed close: it is also full of charged erotic scenes and, to an even greater extent, of graphic violence (sometimes together). Jonathan Romney in *The Guardian* (Romney, 1994) dubbed it 'heritage gore'. Chéreau insists that we watch and come into contact with both the eroticism and the violence, and in the process violence and suffering are, inescapably, eroticized. This is a decidedly disturbing cinematic process. Sometimes the film seems to use the mechanisms of the horror film, both shocking and fascinating, but it uses these mechanisms within the framework of the costume drama. Thus we are not 'prepared' to dismiss what goes on as a genre convention, and are fully aware of it in a way that is rare in films announced as seeking such effects. The process poses questions about the basis of the costume drama genre itself. St Bartholomew's Eve, and indeed the machinations of the Valois, are documented history and cannot be dismissed as imagination. The spectator, presumably (at least the French one) has approached the film with some conception of its historical content, and the expectation that history will be presented as epic, spectacular entertainment. The *authenticity*, or 'physical density', of Chéreau's approach I think does make the audience question their own position (why is this 'entertainment' and what sort?). The film forces us into voyeurism to a much more disturbing degree than the usual sex scenes which most audiences are thoroughly used to by now.

Chéreau certainly intended to make the audience think about historical violence. He said in an interview with *Le Monde* (Chéreau, 1994b) that he had wanted the shots of St Bartholomew to refer to current images:

> To begin with, the reference point was Tienanmen, and also fanaticism, with Khomeiny's funeral. We were to show the Catholic priests whipping up the crowds in the Paris streets. We cut all that, in the end. In the meantime, other images took over, those from ex-Yugoslavia.

(The change in reference reflects the long time which elapsed between the conception and the making of the film.) The distant violent episode thus becomes a reference for the recurrence of mass violence throughout history. This intention raises the problems inherent in the romanticizing of nasty dirty painful history into a comfortably picturesque 'heritage', which can be watched without any need for the audience to be implicated in the content or to take any responsibility at all.

The film was marketed, however, as the conventional historical epic. Chéreau apparently even accepted 'sneak previews' for the US audience (which resulted in 20 minutes being cut, in order to avoid historical confusion, and long explanatory panels being inserted at the beginning, which must even further condition the audience to expect a panorama of history!). Interestingly, *Margot* did better than most in the USA, where it was largely sold as another in the line of French costume dramas. Possibly its relative success was due paradoxically to its *not* being a straightforward mainstream 'heritage' epic, despite the marketing. Since sub-titled French films in the USA have difficulty reaching a truly mass audience who are deterred by the sub-titles and the 'art' reputation of European films, *Margot*'s potentially more challenging approach – in directions incidentally closer to those of the independent American sector than to the French *Nouvelle Vague* tradition – may have worked in its favour.

The costume drama has become the export flagship of France. However, the aftermath of GATT caused worries in the industry not only as regards the international profile of French film but, purely and simply, as regards its success in France. This is always rather puzzling to the UK, but French cinema is in a *good* enough position in its own country to have some realistic hopes of equalling audience figures for Hollywood films, and since it can afford to cherish such hopes it aims for no less. Thus the score of 28.5 per cent of tickets sold obtained by French production for the first eight months of 1994 was considered a disaster, whereas most other film industries in Europe would see this as a triumph. The effect becomes understandable when the figure is compared with the score for the first three months of 1995 – 46.2 per cent (Frodon, 1995b).

This sort of domestic score is also dependent on flagship films, but not in general the same as those exported. The 46.2 per cent was achieved on the back of *Un Indien dans la ville* a comedy with Thierry Lhermitte. The famous victory over *Jurassic Park* in 1993 was finally achieved not by *Germinal* but by another comedy, *Les Visiteurs*. Comedy has always been a lucrative genre in France, the backbone, in the 1960s and 1970s, of the '*cinéma de samedi soir*' (Saturday evening cinema, weekend relaxation for all the family), and of what has progressively replaced it, prime-time scheduling on the popular TV channels. Until very recent years, on the whole, French comedy has not been a big budget tradition, though there have always been exceptions; nor has it aimed for an export market. The great tradition of '*cinéma de samedi soir*' derived its strength from a portrait of its audience, the 'ordinary Frenchman' (and his family) which was certainly slightly satiric, but above all recognizable and, finally, reassuring. M. Toutlemonde, perhaps not all that bright, but good hearted, well meaning, put-upon, and naturally finally victorious, appears regularly in different situations.

The big budget, exportable version was never entirely absent even from the tradition, but generally, the formula does not lend itself to export. Cultural recognition depends on fairly specific traits – and the better the observation, the more successful the comedy and, often, the less transferable the result. Also, the reinforcement and reassurance of M. Toutlemonde led, probably inevitably, to a reactionary tendency. The target audience was sacrosanct, so the real fall-guys had to be somebody else. At its worst the domestic French comedy tapped a vein of xenophobia which never seriously affected its popularity at home, but which clearly rendered it embarrassing as an export proposition.

However, at its best the comic tradition made vast swathes of France laugh, and, in 1993, just after GATT, the genre found itself catapulted to heroism when *Les Visiteurs* outperformed *Jurassic Park* in France. Undeniably, the newest manifestation of this strand of comedy (very dependent on TV, where all its stars make their debuts) has a much greater effect *in France* than the costume epic.

The comic film, then, was clearly to be encouraged by the film industry as a way of retaining its French audience. However, if that encouragement was to go by way of financial support, the flagships of the genre, now bigger scale and with more at stake, also needed to take their chance abroad, and thus become exportable. This has been largely a secondary consideration for comedies; it has, however, altered the chosen mechanisms to some extent. The central situation has tended towards either (a) an outrageous comic situation not dependent on any but the most general cultural assumptions (*Les Visiteurs* with its time travel theme, the 'guardian angels' of Poiré's most recent film, the uncivilized Indian in the city), alongside which more specifically French elements may find their place, or (b) the choice of a cultural milieu which is a recognizable international 'short-cut' to French culture. (There is a third option, which is a treatment so individual that the films find their market on the auteurist principle, as is the case, love him or hate him, with Bertrand Blier.)

One of the few early versions of this genre to be produced with a wider market in mind, *La Grande Vadrouille*, followed option (b), successfully exploiting the myths already grown up around the Resistance. Strategy (a), however, is the more common, and illustrates the secondary importance of export. This sort of film may not do well abroad, but it *is* likely, if reasonably successful at home, to be bought as a plot and reconstituted by the USA (as has happened already with *Un Indien dans la ville*). Strategy (b), like the big cultural scenarios, lends itself with difficulty to remakes, but it risks small success in France which knows itself too well to accept other people's stereotypes, unless they are stereotypes which the French share. (*La Grande Vadrouille*, like *Dad's Army* at a similar period in Britain, exploited an image almost as mythical within the country as outside it.)

It is in this context, I think, that *Grosse Fatigue* becomes exemplary. It was made in 1994, like *La Reine Margot*, and the two films represented the show-pieces of the French film industry at Cannes that year. It enters, more or less, into the comedy genre (at the higher-brow end, certainly); Blanc has been a well-known pillar of the genre since the 1970s and was a TV personality prior to that. It by and large adopts strategy (b), but the short-cut that it chooses is specifically the French film industry.

Now this is making some possibly unjustified assumptions: that the audience (wherever they are) knows enough about the French film industry to get the jokes, and, given the plot, also that the audience agrees that Blanc and Bouquet are famous enough for a story which revolves around their fame to be credible. Significantly, both these points posed some problems in the United States. However, in France, I suspect that the actual situation was *almost*, but not quite, what seems to be assumed. The majority of French spectators would get *most* (but not all) of the inside jokes – but they would be able to pick up on why they missed the ones they missed. They might not feel that they or anyone they knew would react to Blanc or Bouquet like the people in the film (even allowing for caricature), but are prepared to believe that some poor benighted soul in Bled-sur-Ruisseau might. The effect of such half-justified assumptions is to reinforce themselves. If I get most of the jokes, the Average Spectator may think, the guy along the row probably gets all of them; if I feel this story is more or less credible, it's probably because there are French stars big enough to have this effect, even if they might not so affect me.

Grosse Fatigue is a comedy about the production of French comedy, which, almost incidentally, sets up 'the French cinema' as itself a shorthand for French culture (which we feel we should recognize). It presents a strong, unique milieu which is the French cinema, distinctive enough to be decisively caricatured. It apparently assumes that everyone will know what's going on – and of course most people will know something, and absorb a little more in the process. Even as it plays with the nature of celebrity, it presents its stars as having a truly mythical national star status. Whatever you thought of Blanc before watching *Grosse Fatigue*, after it you're in no doubt that he is universally recognised, permanently news value and of major celebrity status. It's a skillful PR exercise. In this context, the final plea for the French cinema becomes a coherent part of the whole (although its rather jarring seriousness, and its apparent appeal to the old xenophobic genre tradition, does strike a somewhat sour note). The film has throughout built up the French film industry as a vital part of French culture, able to bring a small-town no-good-boy instant riches simply because he looks like a star, able – whichever way you turn it – to make the paralytic walk, while, at the same time, being *national*, familiar and loveable. The stars of the French industry are really just like 'us'. Any Patrick Durand may look like Blanc; Carole Bouquet would have supper with your family just out of the kindness of her heart; indeed – the stars could even *be* us! (you too could substitute for Depardieu). It is all this which Noiret in the end declares to be in danger of becoming 'une souris dans un parc' (a mouse in a theme park). By this time, the French audience is implicated: if the film industry is degraded, so too is France. The overblown symbolism of the Arc de Triomphe and the unknown soldier arguably undermines the seriousness of the expressed threat, since it is itself potentially theme-park imagery. It's hard to imagine an audience reacting to this at the first degree after the lightheartedness of the previous hour and a half. Nonetheless, the 'message' (support your film industry or lose it) comes at the end of a film which subtly valorizes it. It is hard not to see *Grosse Fatigue* as an advertisement for French film, aimed at the French public and that part of the foreign cinema audience which – by choosing to see what is unlikely to be a huge success abroad – indicate that they already put value on French films.

The film industry's new-found big budgets then, tend to go one of two ways:

1. to expand market share in the USA (principally): spectacularly expensive films, over-defined as Cultural (classic literature, classic photography, great actors), and/or as Beautiful (scenery, costumes, actors);
2. to expand market share in France: increasing the production values of the perennially successful comedy genre – which, be it said, has undeniably become less insular as the number of productions has decreased and the prospect of export for those that are made is correspondingly increased.

Nonetheless, Luc Besson's *Léon*, the biggest single French success both in France (3.3 million entries, the highest for a French film in 1995) and the USA (32.346 million dollars, twice *Cyrano*'s score) was achieved (at first glance) by following an American model. Shot in English (although released in a French version, but so are most Hollywood films), filmed in America, with a part-American cast; a genre film of a genre which, though certainly not exclusively American, has come to be largely identified with America, *Léon* nonetheless remains, if not distinctively French, at least clearly apart from the films it is modelled on. *Eye Weekly*, a Canadian review, spoke with shock of the America which *Léon* portrays: 'a questionable world... where guns are so omnipresent and natural they seem to sprout organically from the ends of your fingers'.[3] *Cahiers* compared *Léon,* very convincingly, to a spaghetti western. It takes a genre (the violent, urban gangster film) and strips it of its particularities. It presents a non-hero, with no past, no private life, no function but that of a killing machine, and a story stripped to the bone. It was received in America as 'an outsider's eye', and as essentially non-realist. Rather than an image of America, US reviewers saw in it the European myth of America: 'Besson's French vision of the NY underworld is so eerily unreal' (*Time*); 'Frenchman in America, home seen through new eyes' (*Entertainment Weekly*); 'Besson's visual approach gives it a European look – he finds Paris in Manhattan' (*Chicago Sun-Times*).[4]

It is hard to know how to approach *Léon*. From the artistic point of view, it seems to have been perceived as alien in both countries. To the American perceptions quoted above corresponded a certain snobbishness on the part of some of the French reviewers towards this 'American' film. To the industry, however, and as soon as economic matters were under discussion, *Léon* was a French film in France and an American film (albeit independent) in America. At the time when it appeared *Léon* was presented by some as the possible way forward for the French industry, at least avoiding the reclaiming of French scenarios. (It was Besson's disappointing experience with the remake of *Nikita* which persuaded him to make his own American film.) Besson had precedents for his move prior to the GATT negotiations and the accompanying raising of the stakes, notably Jean-Jacques Annaud's *L'Ours*, which made 31 million dollars in 1988. His own previous venture in this direction, *Le Grand Bleu*, had come nowhere near equalling this, although it topped three million. *Léon* represented a bold move in that, unlike *L'Ours*, it took on American culture as well as language and location, with an urban genre-film which nonetheless used specifically French elements – principally the main actor, Jean Reno. Despite *Léon*'s success, however, emulators have been rare. Besson himself is continuing in the same vein, but the possibilities for such cross-cultural work are limited except for rare and well-established film-makers.

The best schemes of the industry don't always work. As Jean-Michel Frodon has pointed out in *Le Monde* (Frodon, 1995a), the French cinema is not rich enough to churn out super-productions at the Hollywood rate: they tend to come at 18-month intervals, and big failures are correspondingly devastating. The other side of this is the films which achieve unexpected success, and which therefore present themselves before an international market that prior to their making had not been anticipated. In the last part of this chapter I should like to look briefly at what happened to *La Haine* in the course of its grooming for international stardom.

Compared with the films we have discussed hitherto, *La Haine* was a mini-production, very low-budget, and made with non-professional actors (with the exception of Vincent Cassel). It was not entirely without ambition; Kassowitz had established himself as a name to watch with his first feature, *Métisse*, and his contacts in the 'auteurist' end of the French cinema were good. The hot subject of the banlieue had already been treated once or twice recently, on an even smaller scale but with some success. Compared with *Hexagone*, a *succès d'estime* made by an amateur on a shoestring the previous year, Kassowitz's treatment represented a move towards the mainstream. Again compared with *Hexagone*, *La Haine* was very anchored in a cinematic tradition, quoting *Taxi Driver* and the big French success of a couple of years previously, *Un Monde sans pitié*, as well as paying its respects to the Spike Lee school of American ghetto films. Nonetheless, the success it achieved after showing at Cannes took its production team by surprise. Its producer Christophe Rossignon said (in Mérigeau, 1995a): 'To begin with, we thought of making 50 copies', but by the 6 June 1995 250 were in circulation and the film was proving a serious rival to *Pulp Fiction* in France. Inevitably, the prospect of export became a reality.

It should be said that *La Haine*'s small scale meant that the logistics of the export process were different – and easier in some ways – than for those involved in flagship productions. Authorial control of the film's image in America was much more possible for Kassowitz than, say, for Chéreau. *La Haine* had recouped its budget in France, and so the producer could afford to hesitate: 'It's not a question of taking the American cheque and saying thanks: we must do all we can to have the film seen by as many people as possible'. From the point of view of the production team, *La Haine* really was a cultural message, not only to America but to the established industry in France. 'It's because they have no right to speak that young people in the banlieues become violent', said the casting director, 'and I am sure that when they make their films, the French cinema will at last become a rival to the Americans' (Mérigeau, 1995b). The wish for a large American audience led the producer to the same tactic as Cleitman for *Le Hussard sur le toit*; that is, to hold out for a dubbed version. Like Cleitman, he failed to get it, and eventually accepted sub-titles.

The sub-titling of *La Haine* is an interesting issue. The enterprise was important enough to merit an article in *Libération* about the team (of Canadians) entrusted with the task of 'translating the *argot* into appropriate American'. The result is more than the translation of the 'argot', however. The sub-titles have the characters speak the language of gangsta rap even when their French is relatively standard ('ami' determinedly becomes 'homeboy'). All specifically French culture is excised – with some hilarious results: a reference to Bernard Tapie is replaced with Mickey Mouse, even though the point of the reference is Tapie's pose as a social idealist, and Mickey Mouse has never been known for visionary speeches. The character nicknamed Astérix becomes Snoopy... also far from equivalent, and the substitution seems fairly pointless given Astérix's international fame. In brief, French cultural references which had a certain significance (depending certainly on knowing a bit about who is involved) are replaced by American references which have no other significance than to be American.

Perhaps more importantly, the insistent gangsta slang – apart from being an essentially spoken language which looks uncomfortably false on subtitles, robbed of its spontaneity and called to provide an equivalent for something quite different – immediately inserts the film into a *genre* within the American cinema. This is absolutely contrary to its position in France, where, despite the existence of *Hexagone*, it came more or less out of the blue. It seems to me that this treatment of *La Haine* can have done it no favours in America (where, incidentally, it polled least well of all the films I have considered). Although there are no doubt similarities between the banlieue as portrayed by Kassowitz and the US 'ghetto-culture', there are visible and vital differences too. As Rappeneau's producer René Cleitman observed (Buob, 1995), in a culture where gun-ownership is a right it's hard to understand why all the action of the film revolves around an illegally held gun. To try to equate them is only to sacrifice credibility, to make the film exist in a non-place when in fact, despite its acknowledged debts to Scorsese and others, *La Haine* is rooted in a specific time and place, and to transpose it to another doesn't make it universal, just potentially inauthentic.

I find the export-treatment of *La Haine* a rather sad comment on the insecurity of French cinema when it is faced with marketing itself outside defined formulae (or perhaps it should be a sad comment on the way in which the US industry conceives of its own audiences, or conceivably a sad comment on the possibility of exporting anything socially 'disturbing' into the industry), and even more disturbing is the fact that – if my queries in FNAC are to be believed – the film appeared on video *in France* or at least in Belgium in its sub-titled version before the original.

Overall, the account of the search for the French blockbuster capable of imposing European cinema as an equal rival to the American industry has not been particularly encouraging. All efforts to conform to the American market have had a strictly limited impact, except the actual invasion of it on its own terms represented by *L'Ours* and *Léon*. Economically this route perhaps represents a real opening, but it is likely to pass by way of a loss of cultural identity. Besson's newest film will be 'French' – or, indeed 'European' – only in a financial sense. The situation in France is considerably more encouraging, and remained so through 1996. As a coda to this, however, should be placed the gradually increasing awareness of other useful international markets. The French showcase in America, the Festival of Sarasota in Florida, recently closed, since the profits which resulted were not enough to justify the expense. France is considering reopening it in Mexico, but in the meantime, an equivalent festival in Yokohama has been, for several years, a great success, and the press commentators have recently begun to suggest that the search for the French blockbuster may in the future ignore the US home market and look to its importers in the East and the Third World. What effect this – if it happens – will have on the kind of films France produces is anyone's guess.

NOTES

1.   *Léon* made over 32 million dollars. For comparison, *Pulp Fiction* reports a gross of 108 million, *Jurassic Park* 377 million in the USA alone (but – according to the ImDB figures – *Reservoir Dogs* only managed three million all told). Source for all US box office figures: the Internet Movie Database (http://uk.imdb.com)
2.   *Eye Weekly*, 30 May 1996. (http://www.eye.net/Arts/Movies/Onscreen/1996/os0530a.htm)
3.   'Me and the Hitman', 12 November 1994. (http://www.eye.net/Arts/Movies/Onscreen/Aisle/1994/ai1117.htm)
4.   *Entertainment Weekly*, 2 December 1994, *Time*, 5 December 1994 (Vol. 144, No. 3), *Chicago Sun-Times*, 18 November 1994. All these reviews can be accessed through the Internet Movie Database: http://uk.imdb.com/cache/urls/title+59776, or at: *EW*: http://pathfinder.com/@@tEI@*AcAGKv03hG7/ew/941202/movies/professional.html *Time*: http://pathfinder.com/@@tEI@*AcAGKv03hG7/time/magazine/domestic/1994/941205/941205.cinema.professional.html *CS-T*: http://www.suntimes.com/ebert/ebert_reviews/1994/11/951622.html

REFERENCES

Buob, J., 'Comment le producteur René Cleitman veut "ouvrir les portes de l'espoir" au cinéma français', *Le Monde*, 21 September 1995, p. 26.

Chéreau, P., Interview in *Cahiers du cinéma*, 479/80, May 1994a, pp. 12–19.

Chéreau, P., Interview, 'Le Temps de vivre l'histoire', in *Le Monde*, 16 May 1994b, p. 8.

Forbes, J., 'Keeping it in the Family', *Sight and Sound*, Vol. 4, No. 5, May 1994, pp. 24–5.

Frodon, J-M., 'L'Année des *Visiteurs*', *Le Monde*, 4 January 1994, p. 22.

Frodon, J-M., 'Une année cinématographique en noir et blanc', *Le Monde*, 4 January 1995a, p. 1.

Frodon, J-M., 'Les Entrées à Paris', *Le Monde*, 18 May 1995b, p. 29.

Hodgson, P., 'Pleurnicherie pour le cinéma français', *Cahiers du cinéma*, 489, March 1995, pp. 44–8.

Jousse, T. and Toubiana, S., 'A la hussarde', *Cahiers du cinéma*, Editorial, 495, October 1995, p. 5.

Mérigeau, P., 'Comment Mathieu Kassovitz a recruté les acteurs de *La Haine*', *Le Monde*, 1 June 1995a, p. 28.

Mérigeau, P., 'Les jeunes de Chanteloup ne se sentent pas trahis par *La Haine* de Mathieu Kassovitz', *Le Monde*, 6 June 1995b, p. 17.

Romney, R., 'Cannes: the shallow cut', *The Guardian*, 2, 24 May 1994, p. 6.

Part II
Media Issues

4 Regulation for Media Pluralism: Issues in Ownership and Competition[1]

Peter Humphreys

THE NEW MEDIA AND THE MARKETIZATION OF BROADCASTING

During the 1980s, the 'new media' of cable and satellite overcame the 'scarcity of frequencies' that had traditionally justified public service broadcasting monopolies (or, as in Britain, duopoly) in Western Europe. Changes of government in Europe's three large broadcasting powers – Britain, France and Germany – opened the floodgates to a Europe-wide deregulation and marketization of the broadcasting sector. In Britain and Germany, conservatives promised 'more market and less state'.

In France, Socialists 'liberated' broadcasting from the state and Gaullists privatized the country's premier public service channel in 1987. In all three countries, a new 'market model' of broadcasting was embraced with enthusiasm. Other countries followed at varying speeds (Humphreys, 1996, pp. 159–98).

The first wave of new media – cable and satellite television – increased the number of television channels in Western Europe from around forty mainly public service channels in 1983 to approaching three hundred by 1996, most of which were commercial. While the number of public service channels has hardly grown, alongside them has appeared a range of new advertising- or subscription-based commercial television services. Most are new national services or networks of local stations. Many services, designated 'generalist', are primarily entertainment channels. Alongside these has appeared a range of new 'thematic' channels, dedicated to sports, music, news, etc. In the late 1990s, a second wave of the new media – digital broadcasting – now promises an imminent further expansion of new services. These developments have been evaluated by many – notably on the neo-liberal Right – as a 'pluralization' of broadcasting.

Across Western Europe, technical change has combined with the new market-orientated political agenda to bring about a paradigm shift in

regulation of the electronic media. A regulatory system that has traditionally given primacy to the social and cultural goals of broadcasting
has given place to one that gives a new primacy to market values
(Hoffmann-Riem, 1986, 1996). Furthermore, the ongoing convergence of
broadcasting with advanced forms of communication more associated with
computing and telecoms appears to many to render public regulation
almost redundant.[2] Multi-channel broadcasting, it is argued, will increasingly resemble 'electronic publishing': it will be characterized by multiple
and diverse products and the rule of consumer sovereignty. Henceforth,
neo-liberals argue, regulation need only be 'light touch'; the free market
will guarantee media pluralism (for an explanation of this argument see
Veljanovski et al., 1989).

As the new market model of regulation has achieved ideological dominance, the safeguarding of key public service values in broadcasting has
arguably become secondary to the pursuit of techno-industrial and commercial goals. Policy-makers increasingly perceive broadcasting to be an
industry 'like any other'. Programmes and programme rights are seen as
internationally tradable commodities, public broadcasting companies like
the BBC as potential national champions in international markets, their
programme libraries as strategic assets, and so on. Regulatory policies are
undergoing a paradigm change: from a conception of regulation as trustee-
ship of the national cultural heritage and of social integration, to (de)regu-
lation as a means of attracting media investment and promoting new
technologies. With regard to media ownership and competition, regulatory
policy is assuming the dimensions of industrial policy, of what economists
call 'location policy' – the word is *Standortpolitik* in German, and it has
been much evoked in discussions about media ownership policy of late.[3]

OWNERSHIP REGULATION AND LOCATION POLICY
(*STANDORTPOLITIK*)

Governments have become keenly aware of the importance of the media
for inward investment and sensitive to the threat of disinvestment. A core
rationale behind the 1980s deregulation of broadcasting by West European
governments had been the race to exploit the industrial and commercial
promise of cable and satellite. More recently, official concern to produce a
regulatory framework that will encourage the take-off of digital terrestrial
broadcasting is explicitly clear from the legislative process culminating in
the British Broadcasting Act 1996 (Department of National Heritage,
1996).[4] Generally, policy-makers are aware that for European economies

on the threshold of the 'Information Society' the media are a very important field of economic activity. The promotion of a strong, dynamic and internationally competitive media sector has become a key policy concern, at national and European level (see, for instance, Bangemann, 1994).

However, relatively few players have the resources to risk investing in the new technical systems, whether cable, satellite or digital TV. Investing in or leasing capacity on a transmission system, marketing the new services and technologies, setting up conditional access systems for pay-TV (e.g. encryption and subscriber management systems), and so forth, all require substantial capital sums. So, too, does the huge amount of programming that is required to feed the burgeoning new private commercial media sector, let alone the expensive kind of strategic programming which will attract the audiences that new operators of 'free-to-air' broadcast services need to deliver to advertisers, or which drives subscriber up-take for pay-TV. Further, increased demand for programming and more competition between broadcasters have significantly inflated the cost of rights to popular sports events, especially football, and recently released movies, such that only concerns with deep pockets can afford them (to the discomfort of the public broadcasters).

Naturally, multiple ownership of TV stations provides multiple opportunities for the commercial exploitation of media products and rights, information resources, media stars, and so on. Multiple ownership of media outlets also produces economies of scale, synergies that can be exploited, and interesting opportunities for cross-media promotion. Joint ventures and strategic alliances allow the pooling of capital, the sharing of information, expertise, media products and rights, and the spreading of risk, as well as access to new markets. Thus, received economic wisdom suggests that the successful, internationally competitive companies of the future will be those that spread their interests across different media and which are able to benefit from the economies of scale and synergies that arise from their conglomerate status. Typically, these concerns will be integrated horizontally, vertically and diagonally (cross-media), controlling both rights to programmes and access to distribution systems through ownership of channels, encryption technologies and subscriber management systems. A leading expert on broadcasting regulation, critical of the neo-liberal viewpoint, readily concedes all the same that 'a high level of international and multimedial concentration is virtually a structural necessity and goes hand in hand with the media *market*' (Hoffmann-Riem, 1996, p. 2; my emphasis).

Because governments are keen to promote media investment, the media industry has had a privileged position of influence over public policy.

The media industry has not even needed to make explicit the threat of regime shopping – that is, relocation to jurisdictions with more (economically) competitive regulatory regimes – as a lever to gain deregulation: as the industry's power is structural, policy-makers are only too aware of the dangers (on the general proposition about the structural power of business, see Lindblom, 1977). At the same time, governments incur little obvious cost from the deregulation of media ownership restrictions in order to encourage media investment. Certainly, this kind of 'industrial policy' incurs no financial cost to the state exchequer, unlike industrial investment subsidies; the only cost falls on cultural and social policy. Under such conditions, media policy easily becomes subsumed into *Standortpolitik.* However, this kind of policy needs to be legitimized politically: hence the need for a symbolic politics of 're-regulation'.[5] But before examining this process, the question needs to be asked: why worry about media concentration?

WHY WORRY ABOUT MEDIA CONCENTRATION?

The consequences of media concentration are more serious than in other industries. Industrial concentration always carries the danger of abuse of market power, monopolistic or oligopolistic pricing, and restrictive trade practices. But media concentration can adversely affect a country's cultural and political life as well. The media are central to public opinion forming and they help determine the mass public's political values: they affect the political culture, no less. They have political agenda-setting and electoral effects, which have been the subject of considerable political science investigation. To state the problem simply: media concentration poses a potential threat to democratic pluralism by concentrating control over information, ideas and opinion forming in the hands of a limited number of media owners. Clearly, media concentration militates against the 'free market in ideas' that underpins the liberal ideal of media freedom. Many media experts have voiced concern about the dangers of media concentration. Thus, Ben Bagdikian author of the classic critique *The Media Monopoly*, notes that ' "market dominant" corporations in the mass media have dominant influence over the public's news, information, public ideas, popular culture and political ideas'. Because of their influence over the audience's perception of public life and politicians, they also 'exert considerable influence within government' (Bagdikian, 1992, p. 5). Lorimer (1994, pp. 94–5), explaining the economic factors that tend to produce media concentration and pointing to certain advantages (e.g. economies of scale – see above), warns that 'conglomerate journalism' may 'discourage in-depth investigative reporting', produce a 'softening of news values' and encourage 'company loyalty rather than journalistic integrity'. Lorimer (1994, p. 97) concludes that a 'highly concentrated media industry...leads to a narrowing of perspective'. Golding and Murdock (1991, p. 24) observe that, in the age of increasingly deregulated and commercialized media systems, the rise of the modern multimedia conglomerate has served to 'increase greatly the potential reach and power of the major communications companies and to reinforce the danger that public culture will be commandeered by private interests' (see also Murdock, 1990). In his major comparative study of broadcasting regulation Hoffmann-Riem (1996, p. 273) notes:

> in view of the massive tendencies to concentration in the broadcasting market, the risks of accumulation of power and thus the absence of equal communicative opportunity are inherent in privately owned broadcasting orders.

In fact, both the *historic* relative 'scarcity of frequencies' and the *enduring* high market entry barriers in the broadcasting field led to an acceptance on the part of policy-makers that private commercial broadcasting requires special regulation in the matter of ownership and control. It has hitherto been generally agreed that ordinary economic competition laws are inadequate for guaranteeing pluralism in the broadcasting sector. The arguments against relying simply on competition law in the broadcasting field are essentially twofold. In the first place, broadcasting has not, *at least until recently*, been viewed as an 'industry like any other'. It fulfils an important democratic opinion forming role. This is very explicitly expressed in German constitutional law where broadcasting is regarded as a 'factor' for democracy as well as a medium. The protection of the key goals of pluralism and diversity in broadcasting is seen as a central justification for special regulation (Ruck, 1992, p. 223; Hoffmann-Riem, 1996, p. 119). Secondly, ordinary economic competition laws have not been adequately tailored to the economic realities of the media sector. Anti-trust laws are usually concerned with larger concerns than most media companies and typically they allow for a generous measure of regulatory discretion.

Thus, in the United States – a country with a long experience of private commercial broadcasting – it has always been an axiom of media policy that cross-ownership between the press and the broadcasters should be restrained. In Britain too the Independent Broadcasting Authority (IBA) had become accustomed to grant its franchises to commercial television companies with key conditions attached regarding media ownership.

In 1990 strict ownership rules – including cross-ownership restrictions – were actually incorporated into statute and became the responsibility of the Independent Television Commission (replacing the IBA) to enforce. Similarly, the introduction of private commercial broadcasting in Germany, during the 1980s, saw the enactment of a whole series of media laws by the individual *Länder* and inter-state treaties between them collectively containing media-specific ownership rules against media concentration. Recently, however, these rules have been extensively deregulated.

THE DEREGULATION OF MEDIA OWNERSHIP RULES IN BRITAIN

Typically, private media industry lobbies have been well organized and well funded, and they have often enjoyed uncommonly close links to government. They have accordingly been highly effective in lobbying for deregulation. For their part, policy-makers, keen to promote media investment and technological development (e.g. digital broadcasting), have been naturally sensitive to the economic and technological arguments for a more relaxed approach to media concentration. In the policy process, therefore, the interests of the large media players have usually prevailed. However, where conflicts of interest have occurred between important media industry players, governments have acted in the interest of the industry at large, as the British case demonstrates.

As noted, the Conservative government's Broadcasting Act 1990, though a liberalizing reform of broadcasting, nonetheless incorporated some strict media ownership restrictions into statute.[6] The Act (partially) opened up the way for the joint ownership of a maximum of two ITV (Channel 3) licences, albeit after an initial moratorium on takeovers, but prevented any holder of an ITV franchise area designated as 'large'[7] from taking over another 'large' region. The Act also contained cross-media restrictions preventing national newspaper owners from taking more than a 20 per cent holding in a domestic television company (Channel 3 or 5) or a national radio service and only a 5 per cent interest in a second holding. Significantly, there were no such restrictions on cross-media ownership between newspaper and satellite services (e.g. those controlled by News International), the government arguing that it did not want to restrict investment and that, in any case, there was sufficient diversity among satellite channels. However, leading ITV (regional Channel 3) companies argued that the takeover restrictions placed them at a disadvantage at a time of increasingly fierce international competition between media companies. Worse, it rendered them vulnerable to takeover by European competitors in the emerging single European broadcasting market.[8] The issue split the ITV network; unsurprisingly, smaller ITV companies argued in favour of retaining takeover restrictions.[9] Predictably, however, the large players' international competitiveness argument won the day. In November 1993 the government liberalized the rules to allow the same company to hold any two ITV licences, except the two London ones. As had undoubtedly been intended, a series of ITV mergers immediately ensued, consolidating the industry (see later).

The structural power enjoyed by large, and especially internationally mobile, media investors – and the increasingly symbolic quality of media ownership regulation – appeared already to be clearly illustrated by the fact that BSkyB, half-owned (since 1995 40 per cent owned) and effectively controlled by Rupert Murdoch's News International, which already had 35 per cent of the British national press market, had been spared the Act's strict cross-media ownership restrictions. BSkyB was even deemed to be a 'non-domestic' broadcasting operation since the Astra satellite carrying BSkyB's service operated from Luxembourg – despite the fact that BSkyB's operation was based in the UK and its audience was British. Moreover, BSkyB had resulted from a controversial merger (of Sky TV) with British Satellite Broadcasting, the latter licensed as a British satellite broadcaster by the IBA. Why did Rupert Murdoch benefit from such apparently privileged treatment? Various explanations have been offered. Murdoch had been a valuable supporter of the Thatcher government and the government did not want to see his business damaged (Belfield et al., 1994, p. 213). Key News International lobbyists proved themselves to be very energetic and effective (Shawcross, 1992, pp. 501–2). Last but certainly not least, Murdoch's media investment must have weighed in the matter. One minister commented that 'the queue to invest in satellite did not go round the block'.[10]

Unsurprisingly, other media concerns in Britain started to lobby for a level playing field. The British Media Industry Group (BMIG) was established in 1993 by a number of Britain's other leading newspaper groups, namely Associated Newspapers (*Daily Mail*, etc.), the Guardian Media Group, the Telegraph Group and Pearson (owners of the *Financial Times*), in order to lobby for a liberalization of the rules which, they maintained, disadvantaged them vis-a-vis both News International at home and European and US multimedia organizations in the increasingly internationalized media markets. The BMIG chairman demanded 'the same rights to invest in British industry as [were] given to [their] foreign competitors'.[11] To illustrate its case, the BMIG presented a model for measuring media power in terms of individual media owners' share of the country's overall media market, including press, radio and television. The model took the share of British 'national voice', in other words the audience share enjoyed by a media company over various media (i.e. national press, local press, TV and radio) as the key measure of a media company's influence. According to this 'audience-share model', the only companies that had a significant share (i.e. above 10 per cent) of Britain's media were the BBC (19.7 per cent), which was in any case strictly regulated to promote a diversity and plurality of media content, and News International (10.6 per cent) (see Peak and Fisher, 1996).[12] The BMIG's audience-share model suggested that the cross-media expansion of other media companies active in Britain presented no threat to the diversity and plurality of the UK media.[13]

Williams (1996, pp. 4–5) suggests that the BMIG 'provides a case study of the effective use of media power'. He notes 'the interplay of discreet lobbying, high profile conferences aimed at opinion formers, and a stream of articles and reports presenting a one-sided case for abandoning ownership restrictions'. In Williams's view, the British government's acceptance of the need to liberalize media ownership rules was in fact 'a "need" created by powerful lobbying and the deployment by media groups of their power, acting in congruence, to shape emerging media policy to their advantage'. The BMIG's influence over public policy certainly appears to have been impressive. The Department of National Heritage (DNH) embraced a version of the audience-share model and the need to liberalize cross-media ownership restrictions in its 1995 Green Paper (proposals for legislation) on media ownership (DNH, 1995) and thereafter in the Broadcasting Act 1996.[14]

The government stated the continuing need for special rules, beyond general competition law, to protect diversity of the media. At the same time, however, it acknowledged the necessity to liberalize the existing ownership regulations. Technological change was breaking down the distinctions between the various media. Diversity was now being supplied by a proliferation of media outlets. Moreover, both the Green Paper and, subsequently, the Broadcasting Act 1996 bore explicit testimony to the government's concern to encourage the growth of internationally competitive media companies and to attract investment in the new technologies that it wanted to promote, notably digital broadcasting.

In essence, the Broadcasting Act 1996 introduced a new set of media ownership rules that put a ceiling on permissible media concentration in order to protect pluralism, yet also allowed companies to diversify fairly extensively across the media (DNH, 1997; also see Gibbons, 1998,

Chapter 5). The Act abolished numerical limits on the holding of TV licences; it also abolished the rules limiting the common control of terrestrial, satellite and cable TV broadcasters. Instead, the Act restricted holdings to 15 per cent of total audience share (share of total viewing time, that of the BBC and Channel 4 included, as measured by the Broadcasting Audience Research Board, BARB). The Act also abolished numerical limits on the total holding of local radio licences by any single group, though aggregate holdings are still restricted to 15 per cent of the total points available in the points scheme operated by the Radio Authority as an overall safeguard of pluralism and diversity. The Act introduced a points system for maintaining plurality and diversity in the supply of digital programme services, restricted any one interest from controlling more than three digital TV multiplex licences, and reserved a significant share of digital terrestrial frequencies for the BBC, ITV, Channels 4 and 5, and S4C. The Act also liberalized cross-media ownership between the press and broadcasting. Newspaper groups, so long as they do not already have more than 20 per cent of the national circulation, were to be allowed to buy mainstream terrestrial television stations (i.e. ITV Channel 3 and Channel 5) so long as the latter did not account for more than 15 per cent of the total television market measured by audience share. Similarly, TV owners could now buy into the press sector as well as, clearly, diversify further within the electronic media – terrestrial, cable, satellite, digital – so long as they did not exceed the 15 per cent limit of total television audience. The Act did, however, provide for a 'public interest test' that gave the regulators (the ITC and the Radio Authority) some discretion to act against individual cases of cross-media ownership that might otherwise comply with the restrictions.

In fact, it was immediately widely observed that the only media groups that this new regulatory model actually prevented from expanding, and only into mainstream terrestrial TV, were Mirror Group Newspapers and News International. Some Conservative MPs had been worried by this apparent provocation of Rupert Murdoch. On the other hand, the Conservative government had pleased the media industry at large, including some powerful players like the Associated Newspapers conglomerate (owners of the *Daily Mail*).[15] Moreover, looked at another way, the Act actually confirmed News International's *existing* scale of cross-media business in Britain and, significantly, held the door open for it to expand into *digital* TV. At the same time, the 1996 Act opened the way for the rest of the British media industry to consolidate. The new regulatory framework for media ownership in Britain clearly had a certain 'symbolic re-regulatory' quality, yet it was not as deregulatory as the German case (Stock et al., 1997, p. 149).

THE DEREGULATION OF MEDIA OWNERSHIP
RULES IN GERMANY

In Germany, as in most of Western Europe, the abolition of the public broadcasting monopoly was a 1980s development. Because broadcasting regulation in Germany is a responsibility of the *Länder* (federal states), regulations with a nation-wide reference have to be negotiated between the *Länder* governments and legislated in the form of inter-*Land* treaties (*Staatsverträge*). The original broadcasting inter-*Land* treaty of 1987 contained few precise anti-concentration restrictions beyond stipulating that a broadcaster be limited to a maximum of two national television channels, only one of which might be a 'generalist' channel (*Vollprogramm*), and that broadcasting companies should be pluralistically constituted in order to prevent any investor gaining dominant influence on programming. A new 1991 inter-*Land* treaty tightened up the restrictions by introducing more precise shareholding limits. Individual investors were now prevented from holding 50 per cent or more of the shares in a single national generalist channel or a national 'information-orientated' thematic channel and the same investor was prevented from holding 25 per cent or more (a blocking minority in German law) in two other such channels. Neither of these inter-*Land* treaties prescribed any precise cross-media ownership restrictions, leaving this matter – and anything else not specified in the inter-*Land* treaties – to individual *Länder* laws. These regulations already seemed sensitive, in their comparative laxity,[16] to the requirements of capital investment in the new commercial broadcasting sector. A major problem was that achievement of an inter-*Land* regulatory framework for nation-wide broadcasting had been rendered difficult by political disagreement over media policy goals between those *Länder* governed by the Social Democrats (SPD) and those governed by the Christian Democrats (CDU/CSU). As a result, some market *faits accomplis* had already occurred, notably the fact that the principal source of investment in the new national commercial television channels were press and other media interests, including some major players like Bertelsmann, CLT, Springer and KirchGruppe (Humphreys, 1994, pp. 239–85).

Moreover, in the implementation of the inter-*Land* treaties' media concentration rules, regional economic rivalries soon brought about a competitive deregulation, as 'soft competition policy' served as an instrument of regional *Standortpolitik* (Heinrich, 1994). The federal structure of German broadcasting meant that a national satellite broadcasting service could apply for and receive a licence in a *Land* where the media regulation was suitably lax; its licence then had to be recognized across the federal republic.

Clearly, then, those *Länder* that provided the most relaxed regulatory conditions were the best placed to attract the new media investment. Therefore, tbe *Land*-based regulatory authorities – the *Landesmedienanstalten* – came under political pressure to prioritize the economic interests of their respective *Länder* which were vigorously competing to attract – or retain – media investment. Thus, Porter and Hasselbach (1991, p. 21) suggest that the regulatory authorities favoured licence applicants who promised to site specific activities in their particular *Land*. Similarly, Hoffmann-Riem (1996, p. 137) notes that the regulatory bodies 'came to see themselves as advocates of "their" companies, that is those headquartered within their jurisdictions'. Soon, the *Landesmedienanstalten* found themselves criticized for being the politicians' 'puppets' or helpless 'paper tigers', incapable of controlling the new multimedia empires.[17] The German political scientist Axel Zerdick (1993, p. 61) neatly summarized the problem:

> the objectives of the *Land* media laws, orientated less towards media policy than towards *Standortpolitik*, [had] led to a state of affairs in which too many *Landesmedienanstalten* controlled too few broadcasters who, at the same time, [were] being courted avidly by the respective *Land* governments.

The outcome was the dominance of the German private commercial broadcasting sector by an oligopoly composed of two broadcasting 'families': Bertelsmann (ufa)/CLT and Kirch/Springer (Europäisches Medieninstitut, 1995).

Before long, there were calls for a re-regulation to tighten up the regulatory framework, and in particular to establish a regulatory body at the national level that would stand above this (economic) competition between the *Länder*. The unions, churches, regulators, media experts, the Greens and the Social Democratic Party (SPD) all demanded action. However, the negotiations over a new inter-*Land* regulatory framework for media ownership were characterized by intensive industry lobbying of the policy-makers. The media industry was largely agreed that the media ownership rules should in fact be relaxed, not be made more strict. The arguments deployed were essentially the same as in the British case; liberalization was necessary for the international economic competitiveness of the German media industry. Further, each of the two leading media concerns had 'special relationships' to Germany's two main political parties: the huge multinational multimedia conglomerate Bertelsmann based in SPD North-Rhine Westphalia, with the left-of-centre SPD; and the KirchGruppe, based in CSU Bavaria, with the right-of-centre CDU/CSU (Kleinsteuber and Peters, 1991, p. 188). In the negotiations, the CDU/CSU broadly supported the media industry's position and linked the issue to a concurrent debate about the future of public service broadcasting and in particular about how much the public service broadcasters' licence fee income should be allowed to rise; this applied pressure on the SPD *Länder* to give way over the liberalization of media ownership rules (Stock et al., 1997, pp. 18–21). Yet, in reality not much separated the most influential policymakers who, regardless of party, catered to considerations of regional economic policy in the media field (*Standortpolitik*).

After a series of negotiations between the CDU and SPD *Länder*, in which the media industry was intensively involved, a new regulatory framework was proposed embracing an audience-share model similar to the one adopted in Britain, but adopting a more generous 30 per cent audience share ceiling for individual investors. Predictably, this limit left the broadcasting interests of the major industry players, Bertelsmann and the Kirch group, entirely unaffected. Indeed, it presented scope for their further expansion, particularly since there were no specific rules for digital TV beyond a requirement that controllers of digital pay-TV platforms should grant non-discriminatory access to all broadcasters (this in line with a European Directive). The new rules did provide for a new inter-*Land* regulatory body to vet broadcasting licence applications and whose task it would be to police the 30 per cent audience share ceiling. However, up to this limit, media investors would now be able to accumulate channels and own them outright, the shareholding limits having been abolished by this new regulatory regime. The new rules did provide for one very interesting re-regulatory element: broadcasters with more than a 10 per cent total audience share are required to relinquish 260 minutes of weekly airtime, including 75 minutes of prime viewing time, to 'window broadcasters' who must be independent of the major broadcasters. This amounted to an innovative device to promote pluralism in an oligopolistic market. However, it could hardly disguise the largely symbolic nature of the 're-regulation' of media ownership rules in Germany. The inter-*Land* treaty of 1996 amounted, in the words of one respected commentator, to a 'capitulation on the part of the policy makers to Germany's most powerful media concerns Kirch and Bertelsmann'. Virtually the only concentration that the latest regulation ruled out now was *their* merger.[18] The German case graphically illustrates how large multimedia companies exert structural power over the politicians and regulators.[19]

THE OUTCOME: THE CURRENT STATE OF CONCENTRATION IN EUROPEAN BROADCASTING

What has been the outcome of the regulatory trends described above? In Britain, even before the Broadcasting Act 1996, there had occurred a series of ITV mergers which led to the commercial broadcasting sector being dominated by several large interests. Following the government's first loosening of the 1990 Broadcasting Act's rules in 1993, Granada took over LWT, Carlton took over Central, and the MAI group (owners of Anglia TV) took over Meridian, all in the course of 1994. By the end of that year, these three players already accounted for over two-thirds of ITV advertising revenue. Then, following the 1996 Broadcasting Act, MAI merged with United News and Media, a large publishing group (owners of the *Express*, the *Express on Sunday* and the *Daily Star*).

Moreover, in December 1997, United News and Media proceeded to take over the HTV group which holds the Channel 3 franchises for Wales and the West of England. Further, some major players in the communications industry now formed alliances for the purpose of launching digital TV. In 1996, BSkyB first announced its intention to provide a digital satellite platform for as many as two hundred channels. This service actually commenced operation in the autumn of 1998. At the same time, BSkyB originally formed part of the British Digital Broadcasting (BDB) consortium, together with the leading British commercial TV companies Granada and Carlton, in order to bid for the licence for the 'multiplexes' that will provide some 35 digital terrestrial channels in Britain. It appeared likely that, whichever technology proved to be successful, BSkyB would replicate in digital broadcasting the commanding position that it currently enjoys in the analogue pay-TV market in Britain. In the event, the Independent Television Commission made it a condition of awarding BDB (Granada/Carlton) the digital terrestrial licence in 1997 that BSkyB withdraw from the consortium. Nonetheless, BSkyB was allowed to remain an important, possibly the most important, programme provider for BDB (Humphreys and Lang, 1997, p. 20). Clearly, Britain's commercial television sector has consolidated considerably in the course of the 1990s.

In Germany, as noted, private commercial broadcasting has been controlled more or less from the outset (when private broadcasting was introduced in the 1980s) by two powerful broadcasting 'families': Bertelsmann (ufa)/CLT and KirchGruppe/Springer. Bertelsmann and Springer were Germany's leading press concerns (in magazines and newspapers respectively); KirchGruppe was the country's leading dealer in film rights for television; the CLT was Europe's best known private commercial broadcaster, based in Luxembourg, which had radio and TV interests (mainly operating under the RTL emblem) in several West European countries. By 1997, most of the German population may have been able to receive numerous new TV channels via cable, satellite and regional terrestrial frequencies, but the three main channels – RTL (ufa/CLT), SAT 1 (KirchGruppe/Springer) and PRO 7 (Thomas Kirch) – accounted for

40 per cent of the total audience market (another 40 per cent going to the public broadcasters, 20 per cent spread across all the other new channels). Further, these three leading commercial channels accounted for 83 per cent of the private television sector's advertising revenue, and three-quarters of the overall German television advertising market (the private broadcasting sector altogether accounted for 90 per cent of television advertising revenue, the other 10 per cent going to the public broadcasters which were allowed to supplement the TV licence fee with limited advertising revenue). Moreover, by 1997, Bertelsmann's TV subsidiary ufa had merged with the CLT, a development which the new media ownership rules seemed almost perfectly designed to accommodate. KirchGruppe had launched a digital TV service and, to assure it attractive programmes, had concluded output deals with five of the six major Hollywood studios. Finally, in June 1997 KirchGruppe and Bertelsmann – 'Bertelkirch' as some observers now playfully referred to them – announced plans to form a digital pay-TV joint venture. This, however, was blocked in May 1998 by the European Commission's competition directorate. Nonetheless, by any standards, the German private broadcasting sector had been allowed to become highly concentrated.

EC COMPETITION RULES

Given the trends towards what might be termed the 'competitive deregulation' of national media ownership rules and increasing media concentration, the EU suggests itself as a more suitable and effective level of regulation. The EU does already possess some instruments for combating media concentration, in the shape of its existing European competition law, applied by Directorate General IV (DG IV) of the Commission, which has the direct authority to intervene and is subject only to judicial review by the European Court of Justice. Articles 85 and 86 of the Treaty of Rome respectively ban anti-competitive practices and the abuse of dominant market position. Moreover, the Community's merger control regulation was enhanced in the run-up to the 1992 Single European Market. From 1990, proposed mergers and acquisitions required DG IV's permission where (i) the aggregate worldwide turnover of all the enterprises concerned is more than ECU 5 billion; and (ii) the aggregate Community-wide turnover of each of at least two of the enterprises concerned is more than ECU 250 million, unless each of the enterprises concerned achieves more than two-thirds of its aggregate Community-wide turnover within one and the same member state (Council of the EC, 1989).

In 1997, EU industry ministers voted to lower these thresholds – so long as three or more member states were involved – to a global turnover of ECU 2.5 billion and an EU turnover of ECU 100 million each, when in each of at least three member states the aggregate turnover of at least two of the merging enterprises is more than ECU 25 million. Again, Commission permission is not required for a merger if each of the enterprises concerned achieves more than two-thirds of its aggregate Community-wide turnover within one and the same member state (Council of the EC, 1997). Thus, mergers with a mainly national impact remain a national affair. For the European Commission to act against mergers there has to be a clear 'community interest' (Fröhlinger, 1993).

The deregulation, commercialization and internationalization of the electronic media – and not least of all the enactment of the 1989 'Television without Frontiers' directive establishing a single community television market – have meant that EU competition law has become increasingly relevant to the sector. In 1990, a section specifically devoted to the media field was opened within DG IV. Several important rulings were made against anti-competitive practices in the field of programme acquisition[20] (Collins, 1994, pp. 145–53). As regards the issue of media concentration, DG IV first demonstrated its authority in 1994 when it ruled against a proposed digital pay-TV joint venture between Bertelsmann, KirchGruppe and Deutsche Telekom (an earlier attempt than the one mentioned at the close of the preceding section). The joint venture, called Media Service GmbH (MSG), had been intended to provide infrastructure, marketing and subscription services for commercial pay-TV, including video-on-demand and a number of other advanced 'interactive' services. After discussions between the Commission and more than 100 companies and industrial bodies, the deal was blocked on the grounds of the threat that it was thought to present to three separate markets. First, the Commission argued that Bertelsmann and Kirch would have dominated the market for pay-TV services in Germany. As seen, Bertelsmann and KirchGruppe already dominated Germany's private television sector. In fact, they also shared between them the country's only existing (analogue) pay-TV channel, *Premiere*. Moreover, KirchGruppe had a leading position in the German market for TV film rights. Second, it was feared that MSG would have dominated the market for the technological services associated with pay-TV, such as the supply of decoders providing conditional access to the system. Third, the Commission felt that the merger would have allowed Deutsche Telekom to reinforce its dominance of the German cable market. Deutsche Telekom had a virtual monopoly of Germany's cable systems and had recently acquired a significant stake in Luxembourg's Astra satellite operation. The 'Community interest' in the merger resided in the fact that MSG, it was felt, would have foreclosed these markets in Germany to other European players.[21]

The second, 1997, proposal for a joint venture between Bertelsmann and KirchGruppe, which also foresaw co-operation with Deutsche Telekom, bore more than a passing resemblance to the MSG venture blocked by the Commission in 1994 (Humphreys and Lang, 1997, p. 23). Therefore, it was hardly surprising that the Commission's competition watchdog took a very close interest in it. While the Commission conducted its investigations, the further expansion of digital TV in Germany remained temporarily halted, a state of affairs that infuriated the industry and also, reportedly, led the German government to lobby the Commission.[22] Germany's own rules against media concentration, it was argued, were adequate. The German media industry complained that while 'Europe' blocked German companies from investing in digital TV, American companies were stealing a lead.[23] The argument was a familiar one. Nonetheless, in May 1998, the European Commission blocked the merger on competition policy grounds very similar to the 1994 MSG case.

THE EUROPEAN COMMISSION AND MEDIA CONCENTRATION RULES

The point has already been made that, in view of the cultural and democratic importance of the media, an argument can be made that competition law can be no substitute for media-specific ownership rules. Indeed, European journalists' organizations have lobbied long and hard for European action that goes beyond competition law. The European Parliament (EP), too, has presented a number of resolutions and reports calling upon the European Commission to draft media-specific legislation on media concentration and pluralism. The Parliament expressed disappointment that the 1989 European Directive 'Television without Frontiers' – creating the regulatory framework for a single European market for television – had contained no media-specific anti-monopoly measures. The Economic and Social Committee echoed this concern. In the early 1990s the pressure on the Commission for some measures on media concentration from the European Parliament became irresistible. The EP's Culture Committee was the originator of this pressure. From 1990 onwards, the EP has produced a series of resolutions urging the Commission to act in order to safeguard media pluralism against growing media concentration in Europe (EP 1990, 1992a, 1992b, 1994a, 1994b).

In 1992 the Commission, apparently responding to these calls, produced a Green Paper entitled 'Pluralism and Media Concentration in the Internal Market' (CEC, 1992). However, it was immediately clear from the content of the Green Paper that the Commission's prime concern was not so much to safeguard media pluralism *per se*, as to address the danger that the disparity of existing national anti-concentration rules might constitute an obstacle to the creation of the Single European Market (Humphreys, 1996, p. 290). The Green Paper presented an extensive comparative study of the disparate national media ownership rules in Europe and highlighted a range of problems that could arise from this disparity. It then offered three options for action. Essentially these were: do nothing, promote increased co-operation between member states, and prepare community action to harmonize these media ownership laws.

The 1992 Green Paper launched a round of consultation with the European media 'policy community'. The European federations of the various media unions were all in favour of community action on media ownership. The business community was divided. Among the voices against pan-European regulation (i.e. favouring the first option) were the European Publishers' Council (EPC), Berlusconi's Fininvest, BSkyB and News International, and the Association of Commercial Broadcasters (ACT). Other media companies argued in favour of EU action to counteract the scope for circumvention of national rules by internationally operative competitors. Those arguing for no EU action tended to be those benefiting from liberal national laws, while those pressing for regulation were those who felt disadvantaged (Hitchens, 1994, pp. 596–7). Unsurprisingly, the European Publishers Council (EPC), the Euro-lobby of Europe's leading newspaper and magazine publishers, was notably active in seeking to obstruct the Commission's attempts to develop a European policy against media concentration (Williams, 1996, pp. 4–6).

In 1994, the Commission published a second Green Paper entitled 'Follow-Up to the Consultation Process Relating to the Green Paper on "Pluralism and Media Concentration in the Internal Market" – an Assessment of the Need for Community Action' (CEC, 1994). In it, the Commission expressed its view that the responses to its first Green Paper now generally supported future EU legislation to harmonize member state laws on media ownership. The Commission noted that the European Parliament and the Economic and Social Committee were both in favour of harmonization. Nonetheless, it was decided that more time was needed for further consultation. National governments, and Germany's *Länder*, were cool about the idea of European rules for media ownership. Moreover, internally the Commission was divided between those (notably in its competition directorate) arguing for a need to curb undue market power and others more concerned that Europe produce 'world class' media companies (for detail on the internal divisions within the Commission see Harcourt, 1996).

In the summer of 1996 DG XV, under the direction of Internal Market Commissioner Mario Monti, who was more enthusiastic about media ownership restrictions than his (economically) liberal predecessor Martin Bangemann, appeared at last ready to produce a draft Directive. DG XV remained primarily concerned to harmonize divergent national media concentration rules in order to create the conditions for cross-border television investment and programme flows. The draft Directive included proposals to limit media concentration by audience share instead of by ownership. The proposed limit was a fairly liberal 30 per cent of a country's television or radio audience, exactly like the German audience-share model. However, in contrast to the German model, the draft Directive established a limit of 10 per cent of total market share permissible for 'multimedia' enterprises combining TV, radio and the press. This proposed cross-media restriction predictably caused a storm of opposition from large European commercial media interests, notably the European Publishers' Council. The draft Directive was withheld for further modification. During the following months, officials in DG XV explored ways of making it more flexible.[24] Meanwhile, the industry pressure on the Commission continued. The European Publishers' Council lobbied Jacques Santer, President of the European Commission, stating that the proposals were both against its long-term interests and the interests of a flourishing European media industry.[25] The industry pressure appeared to be effective; a new draft contained a 'flexibility clause' which would run for an initial ten years and allow member states the discretion to allow media companies to exceed the proposed thresholds in their home countries. However, despite this compromise, much of the media industry – including the EPC – remained opposed to the legislation. Also, some commissioners remained sceptical. The Directive appeared to be hopelessly stalled.[26]

Should it eventually be finalized by the Commission, the point might be made that any draft directive watered down beyond the extent presented by the 'flexibility clause' would hardly deserve to be considered worthwhile. Moreover, the draft Directive would still require European Parliament/Council co-decision. However positive the European Parliament may be about regulating for pluralism, the prospect of reaching even a qualified majority within the Council of Ministers (as a single market issue) remains bleak. Too many member states are hostile to the imposition of European regulation in such a sensitive area. For instance, Chancellor Helmut Kohl is reported to have expressed to Commission President Jacques Santer his view that Germany's rules sufficed to safeguard media pluralism.[27] Finally, the evident 'veto power' of (much of) the commercial media industry suggests that a robust pan-European regulation of media concentration, one that would be far more appropriate to the media as a sphere of cultural activity than that offered by economic competition policy alone, is not a very realistic expectation. The European trend would appear to be towards a deregulation that will permit all but the largest of mergers with a cross-border relevance.

NOTES

1. The research upon which this chapter is based was funded by the Economic and Social Research Council under its Media Economics and Media Culture programme. The three-year research project, which began in January 1996, is entitled 'Regulating for Media Pluralism: Issues in Competition and Ownership'. It examines policy-making relating to media concentration in Britain and Germany, and also at the European level.

2. New services are emerging that arguably do not fit the traditional understanding of 'broadcasting' at all. In the jargon, these services are not 'uni-directional point-to-multipoint' but 'point-to-point' communication. They include video-on-demand, pay-per-view and data services. Currently, therefore, there is debate about whether these new services – including pay-per-view – should be regulated more strictly as mass communication or less strictly as a form of private communication.

3. The centrality of *Standortpolitik* has been one of the key findings of the interviews that we have conducted with German policy-makers, regulators and other interests in the media field in 1996 and 1997.

4. For its part, the media industry was quite frank about the possibility of disinvestment if the regulatory framework provided by the Bill should prove too unattractive. For example, David Elstein, while still head of programming for BSkyB suggested that if cross-media restrictions affecting News International remained in the Bill, the likeliest effect 'would be to make investment outside the UK more attractive than inside' (Elstein, D., 'Stimulating Digital Development', a presentation to the Westminster Media Forum, 6 February 1996, p. 5).

5. On the 'symbolic uses of politics' see Edelman, 1964. Edelman (pp. 38–40) argues that business regulation has often been largely symbolic in function, serving to produce political quiescence. The Federal Communications Commission, claims Edelman, had permitted greater concentration of control to occur. Anti-trust regulation, too, often appeared to promote the growth of large industrial organizations.

6. Previously the IBA had implemented its own strict media ownership rules.

7. Nine of the 15 franchise areas: Anglia, Carlton, Central, Granada, HTV, LWT, Meridian, Scottish and Yorkshire.
8. The moratorium on ITV takeovers was due to end in 1994.
9. Peter Gibbons, 'Big boys' threat to small screen', *Media Guardian*, Monday 14 June, 1993, p. 17.
10. National Heritage Minister Peter Brooke in a speech in January 1994, cited in Williams, 1996, p. 52. Williams points out that this view ignored the bitter competition raging at the time between Sky (as it was) and BSB, the latter handicapped by 'stringent technical and regulatory requirements'.
11. David English, the BMIG chairman, cited in *The Guardian*, Wednesday 22 March 1995, p. 8.
12. Rupert Murdoch's News International was conspicuous by its absence from the BMIG.
13. Other influential media interests also lobbied for a 'level playing field'. For instance, Michael Green, the chairman of Carlton Communications, argued that all companies – not just News International – should benefit from a more liberal regulatory framework. See Michael Green, 'Thinking big about the small screen; media ownership rules must change if Britain is to compete in an exploding world market', *The Guardian*, 20 April 1994, p. 20.
14. When the government's proposals were published, the BMIG announced that it was 'particularly pleased', Matthew Lynn and Rufus Olins, 'Media Melting Pot', *Sunday Times*, 28 May 1995, p. 2.3. On the other hand, Murdoch was distinctly displeased with the proposals which would set limits on News International's further expansion. Rupert Murdoch, 'Cross? You bet', *Media Guardian*, 29 May 1995, p. 14.
15. Michael White, 'Ministers defy Murdoch and agree media bill', *The Guardian*, 26 May 1995, p. 9.
16. Compared with Britain with, until the recent deregulation, its limitations on the multiple ownership of regional ITV franchises and cross-media ownership.
17. Hauch-Fleck, Marie-Luise (1992), 'Marionetten der Macht: Medienanstalten der Länder sehen die Konzentration bei den Privatsendern tatenlos zu', *Die Zeit*, 12 June 1992, p. 29.
18. Ott, K. (1997), 'Der Triumph des Leo Kirch', *Süddeutsche Zeitung*, 9 January 1997, p. 4.
19. For an overview in English of the policy process leading up to this latest regulatory framework, see Ridder (1996). For a collection (in German) of the negotiating positions of the SPD, CDU, media industry, etc., see Kresse (1995). For a critical treatment (in German) of the content of the regulations see Stock et al. (1997).
20. For example, in 1991, DG IV upheld a complaint by W. H. Smith, the main backer of a commercial satellite sports channel called Screensport, against the Eurosport channel which was a joint venture between Rupert Murdoch's Sky TV (as it was then) and the Eurosport consortium, a group of members of the European Broadcasting Union. The joint venture's programme acquisition and sharing arrangements were held to be anti-competitive.
21. See Tucker, Emma (1994), 'Brussels closes off multimedia gateway...', *Financial Times*, 10 November.

22. Ott, K., 'Freund Kohl in geheimer Mission', *Süddeutsche Zeitung*, 17 December 1997; Walker, M., 'Brussels risks war with Kohl', *The Guardian*, 2 February 1998.
23. Kaatz, S., 'Von Eurokraten umzingelt', *Focus*, 2 February 1998.
24. *European Report*, no. 2154, 5 September 1996, pp. 5–6; also Johnstone, Chris, 'Monti retunes media strategy', *European Voice*, 19 December 1996–8 January 1997, Vol. 2, No. 47, p. 1.
25. Tucker, Emma, 'Brussels media plan under fire; industry resists proposals to limit audience share in the European Union', *Financial Times*, 4 March 1997, p. 2.
26. Ibid.; also Tucker, Emma, 'Europe: EU media initiative bogged down', *Financial Times*, 13 March 1997, p. 3.
27. Ott, K., 'Kohl für Kirch und Vaterland', *Süddeutsche Zeitung*, 6 February 1998.

REFERENCES

Bagdikian, B., *The Media Monopoly* (Boston, Beacon Press, 1992; fourth, paperback edition).
Bangemann, M., *Europe and the Global Information Society: Recommendations to the European Council* (Brussels, The European Commission, 1994).
Belfield, R., Hird, C. and Kelly, S., *Murdoch: the Great Escape* (London, Warner Books, 1994).
Collins, R., *Broadcasting and Audio-visual Policy in the European Single Market* (London, John Libbey, 1994).
Commission of the European Communities, 'Pluralism and Media Concentration in the Internal Market' (Brussels: COM (92) 480 final, 1992).
Commission of the European Communities, 'Follow-Up to the Consultation Process Relating to the Green Paper on "Pluralism and Media Concentration in the Internal Market" – an Assessment of Need for Community Action' (Brussels: COM (94) 353 final 1994).
Council of the European Communities, 'Council Regulation (EEC) No. 4064/89 of 21 December on the Control of Concentrations between Undertakings' (OJ L 30.12.1989, OJ L 257, 21.09.1990, 1989).
Council of the European Communities, 'Council Regulation (EC) No. 1310/97 of 30 June 1997' (OJ L 180, 09.07.1997).
Department of National Heritage, 'Media Ownership: the Government's Proposals' (London, HMSO, Cmnd. 2872, 1995).
Department of National Heritage, 'Digital Terrestrial Broadcasting; an Explanatory Guide to the Provisions Introduced by the Broadcasting Act 1996' (London, DNH, 1996; also available from ⟨http://www.culture.gov.uk DTB1.HTM⟩).
Department of National Heritage, 'Guide to Media Ownership Regulation' (London, DNH, 1997; available from ⟨http://www.culture.gov.uk/M1.HTM⟩).
Edelman, M., *The Symbolic Uses of Politics* (Urbana, University of Illinois Press, 1964).

Europäisches Medieninstitut, 'Bericht über die Entwicklung der Meinungsvielfalt und Konzentration im privatem Rundfunk gemäss 21 Abs. 6, Staatsvertrag über den Rundfunk im vereinten Deutschland', in Die Landesmedienanstalten (eds), *Die Sicherung der Meinungsvielfalt* (Berlin, VISTAS, 1995), pp. 127–220.

European Parliament, 'Resolution on Media Takeovers and Mergers' (OJ.C68/137–138, 1990).

European Parliament (1992a), 'Report by the Committee on Culture, Youth, Education and the Media: Media Concentration and the Diversity of Opinion', DOC EN/RR/207249, PE 152.265/fin (Strasbourg, European Parliament, 1992).

European Parliament (1992b), 'Resolution of 16 September 1992 on Media Concentration and Diversity of Opinions' (OJ.C284/44–49, 1992).

European Parliament (1994a), 'Resolution on Concentration of Media and Pluralism' (OJ.C323/157–158, 1994).

European Parliament (1994b), 'Resolution on Pluralism and Media Concentration' (OJ C166/133, 1994).

Fröhlinger, M., 'EG-Wettbewerbsrecht und Fernsehen', *Rundfunk und Fernsehen*, Vol. 41, No. 1, 1993, pp. 59–65.

Gibbons, T., *Regulating the Media* (London, Sweet and Maxwell, 1998).

Golding, P. and Murdock, G., 'Culture, Communications, and Political Economy', in Curran, J. and Gurevitch, M. (eds), *Mass Media and Society* (London, Edward Arnold, 1991), pp. 15–32.

Harcourt, A., 'Regulating for Media Concentration: the Emerging Policy of the European Union', *Utilities Law Review*, October, Vol. 7, Issue 5, 1996, pp. 202–10.

Heinrich, J., 'Keine Entwarnung bei Medienkonzentration. Ökonomische und publizistische Konzentration im deutschen Fernsehsektor 1993/94', *Media Perspektiven*, Vol. 6, 1994, pp. 297–310.

Hitchens, L., 'Media Ownership and Control: a European Approach', *Modern Law Review*, Vol. 57, 1994, pp. 585–601.

Hoffmann-Riem, W., 'Law, Politics and the New Media', in Dyson, K. and Humphreys, P. (eds), *The Politics of the Communications Revolution* (London, Frank Cass, 1986), pp. 125–46.

Hoffmann-Riem, W., *Regulating Media: the Licensing and Supervision of Broadcasting in Six Countries* (New York and London, Guilford Press, 1996).

Humphreys, P., *Media and Media Policy in Germany* (Oxford and Providence, RI, Berg, 1994; second, paperback edition).

Humphreys, P., *Media and Media Policy in Western Europe* (Manchester, Manchester University Press, 1996).

Humphreys, P. and Lang, M., 'Digital Television between the Economy and Pluralism', Chapter 1 in Steemers, J. (ed.), *Changing Channels: the Prospects for Television in a Digital World* (Luton, John Libbey Media/University of Luton Press, 1997), pp. 9–36.

Kleinsteuber, H. and Peters, B., 'Media Moguls in Germany', in Tunstall, J. and Palmer, M. (eds) *Media Moguls* (London and New York, Routledge, 1991), pp. 184–205.

Kresse, H., (ed.), *Pluralismus, Markt und Medienkonzentration: Positionen* (Berlin, VISTAS, 1995).

Lindblom, C., *Politics and Markets* (New York, Basic Books, 1977).

Lorimer, Rowland with Paddy Scannell, *Mass Communications: a Comparative Introduction* (Manchester and New York, Manchester University Press, 1994).

Murdock, G., 'Redrawing the Map of the Communications Industries: Concentration and Ownership in the Era of Privatization', in Ferguson, M. (ed.), *Public Communication: the New Imperatives* (London, Sage, 1990), pp. 1–15.

Peak, S. and Fisher, P., *The Media Guide 1997* (London, Fourth Estate, 1996).

Porter, V. and Hasselbach, S., *Pluralism, Politics and the Marketplace* (London and New York, Routledge, 1991).

Ridder, C-M., 'Germany', in International Institute of Communications (ed.), *Media Ownership and Control in the Age of Convergence* (London, IIC, 1996), pp. 65–82.

Ruck, S., 'The Development of Broadcasting Law in the Federal Republic of Germany', *European Journal of Communications*, Vol. 7, No. 2, 1992, pp. 219–40.

Shawcross, W., *Murdoch* (London, Sydney and Auckland, Pan Books, 1993, first published by Chatto and Windus, 1992).

Stock, M., Röper, H. and Holznagel, B., *Medienmarkt und Meinungsmacht: Zur Neuregelung der Konzentrationskontrolle in Deutschland und Grossbritannien* (Berlin and Heidelberg, Springer, 1997).

Veljanovski, C. et al., *Freedom in Broadcasting* (London, Institute of Economic Affairs, 1989).

Williams, G., *Britain's Media: How They are Related* (London, Campaign for Press and Broadcasting Freedom; second edition, 1996).

Zerdick, Axel, 'Zwischen Frequenzen und Paragraphen: die Landesmedienanstalten als institutionalisierter Kompromiss', *Bertelsmann Briefe*, No. 129, 1993, pp. 60–2.

5 The European 'Goal' and the Popular Press

Pamela Moores

INTRODUCTION

In the early summer of 1996, as the Inter-Governmental Conference in Florence approached, nothing was further from the minds of the majority of British journalists than the goal of European unity. With the BSE crisis at its height, Tory politicians and the right-wing press were voicing grave misgivings about Britain's future in Europe, while Eurosceptics clamoured for withdrawal. The goal of harmony, understanding and close co-operation within Europe fell victim to scientific and governmental uncertainty over BSE, submerged in a confusion of economic threats, vested interests and consumer anxiety. John Major and his ministers were obstructing progress in Europe by widespread recourse to the veto in an effort to save the British beef industry, and the dominant Tory rhetoric, reflected in the columns of the press, was overtly anti-European. As the European Cup football matches got under way, and English expectations rose with successive victories, the tabloids were rapidly carried away by a wave of patriotic fervour. Spurred on by intense rivalry, they seemed to be vying to outdo one another in blatant chauvinism and crude stereotyping of Dutch, Spanish and German opponents in turn. Eagerness for the English football goal became more immediate and emotionally compelling than the possibly noble but elusive European 'goal', and anti-European crusading in the press intensified to an extraordinary degree.

Already on 30 May 1996, speaking in Dublin, Jacques Santer, President of the European Commission, had expressed his anxiety over this divisive phenomenon:

> I am very concerned about the anti-European propaganda – and even xenophobic propaganda – in the British press. But I am also concerned about the anti-British atmosphere in the continental European press. This is not good for the EU.

He is to be congratulated on what was, under the circumstances, a restrained and diplomatic understatement. Choosing his words judiciously, he made a bald distinction nonetheless between 'xenophobic propaganda' on one side of the Channel, and a mere 'anti-British atmosphere' on the continent, a reaction recognized as more subtle and discreet, yet still disturbing. It is these differing national media responses to matters of common European interest which prompt the present study, for they suggest the extent to which newspapers address very specific audiences, defined by shared values and cultural expectations. The readership of a newspaper may be linguistically, socially, politically and geographically determined to varying degrees. Yet, with very few exceptions, such as international titles like the *European* and the *International Herald Tribune*, newspapers are significantly conditioned by national culture.

To examine the substance of Jacques Santer's observations, cross-national comparative research is required, but comparisons are notoriously difficult to sustain in the cultural sphere owing to the absence of direct equivalents. Where comparative data exist, they can be richly revealing. In the case of circulation figures, for example, high consumption of daily newspapers across Northern Europe contrasts strikingly with low circulation in Mediterranean countries such as Italy, Spain and Greece. This can be readily, and also plausibly, attributed to the contrast between long commuter journeys and dark winter nights spent reading at home in the industrialized North, as opposed to sociable outdoor pastimes of the sunnier South, and a café culture in which newspapers are shared and handed around. Yet in order to develop truly scientific comparisons in this field, and pinpoint specific explanations for differences, it is necessary to take account of numerous variables, such as literacy and employment levels, disposable household income, alternative leisure and educational opportunities, to name but a few, with the result that any comparative undertaking may quickly assume unmanageable proportions.

It must be stressed that the comparisons developed in this chapter do not lay claim to scientific validity, and limitations are readily acknowledged. However, British coverage of the beef crisis and Euro 96 appeared so provocatively jingoistic that, in the context of a general political movement towards increasing European unity, it would seem important to examine how far such media treatment constitutes a peculiarly British phenomenon. In view of the complexities of cross-national comparison, investigation has been confined here to two countries, namely Britain and France, her closest continental neighbour.

As a Francophile, and avid reader of the French press, my own instinctive reaction to the distinction which Jacques Santer highlighted was that it rang true. It seemed highly improbable that one would find such flagrant xenophobia in any French newspaper, except perhaps in extreme right-wing titles such as *National hebdo*, *Le Présent* and *Le Français*, which are associated with the National Front and have a limited and very specific audience. Yet in Britain it was precisely in the mass circulation popular press that distasteful and offensive articles appeared, and this can be seen as part of a long established tradition. The *Sun* is notorious for xenophobic campaigns which have been directed against the Germans, Japanese and French. One recalls the 'Hop Off You Frogs' campaign of 1984, or 'Up Yours Delors' in 1990. This aspect of the British tabloid reputation is amply documented in Chippindale and Horrie's *Stick it up your Punter! The Rise and Fall of 'The Sun'* (1990), and Taylor's *Shock! Horror! The Tabloids in Action* (1991).[1] Certainly the mud-slinging has not been entirely one-sided. *Bild-Zeitung* has been known to involve itself in exchanges on the Germans' behalf, while a number of French newspapers, including the popular daily *Le Parisien*, have also retaliated under provocation. The French are not averse to mocking 'les Rosbifs', as they refer to the British, and the beef crisis lent itself especially well to elaboration on that particular theme. However, there is a fundamental difference between the occasional exchange of good-humoured banter, and jingoistic excess and xenophobia which verge on incitement to racial hatred. The intention of this research is to define and compare the mood and character of coverage of the BSE crisis and the European Cup in the early summer of 1996, and examine what this tells us about newspaper culture in the two countries.

Since the two topics themselves are so different in nature, it could be argued that it would be preferable to focus on one or the other. However, the timing and sequence of events in the early summer led to a mounting and mutually reinforcing climate of anti-European feeling. Articles on BSE and football often appeared side by side, and increasingly overt hostility over the beef issue may have paved the way for more xenophobic coverage of the football. To quote the *Economist* of 25 May: 'In the fights they are picking with Europe, many Britons, not led by Mr Major but pandered to by him, are becoming increasingly jingoistic, seeing enemies and injustice wherever there is a European accent.' The Conservatives' belligerent stance in Europe could be seen as having set a precedent for unashamed chauvinism. Mad cows were also finding their way into satirical newspaper articles on a wide range of unrelated topics, both in France and Britain, as a result of journalists' love of punning and cartoons. Plantu's series of mad cow cartoons, appearing on the front page of *Le Monde* over several months, admirably illustrates this point. In the general mood of hysteria, mad cows were never far from readers' or editors' minds, and it therefore seems logical to look for evidence of chauvinism and xenophobia in relation to either topic, rather than attempting to introduce a frequently artificial separation.

A further criticism which might be levelled at this comparison is that, both in the case of BSE and the European Cup, much more was at stake for Britain than France, and to that extent a more excitable British response was to be anticipated. British agriculture, the economy and the health of the nation were potentially much more immediately threatened by BSE, and understandably emotions were running high in June as negotiations in Europe seemed to have reached a stalemate. It was also on English soil that the football matches were played, and there was a surge of nostalgia and patriotic pride in the sense that 'football's coming home', as the nation was repeatedly reminded by the media in song. However, France was directly concerned and emotionally involved in both affairs. Football may well not rank so highly in the hierarchy of French national sports, but there was considerable interest on this occasion since the French team was strongly backed to win the Cup and, like England, in fact succeeded in reaching the semi-finals. On the question of BSE, French consumer organizations, farmers, butchers and restaurateurs were all passionately outspoken. French agriculture and French cuisine are vital elements of national pride and identity. Moreover, since the exposure of the blood transfusion scandal in France, which infected many haemophiliacs with HIV, there has been heightened sensitivity over public health issues and governmental responsibility in such matters. Given that England is the prime source of BSE-infected cattle, and that this may be regarded as the result of irresponsible, intensive farming practices, there was good reason to anticipate that strong anti-British sentiment would be expressed in the French press.

However, since the French press is fundamentally so different in character from the British, it is not immediately obvious which newspaper titles should be used as a basis for comparison. It is entirely feasible to set up a systematic study comparing and contrasting broadsheets such as *The Guardian* and the *Independent* with *Le Monde* and *Libération* or, on the Right, the *Daily Telegraph* and *The Times* with *Le Figaro*. A number of objections might be raised, and parallels would certainly have to be hedged with reservations and ample acknowledgement that these titles do not represent direct equivalents. However, although such a study would be perfectly possible, it would not adequately serve our purpose. Given our starting point, the intention to investigate expressions of chauvinism and xenophobia in the press, it is clear that this was not the sector of the market which prompted accusations of excess in Britain: indeed, it should be the popular press which constitutes the focus of attention. The problem is that there are no mass circulation dailies in France, and certainly no equivalent of the British tabloids and their cut-throat circulation wars. Sales of daily newspapers are low across the board, and by far the best-selling daily paper is a sober regional title *Ouest-France*, well known for its strong moral values and reasoned responses. With average circulation of almost 800 000 copies per day, which is approximately twice the number sold by *Le Parisien*, *Le Figaro* and *Le Monde*, *Ouest-France* is an outstanding success in French terms. Nonetheless, this is a relatively low circulation figure when compared with the millions of copies regularly sold by British tabloids such as the *Sun* and the *Daily Mirror*. In the post-war period, only one French daily, *France-Soir*, has achieved circulation of over a million copies, and this was in the 1950s and 1960s. Since then its sales have fallen steadily, leaving the paper with accumulating deficits in the 1990s. The absence of a thriving national daily press, either popular or populist in character, reflects entirely different habits and tastes as regards newspaper consumption in France, and this poses problems for cross-national comparison. The logical conclusion is that one has to abandon any notion of direct parallels between specific titles, and content oneself with scanning a wide cross-section of newspapers. In the case of Britain, the tabloids remained our natural focus of study. In examining the French press, particular attention was paid to *France-Soir* and also its direct rival *Le Parisien*, which has now replaced it as the most successful 'downmarket' or popular newspaper which has a national circulation and appeals to ordinary people (although, as its title suggests, *Le Parisien* achieves the majority of its sales in the Paris region). However, since these newspapers account for so few readers when compared with the audience of British tabloids, it was also considered useful to scan leading opinion forming titles, *Le Monde*, *Libération* and *Le Figaro*, to provide a fuller picture of French reactions, and situate individual newspaper responses in a broader context.

BRITAIN

Since anti-European sentiment in the British press was the stimulus for the present research, this is our starting point. Following the EU ban on British beef, virulent Europhobia invaded many tabloids and even broadsheets such as *The Times* and the *Daily Telegraph*. On 18 May the pro-European *Economist*, which has an international readership, felt obliged to reassure readers that Britain was 'In to Stay' in the EU, even if the British press appeared to suggest the contrary. The following week (25 May), it talked of Major's 'thuggish supporters in the press' damaging Britain's image abroad, for after the Prime Minister decided, on 21 May, to wield the veto to block key EU business, the *Daily Mail* had welcomed his combative

stance with the jubilant headline 'Major goes to war at last' (22 May),
while the *Sun* took readers back to 1940, claiming this was a 'showdown
on a scale rarely seen since the Battle of Britain' (22 May). Launching a
'Buy British' crusade, the *Sun* offered 20 suggestions as to how to retaliate
against countries which had voted against British beef. Hostilities were thus
declared and, at the end of the month, Geoffrey Martin, the head of the
European Commission in London, complained in frustration: 'The anti-
European press in Britain is not even willing to print letters from the commission correcting factual inaccuracies in their stories. They are impossible
to deal with. It is as simple as that' (*The Guardian*, 1 June).

In explanation, one notes that much of the British press is owned
or edited by anti-Europeans. For Rupert Murdoch and Conrad Black it is
the transatlantic not the European alliance which counts, and Sir James
Goldsmith's powerful anti-European lobby is well known. However, the
picture is not entirely negative, thanks to papers such as the *Economist*,
The Guardian, the *Observer*, the *Independent*. The *Daily Mirror* also
refused to join fellow tabloids, stating firmly in a front page editorial on
28 May, 'If we ever cut ourselves loose from our partners across the
Channel, we would become an isolated irrelevant island.' Yet, when it
came to football, the *Daily Mirror* itself produced what was probably the
most offensive and outrageous coverage of Euro 96. The language widely
used by the tabloids to describe foreign football teams was stereotypical
and insulting: the Dutch referred to as 'Edams', the Scots as 'Jocks', and
the Spanish 'Juans'. Opponents of the English team attracted the greatest
hostility. The Spanish team prompted a barrage of images and puns associated with paella, flamenco dancers, castanets and bull-fighting, for example, a montage of a beefeater executing a matador on the front page of
the *Daily Mirror* (20 June) entitled 'You're done Juan'. Don Juan, Francis
Drake and the Armada figured frequently, the latter reference being clearly
intended to humiliate the opposition, recalling and anticipating Spanish
defeat. The *Daily Mirror* (20 June) also kindled animosity by listing ten
'nasties' the Spanish had given Europe, such as syphilis, Spanish 'flu, the
Inquisition and so on. 'Adios Amigos' declaimed its triumphant front page
banner on 22 June, and a jubilant 'No more mananas'.

It was when it came to the semi-final against the Germans, however, that
the newspaper's supposed humour most blatantly exceeded the bounds of
good taste and decency. Two world wars, the 1966 World Cup final, and
memories of bitter defeat for England in the semi-final against Germany in
1990 make Anglo–German matches especially highly charged. Latent ger-
manophobia is rife in Britain thanks to films and comics perpetuating
images of Hitler, the Gestapo and German forces. It is also exacerbated by

envy of post-war German prosperity and her influential role at the centre of the EU. The uncompromising German position over BSE had intensified antagonism yet further. In this climate, on 24 June, the *Daily Mirror* declared football war on Germany in a front page editorial which parodied Neville Chamberlain's 1939 fireside speech calling for German surrender, next to pictures of warlike English footballers Pearce and Gascoigne in army tin hats, screaming, '*Achtung!* Surrender. For you Fritz, ze Euro 96 Championship is over'. On the inside pages, *Mirror* representatives were shown carrying the invasion to the streets of Berlin. English signposts were modified to point the way home for an enemy supposedly facing defeat.

The use of war imagery to describe political battles and sporting contests has long been commonplace, and not only in tabloid culture. International sporting contests are widely considered less a source of fun, more an opportunity for asserting national prowess, as is patently, and ironically, evident in the case of the Olympics. In 1996, serious pro-European publications such as the *Economist* explicitly developed this symbolic dimension of the football championship, as evidenced in an article entitled, 'World war, national decline and the English football team'.

Following the English defeat, the theme of parallelism between the outcome of the football contest and the state of the nation was to prompt caustic journalism at Britain's expense, in the writing, for example, of Peter Ellingsen in Australia under the title 'Land of little hope and glory' or 'Bilious barracking reflects distasteful political reality'. Returning, however, to the 'distasteful reality' of the *Daily Mirror* coverage, this was the result of a gross miscalculation on the part of the editor Piers Morgan, a former columnist of the *Sun*, a paper notorious for drawing on world war images in coverage of sport and politics. Influenced presumably by habits learned while working for his former newspaper, Morgan went too far in attempting to promote the English at the Germans' expense, misjudging the public mood, as was demonstrated by the public indignation which followed. The political context may have been widely referred to as the 'Beef war'. Nonetheless, to insult sporting opponents by making so explicit a connection with painful episodes in recent history, and to use aggressive imagery likely to incite racial hatred, was widely regarded as overstepping the mark.

The *Daily Star* was in little better taste, with its headline 'Herr we go, Bring on the Krauts' and a front page photo of 'Curvy Claudia Schiffer... German striker' in her '*wunderbra*' next to Terry Venables as Kitchener (24 June). Pictured inside the *Star*, as in the case of the *Mirror*, was the familiar symbolic holiday sunlounger by the pool, now occupied by the British. When German manager Berti Vogts raised doubts about the fitness of player Jurgen Klinsmann, the *Daily Star* quipped, 'Berti Vogts ... more like Berti Jokes' with the headline 'The Jestapo!' (26 June). Silly jokes about sausages and lager abounded, in particular wordplay such as 'We're hunstoppable', and 'England best ... Germany wurst', but truly worst of all was a grossly insulting picture of the *Star*'s German Page Three girl, 'Lederhosen lovely Brunhilde Grossentittiboobs', with the stereotypical accoutrements of beer, sausage and boots (26 June).

The general public and leading national figures complained in force about such coverage. The Press Complaints Commission phonelines were jammed by irate callers, and over 200 written protests were received by the end of the week. The National Heritage Select Committee released a report condemning 'xenophobic, chauvinistic and jingoistic gutter journalism' in 'certain tabloid newspapers', judging that it 'may well have had its effects in stimulating the deplorable riots' which followed England's defeat, and calling upon the PCC to take action. 'MPs say tabloids are to blame for football violence' claimed Alexandra Frean and Arthur Leathley in *The Times*. 'Rioting is blamed on media jingoism' according to Steve Boggan and James Cusick in the *Independent*. Peter Leuprecht, deputy general secretary of the Council of Europe, wrote to Lord Wakeham, chairman of the PCC, to condemn the *Mirror*'s chauvinism, claiming it undermined the Council's efforts to curb soccer violence (Reuters New Service, 25 June). Vauxhall, official sponsor of Euro 96, whose marketing communications director is German, withdrew its advertisements from both the *Daily Mirror* and the *Star*. Condemnation was widespread, and Lord Healey commented disparagingly, 'The grubby little men who write this sort of trash should remember that our monarchy are krauts and that our defence minister is a dago' (*The Guardian*, 25 June). Numerous commentators contrasted the friendly attitudes of players and the majority of supporters with the hostility incited by the press.

A contrite Piers Morgan claimed in his paper's defence, 'Our pro-European stance is well known' (reported by the *Daily Telegraph*, 25 June). According to the *Mirror*'s editor, he 'intended this purely as a joke', and he was quick to apologize. The editor of the *Daily Star*, responding to the PCC, maintained that their jokes were 'good natured, tongue-in-cheek, and designed to raise a smile ... They were never malicious'. The *Sun*, in turn, argued that its coverage too was, 'if robust, intended to bolster national pride and was good-natured' (PCC Report, p. 22). Clearly, in their desire to play to the gallery, the tabloids tread a fine line between puerile buffoonery and more sinister provocation. Some 300 complaints against the three papers received by the PCC on this occasion confirmed that members of the public did not find the jokes funny, and were concerned that coverage was pejorative and prejudicial. The Commission (p. 23) noted that:

> all three newspapers had intended their approach to be seen as a good-natured, humorous entertainment designed to reflect national pride without any malicious intent towards the Germans or any other nationalities

but joined in the universal criticism of coverage which it found 'shrill and poorly judged', condemning serious 'lapses in editorial judgment' (p. 24).

Scanning the tabloids during this period, one is struck by the extraordinarily juvenile nature of many features. The *Daily Mirror*, for example, staged mock torture for their sports journalists, who were clamped in the stocks as traitors to the cause of English football for daring to criticize Terry Venables. 'Tel's No 1 tormentor', Harry Harris, we were told, was on his way to the Tower and his fate was in the hands of readers (20 June). It is evident that neither the journalists nor the readers of such publications take themselves entirely seriously, and in attempting to emulate and appeal to partisan football supporters among their readers, journalists are readily carried away by fantasies of their own creation, losing all sense of proportion. Their hierarchy of news values demonstrates the extent to which they lose sight of the real world. The *Daily Mirror* devoted a dozen front page leads to Euro 96 in June, and nine in a row as the semi-final with Germany approached. On 24 June, the *Sun*, generally regarded as a flimsy publication, devoted a full 21 pages to the football.[2] Yet, as soon as England was knocked out of the tournament, it was suddenly as if the entire championship was over. In the meantime, other important news had been neglected, for the whole climate of 'reporting' was obsessional, semi-hysterical and distorting. This hysteria is no doubt linked to the fierce rivalry between the tabloids in Britain. Condemning the *Mirror* as 'coarse and demented', Matthew Engel in *The Guardian* described the paper as 'sick, failing and desperate'. Robert Harris in *The Sunday Times* mourned the passing of the restraint and clear-sightedness which the *Mirror* had displayed during the Second World War, and put the editor's misjudgement down to a determination to 'out-sun the *Sun*'. The circulation war no doubt contributes to desperate tactics, but it is equally clear that the titillation of readers by flirting with the bounds of good taste and verging on excess has become a mainstay of the tabloid appeal.

The British Embassy in Bonn was deluged with protests and German diplomats commented on the bad taste of the coverage, but no official complaints were received either from the German government or its football authorities. The German press too was relatively restrained in response. *Bild-Zeitung* retaliated briefly in humorous vein with a list of *Sun*-style questions asking:

> If you are the home of soccer, why have you never won the European championship? Why can't you beat your former colonies at cricket? Why do you look like freshly cooked lobsters after one day on the beach?

and so on (reported in *The Times*, 26 June), but this was relatively harmless banter. In the view of a third party, Lucas Delattre, writing in *Le Monde*, the German retaliation did not reach one-hundredth of the level of excesses committed by the English. Nonetheless the exchanges were damaging, particularly to British credibility abroad, as suggested in the following extract from a letter to The *Guardian* (26 June) by a British citizen in Germany:

> it is increasingly clear to me that German opinion links the mindless stupidity of the British tabloids, or football hooligans, and British opposition to European federalism in one package.

It is also possible that national flag-waving was reinforced: after German victory in the final, for the first time since the fall of the Berlin Wall the front page of *Bild-Zeitung* was framed in the colours of the German flag – black, red and gold – asserting their triumph and pride in national identity.

FRANCE

In the French press over the same period it was difficult to detect evidence of chauvinism or offensive national stereotyping. There was criticism of the French press from President Chirac following British announcements in March about the likely link between BSE and CJD (Creutzfeldt-Jakob Disease). Chirac denounced the media for an hysterical reaction likely to exacerbate consumer anxiety. Between 22 and 29 March the French news agency Agence France Presse had devoted 313 dispatches to the topic, and there were dramatic and sensationalist front page headlines accompanying full page images of cows, such as the following in *Libération*: 'Vers l'hécatombe' (23–24 March), 'La vache hésitation'[3] (28 March), 'Le krach bovin' (29 March). However, treatment focused on the disaster for farmers and the meat industry, on issues of public health, and not British responsibility. In the following months BSE was ominpresent in the French media as it was in Britain, and cartoonist Plantu reminded *Le Monde* readers of the issue constantly, even when it was not related to the newspaper's lead item. Mad cows cropped up everywhere. Coverage in *Le Monde* and *Libération* was extensive, with *Le Monde* taking on its traditional investigative role, pursuing scientific reports and exposing any efforts at a cover-up. Treatment in *Le Parisien* was surprisingly anodyne and factual, and was given little prominence, but *France-Soir* provided much greater coverage, used the most emotive language, and might justifiably be considered guilty of the alarmism for which Chirac rebuked the press as a whole. Editorialist Bernard Morrot's consistent line over several months was to denounce the French government's preoccupation with the collapse of the beef market and the economic consequences, instead of focusing on the health of consumers. He attacked unscrupulous commercialism, irresponsible farming methods and vested interests. *France-Soir* could also be accused of scaremongering insofar as it speculated in sensational terms about the potential dangers of BSE.

Following the revelation on 13 June that contaminated animal feed had been exported to France long after it had been banned in Britain, the press did point the finger at Britain, as illustrated by *Le Monde*'s blunt headline (13 June): ' "Vache folle": la Grande-Bretagne a exporté massivement des farines animales contaminées. La France a été l'acheteur principal...' However, as suggested by *Le Parisien*'s titles: 'Scandale de la vache folle', and 'L'élevage modern en accusation' (14 June), coverage still focused primarily on the underlying causes such as modern farming methods, lack of accountability and regulation. Pierre Georges, in a piece in *Le Monde* entitled 'Le crime industriel', stressed that the problem was not British in nature, but was the result of weak government in the face of food and farming lobbies. Numerous articles throughout the press drew parallels with the French blood transfusion scandal where contaminated blood had continued to be used after the dangers had been recognized, simply so as not to waste existing stock. *France-Soir*, however, now attacked the British with passion, leading with 'Le Crime des Anglais', talking of the British having pulled a fast one, 'Les Anglais nous ont roulés dans la farine', and using France as their dustbin, '...la France a servi de poubelle à l'Angleterre' (13 June).

Nonetheless, in general what one detected was latent anti-British resentment, expressed in exasperation, and occasionally disdain, but not xenophobia. Accusations from members of the public were often reported in inverted commas, rather than journalists themselves voicing direct criticism. Factual reports stated that consumer groups were organizing boycotts, that French farmers were protesting in fury, erecting barricades and stopping British lorries, or that an effigy of John Major had been burned outside Parliament in Strasbourg. The French public vented their anger in direct action rather than through their newspapers, where irony, restraint and detached reporting were more apparent. This contrasts strongly with the relationship between the British press and public. The French press seemed tame, French protestors did not, whereas in Britain it was the media, and particularly the tabloids, who whipped up anti-European passions. For French journalists, John Major became the obvious target for their accusations. He crystallized the focus of ill-feelings and served as the butt of humour, a weak figure described as very ordinary in comparison with his predecessor. The French were not impressed by his tactics of obstruction, but expressed serene indifference, given that the combined forces of other European countries were powerful enough to make Britain pay the price of her obstinacy. In *Libération* François Sergent portrayed Major as living in another era, unable to understand Europe today: '*le preux chevalier de l'Angleterre, ferraillant contre ses ennemis européens*', a valiant knight fighting outdated battles by the sword. He was 'Prime loser' rather than Prime Minister in the words of the paper's editorialist Jacques Amalric. His 'nationalist posturing and anti-European threats and bragging' were scorned by Nathalie Dubois and Jean Quatremer, who presented Major as a naked, vulnerable figure being offered a vine leaf by European colleagues. Leading journalists such as Alain Duhamel reiterated the theme that Britain had never been committed to the EU, and that it was time to decide either to stay in or get out. The general impression was that France would not shed many tears either way.

As regards reporting of the football championship, very little attention was devoted to the subject when compared with the British press, and in this context it is worth noting the very different place of sports reporting in Britain and France, in particular the unique position of *L'Equipe*. This is a popular daily devoted exclusively to sport, which is currently in the ascendant, and sells approximately the same number of copies per day as *Le Monde*[4] (which, at the other end of the spectrum, incorporates absolutely minimal reference to sport). Since sport is so essential a component of mass circulation dailies in Britain, not only and yet most especially in the case of the tabloids, it is surprising to note the degree of separation between sports reporting and coverage of current affairs in France. However, the French situation is changing and, for commercial reasons, newspapers are reconciling themselves to acceptance of the popularity of sport as a source of mass appeal. Among generalist newspapers, this is most obviously true of *Le Parisien* (probably the French newspaper closest to the British tabloid 'model'), which devoted several front pages to Euro 96. Much of French interest centred on speculation as to whether or not Eric Cantona would be selected for the French national team. Nowhere, however, was there anything but straightforward, patriotic sports reporting, with no trace of xenophobic sentiments.

What did provoke a strong emotional reaction in the quality national press in France, was British media coverage both of the beef crisis and the football: in *Libération* François Sergent wrote of an hysterical anti-European offensive, which made him wonder whether British editorialists had forgotten that the war was over; his fellow journalist Fabrice Rousselot spoke of an anti-community virus. In *Le Figaro* Jacques Duplouich con-demned the xenophobic anti-German clichés in the English popular press, while Pascal Ceaux in *Le Monde* sketched a scathing picture of the tabloids' warlike rhetoric and anti-German fever. There was general dis-taste at the insulting portrayal of Helmut Kohl. Although the special nature of Anglo–German rivalry was recognized, the French were in no doubt that if they had had to play England, they too would have been the objects of xenophobic abuse.

The only occasion on which the theme of xenophobia in France arose was when Jean-Marie Le Pen, leader of the National Front, attacked the multiracial French football squad, claiming that it was artificial to call upon players from abroad and yet name them the French team. He com-plained that players on the field either did not know the words of the national anthem, or were unwilling to sing it. In a two-page interview with *France-Soir* (25 June), he made matters worse by revealing that he had not made a careless, off-the-cuff remark, but had detailed files on the ethnic origins and status of all the French players. He sought to jus-tify his curiosity in this matter by arguing that his target was not coloured players from former colonies or overseas territories, but those who had acquired French nationality via naturalization. However, his words pro-voked widespread indignation and condemnation throughout the media. This was not an isolated episode, and it underlines a crucial point: how-ever great the contrast between French and British media coverage, there is no reason to suppose that xenophobic discourse is less widespread in France than in Britain, especially in view of the support which Jean-Marie Le Pen and the National Front enjoy. It is rather the case that xenophobia surfaces in a different form and context, because both politi-cal and media culture are configured differently. In France the main-stream media are more restrained, and in particular they are on their guard against xenophobia, precisely because of widespread awareness that the rise of the extreme Right constitutes a genuine political danger. In Britain, where such a threat is less obvious, and where shock tactics appear to be regarded as a legitimate means of selling newspapers in the popular sector of the market, editors feel freer to put the limits of good taste and acceptability regularly to the test, with the inevitable excesses that this involves.

Indeed, our comparative research did confirm that French newspapers, even at the lower end of the market, are altogether more cautious, serious and responsible than some of their British counterparts. In order to find more strident and aggressive journalism, one has to look to satirical weeklies like *Charlie Hebdo* and *Le Canard enchaîné*, while extreme sensationalism is generally confined to Sunday paper *France Dimanche*, and magazines such as *Spécial-Dernière* and *Le Meilleur*. Dailies see their role primarily as imparting information and serious opinion; entertainment figures to a much lesser degree than in British news reporting. This may be linked to dependence on government subsidies and the absence of the fiercely competitive commercial environment one finds in Britain. French newspapers do not display the vitality of the British press, but nor do they enjoy the same following, influence and notoriety.

Nonetheless, common features did emerge: in both countries it was evident that passions are readily aroused by the media in response to perceived threats to national identity. In Britain the inability to reach a satisfactory European solution to the beef crisis led to frustration and anti-European resentment which found an outlet in a wave of aggressive chauvinism during the football championship. In France, the political and media establishment rallied to the defence of Republican values and the concept of national identity in response to xenophobic challenges from the Right. This common rallying factor highlights the problems to be confronted by any supranational European publication. Language barriers and differences in cultural expectations are undeniable obstacles, but such a venture is also limited by the fact that supranational Europe is still in its infancy. As long as the question 'Why Europe?' is still on the agenda, Europe lacks legitimacy in the sense that it remains a goal rather than a living reality and cementing bond in the hearts and minds of the population. The nation remains the natural forum of popular expression.

NOTES

1. Bourdais-Webb (1993) is also particularly relevant as a study of ethnocentric stereotypes in the British tabloids.
2. We owe these statistical observations to Stephen Kelly (1996).
3. A play on words turning on 'vache' denoting a cow, and the adjective 'vache' suggesting contemptible behaviour.

4. For the period 1 July 1995 to 30 June 1996, average daily circulation for *L'Equipe* was 377 098 copies, for *Le Monde* 371 575, and *Le Figaro* 382 021; *Le Parisien* was clearly the frontrunner among national dailies with a circulation of 459 658 copies (Source: *Médiaspouvoirs* (1996), No. 43–4, p. 151).

REFERENCES

Amalric, J., 'Prime loser', *Libération*, 22–23 June 1996.

Boggan, S. and Cusick, J., 'Rioting is blamed on media jingoism', *Independent*, 28 June 1996.

Bourdais-Webb, N., *'The Filthy French' – Examples of Ethnocentric Stereotypes in the British Tabloid Press* (Aston Papers in European Politics and Society, No. 5, Institute for the Study of Language and Society, Aston University, 1993).

Ceaux, P., 'Fièvre antiallemande dans la presse populaire anglaise', *Le Monde*, 26 June 1996.

Chippindale, P. and Horrie, C., *Stick it up your Punter! The Rise and Fall of 'The Sun'* (London, Heinemann, 1990).

De Beer, P., 'La vache folle enflamme la presse britannique', *Le Monde*, 26–27 May 1996.

Delattre, L., 'Bonn, Londres et l'avenir de l'Europe', *Le Monde*, 28 June 1996.

Dubois, N. and Quatremer, J., 'La reculade de John Major soulage ses partenaires', *Libération*, 22–23 June 1996.

Duhamel, A., 'Et si la Grande-Bretagne adhérait à l'UE?', *Libération*, 21 June 1996.

Duplouich, J., 'La balle folle ...', *Le Figaro*, 26 June 1996.

Ellingsen, P., 'Land of little hope and glory', *The Age*, Melbourne, 27 June 1996.

Ellingsen, P., 'Bilious barracking reflects distasteful political reality', *Sydney Morning Herald*, 27 June 1996.

Engel, M., 'A coarse and demented newspaper', *The Guardian*, 25 June 1996.

Frean, A. and Leathley, A., 'MPs say tabloids are to blame for football violence', *The Times*, 28 June 1996.

Georges, P., 'Le Crime des Anglais', *Le Monde*, 13 June 1996.

Harris, R., 'A hideous reflection in the tabloid mirror', *The Sunday Times*, 30 June 1996.

Kelly, S., 'Football crazy', *Free Press. Journal for the Campaign for Press and Broadcasting Freedom*, No. 93, July–August 1996, p. 2.

Press Complaints Commission, Report No. 35, July–August–September 1996.

Rousselot, F., 'Un nouvel avatar du particularisme britannique', *Libération*, 21 June 1996.

Sergent, F., 'L'ultime parade d'un Premier ministre aux abois', *Libération*, 23 May 1996.

Taylor, S. J., *Shock! Horror! The Tabloids in Action* (London, Bantam Press, 1991).

'World war, national decline and the English football team', *Economist*, 8 June 1996.

Part III
Gender and Identity

6 Representations of Feminism in France: Feminism, Anti-Feminism and Post-Feminism[1]

Gill Allwood

It is clear that there are dangers involved in talking of national feminisms. There is a constant fear of falling into the trap of stereotyping and xenophobia. There is also the danger of representing each national feminism as homogeneous, hiding its internal debates and divisions. However, there is also a danger in not recognizing the differences between, and specificities of, national feminisms. And that danger is that we generalize from our own position, claiming (implicitly or explicitly) to speak for all women, denying or obscuring the experience of women who inhabit different cultures from our own, have different priorities and preoccupations, even if we also have much in common. It is as a reaction to being spoken for, ignored or misrepresented by Anglophone feminists that French feminists joined together with other non-Anglophones to hold a conference in Rio in 1995 (*Cahiers du CEDREF*, 1995). This was an attempt to reclaim a space from which dialogue would then be possible with Anglophone feminists, but without the dominance of the English language and the theoretical assumptions which go with it. So how can we talk of French feminism without falling into these traps? In an attempt to do this, this chapter examines some of the ways in which French feminism has been distorted and misrepresented within France and outside, and contrasts these with the way in which French feminists themselves portray feminism in France.

I use the term 'Anglo-American feminism' with great reservation. The term 'Anglo-American' probably became widespread in this context as a translation of the French 'anglosaxon', which is used loosely, often to mean American, but sometimes American and British. Here, I use it as a convenient shorthand for British, American and Australian feminisms, which, although wildly divergent in many respects, have together produced a corpus of theory. This is often referred to as 'feminist theory', despite the fact that it is as culturally specific as any other form of feminist theory. While recognizing that 'Anglo-American' is a problematic term,

111

I find it useful in the context of this chapter as a means of referring to the broadest of trends in British, American and Australian feminisms. I do not intend to suggest in any way that these are homogeneous.

THE REPRESENTATION OF FRENCH FEMINISM OUTSIDE FRANCE

Anglo-American feminists and women's studies departments have been particularly keen to import 'French feminism', but the texts they have chosen for translation, critique and popularization have often been limited to a narrow band of French women theorists, which is sometimes reduced to only three: Luce Irigaray, Hélène Cixous and Julia Kristeva. The construction of 'French feminism' by Anglo-Americans is now well documented, and the recent publication of work by French feminists previously excluded from this definition has gone some way towards correcting the misrepresentation (Jackson, 1996; Adkins and Leonard, 1996). However, it is worth reviewing the process of this construction and some of its consequences, since it has been a powerful obstacle to mutual understanding and to dialogue between French and Anglo-American feminisms. The popularity of French feminism as a subject for study was sparked by the appearance in 1981 of a special issue of *Yale French Studies* on French feminism and a collection of translated articles by French feminists, edited by two Americans and entitled *New French Feminisms* (Marks and de Courtivron, 1981). Both these publications gave prominence to the work of a number of French women intellectuals heavily influenced by psychoanalysis and semiology. As a result, French feminism acquired a reputation for being more theoretical than its British or American counterparts, and its 'exoticism' attracted the attention of many social and literary theorists and critics, particularly in literature departments in American universities.[2]

Of course, this interpretation was not entirely unfounded. As Claire Duchen explains in *Feminism in France* (Duchen, 1986, pp. 68–9), the intellectual context in which French feminist theory has developed differs from the British in its greater interest in psychoanalysis, linguistics and philosophy, in the greater respect accorded to intellectuals in France than in Britain, and in the anti-hierarchical and anti-authoritarian ideals highlighted by the events of May 1968, and present in left-wing and feminist thought. French feminist theory may therefore have a more intellectual appearance than its British or American counterparts. However, this is a broad generalization and one could argue that it does not justify the unbalanced selection of texts which many British and American academics have chosen to call 'French feminism'.

A binary opposition has been constructed between 'French feminism', which is highly theoretical and influenced by psychoanalysis, deconstruction and poststructuralism, and 'Anglo-American feminism', which is empiricist, pragmatic and concerned with producing change at a social and political, rather than a discursive level. This opposition is dependent on maintaining a clear distinction between the two types of feminism. So the aspects of French feminism which are emphasized are those which provide the starkest contrast with the equally reductionist representation of 'Anglo-American feminism', while more familiar forms of feminist theory and practice are ignored. In order to maintain the distinction between French and Anglo-American theory, some curious adjustments have been made to the meaning of the terms 'French' and 'Anglo-American'. Literary critic Toril Moi points out, for example, that the texts which are considered particularly 'French' are those which have more of an 'exotic flavour', rather than the materialist-feminist texts, which in fact have much in common with British socialist feminism (Moi, 1987, p. 6). While materialist feminists are excluded from the category 'French feminism', American feminists can be included in it, by virtue of their style and use of theory. Toril Moi writes:

> A final point: the terms 'Anglo-American' and 'French' must not be taken to represent purely national demarcations: they do not signal the critics' birthplace but the intellectual tradition within which they work. Thus I do not consider the many British and American women deeply influenced by French thought to be 'Anglo-American' critics.
>
> (Moi, 1985, p. xiv)

This has produced the paradoxical situation in which the post-structuralist feminist theory referred to by Anglo-American feminist critics as 'French feminism' is described in France as particularly American (Collin, 1992, pp. 5–9).

The nature of feminism in France is, then, very different to that suggested by many studies of 'French feminism'. Significantly, two of the three theorists most frequently referred to as 'the French feminists' are not seen as important actors by French feminists themselves. Julia Kristeva, a linguist and psychoanalyst, receives little attention from French feminists: 'She is neither a feminist, nor, I suppose, an anti-feminist ... For us, what she writes is outside feminism' (Delphy, 1993). Hélène Cixous, a novelist, playwright and professor of literature at Paris VIII, was involved in the feminist movement in the 1970s, but has not written on the subject for many years. Not only do French feminists pay little attention to the work of these theorists, some even express amazement or incredulity at the thought that this work is considered 'feminist' by otherwise critical British and American feminists. Christine Delphy writes:

> In the United States, Cixous, Kristeva and Irigaray, among others, are studied, and what is more, they are studied as feminists. This is, to say the least, shocking with regard to the first two, who proclaim their distance from feminism high and low.
>
> (Delphy, 1985, p. 151)

In contrast to Cixous and Kristeva, who are labelled 'feminist' only outside France, philosopher and psychoanalyst, Luce Irigaray, has a following in the movement, although she also has many critics, some of them overtly hostile (Guerlais, 1991, pp. 63–92; Planté, 1993, p. 114).

The construction of 'French feminism' has exaggerated the place occupied by Cixous, Irigaray and Kristeva and ignored developments in feminist practice and theory in France. It presents a picture distorted in several respects. First, it groups together theorists whose work has little in common. Second, of the three theorists most often referred to as 'French feminists', two do not refer to themselves as feminists and have expressed differing degrees of hostility towards feminism. As Elizabeth Grosz (1989) argues, this does not justify dismissing their work as irrelevant to feminism. The implications of their theories are highly political, challenging as they do the very basis of male-dominated knowledges. The production of meanings, discourses and knowledges which challenge existing ones is an essential part of the feminist struggle, even though it could not achieve feminism's aims alone. Grosz writes:

> Without a critical feminist awareness of the ways patriarchal knowledges inform everyday language and life and without alternative frameworks of knowledge and representation, women will remain tied to a series of concepts and values which oppress them.
>
> (Grosz, 1989, p. 234)

However, the recognition that the dismantling of patriarchal discourses is an important aspect of feminism's project does not justify its construction as the only, or most important, part of the French feminist struggle, and the fact that the term is applied to women who express hostility towards feminism makes it even more misleading.

Finally, there are now French feminists who have been advised not to refer to themselves as such outside France in case it should mislead

English-speaking readers. But if they cannot call themselves French feminists, then what can they call themselves? Eleni Varikas writes:

> The 'national' modifier thus effaces or trivializes any other feminist positions; it implies that any reference which falls outside those selected and defined as French theory or French feminism, is not theoretical (or is not feminist) and that it therefore does not need to be discussed. However, reducing 'French' feminism to certain theoretical positions not only obscures the fact that the majority of feminist struggles have been led outside and sometimes against these positions; not only does it obscure the most influential theoretical positions in feminist thought in France (Colette Guillaumin, Christine Delphy, Michèle Le Doeuff, Nicole-Claude Mathieu, to cite just a few); it prevents the analysis of the conditions in which these numerous positions emerged, of their relation to the political practice of women, of what makes them socially and academically acceptable or unacceptable, and of their subversive dynamic.
>
> (Varikas, 1993, p. 63)

THE REPRESENTATION OF FRENCH FEMINISM INSIDE FRANCE: ANTI-FEMINISM, POST-FEMINISM AND BACKLASH

The representation of feminism inside France is said by many observers to have become increasingly negative. An empirical study by psychologists Marie-Claire Hurtig and Marie-France Pichevin (1995) claims to demonstrate the increasingly anti-feminist representation of sexual difference in popular publications. They argue that while the theories emanating from the scientific community are marked by their heterogeneity, an unrepresentative selection is used as evidence in popular publications to support the idea that the biological divide between the sexes is clearly defined and plays a determining role in gender relations. Hurtig and Pichevin conclude that this revival of biologism is part of a backlash against feminism, whose other manifestations include attacks on abortion clinics and attempts to encourage women back into the home. While it is clear that anti-feminist (or patriarchal) attitudes, policies and practices are readily identifiable, it is less clear that these can be seen purely as a reaction to feminism, and their portrayal as a straightforward backlash is not universally accepted. Feminism has always met resistance, and this is not surprising, given the radical nature of the feminist project. But this does not mean that all measures which can be read as anti-feminist are deliberately so. Cuts in welfare spending, for example, are anti-feminist in that they are, on the whole, much more damaging for women than for men, but they are motivated not

by opposition to feminism, but by liberal economic policy. The term backlash tends to simplify the relation between the patriarchy, women and feminism (Walby, 1993).

Feminism in France has been accompanied almost from the beginning
by media suggestions that it is over (Duchen, 1987)[3] and that we have
now entered a 'post-feminist' era. The meaning of 'post-feminism' varies
according to the author and the context, but there are two main versions.
The first is that feminism has achieved its aims and is now no longer necessary, and the second is that feminists have realized the errors of their
ways and are now happy to forget it all and re-embrace their femininity.
The media debate around contemporary masculinities, which has gained
popularity since the late 1980s, illustrates a broad consensus that feminism
is a thing of the past. Books such as Evelyne Sullerot's *Quels pères? Quels
fils?* (1992) and Elisabeth Badinter's *XY: de l'identité masculine* (1992) as
well as a growing number of magazine articles and special issues portray
feminism as something which was relevant in the 1970s, but which, having achieved its aims, no longer has a role. It is seen to have caused many
changes, however, including the destabilizing of masculine identity. Many
of the popular interpretations of masculinity are concerned with how men
have coped with this and with their loss of power and rights. Masculinity
is said to have been seriously damaged by feminism, and men are portrayed as victims of excessive feminist demands, who have lost a considerable amount of power.

In fact, feminism's gains are portrayed as so extensive that women are
said to be at an advantage over men in many respects: in particular, they
control decisions about reproduction and invariably 'win' conflicts over
the custody of children after divorce and separation. Elisabeth Badinter,
for example, writes:

> By bringing an end to the distinction between the roles, and by entering
> all the areas previously reserved for men, women have made the univer-
> sal male characteristic disappear: the superiority of men over women.
>
> (Badinter, 1992, p. 17)

The point of many of these post-feminist portrayals of masculinity is to
call for a post-feminist consensus in order to solve the problem of the male
identity crisis. This post-feminist consensus often requires women to be
more 'reasonable' and allow men to behave in more 'masculine' ways.
This has implications for the reception of feminist theories. The reduction
of feminism to one of its historical manifestations, the MLF of the 1970s,
means that today's struggles against men's continuing domination of
women are not recognized as feminist struggles. Feminist debate in all its

diversity is ignored. Instead, individuals such as Elisabeth Badinter are selected to represent feminist ideas, despite the fact that their analyses of changing masculinities are situated in the same post-feminist framework.

AMERICAN FEMINISM AND THE FRENCH ART OF SEDUCTION

The portrayal of a particular way of structuring gender relations as a national characteristic plays an important role in the popular representation of feminism. Implicit or explicit comparisons are often made with 'Anglo-American feminism', which is represented as dangerously and unnecessarily extreme. French women are told that feminism is a threat to national gender relations and fortunately unnecessary in France, where, it is alleged, men and women understand each other better. A national consensus around the rules of gender relations, which include a specifically French gift for the art of seduction, is said to have been temporarily under threat from feminists in the 1970s. Now, however, this threat is no longer seen to be particularly worrying in France. Feminism today is an American excess, which must be prevented from upsetting the understanding which French men and women have for each other. This opposition between French and American feminism undermines the theory and practice of French feminists and the experiences of French women. For example, Elisabeth Badinter (1992) implies that male violence is not a problem in France, as it is in the United States, thus denying the experiences of many French women and silencing those who are trying to raise public awareness of its existence. This has the effect of removing discussions of feminism from the French experience. French citizens are urged to unite against imported American ideas which could contaminate the idealism of French sexual relations. The message is that French men and women have an interest in joining together to resist this external threat. This is evident, for example, in the debates around sexual harassment and political correctness.

The debate on sexual harassment which surrounded the introduction of legislation against it was conducted in opposition to what is represented as the ridiculously extreme situation in the United States. Benoîte Groult, editor of *F-Magazine* in the late 1970s, writes (1994, p. 63), 'In the United States, sexual harassment is talked about a lot, but in France it is a national sport which is played in public! And in our official institutions!' While in the United States, the term sexual harassment was coined to identify the use of sexuality to reinforce gender domination and referred to behaviour based on gender, in France, this definition has been distorted. The law against sexual harassment in France refers only to the abuse of a position of authority to obtain sexual favours. There is a striking absence of an awareness of gendered power relations both in the French legislation and in the debate which surrounded it (Delphy, 1996, p. 152).

The French rejection of political correctness similarly rests on a desire to maintain a specifically French approach to gender relations. In France, political correctness is ridiculed not only by the right, as is the case in Britain and the United States, but also by the left. This is probably due to the fact that the main source of information about political correctness has been the largely conservative American popular press (Ezekiel, 1995). The debate around political correctness, which in the United States is highly politicized and deeply rooted in a specific cultural and historical context, has been removed from this context to become nothing more than a joke and an example of American extremism. Ridicule is used to undermine the recognition of difference, which is at the base of political correctness, and material consequences of difference, including sexism and racism, are ignored.

A partial explanation for the French rejection of political correctness is the influence of the republican tradition of universalism. Within the logic of universalism, according to which all citizens are the same and equal, there is no room for the recognition of difference, for to recognize differences between citizens would provide reasons for inequality. Feminists have criticized the notion of universalism, arguing that what is supposed to be universal is in practice masculine. While there is theoretically no difference between a male and a female citizen, the state has a very different impact on the life of an individual depending on whether or not that individual may want an abortion, may not be able to enter politics because of widespread inequality in the sharing of domestic chores, or may be limited in career choices and earning power because of the feminization of low-paid sectors of the labour market. What French feminists have not done, however, is to focus on the multiple differences among women themselves, and a particularly noticeable difference between French and Anglophone feminism is the level of theorization of multiple identities. This is a source of incomprehension between French and Anglo-American feminists, with the latter unable to understand why differences between women have not been addressed by their French counterparts (Duchen, 1995; Kandel, 1995).

ANTI-FEMINISM WITHIN THE WOMEN'S MOVEMENT

The representation of French feminism has also been affected by 'anti-feminism' within the movement. This improbable position was adopted throughout the 1970s by the group Psych et Po. With its charismatic leader, Antoinette Fouque, and the personal fortune of one member which enabled the group to found a magazine, bookshop and publishing house, Psych et Po exerted a powerful influence within the women's movement. It was also intellectually influential. Luce Irigaray, Hélène Cixous and Julia Kristeva all passed through the group, although Cixous was the only one to maintain any long-term relations with them, publishing all her work with 'des femmes' between 1976 and 1982 (Moi, 1987, p. 4). However, tensions existed between Psych et Po and the rest of the movement. The group was criticized for its élitism and exclusionary practices. But the main problem was Fouque's repeated public claims to represent the MLF, while at the same time viciously attacking the rest of the movement. In 1979 Psych et Po registered the name '*Mouvement de libération des femmes*' and the initials 'MLF' as company trademarks, making it illegal for anyone else to use them. Their review *Des femmes en mouvement – hebdo (FMH)* continued to proclaim their opposition to feminism, which was seen as a reformist compromise with the patriarchy. What Psych et Po advocated was a complete overthrow of 'phallogocentrism', the entire masculine tradition of thought (Kandel, 1980).

Antoinette Fouque's ability to use the media to disseminate her own views in the name of the MLF, while at the same time describing herself, her group and her publication as 'anti-feminist', was initially an effective way of silencing the rest of the movement. It broke an unspoken rule that no one would speak in the name of the MLF and raised questions about the nature of a movement which resists organization and hierarchy, only to find that there is no control over who speaks in its name.

Psych et Po no longer exists as such, but Antoinette Fouque continues to exert a strong influence on the representation of the women's movement and of feminist ideas in France. Fouque's willingness to use the media to her advantage, coupled with the reluctance of the rest of the movement to do this, have meant that she has exerted almost total control over the publicity of feminist actions in France. Pamphlets have been distributed at demonstrations which suggest that they were organized by Fouque and that any other group present is a sub-group of hers (Delphy, 1993). Important feminist actions in the 1990s, including the movement for parity and the expression of solidarity with the women of the former Yugoslavia, were 'hijacked' by Fouque, who is often misleadingly represented as the spokesperson of the movement (Visser, 1993).

However, contradictions have emerged in her relation to the rest of the movement since the creation in 1989 of the *Alliance des femmes pour la démocratie* (Trat, 1996). The *Alliance des femmes* continues to demand the recognition of women's specificity, a position which has been a source of conflict with other feminists since the 1970s, in particular those associated with the journals *Questions féministes* and *Nouvelles questions féministes*. However, Fouque seems to have revoked her total opposition to equality. During the 1970s, Fouque saw the demand for equality as striving to be like men, a strategy which she rejected in favour of a search for the realization of femininity. This implied a total rejection of male power structures, a position which she evidently no longer holds: in the 1994 European elections, Fouque supported Bernard Tapie and was herself elected MEP. She also seems to have revoked her anti-feminism:

> As for feminism, I did not know what it was and now I could say that I regret it. It was a sign of my ignorance of women's struggles throughout history ... I fought to prevent the women's movement becoming the 'feminist movement'. I thought, maybe wrongly, that with the word 'women' we had the chance to speak, if not to all women, at least to the largest possible number.
>
> (cited by Trat, 1996, p. 28)

Josette Trat, writing in *Cahiers du féminisme* (1996), argues, perhaps surprisingly, that Antoinette Fouque should not be condemned outright and excluded from all feminist actions. Trat urges us to see the *Alliance des femmes* not simply as the successor of Psych et Po, but as an association with a feminist agenda. The *Alliance des femmes* supports the struggle of women against fundamentalism in Algeria. It opposes the subordination of women, the rape of women in the former Yugoslavia and the proposed '*salaire maternel*' (an allowance for women who stay at home to look after their children). The solution, argues Trat, is not to exclude them *a priori*, but to enter into a debate with them on the points where their position is different and to insist that they respect the rules of the 'movement'. This is not the position taken by *NQF* and *ANEF* (*Association nationale des études féministes*) who are refusing to co-operate with Fouque and her supporters in the organization of feminist actions (Delphy, 1995, p. 6).

THE REPRESENTATION OF FRENCH FEMINISM BY
ITS THEORISTS AND ACTIVISTS

Feminist activists and historians stress the changes which feminism has undergone since 1968. The period between 1978 and 1981 usually marks the cut-off point in accounts of 'the movement years'. It was a time of change, uncertainty and reflection for the women's movement in France.

The left was on the decline and had suffered defeat in the legislative elections in March 1978; the effects of the economic crisis were worsening and this brought a move from collective struggle to individualism in the search for security. Although many women remained active within the parties and the unions, many feminist groups disappeared, and there was a move from radical activism to feminist research (Remy, 1990, pp. 103–4). In 1979, Psych et Po appropriated the name of the movement and with the name, its actions and visibility. The arrival in power of the left in 1981 posed further problems for the women's movement, with regard to its relationship to institutions and strategies for achieving short-term reforms (*Nouvelles questions féministes*, 1981, p. 5).

While the media portrayed these changes as evidence that feminism was dead, feminists themselves were involved in a struggle over its redefinition and, in particular, its 'institutionalization'. For many, the most potent symbol of this institutionalization was the creation of the Ministry for Women's Rights when the Socialists came to power in 1981. Françoise Picq (1993, p. 332) goes so far as to write that 'the Ministry for Women's Rights replaced the women's movement'. During its short period of existence (1981–6), the ministry achieved a number of reforms. Abortions were reimbursed by Social Security; women's centres were established with ministry funding; projects were set up; and feminist research was introduced into the CNRS (*Centre national de la recherche scientifique*). However, it is clear that these would not have happened had it not been for the preceding decade of feminist struggle, and feminist criticisms of the ministry continued.

The existence of the ministry, the (very limited) insertion of women's studies into universities, the success of some reforms and the ways in which political parties and trade unions took on a number of feminist ideas all contributed to the changes that took place in the movement. Feminists remained active, but the revolutionary fervour of the 1970s was replaced by longer-term projects, such as setting up refuges for women and children and doing feminist research. Since 1981, feminist activity has been more localized and issue-centred. Feminist commentators stress that this is simply an historically specific manifestation of feminism which differs from the movement of the 1970s, but is no less real. For some, evidence of this lies in the widespread acceptance of certain feminist ideas by large numbers of women who, nevertheless, reject the term 'feminist' (Mossuz-Lavau, 1995). Already in 1979, radical feminists were writing:

The movement is spreading and affecting even the most everyday behaviour, as was its aim. This is happening to such an extent that it can pass unnoticed. The feminist tendencies which have appeared within the parties ... and the diffusion by the media of feminist ideas demonstrate the strength of the movement ... The 'co-option' of feminist ideas (for example, the creation of the Secretariat for Women's Affairs) still serves as a pretext for talking of feminism's failure, for which we are held responsible. Historically, however, co-option is in fact indicative of the vitality of the movement: by trying to co-opt feminism, the establishment is in fact recognizing its existence, even as it tries to neutralize it.

(Des féministes, 1979, p. 103)

This gradual spread of feminist ideas throughout society was initially criticized by many feminists for whom it represented the 'watering down' of feminist ideas and their co-option by, for example, political parties. Monique Remy's main thesis in her history of the movement (1990) is that feminism in France lost its strength due to the move from 'revolution to reform'. However, Françoise Picq (1993, p. 349) states succinctly that, 'Reform is not simply the antithesis of revolution, as we believed in the heat of the struggle; it is just as much its consequence'. And in an article published in 1980, Christine Delphy suggests that 'reformism' should not necessarily be seen as negative. She writes:

While we rejoice when a sister, a mother or a friend begins to respond to feminism, we paradoxically condemn the collective expression of this nascent consciousness. How often do we describe the first, timid adoption of feminist positions as the 'watering down', the 'betrayal', or even the 'co-option' of 'our' ideas? This is to misunderstand not only the way in which we achieve a greater consciousness, a process we have nevertheless all been through, and ought therefore to know about, but also of the way in which ideas are spread; it also suggests a desire, which is both unrealistic and politically suspect, to keep control of the ideas which we produce.

(Delphy, 1980, pp. 5–6)

A quick survey of feminist activity in France today reveals small groups of project-orientated feminists working in specific areas, whether this is solidarity with the women of the former Yugoslavia, the campaign for parity, or women and AIDS. Other issue-specific feminist groups are active around male violence towards women (*Association contre les violences faites aux femmes au travail, Collectif féministe contre le viol*); the defence of the right to abortion and contraception (*Mouvement français pour le planning familial*); the problems faced by immigrant women (*Collectif des femmes immigrées*); and solidarity with the women of Algeria.

Feminist research also continues to take place in universities and in the CNRS, although the funding and institutional recognition it receives is minimal. Women's studies has had to struggle for recognition as a legitimate area of teaching and research, and feminist epistemology and methodology have had little, if any, impact in the mainstream disciplines. While this is by no means unique to France, French feminist intellectuals, such as Marie-Victoire Louis (1996) and Christine Delphy (1991), see the resistance to feminist theory as particularly pronounced among French male intellectuals and the institutions whose hierarchies they dominate. The production of French feminist theory has been severely affected by the lack of institutional support, by the lack of funding and by the lack of publishing outlets. That it has taken place at all is attributed by ANEF (1995, p. 702) to the commitment of individual researchers and feminist organizations such as the *Association contre les violences faites aux femmes au travail* (AVFT). While it is difficult to assess the relative impact of anti-feminism in different societies, it is clear that structural reasons prevent French feminist theory from being produced and published in the same quantities as Anglo-American feminist theory.

In some areas of feminist activity in France today the gap between the movement and research is cause for concern. For example, talking about feminist work on male violence towards women, Marie-Victoire Louis of the AVFT commented (1993) that 'There is all this work by activists, but it has nevertheless been completely divorced from the theoretical work of intellectuals'. On the question of violence, there are, she adds, better relations between activists and feminist lawyers, than between activists and researchers. Françoise Collin also describes feminism as split in two:

> French feminism today seems to have fallen back on to just two of its many areas of activity: on the one hand, 'feminist research', which was established at the Toulouse conference, and on the other hand, social services, in which I would include help-groups for battered women or women immigrants. Between the two, despite certain initiatives, there is an absence of thought and political action, which is nevertheless no worse than that which affects the traditional political scene of the parties ... Feminism is no longer, or has not become, the common ground of intellectuals and non-intellectuals, of theory and practice, which it dreamt of becoming. The absence I am describing is hardly ever analysed by researchers, either because they have abandoned their hopes of changing the world or because they believe that the fundamental change in knowledge, which they are attempting to bring about, will of itself change the world.
>
> (Collin, 1989, pp. 163–4)

There are signs, however, that some recent campaigns may be acting as a remobilizing force for feminists in France and could enable the gap between movement and theory to be closed. The right to free and legal abortion, which is increasingly under threat, is still high on the feminist agenda. A demonstration organized by the *Coordination Nationale des Associations pour le Droit à l'Avortement et à la Contraception* (CADAC) brought 40 000 supporters on to the streets of Paris on 25 November 1995. Commentators have remarked not only on the size of the demonstration, but on the breadth of support which it attracted for a wide range of demands in addition to reproductive rights. These included the right to work and sexual equality at work. It is significant that the demonstration was supported by much of the left, which had previously withheld its support from feminist demands (Picq, 1996). Preparations for a national conference on women's rights in 1997 began immediately after the demonstration, which is being presented as a positive opportunity for feminism (Forest, 1996, p. 39).

The campaign for parity, which demands legislation enforcing the equal representation of men and women in political institutions, is similarly seen as the potential site for the remobilization of feminism (Allwood, 1995). However, it is clear that if feminism in France is to be 'remobilized' around reproductive rights or the campaign for parity, it will take a very different form from the movement of the 1970s. It will also involve the resolution of several important conflicts. These include, first, the differences around revolution and reform. While this issue is far less hotly disputed now than it was during the 1970s and early 1980s, it is of particular salience in relation to the question of whether feminists can achieve their goals by bringing women into (male) political institutions. Second, the conflict around 'ownership' or representation of the movement which surrounded relations between Psych et Po and the rest of the MLF is still present and features in the organization and accounts of most major feminist actions. This source of conflict within the movement contributes to the poor reception of feminist theory and practice. Third, the debate around sexual difference continues to take place within French feminism in terms of a binary opposition between sameness and difference, whereas in British and American feminisms, the criticisms of black, Third World and lesbian feminists shifted the terms of the debate at an early stage. There is evidence, however, that some French feminists are searching for ways to move beyond this dichotomy. Feminists on the extreme left have always been aware of the problems of conflicting identities among women involved in both feminist and class struggle politics. Articles in *Cahiers du féminisme* on parity raise the question of identity-based claims for political representation, which could include not only women, but other groups with a shared identity. However, many of the main actors in the parity debate stress that the difference between the sexes has nothing in common with other differences. It remains to be seen, therefore, whether the deeply entrenched divisions around sameness and difference can be overcome.

CONCLUSION

The media portrayal of feminism as 1970s-style activism leaves little room for discussion of current feminist action and theory. Similarly, as long as 'French feminism' is perceived outside France as the writing of an unrepresentative selection of intellectuals largely ignored by feminists in France, dialogue across national feminisms will be limited. Throughout the world, feminists are increasingly organizing, networking and campaigning at an international level. The globalization of the economy, the growing awareness of areas of similarity in women's positions, despite the recognition of diversity and difference, and the lobbying of European and international bodies over women's rights and human rights, have contributed to this trend. French feminists see themselves as isolated in this process, largely because of the dominance of the English language and because of the effects of the construction of 'French feminism'.

If French feminism is to play a part in international feminist practice and theory, then its specificities and similarities to other national feminisms must be recognized. As lesbians, black and Third World feminists pointed out in the 1980s, feminism, in an effort to stress the links between women, has at times been blind to its own cultural and historical specificity. But the identity politics which rose out of this awareness caused their own problems, notably of fragmentation and the accumulation of oppressed identities, leading to a hierarchy of oppression and divisiveness. In an effort to solve these problems, feminists are suggesting that we need to hold on simultaneously to sameness and difference: recognizing that women have common interests at certain specific moments, yet also recognizing the diversity of their existences, experiences and needs. Nira Yuval-Davis (1993) argues for a 'coalition politics' which would achieve specific political aims. She quotes Caryn McTighe Musil who wrote in 1990:

If the seventies were dominated by the exhilaration of discovering and naming ourselves as women, bound together in sisterhood, the eighties have been dominated by the discovery and definition of our differences as women ... The challenge of the nineties is to hold on simultaneously to these two contradictory truths: as women, we are the same and we are different. The bridges, power, alliances and social change possible will be determined by how well we define ourselves through a matrix that encompasses our gendered particularities while not losing sight of our unity.

(cited in Yuval-Davis, 1993, p. 4)

Applying this to national feminisms, we can say that we need to recognize what is specific to each national feminism, but also recognize where the similarities lie. And we need to find points where dialogue is possible between them, without allowing stereotyped representations to block this dialogue. It is holding on to both these differences and similarities at the same time which will make a future feminist politics possible, not only on a European level, but also on a truly international level.

NOTES

1.   This chapter was originally presented as a conference paper while I was writing *French Feminisms: Gender and Violence in Contemporary Theory* (London, UCL Press, 1998). Many of the themes which are raised here are discussed in more detail in the book.
2.   This is well documented. See, for example, the introductions to Duchen (1987) and Moi (1987). It is also often mentioned in books and articles which then go on to concentrate on only one aspect of French theory which has been constructed as 'French feminism' outside France. See, for example, the introduction to Fraser and Bartky (1992).
3.   See for example Giroud (1979) and the response to it, signed by 'Des féministes' (1979).

REFERENCES

Adkins, L. and Leonard, D. (eds), *Sex in Question: French Materialist Feminism* (London, Taylor and Francis, 1996).

Allwood, G., 'The Campaign for Parity in Political Institutions', in Knight, D. and Still, J. (eds), *Women and Representation* (Nottingham, WIF Publications, 1995), pp. 7–20.

Allwood, G., *French Feminisms: Gender and Violence in Contemporary Theory* (London, UCL Press, 1998).

ANEF, 'Etudes féministes et études sur les femmes en France en 1995', in Ephesia (ed.), *La Place des Femmes* (Paris, La Découverte, 1995), pp. 689–703.

Badinter, E., *XY: de l'identité masculine* (Paris, Odile Jacob, 1992).

Cahiers du CEDREF: Continuités et discontinuités du féminisme, Nos 4/5, 1995, Université de Paris VII.

Collin, F., 'Ringard ou ringuèle? La question des stratégies', *BIEF Bulletin d'information des études féminines*, Nos 20–1, 'Le féminisme … RINGARD?', décembre, 1989, pp. 163–7.

Collin, F., 'Théories et praxis de la différence des sexes', *M*, Nos 53–4, avril/mai, 1992.

Delphy, C., 'Nouvelles du MLF: Libération des femmes an dix', *Questions féministes*, No. 7, 1980, pp. 3–13.

Delphy, C., Book Review: 'La passion selon Wittig', *Nouvelles questions féministes*, Nos 11–12, 1985, pp. 151–6.

Delphy, C., 'Editorial', *Nouvelles questions féministes*, Nos 16–17–18, 1991, pp. 1–12.

Delphy, C., interview with author, 1993.

Delphy, C., 'Editorial', *Nouvelles questions féministes*, Vol. 16, No. 3, 1995, pp. 1–6.

Delphy, C., 'The European Union and the Future of Feminism', in Elman, R. A. (ed.), *Sexual Politics and the European Union: the New Feminist Challenge* (Providence, Oxford, Berghahn Books, 1996), pp. 147–58.

Des féministes de 'Collectif féministe contre le viol', 'Elles voyent rouge' et al., 'Des féministes hystériques aux féministes historiques ou de la caricature à l'enterrement', *Questions féministes*, No. 6, 1979, pp. 102–4.

Duchen, C., *Feminism in France: from May '68 to Mitterrand* (London and New York, Routledge, 1986).

Duchen, C., *French Connections: Voices from the Women's Movement in France* (London, Macmillan, 1987).

Duchen, C., 'Féminisme français et féminismes anglo-américains: spécificités et débats actuels', in Ephesia (ed.), *La Place des Femmes* (Paris, La Découverte, 1995), pp. 352–7.

Ezekiel, J., 'Anti-féminisme et anti-américanisme: un mariage politiquement réussi', *Nouvelles questions féministes*, Vol. 17, No. 1, 1995, pp. 59–76.

Forest, I., 'Demain, des assises nationales pour le droit des femmes', *Cahiers du féminisme*, Nos 75/6, hiver/printemps, 1996, p. 39.

Fraser, N. and Bartky, S. L. (eds), *Revaluing French Feminism: Critical Essays on Difference, Agency and Culture* (Bloomington and Indianapolis, Indiana University Press, 1992).

Giroud, F., 'Les voiles flasques du féminisme', *Le Monde*, 8 avril 1979.

Grosz, E., *Sexual Subversions: Three French Feminists* (Sydney, Allen and Unwin, 1989).

Groult B., in *Dialogue de femmes*, le 5 mai 1994, quoted by Louis, M-V., 'A propos des violences masculines sur les femmes: Ebauche d'une analyse féministe du nouveau code pénal français', *Projets féministes*, No. 3, octobre 1994, pp. 40–69.

Guerlais, M., 'Vers une nouvelle idéologie du droit statutaire: Le temps de la différence de Luce Irigaray', *Nouvelles questions féministes*, Nos 16–18, 1991, pp. 63–92.

Hurtig, M-C. and Pichevin, M-F., 'Psychologie et Essentialisme: un inquiétant renouveau', *Nouvelles questions féministes*, Vol. 16, No. 3, 1995, pp. 7–32.

Jackson, S., *Christine Delphy* (London, Thousand Oaks, New Delhi, Sage Publications, 1996).

Kandel, L., 'Post-scriptum: "une presse anti-féministe" aujourd'hui: "des femmes en mouvements"', *Questions féministes*, No. 7, 1980, pp. 37–44.

Kandel, L., 'Féminisme, multiculturalisme, cosmopolitisme: migrations de l'identité dans les mouvements de femmes', in Ephesia (ed.), *La Place des Femmes* (Paris, La Découverte, 1995), pp. 363–9.

Louis, M-V., interview with author, 1993.

Louis, M-V., 'Eléments pour une critique des rapports des féministes françaises au pouvoir', in Viennot, E. (ed.), *La démocratie 'à la française' ou les femmes indésirables* (CEDREF, 1996), pp. 91–107.

Marks, E. and de Courtivron, I. (eds), *New French Feminisms* (Brighton, Harvester, 1981).

Moi, T., *Sexual/Textual Politics* (London and New York, Routledge, 1985).

Moi, T., *French Feminist Thought: a Reader* (Oxford, Blackwell, 1987).

Mossuz-Lavau, J., 'Les Françaises aux urnes', *Modern and Contemporary France*, NS3, No. 2, 1995, pp. 149–57.

Nouvelles questions féministes, 'Féminisme: quelles politiques?', No. 2, 1981, pp. 3–8.

Picq, F., *Libération des femmes: les années-mouvement* (Paris, Seuil, 1993).

Picq, F., 'L'ANEF, la manifestation du 25 novembre 1995 et après', *Bulletin de l'ANEF*, No. 20, printemps, 1996, pp. 1–9.

Planté, C., 'Questions de différences', in Riot-Sarcey, M., Planté, C., Varikas, Eleni et al. (eds), *Féminismes au présent* (Paris, L'Harmattan, 1993), pp. 111–31.

Remy, M., *De l'utopie à l'intégration: histoire des mouvements de femmes* (Paris, L'Harmattan, 1990).

Sullerot, E., *Quels pères? Quels fils?* (Paris, Fayard, 1992).

Trat, J., 'L'Alliance des femmes pour la démocratie: une suspicion légitime', *Cahiers du féminisme*, No. 77, 1996, pp. 27–8.

Varikas, E., 'Féminisme, modernité, postmodernisme: pour un dialogue des deux côtés de l'océan', in Riot-Sarcey, M., Planté, C., Varikas, E. et al. (eds), *Féminismes au présent* (Paris, L'Harmattan, 1993), pp. 59–84.

Visser, W., 'Viols contre les femmes de l'"ex"-Yougoslavie', *Nouvelles questions féministes*, Vol. 14, No. 1, 1993, pp. 43–76.

Walby, S., '"Backlash" in Historical Context', in Kennedy, M., Lubelska, C. and Walsh, V. (eds), *Making Connections: Women's Studies, Women's Movements, Women's Lives* (London, Washington, DC, Taylor and Francis, 1993), pp. 79–89.

Yale French Studies, No. 62, 1981.

Yuval-Davis, N., 'Beyond Difference: Women and Coalition Politics', in Kennedy, M., Lubelska, C. and Walsh, V. (eds), *Making Connections: Women's Studies, Women's Movements, Women's Lives* (London, Washington, DC, Taylor and Francis, 1993), pp. 3–10.

7 Reflections on Gender Issues in Contemporary Europe

Susan Bassnett

Mapping gender issues in Europe today presents us with a series of complex problems, with different histories and different possible solutions. Over the past three decades, since the advent of second-wave feminism, there has been great diversification within what might be loosely termed European women's movements, for the very term 'feminism' has been the source of considerable debate and many women, particularly in Central and Eastern Europe, remain uncomfortable with it, sometimes overtly hostile to its employment.

It needs to be stated from the outset that there is not, and never has been, a single concept that can be described as a 'European feminism'. Differing socio-economic realities, combined with different historical traditions have resulted in diversity rather than any integrated, central set of ideas. There has also been relatively little traffic of ideas, and a great deal of that traffic has been the result of the translation of works written in English into other European languages, rather than any genuine dialogic exchange. Not a great deal of German, Italian, Spanish or Dutch feminist writing has found its way into English, and those texts that have been translated from French have been carefully selected. Nicole Ward-Jouve has commented on the huge discrepancy between a Frenchwoman's perspective of French feminist thought and the perspective presented to the English-speaking public by means of selective translation. She draws attention to the way in which a notion of 'French' feminist theory has been constructed in the English-speaking world:

> In the process of its importation so-called French theory has changed face. Though it has always been recognized that each writer was different, Kristeva from Irigaray from Cixous (not to mention Wittig in the USA) they have tended to be grouped and discussed together, when in France they are, if not at daggers drawn, at least not on speaking terms.
>
> (Ward-Jouve, 1991, p. 48)

Toril Moi (1985) pointed out over a decade ago that the English-speaking world has tended to distinguish trends in feminist thinking as

129

broadly divisble into two worlds: the Anglo-American, which also comprises the British, and the French. In this fairly crude binary opposition the Anglo-American tradition is viewed as taking a more pragmatic approach and being predominantly concerned with questions of sexual politics, gender identity, race and class, with the French tradition tending towards a more theoretical approach, concerned principally with questions of cultural politics, psychoanalysis and history. Ward-Jouve takes issue with this division, arguing that not only does it blur or deface what French writers effectively do, but it also 'says a great deal about the needs from which it stems' (Ward-Jouve, 1991, p. 48). In other words, Anglo-Saxon culture is the determinant factor in the process of constructing an image of French feminist thought.

In 1986, which now seems a lifetime away (and in terms of developments in European culture *is* a lifetime away indeed!) I published a personal account of my experiences with the women's movement in four societies: Italy, the United States, the German Democratic Republic and Britain (Bassnett, 1986). The invitation to write the book had come out of a series of discussions in which I had been struggling to articulate a sense of the difference between women's movements, in contrast to the received notion of cross-cultural similarity in sisterhood. The differences, which the book endeavoured to explain, derived from a belief that sexual politics were always embedded within a cultural context, which ultimately determined how questions would be articulated. So, for example, the violence of Italian feminism in the early 1970s, with its huge protest marches that reflected the pent-up anger of generations of women betrayed, as they perceived it, by both the right and the left, by Church and by state, can be seen as emblematic of the great ongoing debate in Italian political life that has dominated this century: the question of the nature of power. In contrast, the long tradition of individualistic feminism within the British context, whether of the more conservative, philanthropic variety or the socialist feminist strain, combined with the British tradition of grass-roots action-based politics meant that the women's movement operated in smaller, local or regional-based centres rather than on a grand scale in the Italian style.

In the United States, where feminism had a long tradition of links with anti-slavery, suffrage and civil rights campaigns, the prominence of media treatment of feminism contrasted with the fragmentary nature of issues fought for and debated, and the traditional American emphasis on the personal. In complete contrast, the model of GDR feminism was a centralized socialist model, constructed along patriarchal principles that equated women with the family, and hence prioritized child-care and education issues, while marginalizing (some would say completely erasing) issues of sexuality.

The great interest shown by publishing houses and the media in feminism in the 1970s meant that initially a number of texts were translated into several European languages. Simone de Beauvoir, Virginia Woolf and Mary Wollstonecraft were widely translated, as were many contemporary United States authors such as Shulamith Firestone, Betty Friedan, Kate Millett. In the early phase, English-language authors tended to dominate European women's bookshops, but gradually the pattern altered, and readers became more selective, as the gap between Europe and the United States widened. The introduction of courses in Women's Studies in higher education and a greater attention to writing by women at all educational levels also led to an increase in book production. The early reliance on English-language authors declined rapidly, and is a pattern that can be seen right across Europe, from the Nordic countries to the Iberian peninsula. This also seems to bear out the notion that each culture will produce the variety of feminism most suited to its own development, and that although cross-pollination can occur, the context will determine the way in which growth takes place.

Surprisingly little European feminist material, either in the form of theory or creative writing, finds its way into English, a fact which reflects the unwillingness of English-language publishers to offer translations to their readers. It is worth noting that in his recent study of translation politics, Lawrence Venuti points out that a mere 2.4 per cent of the published book market in Britain in 1990 were translations, as opposed to over 25 per cent in Italy (Venuti, 1995). This means that it is difficult for English-language readers to gain any adequate perception of what is happening in Europe as a whole, and it is perhaps not unsurprising that there have been very few books that have attempted to address this problem. One welcome volume appeared in 1991, when Helena Forsås-Scott published a collection of essays on European feminist writing, entitled *Textual Liberation* (Forsås-Scott, 1991).

In her introduction, Forsås-Scott points out that the history of Europe between 1919 and 1939 was largely a history of the emergence of dictatorships. She notes also that without exception, dictatorships repressed feminism, and that the legacy of this repression characterizes feminism in many parts of Europe. The history of Europe since 1945 can therefore be seen as one of refashioning cultures in the aftermath of war and the crumbling of dictatorships, which happened in several waves. The end of Franco's dictatorship in Spain did not come until 1975, and the Berlin Wall only came down in 1989, with the subsequent revolutionary changes across former Eastern Europe.

The first phase of European reconstruction, both literally and psychologically, can be seen as extending from the late 1940s to 1968, the year characterized by student protests across Western Europe and by the Russian invasion of Czechoslovakia. It was in the 1960s also that small but distinct women's groups began to emerge in several Western European countries in the oppositional parties of the left. Although they were often poorly organized and fragmented, these groups provided a means of registering the dissatisfaction felt by many women with what they perceived as patriarchal attitudes of fellow-comrades. In 1970, for example, a small Italian feminist group operating in Rome and Milan produced the famous *Sputiamo su Hegel* (*We Spit on Hegel!*) manifesto, that rejected the Marxist view of the primacy of the class struggle over other forms of social protest and declared that:

> Woman cannot be defined in relation to man. Both our struggle and our freedom are based on this assumption... Equality is an ideological attempt to enslave women on even higher levels. Behind every ideology we perceive a hierarchy of the sexes... Civilization has called us inferior, the church has called us sex, psychoanalysis has betrayed us, Marxism has sold us out to a hypothetical revolution.
>
> (Bassnett, 1986, pp. 109–10)

The need to try and reconcile feminism and Marxism dominated a great deal of feminist thinking in the early 1970s. Since many European feminist movements had a history rooted in nineteenth-century socialist feminism, the process of unravelling undertaken by second-wave feminists was long and painful. But although women looked for support from male colleagues on the left, they were also struggling to redefine the political agenda in ways that prioritized gender issues. Initially the way forward seemed to be the large-scale campaigns centred around divorce or the reform of family law or the right to abortion. The success of those campaigns in the long term is hard to measure, but it is perhaps significant that both Spain and Italy, two strongly Catholic countries, had the lowest birth rates in Europe by the 1990s, and the birth rate in Ireland was also declining rapidly, despite the high profile of the church in state affairs.

The 1980s can be seen as the decade of consolidation, as feminist infrastructures began to develop in many countries, and feminist publishing and media had become a substantial industry. The large-scale mass protests declined, and more women found their way increasingly into public life. A reasonably high proportion of Euro MPs elected were women, and it is possible to argue that the European Parliament has provided a means for many women to be heard that would have been less feasible in their own countries. Iceland and Ireland both elected women as President, Norway and Poland elected women as Prime Ministers, Germany appointed its first woman President of the Federal Constitutional Prime Court, France created a Minister for Women's Rights as early as 1981. But it is also possible to see the emergence of other, more disturbing signs in the 1980s. Fast-growing economies and rising standards of living in many urban areas in Western Europe contrasted increasingly sharply with the emergence of a new underclass of poor dispossessed citizens, often immigrants from former colonies. Countries such as Italy that had always seen itself as non-racist, now found racist politics high on the agenda as the success of right-wing political groups and neo-fascist parties showed. Anti-Semitism and overt racism reappeared across Western Europe. In Britain, the election of Margaret Thatcher as Prime Minister in 1979 on a radical right-wing ticket exposed as a fallacy the myth that the world might be a better place if ruled by women.

The sense of growing uneasiness that characterized much of the 1980s culminated in 1989, with the collapse of the socialist states in former Eastern Europe. The Cold War came to an abrupt end, and the newly expanded Europe engaged in a frenzy of realignment and self-redefinition. The implications for gender politics were enormous. Countries such as Poland, Czechoslovakia (soon to split into the separate states of the Czech Republic and Slovakia), Hungary and the German Democratic Republic, which ceased to exist when it rejoined the German Federal Republic, had placed emphasis on institutionalized welfare services that enabled more women to join the labour force. In the 1980s, for example, some 87 per cent of women in the German Democratic Republic of working age were either in some form of work or education. The provision of nurseries was routine. After 1989, the welfare infrastructure collapsed and free market economic policies decimated the labour force. Restricted access to abortion (which was banned altogether in Poland) and diminished maternity leave provision added to the problems experienced by women once the euphoric months of 1989 and 1990 were over.

However, under socialism the situation for women had not been as easy as socialist propaganda sought to depict. Despite the ostensibly pro-women policies, the lack of access to contraception (or its outright prohibition, as in Romania) meant unwanted pregnancies or abortion, and many women brought up children in cramped living spaces. The material conditions of women's lives in Eastern Europe were drab at best, deprived at worst. It is important to bear this in mind, for on the surface at least, the changes in Eastern Europe have shown that the priority questions for women are not the same across cultures, and may even be seen to be in conflict. Slavenca Drakulic, the Croatian writer, contrasts Western feminist thought with that of women in Eastern Europe, and concludes that the history of culture affects the development of feminist consciousness (Drakulic, 1987). In a collection of essays, ironically entitled *How We Survived Communism and Even Laughed*, Drakulic argues that the interest in the beauty industry, including the beauty pageants so despised by Western feminism, shown by Eastern European women reflects a newly discovered concern with what she terms 'femininity'. She sees this question of femininity as a crucial area of difference between women in Western and Eastern Europe, and suggests that its resurgence is connected to the fact that for decades women were deprived of the trappings of the beauty industry under socialism.

What Drakulic does not discuss, however, is the commodification of what she terms 'femininity' when it is placed in an economic context. The rise of prostitution across former Eastern Europe has grown parallel to the decline in jobs for women; in Turkey and the Eastern Mediterranean the hundreds of young prostitutes who work the bars and the streets are known disparagingly as 'natashas'. Many women training as dancers or performers in the stage schools of the former Soviet Union and other Eastern European countries can find work only in strip clubs. The surge of pornography that followed the collapse of the Berlin Wall, and which earlier had followed the end of the Franco regime in Spain, suggests that 'liberation' perceived in sexual terms takes no count of the debasement of those (predominantly) women forced to rely upon the sex industry for survival.

By the mid-1990s it was clear that within the new enlarged Europe there would be no consensus on questions of gender politics, due to the diversity of histories. Whereas Western feminists had to engage initially with their relationship to Marxism and seek to reconcile class consciousness with struggles for racial and gender equality, in Eastern Europe women had to come to terms with their suspicion of the very term 'feminism' as employed by women in the West, and were quick to reject the version of socialist feminism that had been imposed by the state. However, this seemingly conflictual position did have its positive side: the changes that brought about the removal of the Iron Curtain also called into question some of the more facile assumptions about feminist goals and expectations. Additionally, by initiating a reconsideration of 'femininity', however that term might be understood and interpreted, women in the newly expanded Europe were also able to engage with another rapidly developing area of gender politics: the debates around masculinity and its relationship to feminism.

There has been a great deal of uneasiness within feminism about the prominence given to questions of masculinity in the 1990s, particularly given the resurgence of nationalist politics across Europe and extreme manifestations of masculinism, especially in military conflict zones. In December 1995, the Glass Ceiling debate in the National Theatre, London focused specifically on the relationship between feminism and masculinity. Chaired by Sara Dunant, speakers were invited to express their views on whether the media interest in masculinity should be seen as a retrograde step, and in terms of theatre, whether the large number of roles written for or given to men (including some all-male productions of Shakespeare or *Swan Lake*) was detrimental to the progress women had made in the previous decades. Della Grace, the lesbian artist whose physical appearance deliberately transgresses gender distinct boundaries (she dresses as a man and grows facial hair, while accentuating her breasts) argued cogently for the need to rethink those boundaries, pointing out that the gay and lesbian movement has called into question the concept of gender bipolarity. After a long debate, it was generally agreed that the new emphasis on questions of masculinity and the exploration in theatre terms of traditional concepts of gender representation was a logical next stage in international gender politics. In short, feminist thinking led on logically to the study of masculinity.

In his study of masculinity, R. W. Connell points out that a generalized concept of the masculine is as oppressive to gay men as it is to women:

> Oppression positions homosexual masculinities at the bottom of a gender hierarchy among men. Gayness, in patriarchal ideology, is the repository of whatever is symbolically expelled from hegemonic masculinity, the items ranging from a fastidious taste in home decoration to receptive anal pleasure. Hence, from the point of view of hegemonic masculinity, gayness is easily assimilated to femininity.
>
> (Connell, 1995, p. 78)

This is an interesting argument, for it suggests that, far from being an anti-feminist or post-feminist development, the current interest in exploring concepts of masculinity is a logical next stage in ongoing feminist debates about the cultural construction of gender. Theorizing about gender has moved on from simplistic bipolarities based on equations of male = masculine, female = feminine and the terms within which the discussion can take place have been redefined. In his very useful essay aptly entitled ' "Irresolutions, Anxieties and Contradictions": Ambivalent Trends in the Study of Masculinity', Joseph Bristow argues that there have been two main lines of research in the field, two linked but separate critical genealogies:

> If research emerging from men's anti-sexism has struggled to redefine how men can speak of masculinity self-critically, the studies following Foucault's work have considered how discourses on masculinity were constructed in the first place. In other words, if anti-sexist men have worked hard at finding a pro-feminist means of talking about manhood, then queer theorists have tried to understand more about the cultural conditions that gave rise to the dissident styles of maleness. Likewise, if the anti-sexist men's movement addressed the question of masculinity in terms of *gender*, then queer theory was arguably more concerned with men's relations to *sexuality*.
>
> (Bristow, 1996, p. 169) (emphasis in original)

Bristow demonstrates that just as feminist theory saw femininity and female sexuality as sources of conflict for women, so the new masculinity theorists are exploring the ambivalences and conflicts confronted by men, whether gay or heterosexual. Most importantly, he draws attention to the fact that queer theorists' debates are exploring the 'cultural conditions' that give rise to alternative styles of maleness. We could go further, and suggest that a crucial aspect of what we might term 'masculinity studies' is an investigation of the cultural conditions that determine which concept of masculinity predominates at a given moment in time. In other words, masculinity studies are firmly located within cultural history, as the seminal importance of Foucault testifies.

Feminist theorizing is intimately linked to the material situation of women, hence the differences that appear in feminist thinking across cultures, which reflect the differences in attitudes to women and in the social and economic status of women. The historical dimension to feminism has also varied considerably. So, for example, while Anglo-American feminism, and to a large extent German feminism, led to a systematic rethinking of the contribution of women to cultural history, with the rediscovery of hundreds of women artists, writers, scientists, etc. who had been erased from canonical histories, a similar process did not take place in Italy, nor has anything of the kind happened in former Eastern European countries. Italian feminist historiography focused on the nineteenth and twentieth centuries, and there has never been any serious attempt to reconsider the enormous contribution of women as writers, artists and patrons in the Renaissance, for example. The 'hidden from history' model of so much feminist work in northern Europe or in the English-speaking world has no counterpart in Italy, or in Spain and several other European countries either. The attention of many European feminists has focused on the importance of the personal, on the here and now rather than on archaeological research into the past, and, as Forsås-Scott has pointed out, there has been a great surge of fiction, poetry, autobiography and other forms of literary production, which in many instances derives from a strong existing tradition. This is particularly the case in former Eastern Europe, so that the 1996 Nobel prize-winning poet Wisława Symborska was drawing upon a Polish literary heritage in which women writers had long played a major role.

The emphasis of a great deal of European feminist writing has been placed on the contemporary or on the role played by women in the establishment of the modern democratic state. This is in contrast to Bristow's point about the central significance of tracing the genealogy of gender positions within masculinity studies. And here we encounter another important difference: for the current phenomenon of research into masculinity is not European-wide. Rather it appears to be of greatest importance in those cultures that are engaged in rethinking their own colonial or imperial histories: Britain, the Netherlands and, to a lesser extent, France. In those cultures emerging from dictatorship or other forms of totalitarianism, the debates on masculinity are marginal at best, often virtually non-existent. In Germany, where the homoeroticism of nazism is a well-documented phenomenon, the study of masculinity is less advanced than might be expected. However, just as the importance of fiction, film and autobiography needs to be noted as a major manifestation of European feminism, it is also the case that creative artists across Europe deal with masculinity questions in their work, even if there appears to be a dearth of theoretical material or historical case studies.

In the 1990s, however, debates about gender issues have changed direction somewhat, now that the problem of how to define national culture and identity is firmly back at the top of the agenda, after a century of absence from cultural politics. The conflicts in Bosnia and Chechnya have produced a horrendous polarization of gender issues that are linked to questions of ethnic, religious and nationalist extremism. The use of mass rape against Moslem women by Serbian troops, the adulation of Radovan Karadjic and the regional war-lords, the employment of an ethic based on a supposed tradition of masculine militarism and the apparent willingness of women to collude in this process in the interests of a narrowly defined aggressive patriotism provide shocking evidence of the continuation of the worst kind of nationalistic tendencies. Even as the European community seeks closer economic links and moves towards a single currency, European states are ravaged by war and ethnic violence, the starkest of all reminders of difference.

What seems to be happening as we approach the end of the millennium is that there is a greater plurality of gender concerns in Europe, but that these issues are often subsumed in the broader context of debates about national culture and tradition. Feminism, though no longer in its more public, militant phase, has in no way disappeared, but has broadened and diversified, reflecting the diversification of distinctive contexts. Gender studies, and the study of masculinity in particular, invite further investigation of the ways in which gendered images are constructed in a culture, and how those images relate to the representation of a nation-state.

My own research has led me into studying the relationship between ideals of masculinity and ideas of nationhood, something that I would never have predicted a decade ago but which, with hindsight, appears as a logical development after writing *Feminist Experiences*. In the process of researching that book, I found myself more and more intrigued by the differences between cultural constructions of gender. From an examination of specifically women's issues, the focus widened to take account of gender theories and masculinity studies, a process heightened by personal considerations. For after 18 years of being a mother to daughters, I found myself the mother of a son, and an entirely new line of thinking began. What, we may ask simply, are the role models for a boy growing up at the end of this century, given that the certainties of gender bipolarity that established female in direct opposition to male are undesirable?

Working within an English context, I have concentrated my research on tracing ideas and ideals of masculinity back into the history of imperialism, looking at ways in which a set of images were constructed, marketed and perpetuated for generations, through educational textbooks, boys' books and comics and the cinema. In a recent essay which explored images of heroic Englishness in fiction and in film, I argued that the mythical English hero was an artificial construct, that served a precise purpose at a particular moment in time:

> Today we question that myth because we can see the myth-making as a consciously political act, just as we can see the hegemony of England and Englishness as political. The English gentleman hero was meant to personify order, coherence and British homogeneity. Today, that homogeneity is exposed as illusory, the history of British imperialism is being rewritten, the desirability of a model of heterosexual masculinity has been called into question.
>
> (Bassnett, 1996, pp. 58–9)

So a model of heroic, stiff-upper-lipped English maleness was invented that served (and still does, to some extent) as a cultural icon. The English

hero represses his emotions, sublimates his sexual appetites, while preferring the company of men to women, offers himself body and soul to his
country – a useful model to offer the boys who were being educated to
manage an Empire or serve in its armies. And in tracing the construction
of the model, we can also see the stark contrasts with other models of masculinity invented elsewhere in Europe, models where voracious sexual
appetite is perceived as a positive rather than as a negative attribute, or
where what might be interpreted as extreme barbarity, as, for example, the
case of the Transylvanian Vlad the Impaler demonstrates, is seen as an
heroic demonstration of resisting the enemy.

Homi Bhabha has argued that the new cosmopolitanism, the idea of the
'global', has altered our sense of how we perceive and define national tradition and identity (Bhabha, 1994). The spread of a rhetoric of the global
serves to accentuate the local or national, and culture is increasingly
seen as conferring authenticity and identity. Significantly, in the Bosnian
conflict, the folkloric tradition was used to reinforce supposed cultural
differences between Bosnian Muslim, Serb and Croat, just as the restrained English hero was used to contrast with the excesses of the unde-
sirably foreign. Bhabha sees the dangers of this reliance upon expressions
of cultural difference, and in a more recent essay, he makes a distinction
between what he terms culture as an evaluative activity concerned primarily with the attribution of identity and emphasizing the importance of
tradition, ritual and custom, and an alternative perspective,

> that claims that culture is less about expressing a pre-given identity
> (whether the source is national culture or ethnic culture) and more about
> the activity of negotiating, regulating and authorising competing, often
> conflicting demands for collective self-representation.
>
> (Bhabha, 1997)

This is a view that seeks to move beyond the limitations of divisiveness,
that sees what he terms the new cosmopolitanism as an instrument of
change, in contrast with the model of cultural identity that is bound up
with territory and national tradition. Bhabha's concern is to move away
from the idea of dominant and marginal cultures, a position that reflects
his own position as a theorist of post-colonialism. In the next millennium,
it will be important to move away from ideas of fixed, preordained identities, whether constructed through gender, religion, ethnicity or anything
else, and to focus instead on the actual processes of identity construction.

Once we start to dissolve the categories of central vs peripheral, majority culture vs minority, masculine vs feminine, our perceptions alter.
Europe in the twentieth century has been constantly refashioning itself,

and the reconstruction that is currently taking place with the end of the Cold War is immense. One of the most obvious effects of this latest reconstruction is the dissolution of the category of Eastern and Western Europe, that never made much sense either geographically (Prague is further west than Vienna!) or historically. And just as there has never been a single European consciousness, so there cannot be a single European voice, but always a multiplicity of voices. In terms of gender, we are now experiencing a great range of different priorities: in some contexts, such as the United Kingdom or France, the relationship between colonialism and images of masculinity is a significant issue, linked to the problem of redefining identity in a post-imperial society. Elsewhere, in Spain for example, and to some extent in Italy and in Greece, where memories of patriarchal dictatorships are still vividly alive, the emphasis is still on exploring explicitly feminist questions concerning gender and sexuality. In Hungary or the Czech Republic or Slovenia, reconstructing themselves after decades of oppressive state rulings that virtually prohibited open discussion of gender, there is a great deal of interest in understanding and articulating concepts of the feminine within a programme of political action that could be described as feminist in intent. There are, as there have always been, great differences across European cultures, which is doubtless why no single model could ever be accepted as a norm.

Mapping ways in which gender issues are articulated and debated involves endlessly pausing to reflect on how different perspectives are across Europe. The end of the Cold War highlighted sharp differences in attitudes to gender across the new unified Europe, but there were already great divergencies, as indicated by the ways in which second-wave feminism had developed in the 1970s and early 1980s. Moreover, the transfer of information across cultures, and the partiality of translation practices, has made it even harder to obtain any kind of overview that makes sense or does justice to the plurality of positions. Ultimately, one falls back on subjective impressions: when I wrote *Feminist Experiences* in the 1980s, I thought I was writing about different ways in which feminist activity had developed in four societies. At the time, that position appeared to question the idea of universality based on some kind of common feminist ideal. Rereading the book now, I am struck by how dated it seems, for attention has shifted towards an exploration of in-betweenness, both in terms of gender, language and culture. The empowering space is now the liminal, the threshold space that is neither inside nor outside. Mapping gender issues in contemporary Europe we note the shifting frontiers, the redefinitions, the realignments, and above all, the movement and the interconnectedness that comes from movement and transforms the world we inhabit.

REFERENCES

Bassnett, S., *Feminist Experiences: the Women's Movement in Four Cultures* (London, Allen and Unwin, 1986).

Bassnett, S., 'Crossing Cultural Boundaries. Or How I Became an Expert on East European Women Overnight', *Women's Studies International Forum*, Vol. 15, No. 1, 1992, pp. 11–15.

Bassnett, S., 'Lost in the Past: a Tale of Heroes and Englishness', in Gittings, C. E. (ed.), *Imperialism and Gender: Constructions of Masculinity* (New Lambton, Dangaroo Press, 1996), pp. 47–62.

Bhabha, H. K., *The Location of Culture* (London, Routledge, 1994).

Bristow, J., ' "Irresolutions, Anxieties and Contradictions": Ambivalent Trends in the Study of Masculinity', *Journal for the Study of British Cultures*, Vol. 3, No. 2, 1996, pp. 165–81.

Connell, R. W., *Masculinities* (Cambridge, Polity Press, 1995).

Drakulic, S., *How We Survived Communism and Even Laughed* (London, Hutchinson, 1987).

Forsås-Scott, H., *Textual Liberation: European Feminist Writings in the Twentieth Century* (London, Routledge, 1991).

Moi, T., *Sexual/Textual Politics* (London, Routledge, 1985).

Venuti, L., *The Translator's Invisibility* (London, Routledge, 1995).

Ward-Jouve, N., *White Woman Speaks with Forked Tongue* (London, Routledge, 1991).

8 AIDS Prevention, Gay Identity and National Homophobia in France

Murray Pratt

The AIDS epidemic, now accounting for an estimated 37 000 cases of people with AIDS and 110 000 who are HIV positive, has had a greater effect in France than in any other European country.[1] These figures are in large part due to the inadequacy of national responses to the situation throughout the 1980s, and in particular an inability to mobilize effectively around issues of safer sex for gay men, or even imagine the possibility of a public interpolation of men who have sex with men. AIDS awareness in the 1990s, by contrast, has at times achieved a national profile, with multichannel television funding appeals, major films and autobiographical novels, and print media coverage all capturing, and often directing, public interest in the issue. However, the nature of recent attempts to figure HIV as a preventable danger for gay men, this chapter argues, is such that these too fail to counter the forms of homophobia endemic in French national consciousness, and that safer sex campaigns in the 1990s continue to be restricted by problematic attitudes to representations of homosexuality. As a result, the viability of positive valued identities for gay and bisexual men remains compromised, and the social circumstances in which a managed rate of HIV infection is tolerated can persist.

French society's problems with fully imagining a public discourse about homosexuality and HIV/AIDS are well illustrated by an anecdote told by Daniel Defert about his first attempt at safer sex promotion, in a gay club in 1985. Defert offers the following story:

> The first time we handed out condoms it was in a bar in Marseilles. We had arranged to meet there and I had two bags full of 1000 condoms with me, which I was planning to hand out during the summer school. During the conversation, we realized that we could make a start by handing some out in the bar where we were, which had a backroom. We asked the barman for a container and got on with handing them out. There was an American there, and he congratulated us saying that they should do this in the USA too. Three minutes later, the patron appeared

and started taking the condoms back from the customers, saying, 'How dare you cast aspersions on the sexuality of my clientele!'[2]

(Minella and Angelotti, 1996, pp. 208–9)

Political victories in France throughout the 1970s, largely won by the homosexual action group, the FHAR (*Front Homosexuel de l'Action Révolutionnaire*), helped build a fragile gay movement, but as Guy Hocquenghem (1994) argues, their success was restricted to militating for individual rights, forms of sexuality which would remain firmly within the existing order, and yet do nothing to challenge organically the rigid demarcation of sexuality into the categories of public and private. As Defert's story shows, even in a space used for gay sex in the mid-1980s, official discourse could prohibit representations of users' behaviour which referred to certain forms of sexuality, and even collude in characterizing assumptions of homosexual intercourse as shameful. Hocquenghem's reading of the legal and political advances of the 1970s is one which criticizes a 'liberation' able to secure a gay identity within normalized society, but at the price of accepting that this identity is subjected to existing social regulations around public and private space. Bill Marshall summarizes Hocquenghem's concerns well:

> the changes of the 1970s are seen as part of a redistribution of terms and categories within, rather than beyond, the workings of power... The expected 'liberalisation' of anti-homosexual legislation will be matched by a tightening of the apparatus elsewhere, as regards children's sexuality, public sex, sexological/medical orthodoxies... Society will put up with the homosexual rather than seek to get rid of him, but only by distinguishing between 'good' and 'bad' practices and preventing any disruptions to the dominant order.

(Marshall, 1996, pp. 39–40)

It is a pact of this nature, comprising a 'tightening of the apparatus elsewhere', which seems to explain the paranoid concern with the social control of representations of HIV and AIDS in France, particularly in terms of their associations with homosexuality. Paradoxically, at a time when information was at a prime, and campaigns in Britain and America were targeting 'ignorance' about HIV as one of the main dangers, French public discourse about the virus proved unable to formulate effective ways of depicting its impact on gay male sexual behaviour. There are a number of reasons for the initial blind spots in the 1970s, including a refusal on the part of gay men to believe in rumours about a mysterious new disease which would mean that their new sexual freedom would end as quickly as it had been won. As one commentator puts it, 'It is understandable that gay men reacted quickly to dissociate themselves from the new image of "biological aggressors" with which they were being linked' (Martel, 1996, pp. 216–17).[3] What is illustrated by Defert's story is the continuing sense of counter-logic according to which first, the condoms he wanted to distribute become represented as the threat rather than a means of defence, and second, his attempts to promote safer sex are seen to disrupt a local consensus, so determined to defend its emerging place within the hierarchy of sexual economy (and the silences which maintain this) that acknowledging the existence of HIV as part of their experience seemed more dangerous than the virus itself. This would explain the idea of the 'aspersions' cast on the sexuality of the bar's clientele as revolving around the assumption that their sexuality had something to do with the signifying fields of HIV and AIDS, rather than sexual orientation alone.

Sexualized identity is constructed and reaffirmed through narrative and representational strategies which negotiate and allocate value to behaviours and perceptions. In other words, the sexual identities which people occupy are seldom experienced independently from emotive charges, often to do with senses of the value of the self within wider meta-narrative schemes, such as the development of a family, the establishment of prevalent attitudes among a peer group or the formulation and maintenance of national identity. It is in this latter context that the identities and experiences of gay men in France, as evoked and modified throughout the ongoing AIDS crisis of the 1980s and 1990s, have been subject not only to tolls of illness and death but also to an 'epidemic of signification' (Treichler, 1988, p. 31) which cannot be dissociated from the physical spread of the virus. Discursive interventions, professing to offer and disseminate crucial information about HIV, as state-level immunological responses, can be seen, despite themselves, to have been simultaneously carrying and transmitting attitudes conducive to maintaining self-perceptions and images among gay men which may modify, but ultimately also enable, forms of riskier sexual behaviour. In other words, constructions and self-perceptions of gay male identity contribute to how messages of prevention campaigns are actualized, both in their drafting and in the ways in which their messages are received. The aim of this chapter is to outline some of the ways in which these campaigns were influenced by a national reluctance to figure homosexuality positively within public discourses in France, and to consider the impact of these homophobic attitudes on the safer sex campaigns which impact on the perceptions and self-perceptions of gay men's sexuality in France.

REASONS TO BE CAREFUL?: UNDERSTANDING FRANCE'S
HESITANT RESPONSES

The history of responses to the AIDS epidemic in France can be documented as an ongoing series of hesitations and mistakes, especially with
regard to the absence of effective strategies for protecting gay men from
the HIV virus, resulting in HIV infection rates, numbers of AIDS cases
and AIDS-related deaths higher than any other European country. Various
recent publications[4] by writers, sociologists and AIDS campaigners in
France have revealed the failures of the 1980s in gay male health promotion to be a second national AIDS scandal for the country, of even greater
proportions than the more often commented scandal of contaminated
blood transfusions. These reports offer competing analyses of the situation, pointing the finger at different groups, organizations or specific
social factors and attitudes as responsible for the delayed *mise en place* of
an effective set of campaigns addressed to gay men.

The reasons evoked are many, but each of the strands discussed can be
seen as relating to the ambivalent status of representing homosexuality in
France. Commentators refer to the changing political climate, including
the initial hesitancy of the left to fully tackle the potentially contentious
field of gay rights after their initial implementation on coming to power in
the early 1980s, and again during the electoral campaign of 1985, when
the then prime minister Laurent Fabius helped stifle reference to AIDS for
fear of turning off potential voters (Arnal, 1993, pp. 68, 72). This was to
be followed by a right-wing discourse of mistrust of difference and other-
ness, fanning forms of homophobia such as proposals to censor the gay
press, and allied to the racist agenda of *Le Front national* and its knock-on
influence on the broad right in the late 1980s. Notably the interventions of
Jean-Marie Le Pen and Jacques Médecin around concepts such as contam-
ination and forms of social quarantine or segregation betray the extent to
which their concern is with protecting the spaces of French culture from
the 'homosexual lobby', and reveal their attitude to AIDS as providing
them with a reason to advocate classification, surveillance and ultimately
containment of a form of gay public identity which threatened the myths
of pure French masculinity which they peddled.[5]

Over the same time-scale, national structures for epidemiological
policy-making in France proved equally inflexible in addressing forms of
homosexuality which fell outside manageable stereotypes. Organizations
responsible for health promotion and related matters had emerged in such
a way that homosexuality, conceived of as a matter of private choice, was
left unaccommodated in policy matters, and this rigidity meant crucial

delays in tackling the incidence of HIV among gay men. For instance, as ex *Gai Pied* journalist Frank Arnal documents, an inability of government health organizations to address gay sexuality arose from a structural rigidity which routinely occluded gay men from the categories it used for thinking of sectors of the public. As a result the earliest official campaigns run by the CFES (*Comité Français d'Education pour la Santé*) prioritized raising awareness among the young, but their deployment of this term assumed that they would all be heterosexual, leaving generations of gay youths uninformed (Arnal, 1993, pp. 70–8). Moreover, an institutionalized ignorance of the evolving nature of gay contacts in France is discussed by other social historians of the time, including the civil servant and journalist Frédéric Martel, who illustrates the lack of gay involvement in health policy decisions by detailing a history of misunderstandings, such as the idea advanced at one meeting that there was no need to address possible HIV transmission in saunas, since 'everyone knew that you couldn't become infected by contact with planks of pine' – by a doctor unaware that saunas were used for sex (Martel, 1996, p. 263).[6]

Martel, however, goes on to emphasize the extent to which a collective refusal on the part of militant gay rights groups and gay publications to assume the threat of AIDS in the early years of the epidemic abetted the official incompetences. The reaction of gay rights campaigners in the 1980s is summed up by one *Gai Pied* journalist, Albert Rosse, quoted by Martel:

> We didn't believe in AIDS for one moment. They couldn't keep us in line any more through morality, the Church or the law: from where we stood, it made sense that they should go and invent a virus. AIDS was little green men come to punish homosexuals at the very point when legislation no longer kept them in check. We couldn't stop laughing.[7]
>
> (Martel, 1996, p. 243)

Martel uses comments such as these to implicate militant gays within the French denial of HIV and AIDS, accusing them of 'preferring to sacrifice crucial and imperative health measures in the name of a blind defence of sexual liberation' (Martel, 1996, p. 245). Despite increasing evidence of the reality of AIDS as a disease affecting gay men, Martel's argument runs, gay activists and the *Gai Pied* editorial team in particular, consistently refused to raise the alert about AIDS, and their 'irresponsibility' resulted in France's lag of between two and five years on its European neighbours in developing effective resistance strategies. However, in some ways, the incredulity of the gay press seems a logical reaction in the light of the important gains made by gay rights groups in France prior to the 1980s, resulting in nascent forms of liberation exemplified by legal reforms, an increased sense of tolerance, and the emergence of a gay press and of bars and saunas as organized social cruising areas. The reactions detailed by Martel in effect offer a credible political response to the 'convenience of AIDS' as an instrument of social manipulation which stigmatizes and disposes of gay men at the very moment when they start to emerge as a visible group within French society: to resist the questionable and sketchy reality of 'le cancer gay' for gay groups, and writers such as Guy Hocquenghem, was a coherent and militant stance to take in the early 1980s, their suspicions founded on years of discrimination. It is only with hindsight that the impact of the epidemic can be seen to have far exceeded the clampdown on gay liberation which it was originally quite justifiably feared to represent. A dossier on AIDS from *Le Matin* in the summer of 1983[8] contrasts what was at stake in the collective psychology of the Parisian gay scene by equating survival and life with the continuation of the freedom of sexual expression. 'I'm not going to let this stop me living', is offered as one understandable response to the 'invention' of AIDS at the time.

The diversity of these different versions is enough to suggest that it is highly unlikely that one can identify a single cause of the failures of French strategies for resisting AIDS in the 1980s. Indeed, as suggested by Daniel Selden's essay on AIDS as a mediatized play of 'crisis and solution' (1993, p. 221) on national and supra-national scales, the technique of criticizing past methods of representation from the standpoint of a more informed present only serves to reconfirm a social master narrative aimed at engineering the spectacles by which social values are asserted and replicated through technological progress in medicine. As seen more recently with BSE, CJD and E-coli in Britain, for instance, the emergence of medical disasters is often only acknowledged retrospectively, as part of a bid to confirm a pseudo-competence on the part of governmental structures which ally themselves with the presentation of 'solutions', however superficial or partial these may be. The chapter sequence used in even the most informed of texts, such as Arnal's study of French prevention policies, evokes exactly this kind of sequence of disruption and resolution: a section in Arnal's text which translates as 'The irresponsibility of the French authorities confronted with AIDS infection among gay men from 1983 to 1989' is followed by one headed 'Taking account of the homosexual specificity of the disease …'. Selden's essay argues for a wider approach in accounting for positionings of AIDS as follows:

However indispensable here an analysis of discourse or iconography may be, it is bound to remain tactically limited unless it goes on to address the larger social syntax which links and hence construes such images in relation to specific patterns of response.

(Selden, 1993, p. 223)

Beyond the local failures of policy and social attitudes isolated to account for French failures in fighting AIDS lies a 'larger social syntax' of organized national homophobia. However, while commentators such as Arnal and Martel agree in recognizing the lack of models for representing gay experience in France prior to the onset of the epidemic, and advance clear-sighted analyses of specific erasures, absences or discriminations, their accounts stop short of relating these to any syntactical, or systematic assault on gay representation. As we have seen with Martel's epic history of French homosexuality, *Le rose et le noir*, the line which is consistently taken to explain France's reticence in tackling AIDS is to lay the blame on gay men themselves for what he calls 'le déni homosexuel' (1996, p. 241). Martel's account of these initial responses, however, stops short of addressing the structures of national consciousness which deny homosexuality, and which provide a context of homophobia as an organizing force within French society, within which his thesis needs to be placed to make sense. Ultimately Martel too fails to move beyond the syntax of homophobia, transferring the responsibility for accurate health promotion information and campaigns from national and governmental organizations on to the groups who deserved to be informed rather than blamed for their lack of access to unambiguous information.

Research into the attitudes and perceptions of gay men towards safer sex in the late 1980s goes further in investigating some of the effects of homophobia on behaviour modification, but tends to depict these as largely questions of choice and fate, rather than identifying discriminatory practices and ideologies within a larger national framework. Pierre Bourdieu-trained sociologists, Michel Pollak and Marie-Ange Schiltz have established a significant body of research on AIDS in France, based largely on the interpretation of annual questionnaires distributed chiefly through the gay press. Their major contribution has been the basic step of emphasizing in theory, that sexuality and sexual identity are more than just matters of 'individual choice' (Pollak and Schiltz, 1991, p. 54), as they were hitherto conceived in France. As Pollak and Schiltz correctly recognize, the cultural impasse of this restrictive definition resulted in a biomedical approach to AIDS prevention in France as opposed to the more pragmatic responses established in Northern European countries (Moerkerk with Aggleton, 1990, pp. 184–8), which recognized homosexuality in terms of sets of group behaviour and perception. This was in part due to the absence of integrated gay networks in France. Effective prevention, they argue, can only be based on a recognition of the collectivity of gay experience within society as a group identity. Their explanation for the initial lack of mobilization against HIV and AIDS avoids allocating blame, and instead points to a prevalent culture where sexuality has been exclusively identified in terms of personal choice (1991, p. 54).

Between 1985 and 1990 certain adaptations to the risk of infection could be charted, and the conclusions which they draw from their surveys paint a largely optimistic picture, whereby the sense of group identity among gay men has been reinforced due to the threat of the epidemic, and this in turn has provided for the circulation of information about protection from HIV (Pollak and Schiltz, 1991, p. 63).

Optimistically, Pollak and Schiltz (1991, pp. 62–3) chart the evolution of a set of shared values among the respondents to their questionnaires in 1990, expressed in more vocal demands for equal rights, and recognize a new 'génération safe sex' among the under-twenties who replied to their survey (1991, p. 58). Their positive prognosis of the changing place of homosexuality in French culture is characteristic of accounts of AIDS and gay men in the 1990s, confirming the narrative model of crisis and solution evoked earlier. With the exception of Act Up-Paris,[9] there seems to be a consensus that the deficit in effective action has been remedied in the 1990s. Safer sex provision for gay men is now made by a number of organizations working in the field, and as the surveys cited by Pollak and Schiltz show, there is a corresponding increase in the number of gay men responding to preventive messages by adapting their sexual behaviour towards safer sex practices.

However, the anthropological model which they use to explain the different modifications of sexual behaviour made by gay men in France, in many ways repeats the emerging social consensus, whereby the visibility of certain lifestyle choices is permitted, but at the cost of a dissociation of the signifier 'gay' from actual homosexual activities. As their report itself indicates, 'the stabilization of safe sex knowledge' is not universal, but excludes the working classes and people with few formal educational qualifications. Whereas only 2 per cent of professional respondents in 1990 may have unprotected sex, the corresponding figure is 25 per cent among working-class gay men (Pollak and Schiltz, 1991, p. 59). The one other factor which differentiates gay male behaviour by class, according to Pollak and Schiltz, is the environment in which contacts are made, with working-class men being more likely to meet in those remaining public spaces used for cruising as opposed to more commercialized sites. As a result, information campaigns diffused via clubs, bars and saunas and intended for visible gay groups have often passed by whole sectors of the at-risk population. Paradoxically, the visibility of homosexuality in France has often been a form of licensed invisibility: 'gay' has been privatized to the extent that it is effectively contained within certain lifestyle choices, fashions and physical spaces, and consequently those left 'outside' these parameters are not identified as gay, irrespective of their actual sexuality. It is little wonder that working-class men, people with learning disabilities or low esteem for whatever reason, do not recognize themselves within the models used within safer sex promotions taking place within the closed 'gay community'. Whereas Pollak and Schiltz (1991, p. 63) point to the extent to which AIDS has redefined 'social links and internal solidarity', they admit that this model is highly variable when applied to individuals and specific sub-groups. In other words, as predicted by Hocquenghem, gay liberation has proved to be both partial and a compromise, in as much as it is obtained for those homosexuals who redefine themselves within certain legitimate parameters. AIDS prevention work throughout the 1990s, through its inability to look beyond the official gay population, can be seen as reinscribing this situation through its deployment of a fantasized model of homosexuality rather than one which addresses lived social realities.

AN IMAGE DEFICIT[10]

A further factor in the delayed response to the epidemic in France, and one which impacted directly on the stock of images and representations available to be mobilized in prevention campaigns, was the existence of legislation banning the advertising of contraception in France as a form of birth control, dating from 1920, which hindered attempts to discuss the use of the condom in safer sex publicity (Vidal, 1993, pp. 85–91). Drawing again on an omission of homosexuality, the prioritization of the condom's contraceptive use over its prophylactic function which this represents meant that gay men in France were not fully informed about ways of limiting exposure to HIV until well into the 1990s, years after most other European countries. The legal change can be seen as an evolution in that it finally acknowledged the importance of condoms as a form of prevention for gay men. However, even once the laws were eventually repealed, after a series of challenges dating from 1987 to around 1991, official campaigns by organizations such as the AFLS (*Association Française de la Lutte contre le Sida*), advocating the use of the condom, tended to avoid making clear and direct statements about its role in safer sex for gay men. Early slogans often coyly avoided mentioning condoms or their use directly, and as a result lent themselves to ambiguity. This is the case with a phrase such as 'Today everyone's saying yes' (*'Aujourd'hui tout le monde dit oui'*) from 1992, while the earlier slogan, 'Condoms protect you from everything, from everything except love' (*'Les préservatifs préservent de tout. De tout sauf de l'amour'*), from 1989, in its haste to position condoms within the context of real passion offers a conflicting secondary message about true love being an exception, which could result in dangerous confusions being made.[11] Most pernicious in much of the safer sex material advocating the use of the condom put together in France, however, is the persistence of assumptions of heterosexual modes of sexual relations and address, in terms of the scenes depicted, the values and meanings attached to sex, and the figuring of passive homosexuality as other, in such a way that it is this which comes to stand as the threat – to the point of eclipsing the perceived risk of the HIV virus.

Campaign messages specifically directed at gay men have repeatedly reinscribed French ambivalence around the place of homosexuality in a variety of ingenious and inventive ways. What is astonishing is the extent to which slogans and images, even those formulated as part of gay-run campaigns, can be read ambiguously, to the extent it would be no exaggeration to see national discourses of AIDS prevention in France as having been 'infected' by homophobic sub-texts.

The aim of the earliest campaigns to follow the legalization of advertising referring to the condom, such as the image used by AFLS in 1989 under the heading 'In safer sex, there's first and foremost the word sex' (*'Dans safer sex il y a avant tout le mot sexe'*) (see Figure 8.1), is to offer a sex-affirmative message for gay men. To the extent that the representation of two men sharing intimacy figured in the photograph, this campaign amounted to a huge leap forward for the organization which had proved unable to go so far previously (Arnal, 1993, pp. 107–12), even if this image was only to be published in gay-specific magazines, thereby principally reaching only those sectors of the population already informed about safer sex practice. Yet an analysis of the codes deployed by the campaign reveal a set of more worrying tendencies, which continue to set the tone for prevention material appearing in France in the late 1990s. These tendencies can be considered as, on the one hand, an erasure of specificity about sexual acts, or a desexualization of homosexuality, and on the other, ambiguous slogans which confuse more than they inform, often to the point of apparently advocating practices away from which they fully intend to steer their target groups.

Here, the message *'Dans safer sex il y a avant tout le mot sexe'* conforms to this latter tendency in as much as the prioritization of the word 'sex'

152

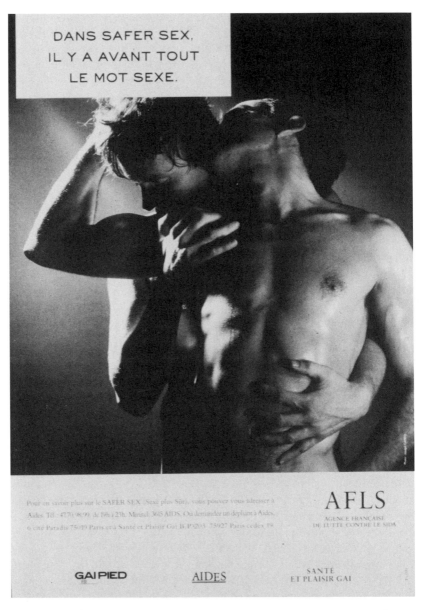

Figure 8.1 Campaign by AFLS, 1989: 'Dans safer sex il y a avant tous le mot sexe'. (Centre Régional d'Information et de la Prévention du Sida.)

necessarily entails the demotion of its complement 'safer', suggesting that sex in itself is somehow the 'product' which the advert is advocating, and the extent to which it is safe is somehow secondary. Coupled with the use of models to provide ideal male body forms, already familiar from underwear marketing in late 1980s France, the effect of this slogan is to engage readers' desire. Rather than directly tackling the myth that sex with a condom doesn't count as real sex, as it aims to do, its connivance with the dominant ploys of the market instead comes closer to offering the message that readers' experience of sex is always already inferior to the 'sex' it is selling, and it is this to which they should aspire, whatever the cost. At the same time, the campaign avoids giving any information about what safer sex is, presumably for fear it might still fall foul of censorship by advocating condom use. The effect of this is to seriously negate the impact of the intended message, by failing to provide the information needed for less aware sectors of the magazine's readerships to equip themselves in attaining the soft focus embrace it promises.

And it is here that this specific campaign can be seen to illustrate the first of the two counter-effective tendencies outlined above. While the slogan hopes to convince gay men that their experience of sex will be just as good with a condom, the image, beset with anxiety about how far it can go in depicting homosexuality, offers in concrete terms nothing more exciting than the depiction of a spot of nape nibbling. As a result, not only does the intimacy depicted fail to convince readers of the merits of safer sex, it once again does nothing in terms of providing information, as the risk factor involved in what is represented is already nil. The process of desexualization can be further discerned in this image in the selected cut off point, around the two men's navels. With this joining the tendency to produce subliminal unsafe desire, the overall effect of the advert is to radically reinforce insecurities and confusions about the places and values of homosexuality as it is lived, and paradoxically help justify ideological pressures about what should be kept silent or invisible, to the detriment of conveying crucial information. Even where campaigns of the period do illustrate condoms, they make no allowance for the fact that after years of religious and secular discourses pretending that these objects didn't exist, people were not informed about how to use them.

AIDS prevention in France, despite the reorganization of health services in 1989 to create a body responsible for overseeing this (AFLS), has often polarized into posters specifically targeted at gay men and produced by gay-specific organizations, but diffused only in very localized situations, and much more substantial campaigns aimed at what gets referred to as the '*grand public*', a homogeneous body which seems not to include any homosexuals at all. Sets of campaigns aimed at public exposure in the early 1990s, such as those illustrated in Figure 8.2, attempt to offer a sense of social inclusivity (even going so far as to figure a black man in one poster), to give the impression that the slogans they provide have relevance to everyone. However, the 1991 posters not only limit themselves to heterosexual couples, but the wording of their slogan 'Condoms. Why hesitate any longer?' ('*Les préservatifs. Pourquoi hésiter plus longtemps?*'), in a deliberate attempt at memorable tricksiness by equating condom use and marriage, could be seen as setting up an equation where homosexuality is not a factor.

The 1992 posters appear to be moving away from the exclusivity of the heterosexual couple, and the chosen slogan 'Condoms. Today everyone's saying yes' ('*Les préservatifs. Aujourd'hui, tout le monde dit oui*') would seem to confirm this. Yet, of the four images collected here by CRIPS (*Centre Régionale de l'Information et de la Prévention du Sida*), only one could be potentially seen as depicting a same-sex relationship, and even this is ambiguous as the two women are noticeably less intimate with each other than the couples in the previous year's campaign. Two of the other posters depict random groups of men, more identifiable as a somewhat antiseptic looking street gang, and some well turned out young entrepreneurs than as recognizably homosexual images. Additionally, by representing a minimum of three men together, sexual intimacy between men figures as an accusation against which the campaign defends itself in advance. The remaining 1992 poster could be construed as two straight men vying for the attentions of a woman, or of an already formed straight couple and another 'unsuccessful' man, in either case positing the idea that the heterosexual couple is the only sexual relationship which functions as a real site of social value. Not only has the prevalence of '*grand public*' campaigns in France diverted funds and energy away from groups of people who might be considered in greater need of information,[12] but this is compounded by the effect on gay men of social exposure to lifestyle images which address the public as universally heterosexual, devaluing anyone outside a straight relationship. Brunet (1993, p. 53) refers to the problem of campaigns using ' "sterilized characters" unlikely to evoke the identification or interest of those most concerned by the risk of the epidemic'.[13] As forms of health promotion found in the mainstream national press and as part of the street geography encountered routinely deny representation of, or denigrate, gay male intimacy, the sense of not participating in forms of national identity considered valuable, and therefore not being fully addressed by the campaigns increases.

Among the slogans addressed to this '*grand public*' are those which carry messages with sub-texts which rely on reaffirming homophobic

→ le préservatif
et la
sexualité
à moindre
risque

102 **Les préservatifs.
Pourquoi hésiter plus
longtemps ?** *1991*
Agence Française de Lutte Contre le
Sida (AFLS) - VANVES
France

103 **Les préservatifs.
Pourquoi hésiter plus
longtemps ?** *1991*
Agence Française de Lutte Contre le
Sida (AFLS) - VANVES
France

104 **Les préservatifs.
Pourquoi hésiter plus
longtemps ?** *1991*
Agence Française de Lutte Contre le
Sida (AFLS) - VANVES
France

105 **Les préservatifs.
Aujourd'hui, tout le
monde dit oui** *1992*
Agence Française de Lutte Contre le
Sida (AFLS) - VANVES
France

106 **Les préservatifs.
Aujourd'hui, tout le
monde dit oui** *1992*
Agence Française de Lutte Contre le
Sida (AFLS) - VANVES
France

107 **Les préservatifs.
Aujourd'hui, tout le
monde dit oui** *1992*
Agence Française de Lutte Contre le
Sida (AFLS) - VANVES
France

108 **Les préservatifs.
Aujourd'hui, tout le
monde dit oui** *1992*
Agence Française de Lutte Contre le
Sida (AFLS) - VANVES
France

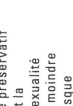

Figure 8.2 Campaigns on condom use by AFLS, 1991 and 1992. Collected by CRIPS (Centre Régional d'Information et de la Prévention du Sida) in their catalogue 'Images & SIDA', Vol. 1, p. 13

identifications of homosexuality as AIDS and AIDS as homosexuality, in the enterprise of policing straight society. Arnal includes some of these in the appendices to his book (1993, p. 167), and the dynamics of denial, defence and sympathy set in play is as much about defending the heterosexual reputation of the subject position offered as it is about enabling clear decisions about safer sex, even for the audiences presumed to be straight. Thus a phrase such as 'AIDS, I won't pass it on' ('*Le sida, il ne passera pas par moi*') from the 1987 CFES campaign functions, by providing a self-congratulatory and ultimately homophobic mantra for people who don't perceive themselves affected by the epidemic, at the same time as it creates a coalition of ill-will towards less 'responsible' others. An apparent reversal of this strategy, in the AFLS campaign of 1989, proclaims, 'AIDS, anyone of us can come into contact with it' ('*Le sida, chacun de nous peut le rencontrer*') does little more than put the general public on a general alert, relying on tactical wording familiar from calls for national unity against Communists, Fascists or immigrants.

Later campaigns have diversified into packaging for condoms, designed to make them trendy and encourage young people especially to 'collect' them, thereby removing any stigma attached to carrying them. This move can be seen as part of France's growing fetishization of the condom as icon since it has begun to figure in the national consciousness. Yet the danger is that the symbolic dimension comes to outweigh its function within safer sex practices, to the extent that the presence of a condom in the wallet or back-pocket can act as a symbolic protection against infection, as a recent article suggests (Mendès-Leite, 1995, p. 101). And, as the examples from the 'Mairie de Paris' collection show (see Figure 8.3), the emphasis is more on providing work for advertising agencies and promoting artists than on meeting prevention needs. More worrying is the fact that while these delectable packets were distributed freely in the gay area of le Marais in Paris in 1996, the condoms inside the wrappings were designated for vaginal and contraceptive use only, and contained no form of lubricant.[14] Irrespective of the real problem of the different strengths of condom needed for anal and vaginal sex, the message communicated is again one about heterosexuality being the assumed norm, and homosexuality an inferior model having to make do with cast-offs.

Even material designed for gay men is obliged to comply with the invisible laws governing national homophobia. A 1995 brochure distributed by the organization 'Aides' and destined for gay male circulation shows on the one hand an evolving sense of the need to address the specificity of gay experience in prevention material (it depicts a situation more familiar

MAIRIE DE PARIS

Une collection de onze étuis personnalisés pour habiller les préservatifs

COLLECTION 94

COLLECTION 95

45.67.01.01. JOUR APRES JOUR, MOIS APRES MOIS, PARIS COMBAT LE SIDA.

Figure 8.3   Condom packaging used in distribution campaign by the Mairie de Paris, 1994 and 1995

to most men having sex with men than the glossy soft-focus embraces of the early posters, and even acknowledges that not all gay men in France are white) but in other ways it confirms tacit conventions about the place of gay male sexuality in discourse. The outside of the brochure (see Figure 8.4), although revolutionary in depicting a gay encounter in public, has nonetheless conveniently cleared the park of any passing women or children for the open air encounter, which seems to consist of nothing more steamy than some furtive pulse-taking. The more graphic acts of sex are reserved for an interior with a divan draped in a rainbow flag (see Figure 8.5),[15] which serves to remind us that the contortions taking place there are marked as gay-identified ones and not the sort of thing which men normally get up to. Most tellingly, the depiction of sex takes place in private, both inside the folded brochure and in a room, whereas the real life versions of the characters in the park would be as likely to head for some nearby bushes. The result is that graphics are designed and advice given for the kind of sex which lends itself to illustration, an orchestrated set of measurable actions, while effective preventive measures applicable in more obscured, entangled encounters, and for relationships where consent and power are less clear issues, are left unformulated. By shifting the sexual behaviour away from the public forum, the Aides brochure misses out on a chance to consider what might constitute safer sex for those gay men left outside the privatized spaces of the gay economy.

As with the earlier poster campaigns, the only possibility of formulating and diffusing HIV prevention messages in France seems to be compromised by the fact that they are so often accompanied with sub-texts which refuse, downgrade or contain gay male experience and identity. The cost of this ongoing national homophobic blind spot needs to be acknowledged alongside those factors which accounted for France's delayed responses to AIDS documented above, since, as the 1986 Ottawa Charter on health promotion stipulates, any effective attempt to promote healthy choices is bound to fail if it proves incapable of at the same time offering no positive images for one of the key groups targeted, nothing to enhance a sense of esteem and foster the ability to make free and informed decisions as valued members of wider communities (Thorogood, 1992, p. 49).

The 'larger social syntax' behind French AIDS prevention campaigns, then, is a sustained ideology which prevents positive figuration of gay male identity, and only sanctions the representation of homosexuality within public discourse when it appears as individual choice. In the field of AIDS prevention, this has led to a series of campaigns which institutionalize an elision of homosexuality as an equal danger to AIDS for the so-called '*grand public*'. This is recognized by Bernard Kouchner

Figure 8.4 Brochure published by Aides, July 1995. Illustration by Stéphane Blot. Front cover

(1993, p. 271), one of the French ministers most concerned with reversing the deficiencies of earlier prevention campaigns:

A phenomenon which we thought we had left behind with the Middle Ages is appearing once again: human rights violations on medical grounds: on every continent and whatever the local culture, this ancient fear has come back into force, offering rejection of the other, of those

Figure 8.5 Brochure published by Aides, July 1995. Illustration by Stéphane Blot. Inside pages

who are contaminated, as an illusory guarantee of one's own protection. The fight against AIDS is also a fight against each discriminatory action.[16]

THE ECONOMICS OF EXCLUSION AND THE NEED FOR GAY AFFIRMATIVE HEALTH PROMOTION

As D. A. Miller has ably demonstrated in his critique of Susan Sontag's refusal of the metaphorization of AIDS, the epidemic already figures in Western consciousness as a highly charged site of cultural and political signification which taps into existing metaphorical and discursive structures around sexual identity. 'AIDS remains', he writes (1993, p. 215), 'centrally a gay disease, the disease of gayness itself', as what he calls (1993, p. 216) 'the homophobic social text' which writes itself into cultural representations of HIV and AIDS, and determines policy decisions and social attitudes which bear materially on the lives on those affected by the virus. For Simon Watney (1993, p. 207), the same drama is played out within the arena of the national media, as the institutional familial society, ever keen to isolate and defend itself against the homosexual body, embraces the 'inestimable convenience of AIDS, reduced to a typology of signs that promises to identify the dreaded object of desire in the final moments of its own apparent self-destruction'.

In France, the forms of discrimination which have spread most corrosively in discourses about AIDS, have taken the form of social exclusion, to some extent mimicking extreme-right discourses which advocate social segregation. An article appearing in a collection which addresses the forms of exclusion experienced by drug users in France provides a credible set of factors rooted in French socio-economic life to explain the 'growing intensity' of national forms of rejection and exclusion (Foucauld, 1993, pp. 257–60). Jean-Baptiste de Foucauld depicts a situation where individuals have become dissociated from wider society to the extent that people have almost acquired the right to exclude, as family relationships and friendships are severed without any great upheaval. The serious consequences of this for those who are unable to support themselves financially are clear. A society which values competition, and where identity is acquired through shopping and other forms of consumer activity, inevitably produces a sub-strata of those who 'fail', and for whom self-destruction can present itself as a logical outcome when self-maintenance is available at too high a price. Foucauld goes on to explore the possibilities of new forms of politics aimed at tackling these problems, since the welfare state as it has evolved in France is not sufficiently nuanced to have an impact upon them. Instead he offers three conditions with which the new politics would have to comply: a sense of the collective community in order to reinvent a sense of responsibility for others, the active participation of those who are excluded within the running of projects concerning them, and the emergence of local forms of economic planning and strategy, to allow for the integration of related actions.

Foucauld's explanation of the growth of exclusion offers one model for understanding the virulence of homophobia in France over the period concerned, and likewise, the solutions he advances provide a principled set of guidelines which social responses to AIDS could follow, as relevant for the provision of care plans, therapeutic projects, advocacy schemes and social and medical networking as for the prevention campaigns considered here. Moreover, by applying his economic model of exclusion to the absence of positive identities and the presence of negative forms of self-perception perpetuated in French AIDS prevention campaigns, a further condition for combating exclusion, discrimination and the prevalence of HIV among gay men can be seen to emerge.

Forms of economic exclusion experienced by gay men in the figuring of the AIDS epidemic in France include statistics which are persistently commented as showing a 'stabilization' in the number of gay men affected as a justification for reducing the gay specific content of preventive and other interventions. Official publications on HIV and AIDS, sharing similar discursive fields as those responsible for allocating funds to 'competing' needs, ally themselves against interpretations which might question their game plan. Thus a general publication entitled *La Séropositivité au quotidien* (*Day to Day Living with HIV*), for instance, can begin by developing an elaborate and tendentious statistical analysis claiming that heterosexual AIDS is under-reported in France as a way of excusing its omission of any consideration of gay lifestyles, dealing with routine discrimination, or legal rights pertaining to same-sex partners.

On a national level, exclusion occurs as part of a similar economic strategy. An article in a magazine produced by a communist anti-AIDS group in Paris points to a similar finding, in its analysis of the sanitized bodies appearing during the 1994 television AIDS appeal screened nation-wide in France. Camille Jove (1995, p. 12) offers the following interpretation:

> The deaths of those who have no productive function: deviants, marginals, victims of police incompetence, tramps who are already 'socially' dead are presented as negligible. Their physical elimination gives the reassuring impression that order is being restored.[17]

Applied to the national place of homosexuality, this translates into a phenomenon strikingly similar to that discerned through the surveys of Pollak
and Schiltz: gay men are accommodated socially as 'productive' to the
extent that they participate within the pink economies, both financial and
symbolic, and find it difficult to become interpolated outside these circuits. In Britain, homophobia has expressed itself in a tendency to deny
that AIDS affects heterosexuals at all, through interventions such as those
made by commentators from the straight community, like Andrew Neil,
for whom the gay lobby simply spoke up heterosexual risks to con the
government into funding their activities (Garfield, 1996, pp. 2–3, 13). In
France, however, the control of public homosexuality has led to a situation
where the only acceptable or 'healthy' representation of AIDS prevention
material is when it is straight-identified, or conforms to national scripts
about the forms of containable homosexuality tolerated. AIDS prevention
campaigns, to become funded, and 'pass' those with the authority to
release these, have been obliged to correspond to this ethic, often to the
point of excluding its negative other, the more dangerous and unhealthy
image of the 'unproductive' homosexual which it works to exclude. Organizations run by gay men and accountable only to themselves, such as Act
Up-Paris, with its more radical demands for fundamental changes in
French health provision, access to information and the urgency of co-ordi-
nated responses to the epidemic, figure in the press as a threat.[18] Jove
again explains this (1995, p. 12):

> A society based on the values of accumulating material wealth (as use-
> less as it is utilitarian) runs the risk of being called into question by
> those who seek more authentic values in their lives, due to the fact that
> they are acutely aware of their mortality.[19]

Yet it is Act Up-Paris and similar organizations which offer a model of
communitarian response more akin to that called for by Foucauld, and
offer the possibility of clear-sighted representations of HIV and homosexuality beyond their imaginary functions in the French national drama of
defending propriety, heterosexuality and ultimately 'Frenchness' against
'aspersions'.

Ironically, for many French men in the 1980s and 1990s, an increasing
public visibility of forms of homosexuality has emerged, but often in tan-
dem with its negative other of the ravaged body of AIDS.[20] From early
denials to the fashionable economy of le Marais, where the privatized
commercial gay scene in Paris often works to exclude or disguise AIDS
by repackaging 'unhealthy' body images (Minella and Angelotti, 1996,
pp. 218–20), opportunities for establishing affirmative gay male identities

have been as effectively monitored and rationed as ever. Self-perception has consequently been rendered problematic, confused or impossible for gay men, who are forced to negotiate complex series of misrecognitions in order for any performance of identity to be acknowledged. Rommell Mendès-Leite (1995, pp. 98–100) points out in his linguistic analysis of a series of interviews with men having sex with men in Paris, that the word 'AIDS' only occurs in their vocabulary when they are talking about public perceptions of homosexuality as opposed to their own self-perceptions. He reports that in their dealings with other gay men there is a tendency for gay men to view other homosexuals from the perspective of public stereotypes, making the possibility of relations, identifications and relationships one which is characterized by suspicion and mistrust. He comments (1995, p. 98):

> the other is represented directly or indirectly as 'dangerous'. When preventive discourse says that you should avoid non-protected relations, or that you should restrict the number of partners, it's putting you on guard against the other.[21]

The conclusion which his survey draws (1995, p. 101) is that prevention has a symbolic dimension and brings with it socio-cultural constructions, meanings and logics, and ought therefore to address the values and self-images of gay men, with a view to empowering them.

This is again borne out by the internationally agreed definitions of the Ottawa Charter on health promotion of 1986, which argues for strategies which enable people to take control over their own health, or the formulation offered by the World Health Organisation of health as 'the extent to which an individual or group is able to realise aspirations and satisfy needs, a resource for everyday life and not an object of living'. Within an American context these needs and aspirations have been identified as the recognition that affirmative models of gay sex and intimacy have to be taught and encouraged as a priority, rather than maintaining the illusion that gay sex can be safely packaged away.[22] In France, these health promotion aims can only be met by fostering opportunities for proliferating positive images, representations, iconographies and vocabularies of homosexuality and AIDS which contest and challenge the boundaries of public and private sexual discourse, and of gendered and ethnic identity within the national consciousness.

Effective AIDS prevention interventions among gay men in France are therefore those which expose and counter the state's panicked policing of psychosocial self-images by openly representing, imagining and valuing homosexuality in ways 'which take account of social relations, geographical locations, ways of life and social classes and appropriate media', as Michael Pollak was seen to be advocating as early as 1989 (Marsan, 1989, p. 101).[23] AIDS prevention is health promotion only when it provides positive images for all forms of homosexuality within the consciousness of the *'grand public'*, and questions the continuing (self-)surveillance of homosexuality in France by addressing realities beyond the economically designated spaces of the rainbow-flag sheets.

NOTES

My thanks to Jean-Pierre Boulé and Dharman Jeyasingham for initially drawing my attention to some of the material used in this chapter.

1.   These figures are based on those available in *Infection par le VIH et sida* (6e édition, octobre 1995, Mutuelle nationale des hospitaliers et Arcat sida) and *Sida: évolution et prise en charge* (Ministère des affaires sociales, de la santé et de la ville, *Solidarité santé, études statistiques*, No. 3, juillet–septembre 1994), especially the statistical annex to the latter of these volumes, 'Le Sida: comparaisons européennes', by Rosemary Ancelle-Park, pp. 89–98.

2.   Defert eventually won this particular confrontation and was allowed to distribute the condoms. The original now reads:

> La première fois que nous avons distribué les préservatifs, c'était à Marseille. Nous avions rendez-vous là ... et j'avais avec moi deux sacs de mille préservatifs que nous avions l'intention de distribuer pendant cette université. Au cours de la conversation, nous nous sommes dit que nous pourrions commencer à en distribuer dans le bar où nous étions – dans lequel il y avait une backroom. On a demandé au barman un récipient et on a distribué, distribué ... Un Américain était là; il nous a félicité, disant que'on devrait faire la même chose aux USA. Trois minutes après, le patron est devenu dans les rangs reprendre les préservatifs à ses clients. Il nous a dit: 'Vous dénigrez la sexualité de mes clients.'

The translation is my own, as are the others included in this article.

3.   The original reads, 'Il est comprèhensible que les gais aient vraiment réagi pour se défaire de la nouvelle image d' "agresseurs biologiques" à laquelle on tentait de les associer'. Martel attributes the phrase 'biological aggressors' to Gilles Deleuze, writing in *L'Autre Journal*, October 1985.

4.   See especially Act Up-Paris, Arnal, Martel, Marsan, Minella and Angelotti and Pollak and Schlitz.

5.   Martel (pp. 281–8) provides a full account of right-wing responses to AIDS in France, including references to Le Pen's acceptance of gay men within his party, as long as they aren't 'queens' ('les folles').

6.   The original reads 'Comment voulez-vous que ces planches de sapin transmettent le virus?'

7. The original reads:

   On ne croyait pas une seule seconde au sida. On ne nous tenait plus par la morale, plus par l'Eglise, plus par la justice: nous nous sommes dit qu'il fallait bien qu'ils inventent un virus. Le sida, c'était des petits hommes verts venus punir les homosexuels au moment où les lois ne les réprimaient plus. On a éclaté de rire.

8. The set of articles by Frédéric Ploquin and Maurice Szafran (20 June 1983, pp. 14–15) contrast the attitudes found in the gay scene in Paris with the more militant responses already emerging in New York.

9. Act Up-Paris includes a 15-point manifesto of measures to be taken against AIDS as a matter of urgency in their publication (1994, pp. 429–36).

10. This phrase (*'un déficit d'image'*) is used as an *Evénement du jeudi* article entitlted 'Le pouvoir homo' by Florence Assouline, Anne-Sophie Mercer and Phillipe Petit (20 June 1996, pp. 22–8, [p. 22]), which considers the 'gains' of gays in recent years alongside what they consider to be less palatable, negative images, such as those generated by Act Up-Paris's 'zaps' and other forms of direct action.

11. The 1989 campaign was run by the now defunct CFES in conjunction with *Gai Pied*; the 1992 version was created by its successor, AFLS.

12 Jean-Baptiste Brunet (1993, pp. 52–3) suggests that arguments as to whether to focus prevention campaigns on groups at risk or risky behaviour are engaged in a false debate, since effective prevention will acknowledge the ways in which these two categories interact.

13. The original reads, 'personages aseptisés' which 'semblaient peu à même de susciter, malgré leur bonne volonté, l'identification et l'intérêt des personnes les plus concernées par le risque épidémique'.

14. They included Durex Jeans condoms and state, 'This condom is designed for vaginal use only'. The original reads 'Ce préservatif est destiné à usage vaginal uniquement'. Parallels with other Francophone countries in Europe can unfortunately be made. A 1995 Belgian campaign offering three condoms for 20 francs in retail outlets was criticized for similar reasons (Anciaux, 1996, p. 16), and it was left to agencies working with gay men, Ex-Aequo and Het AIDS Team, to offer imaginative alternatives, such as a 'Seduction Licence' and a 'Safe Sauna Clip' containing suitable condoms and lubricant.

15. Aides Fédération Nationale juillet 1995, Dessins: Stéphane Blot, Maquette: JYLT.

16. The original reads, 'Un phénomène qu'on croyait révolu depuis le Moyen Age se manifeste à nouveau: l'atteinte aux Droits de l'Homme pour cause de maladie: sur tous les continents et quelle que soit la culture locale, on a vu rejaillir cette peur archaïque qui fait du rejet de l'autre, du contaminé, l'illusoire garantie de sa propre protection. Combattre le sida, c'est aussi combattre toutes les mesures de discrimination'.

17. The original reads: 'Du même est présentée comme négligeable la mort de celui qui n'as pas de fonction dans la production: le déviant, le marginal, la victime de bavures policières, le clochard qui était déjà "socialement" morts. Leur élimination physique donne une impession elle aussi rassurante que tout rentre dans l'ordre.'

18. For an account of the framing of Act Up-Paris's dissent to gay visibility, see my article, 'Culturing Visibility: Images of France after AIDS', *Outword*, May 1997.
19. The original reads: 'Une société basée sur des valeurs d'accumulation de biens matérials c'est-à-dire aussi futile qu'utilitaire court le risque d'être remise en cause par celui qui recherche une valeur plus authentique à sa vie du fait qu'il a une conscience aiguë de sa finitude'.
20. Minella and Angelotti (1996, p. 25) include a description by Jean le Bitoux of how the physical effects of AIDS can become conflated with signs of homosexuality. Being ill with AIDS effectively outs gay men, producing visibility, they argue as both homosexual and dying.
21. The original reads 'l'autrui représente directement ou indirectement "le danger". Quand le langage préventif dit qu'il faut éviter des rapports non protégés ou qu'il faut restreindre le nombre de partenaires, c'est à l'égard d'autrui qu'elle met en gard'.
22. See Preston (1993) for a model of sex education which aims to offer positive self-images for gay men.
23. Marsan describes Pollak's goals in this way. The original calls for actions which 'tiennent... compte de liens sociaux, des lieux géographiques, des modes de vie, des couches sociales et des médias capables de les divulger'.

REFERENCES

Act Up-Paris, *Le Sida, combien de divisions?* (Paris, Editions Dagorno, 1994).

Ancelle-Park, R., 'Le sida: comparaisons européennes', in Ministère des Affaires Sociales, de la Santé et de la Ville, Service des Statistiques, des Etudes et de Systèmes d'Information (1994).

Ancelle-Park, R., 'Sida: évolution et prise en charge', *Solidarité santé, études statistiques*, No. 3, juillet–septembre 1994, pp. 87–98.

Anciaux, C., with the collaboration of Huercano-Hidalgo, G., 'Le business du sida, a qui profite l'argent de la prévention?', *Le Vif, L'Express*, Vol. 14, No. 5, *L'Express* No. 2326, 2–8 février 1996, pp. 12–16.

Arcat sida (6th edition), *Infection par le VIH et sida* (Paris, Editions d'Arcat sida, 1995).

Arnal, F., *Résister ou Disparaître? Les homosexuels face au sida. La prévention de 1982 à 1992* (Paris, Editions L'Harmattan, Collection 'Logiques Sociales', 1993).

Assouline, F., Mercier, A-S. and Petit, P., 'Le Pouvoir homo, ce qu'ils ont gagné, ce qu'ils veulent conquérir', *L'Evénement du jeudi*, 20–26 juin 1996, pp. 22–8.

Brunet, J-B., 'Comportement français', *Les Temps Modernes*, No. 567, 'Toxicomanie / Sida / Exclusion', octobre 1993, pp. 52–6.

Cassuto, J-P. and Reboulot, B., *La Séropositivité au quotidien* (Paris, Editions Odile Jacob, 1991).

CRIPS, *Lettre d'Information*, No. 33, septembre 1995.

de Foucauld, J-B., 'Causes de l'exclusion', *Les Temps Modernes*, No. 567, 'Toxicomanie / Sida / Exclusion', octobre 1993, pp. 256–60.

Garfield, S., 'Now it's the real thing', *The Guardian* 2, 18 July 1996, pp. 2–3, 13.

Hocquenghem, G., 'Towards an Irrecuperable Pederasty', trans. C. Fox, in Goldberg, J. (ed.), *Reclaiming Sodom* (New York, Routledge, 1994), pp. 233–46.

Jove, C., 'En quoi la lutte contre le sida est-elle une lutte politique?', *Combat face au sida*, No. 1, sept.–oct. 1995, pp. 11–12.

Kouchner, B., 'Génération Sida', *Les Temps Modernes*, No. 567, 'Toxicomanie/ Sida/Exclusion', octobre 1993, pp. 270–85.

Marsan, H., *La vie blessée. Sida, l'ère du soupçon* (Paris, Maren Sell and Cie, 1989).

Marshall, B., *Guy Hocquenghem, Theorising the Gay Nation* (London, Pluto Press, Modern European Thinkers, 1996).

Martel, F., *Le rose et le noir. Les homosexuels en France depuis 1968* (Paris, Editions du Seuil, 1996).

Mendès-Leite, R., 'Identité et altérité, Protections symboliques et imaginaires face au sida', *gradhiva*, No. 18, 1995, pp. 93–103.

Mendès-Leite, R. and Busscher, P-O., *Microgographie 'sexographique' des backrooms Parisiennes: appropriation de l'espace et gestion de la sexualité face au vih* (Paris, Les Traboules à l'AFLS, 'Les Rites de Rencontres Gais au Temps du Sida', 1995).

Miller, D. A., 'Sontag's Urbanity', in Abelove, H., Brale, M. A. and Halperin, D. M. (eds), *The Lesbian and Gay Studies Reader* (New York, Routledge, 1993), pp. 212–20.

Minella, A-G. and Angelotti, P., *Générations Gay* (Paris, Editions du Rocher, 1996).

Ministère des Affaires Sociales, de la Santé et de la Ville, Service des Statistiques, des Etudes et de Systèmes d'Information, 'Sida: évolution et prise en charge', in *Solidarité santé, études statistiques*, No. 3, juillet–septembre 1994.

Moerkerk, H. with Aggleton, P., 'AIDS Prevention Strategies in Europe: a Comparison and Critical Analysis', in Aggleton, P. D. and Hart, G. (eds), *AIDS: Individuals, Cultural and Policy Dimensions* (Basingstoke, Falmer Press, 1990), pp. 181–90.

Ploquin, F. and Szafran, M., 'Reportage: La "Maladie" des homosexuels: cette épidémie qui repand la terreur', *Le Matin*, 20 juin 1983, pp. 14–15.

Pollak, M. and Schiltz, M-A., 'Les homosexuels français face au sida. Modifications des pratiques sexuelles et émergence de nouvelles valeurs', *Anthropologie et société*, Vol. 15, Nos 2–3, 1991, pp. 53–65.

Pratt, M., 'Culturing Visibility: Images of France after AIDS', *Outword*, Vol. 3, Issue 5, May 1997, pp. 4–5.

Preston, J., *My Life as a Pornographer* (New York, Richard Kasak Books, 1993).

Selden, D., ' "Just When You Thought It Was Safe to Go Back in the Water..." ', in Abelove, H., Brale, M. A. and Halperin, D. M. (eds), *The Lesbian and Gay Studies Reader*, (New York, Routledge, 1993), pp. 221–6.

Thorogood, N., 'What is the Relevance of Sociology for Health Promotion?', in Bunton, R. and MacDonald, G. (eds), *Health Promotion: Disciplines and Diversion* (London, Routledge, 1992), pp. 42–65.

Treichler, P., 'AIDS, Homophobia and Biomedical Discourse as Epidemic of Signification', in Crimp, D. (ed.), *AIDS: Cultural Analysis, Cultural Activism* (Cambridge, MA, MIT Press, 1988), pp. 31–70.

Vidal, V., *La petite histoire du préservatif* (Paris, Syros Alternatives, 1993).

Watney, S., 'The Spectacle of AIDS', in Abelove, H., Brale, M. A. and Halperin, D. M. (eds), *The Lesbian and Gay Studies Reader* (New York, Routledge, 1993), pp. 202–11.

Part IV
Women in Contemporary
European Societies

9 Class, Gender and Voting in Italy
Anna Bull

INTRODUCTION

This chapter[1] explores a number of issues, one of which concerns specifically the political behaviour of women in Italy today. I am not so much interested in the political behaviour of all women, as of women who live and work in specific localities, characterized until recently by a high degree of party identification, linked to a specific political ideology, either Communist or Catholic. Gender issues, therefore, are explored in the context of changing voting patterns in Italy after the demise, as shown in the 1992 and 1994 political elections, of many of the established parties as well as the weakening of the ex-Communist Party. These electoral and political changes can be explained in part by the end of the Cold War, which has provided a powerful impulse to overcome traditional ideological and political cleavages and has taken away the *raison d'être* for the domination of the Christian Democratic Party. Already in the 1980s, however, a new culture based on personal success and individual values had emerged in Italy as throughout Western Europe and had started to weaken both Communist and Catholic collective solidarities.

At one level the electoral results of the 1990s and the disintegration of old political traditions can be interpreted as signifying the emergence of a more homogeneous, pragmatic and liberal society, where voting behaviour increasingly resembles the attitude of informed consumers (Himmelweit et al., 1985) and is no longer closely linked to party identification, family loyalties and traditional political subcultures (Mannheimer and Sani, 1987, 1994; Revelli, 1994). Voters' mobility is considered to be on the increase, and the trend seems to point in the direction of voters exercising an *individual* rational choice without the constraints of family, class, ideology or religion.

One important aspect of this process is the decline of class voting as a European-wide phenomenon which, in Britain at least, has only in part been attributed to a decline in the size of the working class (Franklin, 1985; Rose and McAllister, 1986). It has also been accounted for on the basis of what has been defined as 'partisan dealignment', i.e. a partial uncoupling between party preference and class (Crewe, 1984; Crewe et al., 1977). Various studies have also found that in modern Western societies generational differences are now more important than socio-economic ones. Indeed for Britain, Heath et al. (1991) found that there is no longer a strong correlation between voting patterns and parents' party preferences. As for gender differences, it has been argued that, in Britain at least, they do not affect the way people vote to any significant extent: 'gender has no influence upon voting in Britain today' (Rose and McAllister, 1990, p. 51; Heath et al., 1985). Rose and McAllister argue (1990, p. 51) that:

> the reason is straightforward. On matters that are salient to voting, men and women tend to share similar political values. On most major political issues men and women divide similarly – along lines of party or class, not gender.

This is a relatively recent phenomenon, although the trend towards a homogenization of gender voting patterns had been detected in the past (Barnes and Kaase, 1979; Sani, 1977, 1979).

Traditionally, women had been found to participate less in politics than men and, in Italy at least, as being more easily influenced by their families and by the Church when casting their votes. Indeed, in the 1960s Dogan (1967) argued that in Italy there was a marked discrepancy between masculine and feminine voting behaviour, for religious reasons. The discrepancy was particularly noticeable, Dogan argued, in the case of peasant and working-class women, who voted in accordance with their Catholic beliefs rather than out of identification with a social class. However, in the large industrial cities the religious effect upon women voters was less noticeable. Since then, the process of secularization of Italian society has weakened the influence of the Church upon voters. Already in the 1970s it was suggested that women's voting behaviour in Italy did not differ substantially from men's. In particular, it was argued, it was probably no longer the case that men voted more to the left and women more to the right (Parisi and Pasquino, 1977).

To return to Italy's current electoral and political changes, a different interpretation from the one that emphasizes the trend towards greater individualism and rational choice voting has also been put forward. According to some analysts, the emergence in Italy of new political divisions along geographical lines and new political parties with a populistic appeal points to the persistence of 'systems of solidarity' or territorially- or class-based subcultures (Cartocci, 1990, 1994; Diamanti, 1994; Putnam, 1993). This is not entirely surprising, given that both Christian Democracy and Communism had for long represented political subcultures, based on both class and regional differences. As political subcultures, Catholicism and social-ism/Communism pre-date the Second World War and even Fascism, going back to the 1880s, and are closely linked to specific social and economic structures, predominantly rural before the First World War, industrial after the Second (Bull and Corner, 1993; Trigilia, 1986).

In this context, the assumption that the dual process of modernization and secularization leads to social and cultural uniformity and political pluralism needs to be revised. Accordingly, it cannot be unquestionably assumed that gender voting patterns have become undifferentiated. Follow-ing the birth of new political parties in Italy, there have been signs that gender-based differences in voting behaviour may have re-emerged. Recent polls have suggested that the electoral success of Berlusconi's *Forza Italia* in the 1994 political elections was due partly to a preponder-ance of female voters, especially housewives (55 per cent women versus 45 per cent men supporters: Diamanti, 1994). Conversely, the electorate of the Northern League was found to be predominantly male in the early days, although the party later attracted female voters in considerable num-bers (Mannheimer, 1991). This is not a development unique to Italy. In the USA, for example, a 'gender gap', in other words, considerable dissimilar-ities between the sexes in terms of political behaviour, was detected throughout the 1980s (Mueller, 1988; Burrell, 1993). Indeed, according to Mueller (1988, p. 12), 'a normative model of gender divergence now char-acterises much public discussion as well as some scholarly discussion'. A gender gap has also been detected in Sweden, where women have voted increasingly for the Left parties, and in Canada (Sainsbury, 1993; Erickson, 1993). As for France, it has been pointed out (Jenson and Sineau, 1995) that in the 1981 presidential elections Mitterrand succeeded by appealing to the female electorate and attracting their votes in considerable numbers. Even in Britain, where its demise had been recorded, the gender gap reappeared at the 1992 general elections, with a considerably higher per-centage of older women voting for the Conservative Party (Norris and Lovenduski, 1993).

In contrast to the USA, however, where the gender gap has taken the shape of a constantly higher level of support for the Democratic Party among women than men, so much so that some commentators have spo-ken of a 'voting bloc' (Mueller, 1988, p. 25), in Italy women voters have been judged to form a 'mobile electorate', responsible to a large extent for the success of the Centre-Right Alliance, the *Polo delle Libertà*, in 1994, and of the Centre-Left Alliance, the *Ulivo*, in 1996.[2] Whereas in the USA the existence of a gender gap was skilfully exploited by the women's movement in the 1980s to increase their political influence and gains, in

Italy women appear to have been unable to make significant progress, particularly in terms of obtaining increased representation in Parliament. Women in Italy now account for only 9 per cent of all MPs, as opposed to 13 per cent in the previous legislature. The number of women Members of Parliament is now roughly the same as it was 50 years ago.

The question therefore arises whether voting behaviour in Italy has become gender-neutral, as is generally maintained, although with increasing reservations, or whether specific gender differences are clearly visible. If a marked discrepancy exists, are women still attached to a traditional party and subculture, have they moved towards rational choice voting, or have they found a new collective political voice? Lastly, if voting behaviour differs substantially by gender, what are the nature of the differences and their consequences in terms of the political influence of male and female voters?

To address these questions, the present chapter looks to the micro-level, and focuses on the political culture of industrial workers in two Northern areas, both in the Lombard region, which until recently were characterized by, respectively, a proletarian/Communist subculture and an interclassist/Catholic one. The two areas are Sesto San Giovanni, an industrial suburb of Milan known in the past as the 'Stalingrad of Italy' for its Communist identity, built around the local concentration of large-scale industry and further cemented by its role in the anti-Fascist Resistance, and Erba (Como), a small town characterized by small-scale industry and located in a predominantly Catholic area previously dominated by the Christian Democratic Party. Both areas have seen the demise of their traditional dominant parties, but in different contexts.

SOCIO-POLITICAL CHARACTERISTICS OF SESTO AND ERBA

Sesto S. Giovanni in the 1994 political elections registered a majority of votes for the Centre-Right Alliance, the *Polo*, for the first time since 1946; yet at the administrative elections that followed in June 1994 the candidate of the Left was elected mayor. At the 1996 political elections the Centre-Left Alliance, the *Ulivo*, won a majority of votes, thus reversing the 1994 outcome. In recent times Sesto has undergone substantial socio-economic changes. Of the large plants set up in the area since the beginning of the century, only one, Falck, remains a major employer. An exodus of industrial workers dismissed from the large factories has been accompanied by an emerging image of the town as a 'residential suburb' of Milan. In 1971, 79 per cent of the local working population was employed in manufacturing industry, by 1991 the percentage had gone down to 43 per cent. These socio-economic changes, in particular the decline in the size of the Sesto working class, can to a certain extent explain the failure of the Left at the 1994 general elections, indicating a pluralistic, 'rational choice' approach on the part of an electorate which has no reasons to feel loyal to a traditional subculture. Left-wing organizations in the town, however, have also started to change, after a period of sterile defence of the status quo in the 1970s and early 1980s. In particular, the Democratic Party of the Left (PDS), the main heir to the Italian Communist Party, has begun to woo the increasingly middle-class electorate. It remains to be seen, however, whether the Sesto 'working class' itself changed allegiances and contributed to a large extent to the success of the Right in 1994, or whether it maintained its loyalty to the Left. Gender differences within this social group will be explored in this context.

Erba on the other hand is representative of the Northern Italian model of 'diffused industrialization', characterized by the prevalence of small and medium-sized industrial plants diffused over the territory. The town has a variety of industries with a predominance of firms employing 100–200 workers. This model, unlike the one prevalent in Sesto S. Giovanni, has not undergone substantial change over the years, yet the political configuration of the town has greatly changed, just like in Sesto. Erba has recently seen an upsurge in support for the Northern League, a party which has been defined variously as populist, subcultural, racist and even fascist.[3] The Northern League, it has been maintained, has made inroads into all social groups, thus re-creating the interclassism which characterized the Christian Democratic Party, whose electorate has shifted in great numbers to the League. Christian Democracy (DC) commanded a comfortable majority after the Second World War and even in 1976 – at a time of increasing support for the Left in Italy – it polled 48 per cent in the town. In 1992 this decreased to 26 per cent, on a par with the Northern League. In 1994 the PPI (the main heir to the DC) polled 11 per cent, the League 26 per cent, and *Forza Italia* 26 per cent. In 1996 the League obtained 32 per cent of votes, the *Polo* 36.9 per cent, the *Ulivo* 31.1 per cent. Christian Democracy's domination thus seems to have been replaced by electoral fluidity. Do we have to conclude that the local subculture has broken down?

In the following sections I intend to assess the extent of the process of partisan dealignment and individualism in voting behaviour or, conversely, the degree to which voters, both male and female, still subscribe to a territorial or class subculture and values. I will also explore the possible emergence of gender-based discrepancies in voting behaviour and values, and examine their significance in terms of electoral outcomes and political influence. First, however, I will briefly describe the survey and the characteristics of the samples upon which it was based.

FIELDWORK

This chapter is based on an analysis of 443 questionnaires distributed among industrial workers in Sesto's remaining large factories and 445 questionnaires distributed in Erba among employees of various medium-sized manufacturing firms, as well as among artisans and small entrepreneurs. The survey was carried out in February and March 1994. The questionnaire focused on multiple social identities as well as political behaviour at local level. Specific questions dealt with voting behaviour of the respondents and their parents in the 1987 and 1992 political elections as well as the 1993 administrative elections, voting intentions for the 1994 political elections, and criteria for party preferences. The role of the two most important integrating forces in society, the family and religion, was explored in some depth. A third factor of social identity, class, was also prioritized in the questions. The main object was to examine the interplay of these social identities, in the knowledge that the process of working-class bonding was inserted into pre-existing structures of social relationships such as kinship and family networks, national and local loyalties, and religious affiliation (Williams, 1983, pp. 166–71). Gendered attitudes were systematically explored. In addition to the questionnaires, interviews with local politicians, administrators, trade unionists and members of various associations were carried out.

As for the characteristics of the samples, roughly two-thirds of the respondents in both localities were men, and one-third were women. In terms of age, the Sesto sample contains a smaller percentage of young people. Although this could be due to a sample quirk, it more probably reflects the fact that large firms in Italy have stopped recruiting in any significant numbers and indeed have been shedding labour. Small and medium-sized firms in Erba appear to have been better able to sustain employment, in line with Italy's successful model of small-scale industry.

The age composition of respondents influences their marital status, with only a quarter claiming single status in Sesto but two-fifths in Erba. Being single and between 18 and 30 years of age does not, however, mean living away from one's own family of origin. The nearly 40 per cent of single people in Erba translates into only 7 per cent of people living on their own or outside the family circle. This is in line with recent findings on the Italian family, which show that children continue to stay at home until they get married (Ginsborg, 1994). The average family size of the samples in both Sesto and Erba is 3.2, above both the local averages as recorded in the 1991 population census and the national average.

The data related to gender, age and family composition indicate a relative stability in terms of personal circumstances in both localities. The divorce rate is very low, young people enjoy the security of their families even in their twenties, and partly thanks to them nearly two members per family are in full-time employment, which indicates relative prosperity as well as stability. In Sesto the stable conditions of the respondents contrast with the general instability of recent demographic and socio-economic changes. Thus, respondents in Erba seem to be a stable cohort living in a stable environment, whereas the Sesto respondents represent a stable cohort living in a very unstable – and above all greatly changed – environment.

MAIN FINDINGS: SESTO SAN GIOVANNI

In Sesto the parties of the Left experienced a dramatic decline between 1987 and 1994. The Communist Party had obtained 34.9 per cent of the votes in 1987, but this went down to only 20.9 per cent in 1992 and 21.9 per cent in 1994, the latter figure rising to 29.7 per cent if the votes for the Democratic Party of the Left (PDS) and those for *Rifondazione Comunista* are put together. Votes for the Socialist Party amounted to 18.6 per cent in 1987, but a mere 1.3 per cent in 1994. The full picture shows that, whereas in 1987 the parties of the Left (including the Greens) obtained almost two-thirds of the votes, they managed only about a third in 1994.

Did the votes for these parties decrease in a similar pattern among industrial workers? The answer, on the basis of the present survey, is no, although there are distinct gender patterns (Table 9.1).

The data suggest the persistence of Communist allegiances among male workers and the failure on the part of both the Northern League and *Forza Italia* to make any considerable inroads among this group. A majority of men respondents voted for the Communist and Socialist parties in both 1987 and 1992, and expressed their intention of doing so at the 1994 political elections. There were, however, signs that the Communist subculture was weakening even among factory workers, although this trend differed considerably in terms of gender. It was women whose voting behaviour showed greater discontinuity and who in 1992 had tended to 'betray' the ex-Communist Party. Whereas in 1987 a majority of women had voted for the Communist and Socialist parties (53.4 per cent), in 1992 this percentage decreased to 40.5 per cent (including *Rifondazione Comunista*).

Table 9.1 Percentage of votes for the main parties in Sesto San Giovanni and among sample of respondents

	1987	*1992*	*1994*
Official results			
PCI/PDS	34.9	20.9	21.9
Rifondazione	–	8.0	7.8
PSI	18.6	15.1	1.3
Verdi	4.2	4.4	2.9
DC/PPI	20.4	15.3	6.7
Lega	1.3	15.7	12.7
MSI/AN	4.6	3.7	5.9
Forza Italia	–	–	27.0
Others	16.0	16.9	13.8
All respondents			
PCI/PDS	49.5	43.0	49.7
Rifondazione	–	6.0	2.4
PSI	12.6	7.9	–
Verdi	3.4	4.9	–
DC/PPI	9.6	7.7	5.0
Lega	4.1	12.6	7.3
MSI/AN	2.7	3.3	3.4
Forza Italia	–	–	9.7
Others	18.1	14.6	1.9
Don't know	–	–	20.6
Total numbers	(293)	(365)	(382)
Male respondents			
PCI/PDS	57.4	50.0	54.5
Rifondazione	–	6.6	1.6
PSI	9.7	8.6	–
Verdi	2.6	3.7	–
DC/PPI	8.2	7.0	5.4
Lega	4.6	10.7	5.8
MSI/AN	3.1	3.7	5.5
Forza Italia	–	–	5.1
Others	13.4	9.7	0.3
Don't know	–	–	21.8
Total numbers	(195)	(244)	(257)
Female respondents			
PCI/PDS	36.4	29.7	39.5
Rifondazione	–	5.4	4.4
PSI	17.0	5.4	–
Verdi	4.5	7.2	–
DC/PPI	12.5	9.0	3.5
Lega	2.5	17.1	10.5

Table 9.1 (Continued)

	1987	1992	1994
MSI/AN	1.1	0.9	3.5
Forza Italia	–	–	21.1
Others	26.0	26.3	4.3
Don't know	–	–	13.2
Total numbers	(88)	(111)	(114)

Sources: Comune di Sesto San Giovanni and 1994 survey.
Note: The number of all respondents is higher than the total number of male and female respondents, due to the fact that some respondents did not specify their sex.

Women seemed to cast their votes in favour of new and/or smaller parties. In 1992 these types of parties (League, Greens, Communist Refoundation, and a variety of 'other' parties) attracted 56 per cent of women's votes, as opposed to 30.7 per cent of men's votes.

Even more interestingly perhaps, a significant number of Sesto women respondents declared their intention of returning/starting to vote for the PDS in 1994, although on the basis of a pragmatic choice rather than on the basis of party loyalty/party identification. Thus men remained loyal to the party throughout the period, while women's voting behaviour appears more varied and changeable. This is confirmed by a comparison between the 1987 and 1992 votes. Asked whether they had voted for a different party in 1992 compared with 1987, less than a fifth of male respondents said yes, as opposed to a third of women. When presented with a list of motivations to account for their party preference in 1992, both men and women indicated 'ideals' and the 'party programme' as important factors influencing their choice. However, men also appeared to have been influenced to a large extent by considerations of loyalty. In fact, a third of all male respondents pointed to 'loyalty' as an important factor behind their vote.

Considerations of loyalty also weighed heavily with men when voting at the 1993 administrative elections. By contrast, only a quarter of women mentioned 'loyalty' as a relevant factor for the 1992 political elections and even fewer referred to it for the 1993 administrative elections. Another substantial difference between male and female voters concerned the importance attributed to the level of competence of party candidates. Only 29 per cent of men gave this factor any consideration, as opposed to 41 per cent of women.

The phenomenon of partisan dealignment among women is nevertheless somewhat questionable, since most women changed party preference between 1987 and 1992 but remained within either the Left or the Right political spectrum. Interestingly though, many more women than men were contemplating crossing the Left/Right boundary in 1994.

The more pluralistic attitude on the part of women workers appears confirmed by other responses related to political socialization and the role of the family and the Church. Despite the fact that many more women than men attended Church regularly and had formed their political ideas in the family, women were only slightly more likely than men to have voted for the Christian Democratic Party in 1992 and much less likely to have voted like their parents. Even young male voters voted largely in line with their parents in 1992, unlike young female ones. These findings appear to indicate a real cleavage between past and present women's political behaviour, since traditionally, as we saw, women were identified with political conservatism which in turn was attributed in great part to their degree of religiosity. The findings also indicate that for men, unlike women, political loyalty extends to their families as well as their class.

Why women should have adopted a more pragmatic attitude than men and freed themselves from their class and families' influence is an interesting question. One answer lies, in my view, in the fact that the Communist working-class subculture was male oriented, in the sense that it took for granted that politics was mainly reserved for men and did not question traditional gender divisions of roles.[4] With reference to the 1970s, Weber (1981, p. 204) suggested that the shift in women's party preferences from the DC to the PCI should not necessarily be seen as:

> an indicator of a secularisation process amongst Italian women. It could easily indicate a lack of information, emotional electoral behaviour and a preference for reassuring ideologies rather than cultural pragmatism.

In retrospect, it would seem that women were opening up to cultural pragmatism to a higher degree than it was judged possible at the time.

The recent collapse in Italy of the traditional ideologies may therefore have had, as one of its major consequences, the effect of freeing women from the old constraints and making it easier for them to become detached from a subculture that has never really represented them directly. On the contrary, for male workers this collapse has marked the end of a dream and has resulted in great disappointment. These two contrasting sentiments – freedom and new illusions on the one hand, disappointment and disillusionment on the other – emerge very clearly from other parts of the survey, which also bring to light the continuing attachment to the old subculture on the part of men but not of women workers.

Table 9.2   Frequency of political discussions
(Sesto San Giovanni) (percentages)

	Men	*Women*
Never	16	11
Occasionally	30	29
Quite frequently	39	45
Very frequently	15	15
Total numbers	(271)	(122)

Table 9.3   Frequency of political discussions
now compared with five/ten years ago (Sesto San
Giovanni) (percentages)

	Men	*Women*
More frequently	37	46
The same	49	44
Less frequently	14	10
Total numbers	(194)	(93)

When asked whether they discussed politics with family and friends a majority of both men and women stated that they did so 'quite frequently' or 'very frequently'. Asked whether they discussed politics more or less often than five–ten years ago, more women than men indicated that they discussed it more often (Tables 9.2 and 9.3).

Table 9.3 is an indicator of women's increased interest in politics after the demise of the traditional ideologies. The findings contrast sharply with those of a national survey carried out among Italian women in the 1970s (a decade of great political participation and turmoil), when 54 per cent of respondents stated that they never discussed politics.[5]

Women in Sesto have also retained faith in a number of social and political institutions, such as industry, banks, political parties, regional government, and Parliament, whereas men expressed predominantly negative judgements, while portraying a much rosier picture of the past. Indeed, unlike men, women do not feel that the past was a 'golden age' compared with the present. It is probably for this reason that they do not appear tempted to retreat into their family network to the same extent as men (Tables 9.4 and 9.5).

Table 9.4   How different associations/environments are valued today compared with five/ten years ago (Sesto San Giovanni) (percentages)

	Men				Women			
	More important	*Same*	*Less important*		*More important*	*Same*	*Less important*	
Family	67	32	1	(257)	57	30	13	(129)
Friend	19	64	17	(181)	31	51	18	(100)
Work	41	42	17	(185)	50	34	16	(96)
Religion	5	66	29	(148)	12	57	31	(77)
Unions	6	51	43	(150)	8	53	39	(74)
Politics	11	39	50	(142)	22	41	37	(76)
Culture/ leisure	27	53	20	(150)	30	56	14	(77)

Table 9.5   What is most important in life? (Sesto San Giovanni) (percentages)

	All	*Men*	*Women*
To succeed personally	16.0	14.1	20.0
Family interests are more important than personal success	44.2	48.7	34.6
Family responsibilities are a handicap for personal success	1.7	1.4	2.3
Solidarity is the most important human value	38.1	35.8	43.1
Total numbers	(407)	(277)	(130)

Table 9.5 is particularly significant, because it suggests, that men have partially lost faith in the value of solidarity, perhaps the single most important value in the 'proletarian' subculture. It is part of the process of increasing disillusionment men have undergone at Sesto. Women show more propensity to subscribe to individual success, although they still believe in solidaristic as well as family values. Despite these gender divisions, in fact, the central role of the family does not appear in doubt, particularly when the issue of individualism is explored.

These different attitudes expressed by men and women workers did not, however, feed into political participation, at least in terms of party politics and trade union activity, which remained high for men but low for women. Women's greater interest in politics and relatively free voting behaviour has not led them to engage more directly in political activity.

To conclude, male workers in Sesto are still committed to the proletarian subculture, mainly out of loyalty, but they are also showing signs of contemplating 'exit' from public activity altogether, retreating to a private network of family and friends, driven by disappointment and disillusionment, according to the classic Hirschman theory (1970). As for women, they appear to have discarded any subcultural allegiances and in so doing have become 'emancipated' from Church influence and partially also from the influence of the family. Politically, this has led them to cast their votes more widely and to change party preferences more frequently. Loyalty to a group or a class is much less in evidence than among men. This does not mean that women will not vote for the PDS. On the contrary, they may be increasingly well disposed towards this party, now that it is striving to lose its subcultural connotations. When the PDS replaced the PCI, women delegates played a significant role in defining the new party, so much so that the new statute stated unequivocally that the PDS was a 'party for men and women' (Guadagnini, 1993, p. 177). Since then, the PDS has shown itself open to women's membership and representation, following a trend already started by the old PCI. In Sesto, too, the PDS impressed me with its will to attract new voters and members and to portray a new image, distancing itself from an all-too-close identification with a traditional working-class subculture. The Sesto findings seem to confirm that women voters have become an increasingly mobile electorate, probably swaying the election results in the town in favour of the Centre-Right in 1994 and of the Centre-Left in 1996. A similar trend at national level is also plausible. Nevertheless, women voters seem to be lacking a collective identity and political 'clout', at least when compared to men's persisting 'bloc voting'.

MAIN FINDINGS: ERBA

In Erba, votes for the Christian Democratic Party – later the PPI (*Partito Popolare*) – went down from 39.2 per cent in 1987 to 27.3 per cent in 1992 and 11.3 per cent in 1994. The Northern League rose from 6.5 per cent in 1987 to 27 per cent in 1992, down to 26.2 per cent in 1994 (Table 9.6).

As Table 9.6 shows, votes for the Northern League among the industrial workers surveyed were considerably higher than the average for the town and suggest that the League may have established roots of a 'subcultural' nature among them, at least among male workers. Given the territorial/ localistic appeal of this party, and the fact that previous studies have shown that support for the League increases, in the North itself, among people born there, I decided to disaggregate the votes to the League in 1992 on the basis

Table 9.6   Percentage of votes to the main parties in Erba and among respondents

	1987	1992	1994
Official results			
DC/PPI	39.2	27.3	11.3
League	6.5	27.0	26.2
PCI/PDS	15.1	7.4	7.7
PSI	16.2	11.8	1.1
Rifondazione	–	3.6	4.0
Verdi	2.5	2.6	2.5
MSI/AN	5.2	3.6	7.2
Forza Italia	–	–	25.5
Others	15.3	16.7	14.5
All respondents			
DC/PPI	29.2	20.3	13.3
League	19.9	40.5	34.2
PCI/PDS	13.3	10.6	15.6
PSI	9.6	3.9	–
Rifondazione	0.8	1.6	–
Verdi	3.7	2.6	–
MSI/AN	7.9	3.9	5.4
Forza Italia	–	–	14.5
Others	15.6	16.6	8.2
Don't know	–	–	8.8
Total numbers	(301)	(385)	(392)
Male respondents			
DC/PPI	26.0	18.8	13.3
League	23.7	46.0	40.0
PCI/PDS	12.7	10.3	14.2
PSI	8.7	3.1	–
Rifondazione	1.2	1.8	–
Verdi	2.9	0.5	–
MSI/AN	7.5	6.3	8.0
Forza Italia	–	–	12.9
Others	17.3	13.2	6.3
Don't know	–	–	5.3
Total numbers	(173)	(224)	(225)
Female respondents			
DC/PPI	33.6	21.8	11.8
League	15.2	33.3	26.7
PCI/PDS	14.4	11.5	18.0
PSI	10.4	5.1	–
Rifondazione	1.6	1.3	–
Verdi	4.8	5.8	–

Table 9.6 *(Continued)*

	1987	1992	1994
MSI/AN	1.6	0.7	1.9
Forza Italia	–	–	17.4
Others	18.4	20.5	14.9
Don't know	–	–	9.3
Total numbers	(125)	(156)	(161)

Sources: Comune di Erba and 1994 survey.
Note: The number of 'Don't knows' in Erba were considerably lower than in Sesto due almost certainly to the fact that the Erba survey took place at a later stage, nearer the time of the 1994 elections.

of geographical origins. The results were quite striking, since there was massive support for the League in 1992 among industrial workers born in the North with Northern parents, while there was a clear rejection of this party among people with Southern origins (even if they themselves were born in the North). It is interesting, though, that this distinction applies primarily to men, since women appear to have voted for the League irrespective of their regional origins. This suggests that the territorial, communitarian, quasi-ethnic appeal of the League was clearly perceived by and directly appealed to male voters, whereas it was not a principal factor among women. At first value, my interpretation of these figures is that they confirm that the League is a new subcultural party (Cento Bull, 1992, 1993), but also indicate that the League enjoys a more limited though also much more clearly focused appeal compared with the old DC. Its appeal among industrial workers focuses sharply on Northern males. As in Sesto, there is little evidence of partisan dealignment among male workers. The party they vote for may have changed; however, political alignments continue to be based on highly partisan criteria (territorial and racialized rather than Catholic/solidaristic). By contrast, as other parts of the questionnaire showed, women's reasons for voting for the League were more pragmatic than men's.

An interesting difference emerged when the attitudes of League voters were compared with those of voters of other parties. Whereas both male and female League voters subscribed to the League's flagship ideas of a federal Italy and greater regional autonomy and supported its programme of privatizations, the orientations of non-League voters differed considerably by gender (Table 9.7).

Table 9.7   How much do you agree with the following policies/objectives?
(Erba) (percentages)

	Men				Women			
	Strongly		Moderately		Strongly		Moderately	
	All voters	League	All voters	League	All voters	League	All voters	League
Wider regional autonomy	51	73	33	21	48	77	32	15
Federalism	46	73	22	19	34	74	14	13
Europe of Regions	29	36	37	43	18	38	27	33
Privatization	35	45	30	31	25	38	43	43
Houses and work to residents	39	52	29	28	34	52	37	31

As Table 9.7 shows, men were generally much more receptive to the ideas and policies put forward by the League, irrespective of their party preference. Indeed a majority of all men subscribed to the idea of a federal Italy (including a majority of supporters of the Socialist, Green and Radical parties, as well as half of PDS and PPI voters) and of a Europe of the Regions (including a majority of PPI and PSI voters). By contrast, women were more clearly split, with only League voters subscribing to the idea of a federal Italy or a Europe of the Regions. This finding suggests that the League may in future widen its appeal among male voters, whereas its female electorate is unlikely to increase. It also indicates that for men communitarian and localistic allegiances and shared values continue to be very important and to cut across political party preferences. Not surprisingly, men respondents in Erba put allegiance to their commune first, and to the nation second, unlike any other group sampled. It is also interesting to note that, when asked why they voted as they did at the 1993 administrative elections, men respondents in Erba indicated that considerations of local interests had greatly influenced their choice, whereas women stated that they had looked at the competence of candidates. The general impression is that in 1987 and 1992 men switched from one subcultural party to another, whereas women were more pluralistic in their voting intentions. The fact that the Northern League was a new party probably explains why many women voted for it and even presented themselves as candidates, despite what has been defined as 'a party culture that favours traditional gender roles' (Guadagnini, 1993, p. 200). Women's positive attitude towards the demise of the old subculture was marked, as in Sesto, by their new interest for political discussion (Tables 9.8 and 9.9).

Table 9.8 Frequency of political discussions
(Erba) (percentages)

	Men	Women
Never	13	9
Occasionally	30	27
Quite frequently	43	46
Very frequently	14	18
Total numbers	(245)	(179)

Table 9.9 Frequency of political discussions
now compared with five/ten years ago (Erba)
(percentages)

	Men	Women
More frequently	46	60
The same	42	32
Less frequently	12	8
Total numbers	(212)	(154)

Finally, there is the issue of the role of the Church and of primary associations, such as networks of family and friends, in determining political socialization. As in Sesto, regular Church attendance in Erba was found to be considerably higher among women than men, yet there no longer appears to be a correlation between religious beliefs and party preference. In Erba the role of the family is more in evidence, however, and exercises a significant influence upon voting patterns of both men and women. Thus in Erba there was evidence of families and even groups of friends voting en bloc. The League, in particular, had been able to attract the votes of entire families, rather than single individuals.

Nevertheless, there were also signs that for men there existed a strong correlation between family and group ties, and that the family was at the centre of a communitarian view of society which found its political counterpart in a subcultural party. By contrast, among women voters this link between the family, society and political representation was more tenuous. Thus, when asked how many of their relatives and friends shared their political preferences and ideas, nearly half of men respondents indicated that a majority did, as opposed to less than a third of women. Also, men's lives in Erba seemed to revolve almost exclusively around family, friends and work, whereas women showed a higher propensity to cultivate other

Table 9.10   How different associations are valued today compared with five/ten years ago (Erba) (percentages)

	Men				Women			
	More important	*Same*	*Less important*		*More important*	*Same*	*Less important*	
Family	63	35	2	(233)	62	36	2	(177)
Friends	22	56	22	(213)	22	61	17	(153)
Work	53	41	6	(213)	38	51	11	(146)
Religion	16	59	25	(189)	22	58	20	(142)
Unions	8	42	50	(161)	4	45	51	(119)
Politics	19	35	46	(168)	23	43	34	(128)
Culture/ leisure	10	52	38	(176)	29	55	16	(136)

Table 9.11   What is most important in life? (Erba) (percentages)

	All	Men	Women
To succeed personally	19.2	22.2	15.1
Family interests are more important than personal success	38.4	45.7	28.5
Family responsibilities are a handicap for personal success	3.6	2.1	5.6
Solidarity is the most important human value	38.8	30.0	50.8
Total numbers	(422)	(243)	(179)

interests outside their circle of family and friends (Table 9.10). Men also indicated that they cherished the family above both individualistic and solidaristic values, whereas women put solidarity first (Table 9.11). Women's understanding of solidarity appeared to be linked to universalistic Catholic values, rather than to a class or a group.

CONCLUSIONS

To conclude, in both localities there were distinct gendered voting behaviours. Male workers showed a high degree of continuity with the past and a determination, particularly in Erba, to preserve a familistic and communitarian society represented politically by a subcultural party.

Female workers continued to subscribe to family values and indeed to be influenced to some extent by the family in their voting allegiances (especially in Erba), but among them the link family ties–group ties–system of solidarity–subcultural party is much weaker. Group ties, in particular, do not seem to exercise the same impact upon women as upon men.

This has two important implications, in my view. First, it indicates that women are increasingly withdrawing their support from political subcultures – whether Catholic or Communist – which have traditionally placed them in a subordinate position vis-a-vis men. Second, it indicates that women have not found a political voice of their own, nor are they likely to find it in the foreseeable future, if by this we intend a collective representation at the political level. My findings show that, unlike men, women in areas previously dominated by subcultural parties are now likely to cast their votes widely across the political spectrum, distrusting collective representation. However, I would contend that in areas such as Sesto and Erba the discarding by women of a subcultural approach to voting does in itself amount to a collective aspiration and can be seen in direct opposition to men's collective political behaviour. In this context, it seems premature, at least for Italy, to speak of an individualistic and gender-neutral voting behaviour. Unlike the USA, however, the type of 'gender gap' that it has been possible to detect in the areas surveyed cannot be easily translated into greater political influence. A similar conclusion has recently been drawn from the outcome of the 1996 elections. Female voters may have contributed decisively to the electoral success of the Centre-Left in 1996, but, to quote an editorial in *La Repubblica*, 'women have come out of the electoral campaign defeated'.[6] The editorial pointed out that women had failed to obtain greater political representation, arguing that this could only emerge as the result of women achieving 'female political subjectivity'. Interestingly, only the Housewives' Association, the *Federcasalinghe*, through their leader Federica Rossi Gasparrini, openly and skilfully publicized their conversion from the *Polo* to the *Ulivo before* the election. An electoral pact then followed, based on ten key demands put forward by the housewives' pressure group. After the elections, Ms Rossi Gasparrini boasted that the support of the association had been decisive for the success of the Centre-Left.[7] At least one political party thus showed itself open to women's demands but only one women's group appears to have been able to use its members' votes as a political lever.

If women's votes are 'unpredictable' and their political orientations vary considerably from one election to the next, men's persistent and reliable 'bloc voting' will continue to ensure that their own collective interests and aspirations are more effectively represented at the political level.

NOTES

1. This chapter contains some of the findings of a research project on social identities and political culture in Italy, which was funded by Bath University Research Strategy Fund in 1993. It originally appeared in *West European Politics*, Vol. 20, No. 2, April, 1997, pp. 73–92. Other findings have appeared in *Modern Italy*. See A. Cento Bull, 'An End to Collective Identities? Political Culture and Voting Behaviour in Sesto San Giovanni and Erba', in *Modern Italy*, Vol. 1, No. 2, Autumn, 1996, pp. 23–43. The author wishes to thank all industrial workers in Sesto and Erba who gave up some of their time to fill in long and detailed questionnaires. Her thanks also go to the local section of the PDS, as well as the Istituto per la storia della Resistenza e dell'eta contemporanea, in Sesto, and the local section of the Northern League in Erba.
2. 'Il voto femminile mobile e scontento', in *L'Unità*, 27 April 1996, p. 6. The article is based on analyses of electoral results conducted by *Directa* and *Abacus*.
3. On the Northern League there is now a fairly vast literature. See especially Mannheimer, R. (ed.), *La Lega Lombarda* (Milan, Feltrinelli, 1991). See also Diamanti, I., *La Lega. Geografia, storia e sociologia di un nuovo soggetto politico* (Rome, Donzelli, 1993) and Cento Bull, A., 'Ethnicity, Racism and the Northern League', in Levy, C. (ed.), *Regionalism in Italy: Past and Present* (Oxford, Berg, 1996), pp. 171–87.
4. A recent study on women factory workers at Sesto San Giovanni during the fascist and the Resistance period has shown very clearly that women's participation in politics was restricted to traditional roles, and that these roles were sanctioned by the Communist subculture and organizations: see Willson, P., *The Clockwork Orange: Women and Work in Fascist Italy* (Oxford, Clarendon Press, 1993).
5. Weber, M., 'La partecipazione politica femminile in Italia: evoluzione, determinanti, caratteristiche', in *Rivista italiana di scienza politica*, 11, 1981, pp. 281–311. See also Weber, M., *Il voto delle donne* (Turin, Biblioteca della Libertà, 1977); Weber, M., 'Le casalinghe e la politica', in *Argomenti radicali*, 2, 1978, pp. 45–56. For a general discussion on women (particularly Italian women) and politics see Zincone, G., *Gruppi sociali e sistemi politici: il caso donne* (Milan, Angeli, 1985).
6. 'Le donne e il voto' in *La Repubblica*, 19 April 1996, p. 10. An electoral survey conducted by *Abacus* after the 1996 elections indicated that, with the exception of *Forza Italia*, the electorate of the parties of the Right and Centre-Right was predominantly male. See 'Italia: composizione elettorato voto proporzionale 1996', 3 October 1996, *Abacus*. The survey was based on 14 300 interviews and was directed by Paolo Natale.
7. 'Casalinghe determinanti', in *La Repubblica*, 23 April 1996, p. 6.

REFERENCES

Barnes, S. H. and Kaase, M. (eds), *Political Action* (Beverly Hills and London, Sage, 1979).

Bull, A. and Corner, P., *From Peasant to Entrepreneur: the Survival of the Family Economy in Italy* (Oxford, Berg, 1993).

Burrell, B. C., 'Party Decline, Party Transformation and Gender Politics: the USA', in Lovenduski, J. and Norris, P. (eds), *Gender and Party Politics* (London, Sage, 1993), pp. 291–308.

Cartocci, R., *Elettori in Italia: Riflessioni sulle vicende elettorali degli anni ottanta* (Bologna, Il Mulino, 1990).

Cartocci, R., *Fra Lega e Chiesa* (Bologna, Il Mulino, 1994).

Cento Bull, A., 'The Lega Lombarda. A New Political Subculture for Lombardy's Industrial Districts', *The Italianist*, Vol. 12, 1992, pp. 179–83.

Cento Bull, A., 'The Politics of Industrial Districts in Lombardy. Replacing Christian Democracy with the Northern League', *The Italianist*, Vol. 13, 1993, pp. 209–29.

Crewe, I. M., 'The Electorate: Partisan Dealignment Ten Years On', *West European Politics*, Vol. 6, 1984, pp. 183–215.

Crewe, I. M., Sarlvik, B. and Alt, J., 'Partisan Dealignment in Britain 1964–74', *British Journal of Political Science*, Vol. 7, 1977, pp. 129–90.

Diamanti, I., 'Lega Nord: un partito per il periferie', in Ginsborg, P. (ed.), *Stato dell'Italia* (Milano, Mondadori, 1994), pp. 671–7.

Dogan, M., 'Political Cleavages and Social Stratification in France and Italy', in Lipset, S. M. and Rokkan, S. (eds), *Party Systems and Voter Alignments* (New York, Free Press, 1967), pp. 129–95.

Erickson, L., 'Making Her Way In: Women, Parties and Candidacies in Canada', in Lovenduski, J. and Norris, P. (eds), *Gender and Party Politics* (London, Sage, 1993), pp. 60–85.

Franklin, M. N., *The Decline of Class Voting in Britain* (Oxford, Clarendon Press, 1985).

Ginsborg, P. (ed.), *Stato dell'Italia* (Milan, Mondadori, 1994).

Guadagnini, M., 'A "Partitocrazia" Without Women: the Case of the Italian Party System', in Lovenduski, J. and Norris, P. (eds), *Gender and Party Politics* (London, Sage, 1993), pp. 168–204.

Heath, A., Jowell, R. and Curtice, J., *How Britain Votes* (Oxford, Pergamon Press, 1985).

Heath, A. et al., *Understanding Political Change: the British Voter, 1964–1987* (Oxford, Clarendon Press, 1991).

Himmelweit, H. T. et al., *How Voters Decide: a Longitudinal Study of Political Attitudes and Voting* (Milton Keynes, Open University Press, 1985).

Hirschman, A., *Exit, Voice and Loyalty* (Cambridge, MA and London, Harvard University Press, 1970).

Jenson, J. and Sineau, M., *Mitterand et les Françaises: un rendez-vous manqué* (Paris, Presse de Sciences Po, 1995).

Mannheimer, R. (ed.), *La Lega Lombarda* (Milan, Feltrinelli, 1991).

Mannheimer, R. and Sani, G., *Il mercato elettorale* (Bologna, Il Mulino, 1987).

Mannheimer, R. and Sani, G., *La rivoluzione elettorale: l'Italia tra la prima e la seconda reppublica* (Milano, Anabasi, 1994).

Mueller, C. M., *The Politics of the Gender Gap: the Social Construction of Political Influence* (Beverly Hills and London, Sage, 1988).

Norris, P. and Lovenduski, J., 'Gender and Party Politics in Britain', in Lovenduski, J. and Norris, P. (eds), *Gender and Party Politics* (London, Sage, 1993), pp. 35–59.

Parisi, A. and Pasquino, G., *Continuità e mutamento elettorale in Italia* (Bologna, Il Mulino, 1977).

Putnam, R. D., *Making Democracy Work: Civic Traditions in Modern Italy* (Princeton, Princeton University Press, 1993).

Revelli, M., 'Forza Italia: l'anomalia italiana non è finita', in Ginsborg, P. (ed.), *Stato dell'Italia* (Milan, Mondadori, 1994), pp. 667–70.

Rose, R. and McAllister, I., *Voters Begin to Choose* (London, Sage, 1986).

Rose, R. and McAllister, I., *The Loyalties of Voters* (London, Sage, 1990).

Sainsbury, D., 'The Politics of Increased Representation: the Swedish Case', in Lovenduski, J. and Norris, P. (eds), *Gender and Party Politics* (London, Sage, 1993), pp. 263–90.

Sani, G., 'The Italian Electorate in the Mid Seventies: Beyond Tradition?', in Penniman, H. E. (ed.), *Italy at the Polls* (Washington, American Enterprise Institute, 1977), pp. 81–122.

Sani, G., 'Italy: Continuity and Change', in Almond, G. A. and Verba, S. (eds), *The Civic Culture Revisited* (Boston, Little, Brown, 1979), pp. 273–324.

Trigilia, C., *Grandi partiti e piccole imprese: comunisti e democristiani nelle regioni a economia diffusa* (Bologna, Il Mulino, 1986).

Weber, M., 'Italy', in Lovenduski, J. and Hills, J. (eds), *The Politics of the Second Electorate: Women and Public Participation* (London, Boston and Henley, Routledge, 1981), pp. 182–207.

Williams, R., *Towards 2000* (London, Chatto and Windus, 1983).

10 Women, Work and Family in Post-Communist Germany[1]

Eva Kolinsky

The socialist order that prevailed in the GDR seemed to address the age-old conflict between emancipation and domesticity by requiring all citizens to work. The employment of women was seen as institutionalizing equality and ending all discrimination based on gender. In fact, the East German 'employment society' drew on female labour to alleviate persistent manpower shortages arising from low productivity, population loss and the determination to rival the West German economic miracle (Smith, 1994, pp. 37–44). At the workplace, special measures to assist women in their careers, *Frauenförderung* did not exist. On the contrary, the GDR moved increasingly towards separate employment tracks and occupational routes for women with lower educational and vocational qualifications. Forty years of integration into the socialist labour market had not secured women's emancipation as equals in the workforce but had established a separate, usually lower tier. After unification, women found themselves disadvantaged by these hidden inequalities.

Women also found themselves disadvantaged by their family roles. On the one hand, traditional gender divisions in the home remained largely unchanged. On the other hand, GDR social policy favoured working mothers by a range of financial benefits and other concessions. These not only blunted the conflict between employment and motherhood that had persisted in the West; they also enabled women with children to add child-related benefits to their income and virtually obliterate the pay gap between men and women that persisted in the GDR. After unification, the *Muttipolitik* of the GDR turned into the disadvantage of the relatively large families and low incomes while the economic transformations to a market economy produced their own agenda of disadvantage for women generally and in particular for women who wished to combine employment and motherhood.

WOMEN, WORK AND FAMILY IN THE GDR

In the first 20 years of GDR history, the labour market participation of women was hampered by their lower skills and a lack of child-care facilities outside the family. From the mid-1960s onwards, both shortcomings were being dispelled. Women of working age had their skills updated while compulsory education up to the age of 16 and vocational training for every young East German ensured that women of the post-war generations enjoyed better access to qualifications than their mothers or grandmothers had done (Bertram, 1994). In principle at least, East German women were as well educated and trained as men. When the GDR collapsed, women constituted half the labour force, virtually all held vocational qualifications and the dead-end of remaining unskilled had become a thing of the past (Winkler, 1990, pp. 37ff.). Although access to higher education was restricted compared with West Germany and more determined by political conformism than academic ability, women and men were represented in equal numbers in all but the most advanced level of doctoral studies that led to top leadership positions in the party state and the university sector.

The German state undertook to remove the conflict between employment and family roles by a system of institutional and financial support for mothers and children. Women (not men) were entitled to paid leave during the first year of the child's life and could take up to three years' leave before returning to work. The state was responsible for ensuring that children were cared for during working hours and that women could be workers as well as mothers. Employers including universities and colleges ran crèches and nurseries for pre-school children while schools and the state youth organization provided supervision and entertainment after school hours and also during holiday periods. On the eve of unification, 80 per cent of children under the age of three and some 97 per cent of older children attended full-time day care institutions (Winkler, 1990, p. 141).

The majority of East German women accepted full-time child-care outside the home without reservations and even formed the view that institutions were better able than the nuclear family to encourage a sense of solidarity and teach their children desirable behaviour such as 'motivation to work', 'a positive attitude towards the state', 'comradeship', 'reliability' and a sense of responsibility and duty (Helwig, 1984, p. 66). It has been suggested that the extensive provision of child-care facilities was also designed to reduce the influence of families on the socialization of their children and allow the state to mould the young generations into 'socialist personalities' who would be conformist in their views and compliant in their actions. West German critics held that families in East Germany had delegated too many tasks to public bodies and become little more than places to 'sleep and watch television' (Niermann, 1991, p. 12). The fact that several thousand East German children were left behind during the exodus of 1989 and 1990 suggests that some families at least had relinquished traditional care functions to the state and its institutions.

TRADITIONAL MODERN WOMEN: EAST GERMAN CONTRADICTIONS

In the course of social modernization, the range and duration of education and training have been extended for an increasing number of people while employment opportunities, incomes and lifestyles produced a more complex social structure than that of class society (Hradil, 1983). The emergence of advanced industrial democracies entailed a pluralization of lifestyles and an individualization of biographies. Women have benefited from the weakening of traditional role prescriptions and the diversification of opportunities although many expectations of equal treatment have not been met.

In the GDR, the organization of society and individual biographies in it took a different course. At the macro-level of social structure, official statistics designated eight out of ten East Germans to be 'working class' (Geißler, 1992a, pp. 79ff.). While West German society seemed dominated by a large middle sector, East German society was polarized between a sizeable upper stratum of administrators and bureaucrats and an even bigger working-class sector while the middle sector hardly mattered (Vester, 1995). The majority of the population lived at a relatively uniform level with regard to earnings, education, training qualifications and housing conditions although the upper strata enjoyed the Western style living conditions to which everyone aspired (Vester, 1995, pp. 48–50). Geißler argues that the prescribed homogeneity generated immobilism and impeded social modernization (Geißler, 1992b). In his view, East German women escaped this modernization deficit and even enjoyed a modernization bonus compared with women in the West: all had access to employment, education and training and the gender gap had ceased to matter. On closer examination, however, it appears that women's biographies in the GDR lacked key landmarks of modernity and resembled those of West German women in the 1950s despite their 40-year history of employment.

The Shell youth study of 1992 compared the biographies of young East German and West German women who were born in 1969, i.e. were in their early twenties when the research was conducted (*Jugend '92*, 1992, pp. 207ff.; Kolinsky, 1995a, pp. 277–81). In the East, biographies were more predictable and young women reached landmarks of adult life earlier than in the West. For example, by the age of 16, nine out of ten East German women had left school. By the age of 17, 85 per cent had decided on their career and had found an employer. In West Germany, most 17 year olds continued in full-time education and few had clear career plans. Most remained dependent on their parents. In East Germany, most earned their own money. By the age of 19 most East German women were in full-time employment, and seven out of ten had achieved financial independence from their parents; in the West, just 40 per cent earned enough to live on. Of the cohort born in 1969, most East German women were married by the time they were 21 and had at least one child by the time they were 22 (Gysi and Meyer, 1992, p. 144). Their West German peers were only just completing their education and were some five years older before getting married and older still before starting a family.

In the East, the ideal family was held to consist of a couple and their two children (although the state tried to advocate the three-children family). Having children remained an accepted social norm throughout the GDR era. Most families were complete when the woman was in her mid-twenties. Seventy per cent of East German women had children, normally (68 per cent) two or more (Winkler, 1990, p. 29). From the mid-1980s onwards, one in three children was born to unmarried mothers (*Datenreport*, 1994, p. 29). Many of these unmarried mothers lived in a trial relationship and married their partner after the birth of their first or subsequent children. One in three single mothers in the GDR, however, had never been married and appeared to have chosen single parenthood as an alternative to married life (Gysi and Meyer, 1992, p. 146). Since 40 per cent of marriages ended in divorce, an increasing number of households consisted of a single parent and children. In 1989, one in five East German households was headed by a single parent, almost always a woman (Hölzler and Mächler, 1992, pp. 34–5).

Despite their traditional path into early marriage and motherhood, East German women had begun to break away from traditional family structures by opting for single motherhood or raising their children as head of household after a divorce. State policies in support of working mothers protected East German women from the risk of poverty although partner households with two incomes were significantly better off in material terms than single parent households since women in the GDR contributed some 40 per cent of household income (Gysi and Meyer, 1992, p. 154).

GENDER ROLES AND EMPLOYMENT TRACKS

Women's participation in employment did not in itself signify a break with traditional gender roles. The 'baby-year' enabled East German women to interrupt their employment although they remained officially listed as employed. In a modified form, the East German system instituted family phases of the type envisaged by Myrdal and Klein (1957). In order to fulfil their family duties, women interrupted their employment and returned to it when their children no longer needed constant care.

Combining work and family had become an accepted dual role for women. Surveys of attitudes to employment before unification revealed that women voiced more modest career motivations than men. One in three women worked part-time but up to 80 per cent would have preferred to reduce their hours to part-time if such work was available (Bertram, 1993, p. 35).[2] Given that a full working week amounted to nearly 44 hours compared to around 35 in the West and women like men were required to do shift work in the state's bid to increase economic output, employment itself was more time consuming than in the West, although anecdotal evidence suggests that most East Germans had nothing to do for the better part of a working day since raw materials and supplies tended to run out by mid-morning.

Women were faced with a society that utilized them as a labour force yet had failed to undergo a process of modernization that might have eased everyday duties such as shopping or transport. Obtaining everyday provisions was a daily battle against shortages or a hunt for surprise bargains. After work, most women shopped, collected their children from their day care, prepared the meal and performed domestic duties such as cooking, mending or doing the laundry:

> In morning tired out of bed, get the little one ready, grab something quick to eat, hurry to the bus, to the nursery, to the bus again, to work where I can sit down and have a coffee at leisure. Work, end of work, to the bus, into the *Kaufhalle,* to the nursery, back home with the little one. When she is finally tucked up in bed, I have to do mending or some laundry, and flop in front of the television to let myself be entertained.
> (Schröder, B., *Barfuss durch die Wiese* quoted in Helwig, 1984, p. 68)

Everyday life in the GDR was steeped in traditional assumptions about men's and women's roles. In the family, male and female roles differed sharply. Women were in charge of most domestic duties while men carried out domestic repairs or played with the children. After work, women had considerably less free time than men. In households where both partners were university graduates, chores were shared more evenly than in working-class households. Even children appear to have been groomed for gender specific roles in the family: most girls were expected to help at home while most boys were not (Helwig, 1984, p. 47). Women's larger contributions to the household made it more difficult for them to undertake the additional political and public duties required to secure advancement at work. Women, it seems, were more dissatisfied with the persistence of traditional role patterns in their private sphere and vented their dissatisfaction by petitioning for divorce or refraining from marriage. In retrospect, it can be argued that the persistence of traditional gender roles in the home turned into a structural disadvantage for women in their employment opportunities and their competitive chances after unification.

East Germans did not challenge the gender stereotypes that persisted in their society. Accepting that women should be employed and that homemaking constituted only a facet of a woman's life, they deemed employment and motherhood, work and family, to be without conflict. In assuming that a woman's place is at work and in the family, East Germans continue to differ from West Germans and from most other West Europeans. A comparative study of attitudes towards the family and employment showed in December 1994 that 45 per cent of East Germans and only 12 per cent of West Germans disagreed with the statement: 'a pre-school age child will be harmed if his mother goes out to work' (*Eurobarometer 42*, 1995, p. 71). Twice as many East Germans (73 per cent) as West Germans (36 per cent) objected to the claim that 'being a housewife is as satisfying as working in paid employment' and similar prescriptions of traditional women's roles (ibid., p. 72). In the GDR, women had not been forced to choose between traditional and non-traditional roles, between family duties and employment but had been expected to perform both. The biographies of East German women were 'modern' in making education and employment standard trajectories, yet their 'modernity' was limited by comparatively low levels of formal education, by early and sizeable family duties and a society saturated with concealed traditionalism and gender stereotypes.

THE HIDDEN AGENDA OF INEQUALITY

In employment, the gender stereotypes amounted to a hidden agenda of inequality (Kolinsky, 1993, pp. 259–94). In their choice of qualification, women were directed by the state into an increasingly narrow and genderized range of occupational and professional fields such as telecommunication, retailing, health care, teaching and administrative tasks in industry and public administration (Rink, 1995, p. 74). Within each area, women performed mainly unskilled or semi-skilled work while only a handful reached skilled or leadership positions. Overall, about 2 per cent of East German women held top management positions, although one in four had risen to intermediate management posts (Winkler, 1990, pp. 90–4). Even service sector and administrative employment caught women in a modernization trap since their functions consisted predominantly of support services to compensate for the lack of technology and can be classified as unskilled or semi-skilled labour.[3]

While the women's prevalence at the lower end of the GDR labour market and their deficit in leadership positions may be explained by a lack of career motivation or insufficient political activism, the inequalities of pay in the GDR can only be explained as the result of discrimination. At all levels of seniority and in all areas of the economy, women were concentrated in the lower bracket of the relevant wage band, men in the top bracket (Kolinsky, 1995d, pp. 188–9). The overall effect of this institutionalized wage discrimination was that women earned on average one-third less than men although the GDR claimed to have made equal pay a statutory right of all citizens.

The wage discrimination went unnoticed partly because information about gender specific pay levels was kept out of the public domain and because the so-called 'second wage packet' served to obfuscate the pay differentials between men and women. The 'second wage packet' consisted of child benefit and other allowances to encourage child bearing and assist with child-care. Compared with women's income, child allowances were generous. Thus a woman with two children could increase her monthly earnings by 50 per cent (Kolinsky, 1992, pp. 272–3). Although badly paid for her employment, her actual income was often no lower than that of men. Until the end of their state, East German women had not perceived the hidden agenda that curtailed their equality. They took it for granted that they were equal with men and had not suffered discrimination. They also took employment for granted and that they would be free to balance their family and employment duties in their own way. There is no evidence that East German women anticipated the collapse of their employment society or were prepared for its effect on their personal lives.

SOCIAL TRANSFORMATION AND OPEN DISADVANTAGE

The transformation that turned the former GDR into the Germany of the new *Länder* met some of the expectations that had inspired East Germans to opt for unification: it put an end to the socialist shortage society and brought the onset of consumerism as Western goods became freely available; it put an end to restrictions and opened choices to travel, to voice political and personal views in public without fear of reprisals. The social transformation since 1990, however, also put an end to the East German employment society and rocked the very foundations of everyday life by making employment itself uncertain. For women, the collapse of the employment society was doubly momentous since it turned hidden inequalities into open disadvantages and ended the institutional and financial support that had favoured women with children in the GDR.

THE RISK OF UNEMPLOYMENT

The unification treaty confirmed the introduction of a market economy and the currency union of July 1990 but merely hinted at the risk of unemployment when it stipulated that East Germans over the age of 55 (originally 57) should take early retirement. When this programme came on stream in 1992 it was phased in more effectively for women than for men. By 1994, 70 per cent of women in the early retirement bracket and only 50 per cent of men had been excluded from the labour market (Kolinksy, 1995c, pp. 26–7).

During the first years of transformation, unemployment was cushioned by a range of labour market measures. For the individual, participation in these measures ensured that their employment status was protected and their entitlement to benefit retained. Women were outnumbered by men in all such programmes except retraining courses. Initially, short-time working constituted the main device of stabilizing the labour market. At times, it affected half the labour force. With some regional variations, the programme had 70 per cent male and 30 per cent female recipients. The same applied to the work creation schemes *(Arbeitsbeschaffungsmaßnahmen)* that took effect in 1992. Initially, men obtained seven out of ten of the new (albeit temporary) placements. It took the protests of Equal Opportunities Commissioners at local level and representations to labour exchanges and potential employers to increase women's participation to over 40 per cent before the programme itself was scaled down in 1994. From the outset, women constituted a majority – between 65 and 80 per cent – on retraining courses. This high participation rate reflects women's motivation to upgrade their skills and meet the competitive demands of the new labour market. Even more important appears to be that participation in such courses was the only means open to women to retain their place on the unemployment register and their entitlement to benefit.

In 1995, unemployment in the new *Länder* stood at 15 per cent and had, for the first time, overtaken unemployment levels in the old *Länder*. However, since unification, the workforce in the new *Länder* had already been reduced by one-third as people were phased into non-employment or migrated west. The figure of 15 per cent, therefore, only points to the sharp end of employment society collapse.

Like employment opportunities, unemployment has shown clear gender differences. In 1995, 10 per cent of the male workforce and 20 per cent of the female workforce were unemployed. Of the unemployed themselves, two-thirds were women. Given the genderized employment policy of the GDR, the closure of a *Frauenbetrieb* such as textile production could drive female unemployment levels in affected regions much higher. There is evidence that women lost their employment in greater numbers during the first years of the social transformation when short-time working tended to favour men. Since then, gender differences at the point of entering unemployment have receded (Nickel and Schenk, 1994, p. 262). Yet, since women have found it more difficult than men to return to the labour market, their share among the unemployed has remained higher. Women constitute a clear majority among the long-term unemployed. In 1993, 55 per cent of the short-term unemployed who had been out of work for less than one month but 70 per cent of the long-term unemployed who had been out of work for six months or more were women.

Despite these adverse conditions, the employment motivation of East German women has not wavered. Most perceive themselves as active in the labour market and do not accept being sidelined into homemaking. In the old *Länder*, the *Alternativrolle Hausfrau* has long been regarded as a viable second choice for women who cannot find employment and in particular for women who have lost their entitlement to benefit. In 1993, 60 per cent of West German women who were not in employment referred to their own status as that of 'housewife' and just 23 per cent were looking for work or planned to do so. In the new *Länder*, no such *Alternativrolle* had been accepted. Just 8 per cent of women without employment gave their status as 'housewife'. Nine out of ten were either looking for work (76 per cent) or intended to look for work in the near future (*Datenreport*, 1994, p. 481). Women's employment motivation in the new *Länder* is also evident in the continued high labour market participation. Despite the battering inflicted by unemployment and persistent uncertainties, women's share of the labour force in the age groups between 25 and 55 has remained higher in the new *Länder* than in the old (see Table 10.1). In the middle age groups, over 90 per cent were in work or looking for work, fewer than had been employed in the GDR but considerably more than in the West and all but matching labour market participation of men.

Despite their employment motivation and intense labour market participation, only about one in four women have been employed without interruption since 1990 while the remaining three out of four have moved in

Table 10.1   Labour market participation of women by age groups in the old and
the new *Länder* (percentages)

Age group	Old Länder 1992	Old Länder 1993	New Länder 1992	New Länder 1993
15–20	34	33	43	37
20–25	73	71	85	83
25–30	73	72	95	94
30–35	68	68	97	96
35–40	70	70	97	97
40–45	73	73	97	96
45–50	69	70	96	95
50–55	61	62	90	91
55–60	46	47	27	27
60–65	12	12	3	3
65–70	4	4	–	–

Note: Percentage figures are rounded and may not add up to 100.
Source: *Datenreport*, 1994, p. 80.

and out of work and retraining measures in a determined bid to avoid labour market exclusion (Berger and Schulz, 1994, p. 6).[4] Even for those in work, employment has lost its erstwhile certainty while fears of unemployment are all-pervasive. While older women dread that they may never work again if they were to become unemployed, many younger women doubt that their educational and vocational qualifications are good enough to withstand the new competitive pressures of the labour market. From being a normal part of life, employment has turned into a prime area of concern. In order to optimize their chances of advancement and in particular escape exclusion from the labour market through unemployment, East German women (and men) have tended to enhance their skills or work longer hours. Five years after the collapse of the GDR employment society, employment had gained a greater centrality in people's lives and a greater urgency than it ever had in the past. More than ever in the past, employment had become a dividing line between integration and exclusion, between material life-chances and poverty.

INCOMES AND THE RISK OF POVERTY

In recasting East German society, unification also dismantled the web of state subsidies that had kept rents and energy prices at their 1940s' level and made goods of the so-called *Grundbedarf* very cheap to buy. While so-called luxury goods absorbed a huge proportion of earnings and included most attributes of modern living from television sets or refrigerators to washing machines and cars, people could get by with very little money if their needs did not stray beyond the basics deemed essential by the state. Since nobody could fall through the social net into homelessness or starvation and money mattered less than in the West, poverty did not exist. It arrived with unification in the wake of income developments and earning differentials that blew the relative uniformity of the GDR wide open.

Initially, incomes in the new *Länder* kept their GDR uniformity and were pitched at 65 per cent of those in the old. Provided their employment situation remained unchanged or they were shielded from unemployment by short-time arrangements, most people perceived the scope afforded by the new currency as an improvement although comparisons with the West also gave rise to fears that East Germans had entered the new Germany as underpaid second class citizens. Women with children suffered an immediate reduction of income since their new earnings were calculated only on the basis of their GDR pay without taking heed of the second wage packet of allowances. Widows, however, enjoyed a windfall as they became eligible to a part of their husband's pension in addition to their own.

From about 1993 onwards, incomes lost their GDR uniformity. While all incomes rose, white-collar incomes rose faster (see Figure 10.1). Between 1991 and 1994, blue-collar pay more than doubled from DM 1300 to DM 2900 while white-collar pay grew to nearly three times its 1991 level and reached an average of DM 4600. In 1991, the pay difference between the two occupational groups had been DM 380; in 1994, it had quadrupled to DM 1600 (*Leipziger Statistik* IV, 1994, p. 15).

As the social transformation gathered pace, incomes rose and so did their diversity. In 1992, average earnings in Saxony for example stood at DM 2000 per month, 18 months later at DM 3205 (*Leipziger Statistik* IV, 1994, p. 3). Compared with the old *Länder*, income levels remained bunched in the lower half of the range. In 1992, 48 per cent of households in the old *Länder* but only 24 per cent in the new had a monthly income of over DM 3000 (see Figure 10.2). Since then, the balance has shifted further towards higher incomes. In 1995, 61 per cent of households in Leipzig recorded monthly incomes above DM 3000 compared with just 18 per cent 1991. Individual earnings showed a similar surge. In 1991, 44 per cent of Leipzig's inhabitants had earned less than DM 1000. By 1995, that number had decreased to 14 per cent (ibid., pp. 20–1).

After unification, as before it, women's earnings were about one-third lower than those of men. The conversion into Deutschmark extended the

Monthly Incomes (in DM)
New Länder, 1991 and 1994

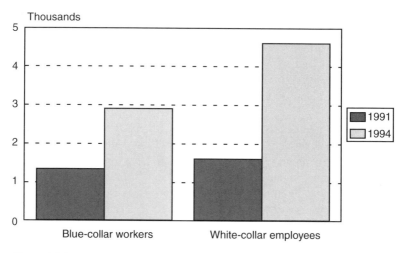

Figure 10.1   Monthly incomes in the New *Länder*
Source: *Datenreport 1994*, p. 105.

genderized wage levels of the GDR into the new Germany. Moreover, the troubled employment history of women since unification and their greater exposure to unemployment meant that most women's earnings rose less rapidly than those for people with an uninterrupted employment history. Since few women succeeded in gaining employment in or promotion to managerial and higher civil service positions or became self-employed, their stake in the highest income brackets has remained small. Data for Saxony show that in 1992, 56 per cent of women in employment and 28 per cent of men were in the lowest income brackets earning less than DM 1000 a month. At the opposite end of the pay spectrum, 11 per cent of women but 29 per cent of men earned more than DM 1400, the highest income bracket at the time (Kolinsky, 1995d, p. 189).

Unemployment benefit mirrors inequalities of pay and exacerbates them. The maximum entitlement amounts to 67 per cent of earnings for one year, falling to 53 per cent after that (Hanesch, 1995, p. 16). Without entering into a detailed analysis of benefit entitlement, it is important to emphasize that all unemployment entails a significant reduction of income. Long-term unemployment, moreover, entails the risk that benefit entitlements cease altogether. In 1992, 64 per cent of unemployed women

Household Incomes, 1992
New and Old Länder

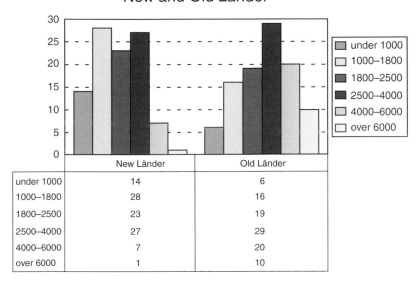

	New Länder	Old Länder
under 1000	14	6
1000–1800	28	16
1800–2500	23	19
2500–4000	27	29
4000–6000	7	20
over 6000	1	10

Figure 10.2   Household incomes in 1992
Source: Calculated from *Datenreport 1994*: 104 and *Statistisches Jahrbuch der Bundesrepublik Deutschland, 1995*.

and 37 per cent of unemployed men received less than DM 600 per month. At the time, average income stood at DM 1500 in the new *Länder* generally and at DM 2000 in Leipzig. The poverty line has been defined as 50 per cent of average income and thus lay between DM 750 and DM 1000 at the time. By this yardstick, four out of five unemployed women (and half the unemployed men) had fallen into poverty (Kolinsky, 1995d, pp. 188–91).

The correlation between unemployment and poverty is borne out by data on income development between 1991 and 1995 (see Figure 10.3). Incomes of the unemployed have been lowest throughout the period. Although they increased by about one-third, increases for other groups have been steeper and the gap widened (*Leipziger Statistik* II, 1995, p. 22).

As mentioned earlier, poverty did not figure in GDR society where earnings were pegged and daily living underpinned by a state policy of minimum provisions. Within two years of unification, however, poverty levels in the new *Länder* resembled those which had been familiar in

Personal Incomes in Leipzig
1991–5

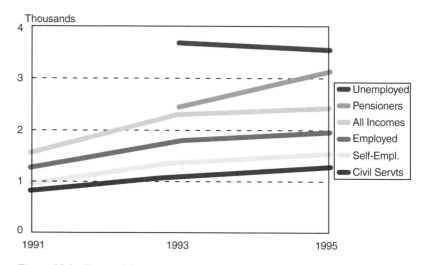

Figure 10.3   Personal incomes in Leipzig
Source: Calculated from *Leipziger Statistik, Statistische Berichte II*, 1995, p. 22.

West Germany for a decade (Krause, 1992, p. 9). East Germans who had been phased out of employment were unable to reap the benefits of wage and salary changes and tended to remain at the bottom end of an increasingly disparate income spectrum. In his *Armut in Deutschland*, Hanesch compares poverty in East and West by measuring under-provisions in key areas such as income, employment, housing or education. He argues that East Germans were hit much harder than West Germans by under-provision of income and employment (Hanesch, 1994, p. 173). They were also more likely than West Germans to experience under-provision in more than one area and for a longer duration. By his measure, women were more affected by poverty than men and 12 per cent of East German women could be classified as poor (Hanesch, 1994, p. 178). The risk of poverty was highest for single parents, most of whom were women. In the new *Länder*, 19 per cent of single parents were affected by poverty. In the GDR, a normal household included one or two working adults. In the transformed Germany of the 1990s the number of such 'normal' households dropped to 42 per cent while the remainder have one or two non-working adults. In the past, 80 per cent of households with children included two working adults/parents; in 1992, just 57 per cent did (Berger and Schulz, 1994, pp. 8, 13). After unification, households with three or more children were more affected by unemployment and 42 per cent of these households lived in poverty (Hanesch, 1994, p. 179).

Recent research has suggested that most poverty in modern society is transitory although it may be recurrent. In a stable society such as that in the old *Länder*, moving in and out of poverty appears to have become a regular occurrence that causes no undue alarm or despondency (Krause, 1992, pp. 11–14). In the transformed society of the new *Länder*, exclusion from employment and relegation into poverty cannot yet have the normality ascribed to them in the West and are more keenly perceived as devastating life-plans and expectations. Women, women with children and especially women with several children have proved especially vulnerable to the unfamiliar risks of unemployment and social exclusion.

RECASTING BIOGRAPHIES

Women who had already passed the landmarks of East German normality, had to adjust to their transformed society after 1990 as best they could. They had left school early, trained in the field into which they were directed by the state, worked in a lower skilled or intermediate position, married early or resolved to remain unmarried, had children, possibly divorced and lived the life between employment and family that all women in the GDR took for granted. After unification, each of these landmarks turned into a potential disadvantage in the newly competitive era.

Early fears that child-care facilities would collapse proved unfounded. Although some crèches and nurseries closed down when firms refused to finance them, local authorities took over. With temporary support from central government and guaranteed support from regional governments who cover 40 per cent of the cost, local authorities in the new *Länder* succeeded in maintaining a comprehensive network of day care institutions and offer a place to each child who requires one. Yet, the system is no longer the same. Charges increased from 35 Pfennig (East German currency) a day to at least ten times that amount. New guidelines about staffing levels and provisions resulted in closures of facilities, amalgamations and staff cuts. In the past, women could be sure to have access to child-care near their home or their workplace; now facilities may be anywhere and their location changes frequently as further closures and amalgamations take effect. Despite comprehensive provisions, women perceive child-care as under threat and less reliable than in the GDR (Kolinsky, 1996).

One of the main reasons for the contraction of the sector has been a rapid decline in the birth rate in the new *Länder*. It is here that the social transformation recast biographies. As we have seen earlier, women have retained a keen employment motivation and done their utmost to continue in employment. While the desire to have children remained as high as it had been in the GDR, women shunned or postponed motherhood. Between 1990 and 1991, the birth rate fell by 50 per cent; by 1995, it had dropped to just 40 per cent of its 1989 level, less than half that in the old *Länder* (Martin, 1995, p. 13). A slight increase in 1996 points to a degree of social normalization as women who postponed childbirth after unification became mothers. Now, East German women were over 27 years old on average when they had their first child, several years older than in the GDR, and only about one year younger than in West Germany. Single motherhood, however, continued at a high level. In the mid-1990s, every second new baby was born to a single mother. In the GDR, of course, single mothers had been able to rely on additional support such as reduced working hours, paid leave to care for their children in case of illness and provisions for their children during illnesses or school holidays. None of these special measures applied in the new *Länder*. In the GDR, single motherhood signalled self-reliance and a disdain for the traditional values and behaviour patterns that appeared to beset most conventional families. In post-unification society, this emancipatory spirit bears all the hallmarks of social risk-taking as single mothers have been among the first to lose their employment and face a higher risk of poverty than other groups. In Leipzig, for instance, 40 per cent of those on income support in 1994 were single mothers and they constituted the fastest growing group of welfare recipients in the city (Kolinsky, 1995d, p. 191). There is nothing to suggest that conditions were better for single mothers elsewhere.

For women with children generally, unification has made things worse. With the abolition of the second wage packet children turned more visibly into a financial burden. Counting all GDR benefits and special allowances together, it has been estimated that before unification, the state contributed about 85 per cent of the cost of a child (Gysi and Meyer, 1992, p. 155). After unification, most of these costs had to be borne by the household. In addition, unification diversified and individualized standards about how children should be brought up, treated and provided for. In the GDR, state institutions and an endorsement of the 'socialist personality' made for collective standards with little scope for choice. After unification, families were thrown back on their own resources of defining values and meeting standards. In retrospect, things appeared to have been easier and better for families in the GDR. A 1994 survey showed that women

Table 10.2   Living conditions of children in the old and the new *Länder*. Married women with children were asked: 'Does your child have too little, enough or too much of the following…?' Listed in the table are responses of 'too little' (percentages)

Too little provision of:	New Länder	Old Länder
Space in the apartment	23	14
Healthy environment	42	29
Facilities to play outdoors	41	15
Contact with other children	7	5
A happy childhood	2	1
Contact with the father	22	11
Contact with the mother	7	3

Source: Jürgen Sass, 'Leben mit Kindern', quoted in *Leipziger Statistik, Statistische Berichte IV*, 1994, p. 9.

remembered the East German state, motorists, child-care institutions, neighbours and their place of work, as *kinderfreundlich*, as accepting of children (Fischer, 1994, pp. 9–10).[5] With the exception of doctors, children's playgrounds and restaurants, conditions generally seemed worse after unification and more hostile to children. In addition, GDR legacies such as cramped housing, environmental pollution and the lack of amenities added to women's concerns about the quality of life for their children (see Table 10.2). As they compared their own situation with that in the West, women with children in the new *Länder* found their flats too small (23 per cent), their environment too polluted (42 per cent), outdoor playing facilities too scarce (41 per cent) and relations with absent parents, especially fathers, unsatisfactory (22 per cent). The same study showed that women with children in the old *Länder* were more at ease with their situation and more assured about their family's quality of life.

MARRIAGES AND DIVORCES

No less momentous than the decline in the birth rate after unification was the drop in marriages and in divorces. Both developments were responses to a climate of social uncertainty and, more specifically, to the introduction of federal German law. In the GDR, most people married to confirm an existing relationship or even to stake a claim on the housing list. Marriage had no bearing on property rights, tax benefits or other aspects of personal or financial security. By contrast, marriage in federal German legislation entitles both partners to material benefits from the union. East Germans had not perceived marriage in these terms and were reluctant to accept the new strictures, not least since cohabitation and child-bearing had long become accepted without the prerequisite of marriage. At a time when controlling and reducing social risks became all-important, few chose to undertake the unknown commitments that were now linked to marriage. Between 1990 and 1993, marriages dropped to half their former level and, as mentioned earlier, the average age on marriage for both women and men jumped by half a decade *(Datenreport,* 1994, p. 33). In 1992, 48 000 couples were married; five years earlier, there had been three times that number.

Existing marriages, however, gained unprecedented stability. Divorces dropped to a record low in post-war Germany, East or West (*Datenreport,* 1994, p. 35). In 1992, 10 000 marriages in the new *Länder* ended in divorce; in the late 1980s, the number of divorces had been five times higher. Indeed, the divorce rate in the GDR had ranked among the highest in the world. Then, divorce entailed no obligations of maintenance and divorcees could even expect to be allocated a new flat after their marriage had broken down. Since women were in employment and could expect work-related pensions later in life, divorce in the GDR was treated as an arrangement of convenience. In the Federal Republic, the divorce law reform of 1977 ruled that each partner was entitled to a fair share of the joint assets as well as maintenance payments. Introduced to protect the financially weaker partner, normally the woman, from material disadvantage arising from periods of non-employment, family roles and child-rearing, the legislation was radically different from the 'clean break' concept in the East. Amidst the material upheavals after unification, East Germans shied away from taking on these additional commitments, as they shied away from the commitment of marriage. Of the divorces that did take place in the new *Länder*, two-thirds involved children under the age of 18, thus entailing maintenance arrangements and unfamiliar material liabilities.

WOMEN, WORK AND FAMILY: FUTURE PERSPECTIVES

In an historical perspective, it is not unknown for periods of economic stress and uncertainty to reduce the frequency of marriages and births. During the mass unemployment of the late 1920s and early 1930s, for example, Germans responded to the economic hardship by delaying marriage. As soon as material circumstances improved, things got back to normal. Postponed marriages took place and the birth rate which had declined faster than in earlier years actually increased until the mid-1930s (Kröllmann, 1985, pp. 100–3). 'Normality' at the time implied that families were based on the marriage of a couple and that children were born within marriage. Although the Second World War and the social dislocations that followed it drove the divorce rate to record levels and established one-parent families as a regular facet of daily life, the nuclear family of a married couple and their children retained normative status well into the 1960s.

Since then, attitude changes between generations and in the wake of socio-economic modernization modified the normative function of the nuclear family and favoured a pluralization of family forms in line with a more general pluralization and individualization of lifestyles and social expectations in society. In the GDR, state support for child-care functions reduced the material effects of child-rearing on the family budget and freed families from many supervisory and educational responsibilities. Women could take motherhood for granted since it did seem compatible with employment and did not constitute a 'massive investment' of time and money (Fischer, 1994, p. 9). In fact, the GDR *Muttipolitik* of financial incentives for mothers and child allowances kept the birth rate higher than it would have been in a less pronatalist setting. A decline of the birth rate in the mid-1970s was reversed by introducing more generous allowances and more concessions for single mothers. The abolition of GDR social policy after unification made children unexpectedly expensive in an environment where the state had subsidized or provided free of charge regular day care, entertainment, leisure activities, holiday camps and many other items of child-related cost.

East German women reacted to the post-unification uncertainties by asserting established priorities. These established priorities had been to combine employment and motherhood. Nickel and Schenk have shown (1994, p. 278) that the majority of women in the new *Länder* prefer to balance both areas of their lives without choosing between them. Under the transformed conditions of unified Germany, the motivation to combine employment and motherhood amounts to a rejection of a role as full-time housewife and priority of work over family. Some younger women already relish the new occupational opportunities and the prospect of building a career based on ability and qualifications.

The demographic transformations since unification reflect the individual answers of East German women about how they hope to combine employment and motherhood in the future. Family developments in the new *Länder* resemble those in the old in their plurality of structures and the imprint of individual choice. Yet, women's choices in the new *Länder* have remained distinctive in several ways. First, their employment motivation has remained unbroken. Adjustments in their family situations and personal lives are determined by their perception of how this employment motivation can best be realized. Postponing childbirth and opting for or against marriage reflect women's perceptions of how to succeed in the transformed social environment. Second, women continue to see themselves as working mothers. In the old *Länder*, one in four women did not wish to have children. In the new *Länder*, only one in ten women did not wish to have children. Studies of young East Germans found that the wish to have children has declined a little since the days of the GDR but still holds its place among the top priorities alongside the wish to find a partner for life and to find employment (Starke, 1995, p. 163). Faced with the conflict of combining motherhood and employment, women in the new *Länder* have opted to delay motherhood, not in order to remain childless but in a bid to combine employment and motherhood when they can manage to do so.

Third, women in the GDR had begun to perceive the choice for single parenthood as a means of evading the unresolved gender conflicts that had soured a considerable proportion of partner and family relations. The choice for single parenthood indicated that a woman felt able to organize her life and combine employment and motherhood in line with her own abilities and inclinations. All economic indicators suggest that households consisting of two adults and children are better off financially than single parent households. Moreover, unification added the risk of poverty to social hardship linked to low incomes even before unification. Yet, a growing number of women have opted for single parenthood. Between 1990 and 1994, the number of children born to unmarried mothers in the new *Länder* increased by more than one-third, constituting more than half the births (Gysi and Meyer, 1992, p. 32). Although fewer children are born than before unification, more children are born to unmarried mothers.

In the new *Länder*, single parenthood has attained a normality it did not possess in the old. The payment of educational allowances, the benefit payable to a new parent for up to three years after the birth of a child, is a good example of these developments. In 1994, 42 per cent of recipients in the new *Länder* were single mothers compared with just 11 per cent in the old *Länder* (*Datenreport*, 1994, p. 213).

In their bid to secure their dual role in work and family by defying traditional family arrangements and opting for unmarried motherhood, women in the new *Länder* cling to the values and social preferences that had emerged in the GDR. More than half a decade after unification, the social risks associated with single parenthood have failed to deter women from choosing a lifestyle that held a promise of self-determination and emancipation in the GDR era. In the old *Länder*, most women (and couples) tended to marry as soon as a child was on the way (Strohmeier, 1993, pp. 11ff.). In the new *Länder*, women have refused to see motherhood as entry point to full-time homemaking. In staking their independence as single mothers, they try to infuse the GDR norm of working mothers into their new environment. In post-communist Germany, this blend of GDR rules and personal motivations has come to entail unfamiliar risks of social exclusion and poverty for East German single mothers and their families.

NOTES

1. An earlier version of this chapter was published in Kolinsky, E. (ed.), *Social Transformation and the Family in Post-Communist Germany* (London, Macmillan, 1998), pp. 118–40.

2. The information on the demand for part-time working is based on unpublished studies conducted by the Institut für Jugendforschung, Leipzig, and was provided to the author by Barbara Bertram in an interview on 22 August 1992 in Leipzig.

3. In Leipzig, for instance, 80 per cent of the female labour force worked in the service sector and women constituted 90 per cent of unskilled white-collar employees. A considerable proportion of clerical employment consisted of auxiliary tasks such as filing and often compensated for lack of technological equipment. After unification, these seemingly 'modern' white-collar positions had no future in the changed working environment.

4. The authors report that, overall, 31 per cent had been with the same employer; 24 per cent in manufacturing, 19 per cent in agriculture, 52 per cent in transport and postal services, 44 per cent in banking and insurance and 43 per cent in building construction. Unemployment affected women more strongly in all areas.

5. Sass, J., 'Leben mit Kindern', quoted in Fischer, J., 'Rückblick auf das Jahr der Familie 1994', pp. 9–10. Seventy-five per cent thought that the East German state had been *kinderfreundlich*; only 11 per cent thought that of their post-unification state. In a similar vein, 70 per cent remembered their workplace in the GDR as *kinderfreundlich* but just 25 per cent felt this about their workplace in unified Germany.

REFERENCES

Berger, H. and Schulz, A., 'Veränderungen in der Erwerbssituation in ostdeutschen Privathaushalten und Befindlichkeit der Menschen', *Aus Politik und Zeigeschichte*, B 16, 1994.

Bertram, B., 'Die Entwicklung der Geschlechterverhältnisse in den neuen Bundesländern', *Aus Politik und Zeitgeschichte*, B 6, 1993.

Bertram, B., ' "Nicht zurück an den Kochtopf" – Aus- und Weiterbildung in der DDR', in Helwig, G. and Nickel, H. M. (eds), *Frauen in Deutschland 1945–1992* (Berlin, Akademie Verlag, 1994), pp. 191–214.

Datenreport 1994. Zahlen und Fakten über die Bundesrepublik Deutschland, Statistisches Bundesamt (ed.) (Bonn, Bundeszentrale für politische Bildung, 1994).

Europeans and the Family. Results of an Opinion survey. Report prepared in conjunction with the Commission of the European Communities by N. Malpas and P.-Y. Lambert (Brussels, December, 1993).

Eurobarometer. Die öffentliche Meinung in der Europäischen Union. Ed. Europäische Kommission (several issues per year).

Fischer, J., 'Rückblick auf das Jahr der Familie 1994', *Leipziger Statistik, Statistische Berichte* IV, Quartal, 1994.

Geißler, R. (1992a), *Die Sozialstruktur Deutschlands* (Opladen, Westdeutscher Verlag, 1992).

Geißler, R. (1992b), 'Die ostdeutsche Sozialstruktur unter Modernisierungsdruck', *Aus Politik und Zeitgeschichte*, B, 1992, pp. 29–30.

Gysi, J. and Meyer, D., 'Leitbild: berufstätige Mutter – DDR-Frauen in Familie, Partnerschaft und Ehe', in Helwig, G. and Nickel, H. M. (eds), *Frauen in Deutschland 1945–1992* (Berlin, Akademie Verlag, 1992), pp. 139–65.

Hanesch, W., *Armut in Deutschland* (Rowohlt, Reinbek, 1994).

Hanesch, W., 'Sozialpolitik und arbeitsmarktsbedingte Armut', *Aus Politik und Zeitgeschichte*, B, 1995.

Helwig, G., *Jugend und Familie in der DDR. Leitbild und Alltag im Widerspruch* (Edition Deutschland Archiv, Cologne, Kiepenheuer and Witsch, 1984).

Helwig, G. and Nickel, H. M. (eds), *Frauen in Deutschland 1945–1992* (Berlin, Akademie Verlag, 1992).

Hölzler, I. and Mächler, H., *Sozialreport 1992. Daten und Fakten zur sozialen Situation in Sachsen Anhalt* (Magdeburg, Institut für Soziologie, 1992).

Hradil, S., *Sozialstrukturanalyse in einer fortgeschrittenen Gesellschaft* (Opladen, Leske and Budrich, 1983).

Jugend '92. Gesamtdarstellung und biographische Porträts. ed. Jugendwerk der Deutschen Shell (Opladen, Leske Budrich, 1992).

Kolinsky, E., 'Women in the New Germany – the East–West Divide', in Smith, G. et al. (eds), *Developments in German Politics* (London, Macmillan, 1992), pp. 264–80.

Kolinsky, E., 'Women in the New Germany', in Kolinsky, E., *Women in Contemporary Germany* (Oxford, Berg Publishers, 1993), pp. 259–94.

Kolinsky, E. (1995a), *Women in 20th Century Germany* (Manchester, Manchester University Press, 1995).

Kolinsky, E. (ed.) (1995b), *Between Hope and Fear. Everyday Life in Post-Unification East Germany* (Keele, Keele University Press, 1995).

Kolinsky, E. (1995c), 'Everyday Life Transformed', in Kolinsky, E. (ed.), *Between Hope and Fear* (Keele, Keele University Press, 1995), pp. 17–38.

Kolinsky, E. (1995d), 'Women after *Muttipolitik*', in Kolinsky, E. (ed.), *Between Hope and Fear* (Keele, Keele University Press, 1995), pp. 177–200.

Kolinsky, E., 'Women in the New Germany', in Smith, G. et al. (eds), *Developments in German Politics*, 3rd edition (London, Macmillan, 1996), pp. 267–85.

Krause, P., 'Einkommensarmut in der Bundesrepublik Deutschland', *Aus Politik und Zeitgeschichte*, B 49, 1992.

Kröllmann, W., 'Die Bevölkerungsentwicklung der Bundesrepublik', in Conze, W. and Lepsius, L. R. (eds), *Sozialgeschichte der Bundesrepublik* (Stuttgart, Klett Cotta, 1985), pp. 66–114.

Leipziger Statistik, Statistischer Bericht, quarterly since 1990.

Martin, A., 'Entwicklung der Geburtenkennziffern in der Stadt Leipzig 1989 bis 1994', *Leipziger Statistik, Statistische Berichte* I, Quartal, 1995, pp. 10–11.

Myrdal, A. and Klein, V., *Die Doppelrolle der Frau in Familie und Beruf* (Cologne, Wissenschaft and Politik, 1957).

Nickel, H. M. and Schenk, S., 'Prozesse geschlechtsspezifischer Differenzierung im Erwerbssystem', in Nickel, H. M. et al. (eds), *Erwerbsarbeit und Beschäftigung im Umbruch* (Berlin, Akademie Verlag, 1994), pp. 259–82.

Nickel, H. M., Kühl, J. and Schenk, S. (eds), *Erwerbsarbeit und Beschäftigng im Umbruch* (Berlin, Akademie Verlag, 1994).

Niermann, J., 'Identitätsfindung von Jugendlichen in den neuen Bundesländern', Bonn, 18 September 1991 (unpublished report to the *Bundestag* commission on *Youth and Women*).

Rink, D., 'Leipzig: Gewinnerin unter den Verlierern?', in Vester, M., Hofmann, M. and Zierke, I. (eds), *Soziale Milieus in Ostdeutschland. Gesellschaftliche Strukturen zwischen Zerfall und Neubildung* (Cologne, Bund Verlag, 1995), pp. 51–90.

Smith, E. O., *The German Economy* (London, Macmillan, 1994).

Starke, U., 'Young People: Lifestyles, Expectations and Value Orientations since the *Wende*', in Kolinsky, E. (ed.), *Between Hope and Fear* (Keele, Keele University Press, 1995), pp. 155–76.

Strohmeier, K. P., 'Pluralisierung und Polarisierung der Lebensformen in Deutschland', *Aus Politik und Zeitgeschichte*, B 17, 1993.

Vester, M., 'Milieuwandel und regionaler Strukturwandel in Ostdeutschland', in Vester, M., Hofmann, M. and Zierke, I. (eds), *Soziale Milieus in Ostdeutschland. Gesellschaftliche Strukturen zwischen Zerfall und Neubildung* (Cologne, Bund Verlag, 1995), pp. 7–50.

Vester, M., Hofmann, M. and Zierke, I. (eds), *Soziale Milieus in Ostdeutschland. Gesellschaftliche Strukturen zwischen Zerfall und Neubildung* (Cologne, Bund Verlag, 1995).

Winkler, G. (ed.), '*Frauenreport '90*' (Berlin, Verlag Die Wirtschaft, 1990).

11 Women in Russia and the Former USSR: Politics, Society and Culture

Rosalind Marsh

Seven years after the fall of the Soviet Communist Party, which had the emancipation of women as one of its overt aims, it is time to take stock of the contemporary situation of women in post-communist Russia and the former USSR. This chapter will propose a theoretical and historical framework within which the experience of post-Soviet women can usefully be analysed, then provide an overview of some key issues affecting women in Russia and the Soviet successor states, focusing particularly on women's role in politics and the economy, and the social position and cultural representation of women, notably the increase in pornography, prostitution and violence against women. Other important issues, such as nationalism and the women's movement, will be referred to only briefly, since they have been extensively discussed elsewhere (Funk and Mueller, 1993; Bridger et al., 1996; Marsh, 1998b; Konstantinova, 1994, Kay, forthcoming). The discussion presented here makes no claim to be comprehensive, but simply to complement and update previous research (Buckley, 1992; Corrin, 1992; Posadskaya, 1994; Marsh, 1996; Rule and Noonan, 1996), and to stimulate debate on some vital questions.

THE THEORETICAL AND HISTORICAL CONTEXT

In considering the current position of women in Russia and the post-Soviet states, it is necessary to bear in mind certain general points. First, women cannot be analysed as one single 'category', either throughout the world or in individual countries or cultures. This is, however, the approach still adopted by the majority of post-Soviet politicians, sociologists and journalists, following the Soviet ideological tendency to develop policies based on an abstract collective identity – 'women'. The political leaders in the newly independent states, many of whom are ex-communists, and all of whom are men, have chosen to perpetuate this myth. Policies towards women in post-Soviet Russia continue to be formulated largely in relation to the family and demographic problems, as was demonstrated by the name given to the Commission for Women, Family and Demography attached to President Yeltsin's office in 1993.

Second, it is impossible to generalize about women's experience in the former Soviet Union, which is an area of tremendous disparity, chaos and dislocation. It has been estimated that by 1996 approximately six million former Soviet citizens had been displaced from their homes (Vladimirov, 1996); and that in the years 1989–95, 2 159 200 ethnic Russians (out of a possible total of 25 289 700) migrated from other states of the former USSR back to the Russian Federation (Grafora, 1997, p. 12). After the breakdown of the unitary state and the monolithic vision of the Communist Party, a range of differences now exists in women's experience, both between the multinational post-Soviet states and between women of different ethnic groups, ages, classes and professions within the Russian Federation itself. Such diversity is potentially liberating, but it also makes it well-nigh impossible to create any unity within the emerging women's movement, thus limiting women's influence in mainstream politics.

For all their diversity, Russia and the other post-Soviet states do share two common features: the revival of nationalism and a situation of economic crisis during the period of transition to a market system. Both these factors – a developing nationalism and economic crisis – seem historically to have been conducive to a conservative approach to the position of women. During a period of national revival (whether German Nazism, Italian Fascism, Islamic fundamentalism or the national resurgence in contemporary East-Central Europe and the Soviet successor states), emphasis is generally placed on women's reproductive and nurturing roles, rather than their role in the workforce. If a period of national revival coincides with a serious economic crisis, women are the first to be driven out of the labour market; and the number of women in top professional positions and representative bodies decreases. Sometimes the issue of abortion is revisited, with some sections of society seeking a total ban in order to increase the indigenous population and prevent it from being overwhelmed by alien immigrants.[1] All these elements are present in the national revival in Russia and the Soviet successor states.

In Russia, the catastrophic decline in the birth rate, which in 1993 was one of the lowest in the world (9.2 per 10 000 members of the population), the increase in the mortality rate (from 10.5 per 10 000 in 1987 to 14.6 in 1993: Khudyakova, 1994a), along with the diminishing proportion of ethnic Russians in the population, has helped to reinforce this nationalistic message (Pervyshin, 1993). The readiness of many Russian women to accept the link between nationalism and conservative propaganda

(Lipovskaya, 1992a) has been demonstrated by their participation in the new discourse of national survival which regards women as self-sacrificing mothers and 'saviours of the nation' (*Predvybornaya platforma...*, 1993; Khamrayev, 1995; Pilkington, 1996b, pp. 169–71).

Another factor which links the numerous ethnic groups, classes, professional groups and both sexes in the post-Soviet states is the search for new identities and values to fill the ideological vacuum created by the collapse of communism. In the case of women, the general psychological and intellectual confusion of the post-Soviet period has been aggravated by the sexual revolution and changing propaganda about gender roles. Nevertheless, an alternative way of looking at these changes is that they could help to promote 'cultural individualization', a process in which the transformation of gender identities might be accelerated (Rotkirch and Haavio-Mannila, 1996; Bridger et al., 1996).

It has, however, become clear by the late 1990s that, whatever the political system in Russia, it has always had negative consequences for women. Under the tsars, the Soviet regime and the new post-communist rulers, power has always been in the hands of Russian men who have legislated for women. The new political parties and movements of the perestroika and post-perestroika eras have primarily been interested in liberating people from the communist system, and have little interest in women's rights; and these attitudes have been carried on into the post-communist governments. Some Russian feminists have called the system which has developed since 1990 'male democracy' (Lipovskaya, 1992c), or a 'men's club' (Semenova, 1992). Certainly, democratization in Russia does seem to have been a gendered concept (Pilkington, 1992, p. 218), granting men and women equal rights in the formal sense, but suggesting that their duties were to be very different: women's would be based predominantly in the moral and spiritual realm, or more precisely, in the sphere of private life.

In spite of the disturbing contemporary situation, Western feminists must be careful not to impose their own modes of thinking uncritically on women from the former USSR. Many women in the post-Soviet states are highly suspicious of Western *feministki* who, in their opinion, have an easy life and cannot possibly understand their problems (Tolstaya, 1990; Lipovskaya, 1992b). The reasons why Russian women have so little sympathy for Western-style feminism have often been explored (Lissyutkina, 1993; Marsh, 1996), but perhaps the main reason for their continuing hostility in the post-communist period is that 'feminism' has been constructed as intimately linked with discredited Soviet socialism, as yet another repressive 'ideology' hostile to the individual (Erofeyev, 1995, p. xxiv), and, increasingly, as a Western import alien to the true interests of Russian society (Rasputin, 1990; Goryachev, 1997).

The conservative attitudes to women propagated in the post-communist era can be traced to long-standing patriarchal Russian and Soviet attitudes towards women (Stites, 1978; Buckley, 1989; Clements et al., 1991). More immediately, they hark back to the pro-natalist policy espoused by the Brezhnev regime in the 1970s, and the backlash against female emancipation characteristic of the perestroika era, when Gorbachev announced his desire to rectify the 'sincere and politically justified desire to make women equal with men in everything' (Gorbachev, 1987, p. 117).

However imperfect women's emancipation was under the Soviet regime, in the post-Soviet period the collapse of the Communist Party and the rise of nationalism have led to many changes in women's lives which are retrogressive from a Western feminist point of view. The former image of women and men as equal partners in the building of socialism has been replaced by that of the traditional family in which men work outside the home and women devote themselves to child-care and domestic duties (Khudyakova, 1991).

WOMEN AND POLITICS

Under Gorbachev and Yeltsin, women have possessed even less power in mainstream politics than in earlier periods of Soviet history. Gorbachev's democratization reforms actually reduced the percentage of women at the highest level of government, which dropped to a low point of 5.4 per cent in the 1990 elections to the RSFSR Congress of People's Deputies, since no seats were now reserved for official women's organizations (Buckley, 1992, pp. 54–71). Nevertheless, since the late 1980s women have played a prominent part in grass-roots political movements, attending demonstrations, organizing meetings, electioneering and voting. In Lithuania, for example, they were seen as particularly important in the 'singing revolution', which led to the declaration of independence in March 1990 (White, N., 1993). However, a highly symbolic episode occurred during the attempted coup of August 1991, when women were requested to withdraw from the Russian parliament and leave its defence to men. Some women left, but the rest indignantly refused to go, arguing with the soldiers on their tanks and protesting that they had an equal right to participate in the political life of their country (Posadskaya, 1994, pp. 1–2).

It is, however, a fact that when the post-communist governments and new power structures were being formed, women seemed to fade out of the picture. The few women in Yeltsin's successive administrations have not survived for long. Galina Starovoitova, his adviser on nationality issues, was dismissed in 1992; and Ella Pamfilova, the Minister of Social

Protection of the Population, resigned in January 1994 because she felt unable to tackle social problems effectively, or even to gain access to the Prime Minister Chernomyrdin (Valyuzhenich, 1994).[2] Subsequently, there have been only token women ministers, in traditionally 'feminine' areas of interest. Lyudmila Bezlepkina was appointed Minister of Social Protection in May 1995; but by mid-1997 there was only one woman minister in Yeltsin's government, Tatyana Dmitrieva, the Minister of Public Health (appointed in August 1996 and reappointed in the March 1997 reshuffle). Since about February 1996, during Yeltsin's re-election campaign and his subsequent illness, probably the most powerful woman in Russia has been one who possesses no formal political position – Yeltsin's daughter, Tatyana Dyachenko (sometimes dubbed 'Princess Tatyana') – a situation which has proved unacceptable to many Russians (Koshkareva, 1996).[3] By February 1997, according to an opinion poll, no woman politician figured in the list of the top hundred leading Russian politicians ('100 vedushchikh politikov ... ', 1997).

The reasons why women are not more prominent in mainstream politics vary across the post-Soviet states, but two important factors are the persistent belief that politics is a 'man's world' (Popov, 1989; Aivazova, 1991), and the fact that women have other priorities, not least the daily struggle to feed their family. One commonly articulated belief is that Russians will not vote for women (Vasileva, 1989). Women are still much more acceptable as behind-the-scenes organizers, while men carry out frequently less demanding public duties.

Even in the 1990s, women prominent in public life are often treated with patronizing sarcasm (Kirpichnikov, 1994; Starovoitova, 1998a). A typical recent example was an interview in 1996 with the newly appointed Minister of Health Tatyana Dmitrieva, which ignored her policies, but included questions about her looks, her husband and her domestic arrangements ('The Woman in Yeltsin's Cabinet', *Rossiiskaya gazeta,* 24 August 1996). The fact that such questions could be asked with impunity, and that the interviewee did not seem to mind, speaks volumes about contemporary Russian attitudes towards women politicians.

Until the post-communist period there was little agreement among women activists as to whether they should form political parties, or simply act as an interest group lobbying the government. At the Second Dubna Forum of November 1992, many Russian women expressed a reluctance to participate in the patriarchal power structures, but others argued that, unless women sought power, their political influence would remain so weak that women's issues (such as female unemployment, rape, contraception and abortion) would either be kept off political agendas or, at best, be accorded low priority.

After Yeltsin's suspension of Parliament in September 1993, the 'Women of Russia' political movement was formed. This bloc managed to achieve relative success in the December 1993 elections, taking 8.1 per cent of the vote for the 225 seats in the Duma (Parliament) awarded on the basis of proportional representation from party lists, which meant that 21 candidates were elected; and at least two of the 26 women candidates elected according to a system of first past the post in single-mandate districts (and another two were sympathizers: overall there were 23 or 25 Women of Russia deputies: Slater, 1994; Pilkington, 1996b; Rule and Shvedova, 1996).[4] The total number of women candidates in the Duma amounted to 60 (13.5 per cent); but it was only because of the moderately good showing of the Women of Russia political movement that the proportion of women was greater than in the preceding Parliament of 1990–3. This achievement suggested that some Russian women at least were prepared to vote for other women, and that women's issues would have some airing in post-communist Russia. The Women of Russia bloc, however, is by no means a radical feminist movement, but a descendant of the Committee of Soviet Women (the official women's organization under the Communist regime), a centrist party whose main concerns are traditional feminine values of home and family[5] – the only kind of women's politics acceptable to the majority of Russian women.

THE DUMA ELECTIONS OF DECEMBER 1995

A new low in women's representation in Russian politics occurred in December 1995, in the elections to the Duma. Before the elections, Ekaterina Lakhova, co-leader of Women of Russia, had made a confident prediction on Russian Public Television that her movement would achieve a vote of 5.5 per cent ('Women of Russia leader ... ', 1995). However, her bloc failed to clear the 5 per cent barrier to representation in the Duma through the list system (the final result was 4.62 per cent of the vote). Of all the associations which were unsuccessful in the elections (and only four were successful), the Women of Russia movement appears to have been the most unfortunate, since it cleared the 5 per cent barrier in 44 regions of the Russian Federation. That was more regions than gave 5 per cent to Yabloko ('Apple', the democratic Yavlinsky-Boldyrev-Lukin Bloc), which did get into parliament, but the 'women's regions' were less populous or had a lower turnout than Yabloko's regions (Lavrov, 1996). The reduced fortunes of 'Women of Russia' in the 1995 elections may demonstrate some disillusionment among Russian women with the movement's marginality and ineffectiveness in Russian politics (and also, perhaps, its initial support for the intervention in Chechnya in 1994). Their poor showing might also reflect the fact that by 1995 their programme had become virtually indistinguishable from that of other moderate nationalist movements with essentialist views of women.

Another reason for their failure was that by 1995, in order to compete with Women of Russia, male-dominated political parties had attempted to incorporate women into their movements, with considerable success. Several other parties (the Communist Party of the Russian Federation, Forward, Russia!, Russia's Democratic Choice, Power to the People and Yabloko) included a woman among their top three candidates (an important position, because the actual ballot paper lists only the top three names for each state). Thus, ostensibly, women were playing a larger part in these elections than they had done in the past, but this advantage was more apparent than real, since women had a low representation in most party lists, ranging from 5.8 per cent in Zhirinovsky's Liberal Democratic Party to 20.6 per cent in Ryzhkov's 'Power to the People' (not a very significant party which gained little support in the elections), with 13.4 per cent in Chernomyrdin's centrist party 'Our Home is Russia' (*Rossiiskaya gazeta*, 6 September – 17 October 1995). In consequence, there are only 46 women in the current Duma – 10 per cent of the total number of Deputies. Moreoever, after the elections, only parties which cleared the 5 per cent barrier were allowed to obtain the chairmanship of Duma committees. As a result, in the years 1996–7 there were only two women chairs of Duma committees: Alevtina Aparina (Russian Federation Communist Party) chaired the Committee on Women's Affairs, and Tamara Zlotnikova (Yabloko) chaired the Committee on Ecology (Yuriev, 1996).

THE PRESIDENTIAL ELECTIONS OF JUNE/JULY 1996

A similar picture emerged in the presidential elections of 1996. Of the 78 people originally nominated as 'candidate for candidate for the presidency' in January 1996, there were only four women: Irina Khakamada, who stated that she would support Yeltsin; Galina Starovoitova, who said that she would support Yavlinsky; and two lesser-known figures, Tamara Bazyleva, the President of Human Ecology International Concern, and Galina Sharova, the General Director of the Nord-Komplekt Firm, a closed-type, joint-stock company. Of these, only Starovoitova cleared the next hurdle by obtaining one million signatures.[6] However, in May the Supreme Court upheld the Central Electoral Commission's decision not to register Starovoitova as a candidate for President, since they claimed that 283 315 signatures on her registration documents 'had been falsified' ('Verkhovnyi Sud...', 1996). Eventually, therefore, no woman candidate stood in the presidential election.

WOMEN'S POLITICAL INFLUENCE

Recent political experience in Russia in the years 1995–6 suggests that women are likely to wield even less power in mainstream politics than in the past. However, the tradition of women's grass-roots political activity (Lipovskaya, 1992a; Konstantinova, 1994) has continued into the post-communist period: during the Russian intervention in Chechnya in 1994–6 in which, according to official statistics, an estimated 80 000 people were killed and 240 000 were wounded and disabled (although the real figure may be far higher: 'Chislo ubitykh...', 1996), Chechen and Russian women mounted separate non-violent protests against military action (Meek, 1994; Zabelina, 1996).

It is now clear that democratization in Russia has not entailed the gaining by women of a political voice, since the balance has shifted to the male-dominated arenas of formal politics. Post-communist Russia in crisis has been even more inhospitable to the political participation of women than the former Soviet Union, for a number of reasons. First, the elimination of official quotas for women has diminished both the number of women who stand for election and those who get elected into Parliament. Second, the majority of women continue to have a negative attitude to mainstream politics, and choose to concentrate on other, local activities which they perceive as more immediate and valuable. They doubt the efficacy of local and national political bodies, and in any case have no time for political involvement: others remain sceptical about the value of a separate women's party. Third, economic crisis and nationalist propaganda have driven many women back into the home: the overwhelming preoccupation of most women is simply to survive and support their families. Finally, many women have become disillusioned with the marginalization and powerlessness of the small minority of women who have managed to achieve some representation in the national arena.

It could, however, be argued that in a system which gives so much power to the presidency and the government, representation in Parliament is relatively ineffectual for all Russians, regardless of gender, and that exerting direct influence on the President is more important. Yeltsin and his government have made some attempt to incorporate women's issues into their political programme. At the end of 1992, a 15-strong 'Group of Gender Expertise' was established within the Supreme Soviet of the Russian Federation, with the aim of helping Russian parliamentarians and legislators to create laws which would take into account the specific interests of both sexes. This objective was significant, because all Russian laws had previously been non-gender specific.

Members of the Women of Russia movement claim that they have been successful in influencing government policy, especially through Ekaterina Lakhova, a long-time associate of Yeltsin's from Sverdlovsk, who in 1992 was appointed chair of the Commission for Women, Family and Demography attached to the President's office, and, according to one Russian feminist (Posadskaya, 1994, p. 192), played a 'relatively positive' role. However, others might take a less optimistic viewpoint. Yeltsin's female political advisers have undoubtedly achieved some success in obtaining the reconsideration of new labour and family laws which would have made women unprofitable employees (Sargeant, 1996). Perhaps their greatest achievement to date has been to get the draft law 'For the Protection of the Family, Motherhood, Fatherhood and Children' re-examined and finally shelved in 1993, on the grounds that it violated the norms of the constitution of the Russian Federation, the European Commission of Human Rights and the United Nations Convention on the Elimination of Discrimination against Women (Lyuka, 1992; Khudyakova, 1992; Pilkington, 1996b). This can be partially ascribed to the combined influence exerted by Lakhova, other members of the Group of Gender Expertise who later joined the Women of Russia political movement, and liberal feminists associated with the Moscow Gender Centre. A more important factor, however, may simply have been the unstable political situation of 1993. Yeltsin's female political advisers also helped to formulate the new family code, signed by Yeltsin on 1 March 1996, which, despite the great opposition it aroused from some male activists (Tyurin, 1995), does not include many revolutionary provisions, although it does contain certain new regulations about divorce, alimony, adoption and guardianship (*Semeinyi kodeks...*, 1996). It also introduces the possibility of concluding pre-nuptial agreements (Polenina, 1996), which may be of significant value to housewives abandoned by their 'new Russian' husbands. In general, however, women political advisers in post-communist Russia have played a predominantly defensive role, rather than a positive role in initiating new policy on women's issues.

Although, as Azhgikhina (1997) comments, the year 1996 was marked by 'unprecedented lawmaking activity in the area of "supporting women" ' in Russia, the Budget of 1997 did not envisage the expenditure of a single rouble to implement the numerous women's programmes. Ironically, it is possible that the appointment in May 1997 of a man, the Deputy Prime Minister Oleg Sysuev, to head a special commission on the role of women, might demonstrate the Yeltsin government's greater readiness to take women's issues more seriously in future. Nevertheless, a spokeswoman for the Russian government found this decision rather puzzling: 'It is strange, as a woman would be in a better position to address these issues, but that's how things work around here' ('Man-sized solution...', 1997).

WOMEN AND ECONOMIC CRISIS

Since the late 1980s, women have borne the brunt of the economic crisis, and, as they still do most of the shopping, they have been most affected by the deficits and hyper-inflation of the post-communist era. Since the price rises of April 1991 and January 1992 and the 'shock therapy' implemented by the Gaidar government in 1993–4, poverty and unemployment have had a disproportionate effect on women, particularly among elderly women (Millinship, 1993, pp. 25–9; Gerasimova, 1996), rural women (Terekhov, 1993, Sukhova, 1998), and those in low-paid service jobs. In a series of recent interviews, Russian women have expressed their feelings about the sharp cut in the quality of their lives in such terms as 'catastrophe', 'fear', 'disaster', 'demolition', 'anarchy', and so on (Eremicheva, 1996, p. 154).

Unemployment

One of the proudest boasts of Soviet socialism was that over 90 per cent of women were in paid employment. Under Gorbachev and Yeltsin, however, the state's economic needs have been conveniently defined to coincide with the aspiration to return to traditional gender roles. The economic rationale behind the powerful campaign urging women to go back to the home became abundantly clear in 1993, when the Russian Minister of Labour posed the rhetorical question: 'Why do we have to give work to women when there are men unemployed?' (*Moscow Times*, 16 February 1993). Whether by accident or design, recent protective legislation concerning women's employment and benefits, particularly the enforcement of the law on women's entitlement to three years' maternity leave, has placed women in a more unfavourable competitive position with respect to men in the transition to a market economy. Moreover, since crèches and kindergartens have either closed altogether or are prohibitively expensive for most families because of the removal of state subsidies in January 1992 (Millinship,

1993, pp. 4–5), many women have little choice but to stay at home. By 1996, since the number of pre-school institutions had been almost halved, the only alternative was for working mothers to lock their children in all day (Nadezhdina, 1996). While statistical data are variable and unreliable, the general consensus among commentators is that unemployed women outnumber men in a ratio of about 70:30 (Pankova, 1993; Nadezhdina, 1996; Rotkirch and Haavio-Mannila, 1996; Bridger et al., 1996).

Few Russian policy-makers or journalists have bothered to discover the views of women on 'returning them to the home'. A recent study does suggest that many women are initially relieved at being able to shed their 'double burden' of paid work and domestic duties, but that subsequently it is easier for younger women (and particularly for women from the wealthy class of 'new Russians') to adjust to their lack of employment outside the home than for older women brought up under the Soviet system (Zdravosmyslova, 1996). For many women in Russia and the post-Soviet states, employment is closely linked with their sense of identity.

Feminized Poverty and Hardship

In 1993, it was estimated that women's average real pay was one-third lower than men's, while their pensions were only worth 70 per cent of the value of men's (Pankova, 1993). Although in 1996, in the run-up to the presidential election, the minimum pension was raised to 82 per cent of the minimum living standard (on 1 August 1996 the Duma passed a law raising it again), the position of elderly women is likely to remain critical in the future, especially as one out of five people in Russia is now over 60 ('Russians are Beginning ... ', 1996).

In the mid-1990s, daily life continues to be as hard, or harder than ever for many women in Russia and the post-Soviet states. Even with the introduction of the market system, many women do not have access to all the essential convenience products and services taken for granted by women in the West. By no means all homes yet possess labour-saving devices such as washing machines; tinned baby food is in short supply (Likhanov, 1996); and tampons are very expensive and not available throughout the country. Horrific conditions still prevail in maternity hospitals (Shafran, 1994; Tutorskaya, 1996); and although official abortion statistics are decreasing (Timashova, 1995),[7] it is still true that 'given the backwardness of the country's pharmaceutical industry, the main method of terminating a pregnancy is abortion' (Baiduzhii, 1994, p. 19; see also Borzenko, 1994). Although by the mid-1990s both contraceptives and information on family planning had become more readily available (although the pill remains in short supply), many women and couples still find contraceptives either psychologically unacceptable, unreliable, unavailable or very expensive (Remennick, 1993, p. 56; Baiduzhii, 1994; Kigai, 1996).

Women's Economic Activity

In Russia and the post-Soviet states the interests of many women are being sacrificed to the transformation from a 'full employment' economic and political system to a quasi-capitalist system. The market system has emphasized traditionally 'masculine' qualities, such as aggression and rationality, independence, competitiveness and the willingness to take risks (Attwood, 1996). On the positive side, women who exhibit such characteristics now have the opportunity to start up their own businesses – if they also have money and know-how. It should not be assumed that all Russian women are simply passively returning to the home; many have been engaged in formal or informal economic activity (Bridger et al., 1996). Since 1994, however, many previously successful women's businesses have been forced to close because of high rents and interest rates (not to mention protection money) and those that remain have been concerned almost solely with survival strategies (Bridger and Kay, 1996).

Nevertheless, Russian women frequently speak highly of their own potential, and complain about the general helplessness of Russian men. Although such feelings could simply be dismissed as anti-male rhetoric, by the late-1990s such protestations are taken increasingly seriously in some quarters. Women's greater reliability, honesty and organizational skills are being increasingly valued by foreign firms (Bruno, 1996, pp. 53–4) and by commercial enterprises and banking (Sklyar, 1994). In October 1994, for example, Tatyana Paramonova was appointed acting head of the Central Bank, and at the time it seemed possible that such appointments might mark the beginning of a shift in social and economic attitudes towards women. However, the subsequent swift rejection of Paramonova as head of the bank demonstrated that, even when Russian women do attain positions of power in the economy, their jobs are far from secure.

THE SOCIAL POSITION AND CULTURAL REPRESENTATION OF WOMEN

The current status of women has also been lowered by the manner in which social problems affecting women – pornography, prostitution, rape and violence against women – have been publicized, propagating an image of women as sex objects and victims of violence (Attwood, 1993, 1996). Previously, Western feminists had praised the absence of such images, which stemmed from the ban on pornography and lack of advertising in the USSR, and had favourably contrasted Soviet restraint with the wide-spread denigration of women as sexual playthings, victims or temptresses in the West. However, this situation changed rapidly under glasnost, demonstrating that, as in the case of national enmities, such feelings had simply been repressed, not eradicated. Yet whereas glasnost and the limited freedom of speech which followed it (White, S., 1993, pp. 94–101) allowed the Russian press to discuss many issues affecting women's health and reproduction which could formerly only be discussed in *samizdat*, such as abortion, contraception, venereal disease and AIDS (Buckley, 1990), issues which concerned male behaviour, such as domestic violence and rape, only came to be widely discussed in the 1990s.

Hitherto the freedom brought by the 'sexual revolution' in Russia has mainly affected the male half of the population at the expense of the female half, since the society experiencing the revolution was male dominated in the first place. In culture and the media, men are generally presented as the subjects of sexual relations, women are primarily seen as the victims of male sexuality or as sexual deviants themselves. In the mid-1990s, issues of primary concern only to women, such as lesbianism (Toktaleva, 1989; Alenin, 1994) and feminism (Posadskaya, 1994; Kravchenko, 1995), are frequently still treated in a superficial or sensationalist manner.

PORNOGRAPHY

One depressing aspect of the cultural representation of women in contemporary Russia is the dissemination of pornography, which began in about 1989 and has proliferated in the 1990s throughout the former Soviet Union (Goscilo, 1993; Attwood, 1996). Although forbidden by law, pornography has not been satisfactorily defined, so it has been difficult to challenge. Since the late 1980s, debates about pornography have generally failed to examine the objectification of women or the mentality of the consumer, but have generally concentrated on the imputed immorality of the women who are being portrayed. Russian feminists have been faced with the same dilemma as many of their Western counterparts: while generally regretting the prevalence of pornography in their society, they dislike censorship even more, and believe that individuals must be free to reject it for themselves (Posadskaya, 1994, p. 199; Stishova, 1996).

Some Russian feminists have spoken out against pornography. Tatyana Klimenkova, for example, has argued (1994, pp. 21, 31) that the aim of the current 'sexual revolution' in Russia is not to emancipate women through sex, as in the West in the 1960s, but to 'make society sick through pornography' and present sexuality 'as man's natural right deliberately to degrade women through sex'. However, most Russian feminists have chosen not to campaign actively against pornography, but have simply expressed the vague (and vain) hope that over-exposure will ultimately lead to boredom.

The dilemma for Russian feminists became particularly acute in 1994, when, in a new government attempt to clamp down on pornography, the publisher of the erotic magazine *Eshche*, Aleksei Kostin, was arrested and interrogated for three months in Butyrki prison. A 'round table' discussion of this issue by avant-garde intellectuals indignantly defending freedom of the press included only one woman, Mariya Arbatova, a writer and president of the international feminist club 'Harmony', who condemned the magazine as 'untalented' and did not sign the protest letter demanding Kostin's release ('Erotika i vlast', 1994).

Although pornography has not been at the centre of attention in the former Soviet Union, it has reinforced images of male power and female passivity. There are still relatively few positive sexual images of women in Russian culture: although some recent stories by women writers are beginning to treat women's sexuality in a non-judgemental way (for example, Valeriya Narbikova's *The Equilibrium of Diurnal and Night-time Stars* (1988), Marina Palei's *Cabiriya from the Bypass* (1991) and Lyudmila Ulitskaya's *Lyalya's House* and *Gulya* (1994)), such representations are relatively rare, and have often been critically received. Male psychologists in contemporary Russia often take a negative view of female sexuality, analysing women's role as simply the satisfaction of men's needs (Shchogolev, 1990), while many works of fiction by Russian men, such as Viktor Erofeyev's *Russian Beauty* (1990) and Anatoly Kurchatkin's *The Watchwoman* (1993), depict women fulfilling male fantasies.

Although in the late 1990s there seems to be less low-grade pornography of the native Russian variety available on the streets, this gap has been filled by glossy foreign imports. In June 1996, feminists of the Petersburg Centre for Gender Issues filed a suit against the Russian edition of *Playboy* because of its series of pornographic pictures of famous women in Russian history, including a topless Catherine the Great, and a masturbating Sofya Kovalevskaya (the famous mathematician).

PROSTITUTION

Another aspect of the sexual revolution, which has eroticized male domination, is the enhanced cultural role of the prostitute. The most prevalent image in the press and films has been of a brazen young woman who picks up foreign businessmen at Intourist hotels, motivated by the possibility of earning foreign currency, or, if she is particularly fortunate, of marrying her way out of the country (as in Petr Todorovskii's film *Interdevochka* (*International Girl*, 1989)). Western commentators have generally argued that prostitution, which can no longer be attributed solely to the evils of capitalist society, has been presented in the Russian press as an example of the moral dissoluteness or sexual deviancy of women (Pilkington, 1992, pp. 226–7; Heldt, 1992), since in the perestroika era little attention was paid to the dangers faced by prostitutes, the poverty which often drove women, particularly single mothers, into prostitution, or, most importantly, the responsibility of the client, as opposed to the prostitute herself. In the post-communist era, however, some articles have reported more frankly on the violence suffered by prostitutes and their exploitation by pimps (Baranovskii and Aleinik, 1993).

According to some Russian commentators, a transformation has taken place in Russian society's view of prostitution:

> Previously, the 'most ancient profession' was publicly condemned; now it's becoming more accepted. Some specialists of sociology and sexology even speak through the media about the positive social aspects of it.
>
> (Lipovskaya, 1992c, p. 24)

Elena Stishova (1996) has emphasized the extraordinary reversal of values which has allowed hard-currency prostitutes to enjoy great prestige in contemporary Russia, a view borne out by a 1989 survey of schoolgirls who reportedly regarded the profession of hard-currency prostitute as an attractive one, preferable to that of school teacher (*Literaturnaya gazeta*, 8 February 1989). Similarly, an article of 1990 claimed that 25 per cent of prostitutes have a higher degree, 8.5 per cent are university students and 26 per cent are married and practising prostitution with their husband's approval (*Izvestiya*, 24 March 1990). In Russia the prostitute has even been regarded as an example of an 'independent businesswoman' ('Eshche odna ... ', 1990). By the mid-1990s, prostitution had become a widespread business – the third-largest sphere of criminal activity in terms of the amount of money involved, after gambling and the drug business (Bateneva, 1996).

Whereas lurid stories of prostitution and international trafficking in women have proliferated in the post-communist press, an even more widespread problem in Russia is the 'undercover prostitution' practised by many ordinary women in order to gain jobs, housing and consumer goods (Bridger and Kay, 1996). Another important issue which has only just begun to be discussed in Russia in the mid-1990s is sexual harassment at work, which affects a large number of Russian women, although it is not usually taken seriously by Russian men (Shtyleva, 1996).

RAPE

Glasnost also introduced discussion of women as victims of sexual abuse: statistics released by the Ministry of Internal Affairs showed a 120 per cent increase in the incidence of rape in 1989 as compared with 1988, and the figures up to 1990 also showed a marked increase (*Zhenshchiny...*, 1992, p. 771). In the 1990s the alarming increase in gang rape has been a particular cause of concern (Yakov, 1993); child sexual abuse and juvenile rape are also widespread, but frequently remain unreported (Bateneva, 1996).

Although it is generally agreed that the apparent decrease in official rape statistics in the early 1990s was a false trend (Pilkington, 1996b, p. 11), the figures are still misleadingly low. In 1993, for example, almost 14 500 rapes and violent sex crimes were reported in Russia, but this probably represented only a fraction of the real number (Yakov, 1993). In 1995, when a lower figure of 12 500 rapes was officially recorded in the Russian Federation, women working at 'Sisters', one of the two women's crisis centres in Moscow, claimed that only 2 per cent of victims of sexual aggression turn to the police. The widespread failure to report the crime has been explained by one female journalist as being a result of the 'paradox' that 'for some reason, in the eyes of public opinion, rape victims almost always bear some of the blame for what happened' (Sotnikova, 1996). Similarly, Natalya Gaidarenko, founder of 'Sisters', quoted one rape victim as saying that a police officer had dismissed her complaint with the remark: 'What are you so upset about? It's not as if you're a virgin, after all' (*Nezavisimaya gazeta*, 18 January 1996, p. 16). Even when rape is discussed in the media, the tone is frequently unfavourable to women (Attwood, 1997): the moral virtue of the woman often appears to be of more interest to journalists – and the judiciary – than male violence against women.

DOMESTIC VIOLENCE

The implication of women in male aggression can also be seen in discussions of domestic violence, a persistent problem in contemporary Russia. In 1993 alone, 54 400 women reportedly received serious injuries at the hands of their husbands, and 14 500 died (Zabelina, 1996, p. 181). Male violence in Russia is often ascribed to drunkenness, and, directly or indirectly, includes criticism of wives for not finding time to be loving enough to their husbands, thus driving them to the bottle. One positive development, however, is that some women have been stung to protest publicly that they should not be held responsible for men's dissolute behaviour and neglect of their families (Ronina, 1988).

Recent developments in the field of domestic violence have been slightly (but only slightly) more promising than those related to rape. A draft federal law, 'On Preventing Domestic Violence', was presented to the State Duma in October 1995 by women members of the Committee on the Affairs of Women, the Family and Young People, but its consideration was postponed, since the majority of the Parliament (which was almost 90 per cent male) regarded domestic violence not as a real social problem, but simply as petty domestic squabbling. The law was further postponed by the Duma in 1996 (Alimamedova, 1996).

The Duma deputy Mariya Gaidash argued in October 1995 that it was intolerable that Russian society did not recognize this problem, when 20 to 30 per cent of murders occurred within the family, every year about two million children suffered domestic abuse, and the situation for women was deteriorating because:

> we now have a large number of non-working women who are totally dependent economically on their husbands. Subjected to humiliations and sometimes even beatings by their husbands, they frequently see no other escape for themselves besides death.
>
> (Adamushkina, 1995)

In May 1996, the first crisis centre for battered women in St Petersburg, 'Women at Risk', was opened. The journalist Tatyana Kharlamova (1996), welcoming this development, nevertheless claimed that Russia was still far behind Western countries, and that every year, 14000 women died in Russia as a result of domestic violence (the figure in the US was 75 per cent lower).[8] The director of the new centre, psychologist Marina Pislakova, expressed views similar to those of Western feminists, stating that part of the problem was the socialization of children in Russia, where boys were brought up to be 'macho' and girls to be meek. In her opinion, there are many myths to be overcome in Russian culture before this problem can be satisfactorily dealt with: the myths of female provocation and masochism, and the myth that violence only takes place in socially disadvantaged families (Kharlamova, 1996). It could be added that, harking back to patriarchal Russian traditions (notably to the sixteenth-century manual *Domostroi,* or *Book of Household Management*), many Russian men appear to see nothing wrong in beating their wives – a view confirmed

by some recent fiction by Russian men, such as Vyacheslav Petsukh's
Central Yermolaevsk War of 1988 (Lipovskaya, 1994, p. 130).

MEDIA IMAGES

The post-Soviet states now propagate a contradictory mixture of age-old
traditional values and unprecedented, sometimes alarming new ideas on
the role and status of women. One Russian feminist has noted with dismay
that the image of womanhood propagated in contemporary Russian media
is 'a model as old as the world: the dualistic image of Madonna and
whore' (Lipovskaya, 1992c, p. 24). The current role models for women – the
strong, suffering mother, the virtuous woman or the sexual being – revive
the typology of the folk tale and traditional images in Russian culture
(Einhorn, 1993, pp. 40, 226; Marsh, 1998a), but whereas the Virgin Mary
and Mother Russia are ancient images in Russian culture, the current representation of the seductive whore as a Cinderella figure gives a new twist
to an old image. The Russian press also propagates an invented myth about
allegedly traditional Russian values of femininity and masculinity, frequently lamenting their loss (Lissyutkina, 1993), although a study of nineteenth-century Russian culture, with its emphasis on the 'superfluous man'
and the 'strong woman', would make one wonder whether such types ever
existed in reality. Although there are currently many women's newspapers
and magazines in Russia, these tend to depict traditional, conformist
images of women. The Barbie doll stereotype of femininity, formerly
ridiculed in Russia, is now heavily promoted.

The campaigns promoting women's traditional role and the images
of violence against women can be interpreted as different facets of the
same contemporary project of reasserting male dominance in the post-
Soviet states after decades of concern that women were challenging
male supremacy (Attwood, 1996). *A fortiori*, the current 'sexual counter-
revolution' of the mid-1990s, which has attempted to establish control over
women's bodies through imposing fees on abortion (Frolov, 1994) and
questioning the value of contraception and sex education (Kon, 1997),
along with the campaign to return women to the home, are an expression
of post-Soviet men's newly acquired control over what they perceive as
their own 'possessions', a reappropriation of male collective identity and a
symbol of having won back freedom and power from the Communist state.

CONCLUSION

Post-Soviet Russia in crisis has proved more inhospitable to women's interests than the Soviet regime. Women's status in Russia and the post-Soviet

states has been reduced because of the resurgence of nationalism, political instability, economic crisis and radical cultural change, particularly the propagation of essentialist views of women and the proliferation of pornography, prostitution and sexual violence.

Although by the late 1990s women's concerns have come to be discussed more frequently in the general media, there is little evidence that the flood of words on women's issues unleashed by glasnost and the freedom of speech which followed it has led to effective *action*. In the 1990s, the nationalist revival and transition to a market system have become the key values of the Russian Federation and the post-Soviet states, as opposed to the ideal of democratization formerly espoused by Gorbachev. 'Women's issues' in the post-Soviet states are still considered irrelevant or secondary to political, national and economic problems, and feminist questions are usually strongly opposed, silenced or ridiculed.

Although Yeltsin's government has taken some notice of women's opinions in formulating his policies, by the late 1990s it has become obvious that the problems of Russian women cannot be solved simply by the issuing of laws and presidential decrees, most of which are ignored (Azhgikhina, 1997). Nevertheless, Russian women's continuing reluctance to problematize gender roles is constantly challenged by the concrete transformations in everyday life. Recent interviews with Russian women, particularly businesswomen and activists in the women's movement (Rotkirch and Haavio-Mannila, 1996; Kay, forthcoming), demonstrate the great resilience and adaptability of many women who are developing new strategies in their personal and working lives to survive the process of rapid, often painful change in their society.

NOTES

1.   In both Russia and Lithuania, debates on abortion have taken place, although it has not yet been banned (Sazonov, 1993; White, N., 1993; Kon, 1997).

2.   In May 1994 Pamfilova took up a new post as director of a Council for Social Policy under Yeltsin (Khudyakova, 1994b). In the December 1995 elections she stood as the first candidate on the slate of the small Republican Party.

3.   In 1997 it was rumoured that Dyachenko had been invited to stand for election as Governor of Tula Province.

4.   There is some doubt about the exact figures, since the allegiance of some deputies is difficult to classify. Compare *Rossiiskaya gazeta*, 12 November 1993 and *Novaya ezhednevnaya gazeta*, 18 January 1994. For a critical assessment of Women of Russia, see Pilkington, 1996b; Rule and Shvedova (1996) take a more positive view.

5. It was formed from the Union of Women of Russia (the renamed Committee of Soviet Women), the Association of Businesswomen of Russia, and the Union of Women in the Navy.

6. Recent polls suggest that Starovoitova was positively viewed by democrats, but was not particularly popular among more conservative Russian women (*Segodnya*, 17 April 1996, p. 1; Temkina, 1996, p. 233). In 1997 Starovoitova, elected as an independent, was deprived of the right to speak at the Duma until the end of the session of 21 March because she had distributed to deputies allegedly insulting statements about Lenin and Stalin.

7. Timashova (1995) states that, according to official statistics, approximately 2.5 million abortions are performed in Russia every year, and the number has dropped by half in the past seven years. However, doctors consider this figure to be rather a low estimate, since it ignores illegal abortions. See the posthumously published interview with Starovoitova (1998b) for evidence that she was becoming increasingly aware of the discrimination against women in Russian politics before her murder in November 1998.

8. Moscow feminists helped to publicize this problem in August 1996 by publishing the first book ever produced in Russia on the subject of domestic violence and rape, Nadezhda Azhgikhina (ed.), *Who Defends Women?*

REFERENCES

'100 vedushchikh politikov Rossii v fevrale', *Nezavisimaya gazeta*, 4 March 1997, p. 1.

Adamushkina, M., 'Nasilie v seme? Net problemy', *Nezavisimaya gazeta*, 31 October 1995, p. 6.

Aivazova, S., 'Zhenshchiny v politike: norma ili iskliuchenie?', *Literaturnoe obozrenie*, No. 3, 1991, pp. 3–8.

Alenin, A., ' "Muzh moi Tanya" ', *Trud*, 16 February 1994, p. 4.

Alimamedova, L., 'Bitye deti', *Trud*, 29 May 1996, p. 6.

Attwood, L., 'Sex and the Soviet Cinema', in Kon, I. and Riordan, J. (eds), *Sex and Russian Society* (London, Pluto, 1993), pp. 64–88.

Attwood, L., 'The post-Soviet Woman in the Move to the Market: a Return to Domesticity and Dependence?', in Marsh, R. (ed.), *Women in Russia and Ukraine* (Cambridge, Cambridge University Press, 1996), pp. 255–66.

Attwood, L., ' "She was asking for it": Rape and Domestic Violence against Women', in Buckley, M. (ed.), *Post-Soviet Women: from the Baltic to Central Asia* (Cambridge, Cambridge University Press, 1997), pp. 99–118.

Azhgikhina, N. (ed.), *Who Defends Women?* (Moscow, Moscow Gender Centre, 1996).

Azhgikhina, N., 'Heaven's Better Half', *Current Digest of the Post-Soviet Press* (henceforth *CDPSP*), Vol. 49, No. 3, 1997, p. 20.

Baiduzhii, A., 'Demographic Catastrophe has Become a Reality', *CDPSP*, Vol. 46, No. 5,1994, pp. 18–19.

Baranovskii, I. and Aleinik, L., 'Bordel Under the Open Sky', *Moscow News*, 24 September 1993, p. 14.

Bateneva, T., 'Deti riska', *Izvestiya*, 14 August 1996, p. 5.

Borzenko, V., 'Abortion in Russia: in the Light of Public Opinion', *CDPSP*, Vol. 46, No. 10, 1994, pp. 16–17.

Bridger, S., 'The Return of the Family Farm: a Future for Women?', in Marsh, R. (ed.), *Women in Russia and Ukraine* (Cambridge, Cambridge University Press, 1996), pp. 241–54.

Bridger, S. and Kay, R., 'Gender and Generation in the New Russian Labour Market', in Pilkington, H. (ed.), *Gender, Generation and Identity in Contemporary Russia* (London, Routledge, 1996), pp. 21–38.

Bridger, S., Kay, R. and Pinnick, K., *No More Heroines? Russia, Women and the Market* (London and New York, Routledge, 1996).

Bruno, M., 'Employment Strategies and the Formation of New Identities in the Service Sector in Moscow', in Pilkington, H. (ed.), *Gender, Generation and Identity in Contemporary Russia* (London, Routledge, 1996), pp. 39–56.

Buckley, M., *Women and Ideology in the Soviet Union* (Hemel Hempstead, Harvester Wheatsheaf, 1989).

Buckley, M., 'Social Policies and New Social Issues', in White, S., Pravda, A. and Gitelman, Z. (eds), *Developments in Soviet Politics* (London, Macmillan, 1990), pp. 185–206.

Buckley, M. (ed.), *Perestroika and Soviet Women* (Cambridge, Cambridge University Press, 1992).

'Chislo ubitykh v Chechne rossiyan mozhet privysit 80 tysyach', *Izvestiya*, 5 September 1996, p. 1.

Clements, B. E., Engel, B. A. and Worobec, C. D. (eds), *Russia's Women: Accommodation, Resistance, Transformation* (Berkeley and Oxford, University of California Press, 1991), pp. 1–13.

Corrin, C. (ed.), *Superwomen and the Double Burden* (London, Scarlet Press, 1992).

Einhorn, B., *Cinderella goes to Market: Citizenship, Gender and Women's Movements in East Central Europe* (London and New York, Verso, 1993).

Eremicheva, G., 'Articulating a Catastrophic Sense of Life', in Rotkirch, A. and Haavio-Mannila, E. (eds), *Women's Voices in Russia Today* (Aldershot and Brookfield USA, Dartmouth, 1996), pp. 153–63.

Erofeyev, V., 'Introduction: Russia's *Fleurs du Mal*', in *The Penguin Book of New Russian Writing* (Harmondsworth, Penguin, 1995), pp. ix–xxx.

'Erotika i vlast', *Ogonek*, Nos 17–18 (May), 1994, pp. 12–18.

'Eshche odna "zakrytaya" tema', *Argumenty i fakty*, No. 16, 1990, p. 7.

Frolov, D., 'Bureaucrats Show Concern for Multiplying the Nation. By Making All Abortion Clinics Charge Fees', *CDPSP*, Vol. 46, No. 10, 1994, pp. 16–17.

Funk, N. and Mueller, M. (eds), *Gender Politics and Post-Communism: Reflections from Eastern Europe and the Former Soviet Union* (New York and London, Routledge, 1993).

Gerasimova, T., 'Elderly Women – a Challenge to Russia', in Rotkirch, A. and Haavio-Mannila, E. (eds), *Women's Voices in Russia Today* (Aldershot, Dartmouth, 1996), pp. 175–85.

Gorbachev, M., *Perestroika: New Thinking for our Country and the World* (New York, Harper and Row, 1987).

Goryachev, V., 'Rhapsody Played From Someone Else's Score', *CDPSP*, Vol. 49, No. 5, 1997, pp. 18–19.

Goscilo, H., 'New Members and Organs: the Politics of Porn', *Carl Beck Papers*, No. 1007 (Pittsburgh, University of Pittsburgh, 1993).

Grafova, L., 'How Can We Save the Russians Still in Chechnya?', *CDPSP*, Vol. 49, No. 1, 1997, pp. 11–12.

Heldt, Barbara, 'Gynoglasnost: Writing the Feminine', in Buckley, M. (ed.), *Perestroika and Soviet Women* (Cambridge, Cambridge University Press, 1992), pp. 160–75.

Kay, R., "It's about Helping Women to Believe in Themselves": Grassroots Women's Organisations in Contemporary Russian Society', in Bull, A., Diamond, H. and Marsh, R. (eds), *Feminisms and Women's Movements in Contemporary Europe* (Basingstoke, Macmillan, forthcoming).

Khamrayev, V., '"Women for Solidarity" Want to Calm "Nervous" Society', *CDPSP*, Vol. 47, No. 13, 1995, p. 14.

Kharlamova, T., 'Sindrom unizheniya na fone lyubvi', *Rossiiskaya gazeta*, 31 May 1996, p. 27.

Khudyakova, T., 'Zhenshchiny ukhodyat s politicheskoi stseny', *Izvestiya*, 23 October 1991, p. 2.

Khudyakova, T., 'Gosudarstvo mozhet zadushit semyu v obyatiyakh lyubvi', *Izvestiya*, 25 November 1992, p. 2.

Khudyakova, T. (1994a), 'We Could Turn Into a Country of Pensioners', *CDPSP*, Vol. 46, No. 5, 1994, p. 19.

Khudyakova, T. (1994b), 'Ella Pamfilova reanimiruet ideyu sotsialnoi reformy i nadeetsya na podderzhku prezidenta', *Izvestiya*, 24 May 1994, p. 2.

Kigai, N., 'Family Planning, Russian-style', *CDPSP*, Vol. 4, No. 31, 1996, pp. 10–11.

Kirpichnikov, Aleksei, 'Social Sphere Left "With a Hat but no Pants"', *CDPSP*, Vol. 46, No. 16, 1994, p. 18.

Klimenkova, T., 'What Does Our New Democracy Offer Society?', in Posadskaya, A. (ed.), *Women in Russia: a New Era in Russian Feminism* (London and New York, Verso, 1994), pp.14–36.

Kon, I., 'Sexual Counter-revolution in Russia', INFO-RUSS list, 9 March 1997.

Konstantinova, V., 'No Longer Totalitarianism, But Not Yet Democracy: the Emergence of an Independent Women's Movement in Russia', in Posadskaya, A. (ed.), *Women in Russia: a New Era in Russian Feminism* (London and New York, Verso, 1994), pp. 57–73.

Koshkareva, T., 'Sostoitsya li politicheskaya reabilitatsiya Borisa Eltsina?', *Nezavisimaya gazeta*, 10 November 1996, pp. 1–2.

Kravchenko, T., 'Ne tak strashen chert', *Literaturnaya gazeta*, 17 May 1995, p. 4.

Lavrov, A., 'Polovina regionov strany ne predstavlena v Dume', *Rossiiskie vesti*, 2 April 1996, pp. 1–2.

Likhanov, A., 'Social Factor: the Situation of Children in Russia', *CDPSP*, Vol. 48, No. 48, 1996, pp. 8–10.

Lipovskaya, O., 'New Women's Organisations', in Buckley, M. (ed.), *Perestroika and Soviet Women* (Cambridge, Cambridge University Press, 1992a), pp. 72–81.

Lipovskaya, O., 'Left/Feminism – Where To?', in Ward, A., Gregory, J. and Yuval-Davis, N. (eds), *Women and Citizenship in Europe* (Stoke-on-Trent, Trentham Books and European Forum of Socialist Feminists, 1992b), pp. 99–100.

Lipovskaya, O., 'Gender Bender', *This Magazine*, No. 25 (May), 1992c, pp. 24–5.

Lipovskaya, O., 'The Mythology of Womanhood in Contemporary "Soviet" Culture', in Posadskaya, A. (ed.), *Women in Russia: a New Era in Russian Feminism* (London and New York, Verso, 1994), pp. 123–34.

Lissyutkina, L., 'Soviet Women at the Crossroads of Perestroika', in Funk, N. and Mueller, M. (eds), *Gender Politics and Post-Communism: Reflections from Eastern Europe and the Former Soviet Union* (New York and London, Routledge, 1993), pp. 274–86.

Lyuka, G., 'Russian Authorities Decide to Concern Themselves with Children and Parents', *CDPSP*, Vol. 44, No. 23, 1992, p. 25.

'Man-sized Solution for Women', *The Guardian*, 8 May 1997, p. 16.

Marsh, R. (ed. and transl.), *Women in Russia and Ukraine* (Cambridge, Cambridge University Press, 1996).

Marsh, R. (1998a), 'An Image of their Own? Feminism, Revisionism and Russian Culture', in Marsh, R. (ed.), *Women and Russian Culture: Projections and Self-Perceptions* (Oxford and Providence, RI, Berghahn, 1998), pp. 2–41.

Marsh R. (1998b), 'Women in Contemporary Russia and the Former USSR', in Wilford, R. and Miller, R. (eds), *Women Ethnicity and Nationalism* (London and New York, Routledge, 1998), pp. 87–119.

Materialy XXVIII Syezda KPSS (Moscow, Politizdat, 1990).

Meek, J., 'Mothers Weep for Russia's Sons and War's Eternal Hunger', *The Guardian*, 28 December 1994, p. 11.

Millinship, William, *Front Line: Women of the New Russia* (London, Methuen, 1993).

Nadezhdina, N., 'Strana bezdetnaya', *Trud*, 31 May 1996, p. 4.

Pankova, M., 'Alevtina Fedulova: "Zhenshchina tozhe chelovek"', *Nezavisimaya gazeta*, 6 March 1993, p. 6.

Pervyshin, V., 'Unichtozhenie', *Molodaya gvardiya*, No. 8, 1993, pp. 3–8.

Pilkington, H., 'Russia and the Former Soviet Republics', in Corrin, C. (ed.), *Superwomen and the Double Burden* (London, Scarlet Press, 1992), pp. 180–235.

Pilkington, H. (ed.), *Gender, Generation and Identity in Contemporary Russia* (London, Routledge, 1996a).

Pilkington, H., 'Can "Russia's Women" Save the Nation?: Survival Politics and Gender Discourse in Post-Soviet Russia', in Bridger, S. (ed.), *Women in Post-Communist Russia* (Interface, Bradford Studies in Language, Culture and Society, No. 1, University of Bradford, 1996b), pp. 160–71.

Polenina, S., 'Brachnyi kontrakt mozhno teper zakliuchit i v Rossii', *Izvestiya*, 6 March 1996, p. 11.

Popov, A., 'Eta drevnyaya igra', *Moskovskii komsomolets*, 18 August 1989, p. 4.

Posadskaya, Anastasiya (ed.), *Women in Russia: a New Era in Russian Feminism* (London and New York, Verso, 1994).

Predvybornaya platforma obedineniya 'Zhenshchiny Rossii', pre-election pamphlet (Moscow, Women of Russia, 1993).

Rasputin, V., 'Cherchez la femme', *Nash sovremennik*, No. 3, 1990, p. 169.

Remennick, L. I., 'Patterns of Birth Control', in Kon, I. and Riordan, J. (eds), *Sex and Russian Society* (London, Pluto, 1993), pp. 45–63.

Ronina, G., 'Chernoe i beloe', *Selskaya nov*, No. 1, 1988, p. 28.

Rotkirch, A. and Haavio-Mannila, E. (eds), *Women's Voices in Russia Today* (Aldershot, Dartmouth, 1996).

Rule, W. and Noonan, N. (eds), *Russian Women in Politics and Society* (Westport, CT, Greenwood, 1996).

Rule, W. and Shvedova, N., 'Women in Russia's First Multiparty Election', in Rule, W. and Noonan, N. (eds), *Russian Women in Politics and Society* (Westport, CT, Greenwood, 1996), pp. 40–59.

'Russians are Beginning to Die at a Slightly Lower Rate', *CDPSP*, Vol. 48, No. 6, 1996, pp. 18–19.

Sargeant, Elena, 'The "Woman Question" and Problems of Maternity in Post-Communist Russia', in Marsh, R. (ed.), *Women in Russia and Ukraine* (Cambridge, Cambridge University Press, 1996), pp. 269–85.

Sazonov, V., 'Novyi simbioz: obshchestvennoe mnenie o zhizni, prervannoi vrachom, i svoboda propovedi', *Nezavisimaya gazeta*, 12 August 1993, p. 5.

Semeinyi kodeks Rossiiskoi Federatsii (Moscow, SPARK, 1996).

Semenova, G., 'Zhenshchiny i rynok: vyzhivat – ne vyzhidat', *Rynok*, No. 16, September 1992, p. 1.

Shafran, E., 'Izgnanie ploda: pochemu zhenshchiny v Rossii boyatsya rozhat', *Izvestiya*, 26 January 1994, p. 8.

Shchogolev, A., 'Lozhnaya zhenshchina', *Leningradskii Universitet*, 16 March, 23 March, 13 April 1990.

Shtyleva, L., ' "Ya – nachalnik, ty – raba!". Seksualnye domogatelstva na rabote: rossiiskii variant', *Nezavisimaya gazeta*, 28 November 1996, p. 6.

Sklyar, I., 'Zhenshchiny pri dengakh', *Rabotnitsa*, No. 3, 1994, pp. 16–17.

Slater, W., 'Female Representation in Russian Politics', *Radio Liberty/Radio Free Europe Bulletin*, Vol. 3, No. 22, 3 June 1994, p. 27.

Sotnikova, T., 'Raskryvat prestupleniya protiv lichnosti meshaet kadrovyi vopros', *Segodnya*, 17 January 1996, p. 6.

Starovoitova G., 'Women's Choice in Russian Politics', in *CDPSP*, Vol. 50, No. 10, 1998a, p. 16.

Starovoitova, G., ' "Vlastiam ne khvataet mozgov i sovesti": Iz neopublikovannogo interv'iu', *Argumenty i fakty*, No. 48, November 1998b, p. 3.

Stishova, Elena, ' "Full Frontal": Perestroika and Sexual Policy', in Marsh, R. (ed.), *Women in Russia and Ukraine* (Cambridge, Cambridge University Press, 1996), pp. 188–95.

Stites, R., *The Women's Liberation Movement in Russia: Feminism, Nihilism and Bolshevism* (Princeton, Princeton University Press, 1978).

Sukhova, S., 'She Can Rein in a Horse at Full Gallop Without Leaving her Burning Hut', *CDPSP*, Vol. 50, No. 7, 1998, p. 16.

Temkina, A., 'Entering Politics: Women's Ways, Gender Ideas and Contradictions of Reality', in Rotkirch, A. and Haavio-Mannila, E. (eds), *Women's Voices in Russia Today* (Aldershot, Dartmouth, 1996), pp. 206–34.

Terekhov, V., 'Rossiiskie selyanki odni nivu ne podnimut', *Nezavisimaya gazeta*, 12 August 1993, pp. 1–2.

'The Woman in Yeltsin's Cabinet', *OMRI*, 6 September 1996, http://www.cdi.org/mailing/Russia

Timashova, N., 'Authorities Decide to Make Maternity Safe in Moscow', *CDPSP*, Vol. 47, No. 38, 1995, pp. 18–19.

Toktaleva, G., 'Olya i Yulya', *Sobesednik*, No. 46, November, 1989, p. 11.

Tolstaya, T., 'Notes from Underground', *New York Review of Books*, Vol. 37, No. 9, 31 May 1990, pp. 3–7.

Tutorskaya, S., 'Mama, vse li ty produmala, kogda reshila menya rodit?', *Izvestiya*, 30 January 1996, p. 5.

Tyurin, G., 'Kodeks stroitelei matriarkhata', *Nezavisimaya gazeta*, 10 November 1995, p. 6.

Valyuzhenich, G., 'Pochemu ushla Ella Pamfilova', *Argumenty i fakty*, No. 5, February, 1994, p. 3.

Vasileva, L., 'Pervye lastocki na tsirkulyare. Razmyshleniya posle Sezda o roli zhenshchiny v obshchestve', *Pravda*, 24 June 1989, p. 3.

'Verkhovnyi Sud ne udovletvoril zhalobu Galiny Starovoitovoi', *Segodnya*, 6 May 1996, p. 1.

Vladimirov, I., 'Obsuzhdayutsya problemy peremeshchennykh lits', *Nezavisimaya gazeta*, 2 April 1996, p. 3.

White, N., 'Women in Post-Independence Lithuania: the Slow Road to Gender Consciousness', unpublished paper presented to conference 'Women in Russia and the former USSR', University of Bath, 1993.

White, S., *After Gorbachev* (Cambridge, Cambridge University Press, 1993).

'Women of Russia Leader Confident of Crossing 5 per cent Barrier', *Summary of World Broadcasts*, 20 December 1995, SU/2491 A/8.

Yakov, V., 'MVD preduprezhdaet: nachalsya rost prestuplenii na seksualnoi pochve', *Izvestiya*, 12 August 1993, p. 8.

Yuriev, E., 'The Landscape after the Battle', *CDPSP*, Vol. 48, No. 3, 1996, pp. 18–19.

Zabelina, T., 'Sexual Violence towards Women', in Pilkington, H. (ed.), *Gender, Generation and Identity in Contemporary Russia* (London, Routledge, 1996), pp. 169–86.

Zdravomyslova, E., 'Problems of Becoming a Housewife', in Rotkirch, A. and Haavio-Mannila, E. (eds), *Women's Voices in Russia Today* (Aldershot, Dartmouth, 1996), pp. 255–66.

Zhenshchiny v SSSR (Moscow, Finansy i statistika, 1992).

Part V
Youth and Education

12 Warfare by Other Means: Unity and Fracture in European Education

David Coulby

UNITY AND FRACTURE IN EUROPE AND IN EUROPEAN CURRICULA

The boundary politics of Europe in the last two decades of the century are following two apparently opposite trends: towards fracture and towards unity. Three supranational states have already broken up: Yugoslavia, Czechoslovakia and the Soviet Union. Other supranational states face pressures towards similar fracture: France, Spain, the United Kingdom, Italy and Russia. These fractures have been partly produced by that antagonism between the state and the nation (Appadurai, 1990) which has been a major cause of conflict in the continent at least since the French Revolution.

The trend towards unity in one case at least, that of Germany, has had a similar rationalization. Other potential national unions in Europe might strike readers as less unproblematic: that of Macedonia, say, or Ireland or the union of Romania and Moldova. The other case of the trend towards unity, that of the European Union, is apparently a movement driven not by nationalism, but, in terms of its rhetoric at least, driven against nationalism. The Commonwealth of Independent States might provide a parallel. Nationality remains an important component in the construction of identities in Europe (Coulby and Jones, 1996). Each nationalism embodies itself through particular configurations of language, religion, cultural manifestations (from epic poems to folk dance), historiographies, sacred landscapes and townscapes, etc. This is not to say that it is the only component in the construction of identity, as against gender and sexuality, say, or indeed that European identities cannot be structured in opposition to nationality and nationalism, around social class perhaps, around pan-Europeanism or even internationalism. It is, however, to assert that nationality and nationalism have not disappeared; that, if anything, they are resurgent factors in both the politics of Europe and in the shaping of the various European identities.

At the centre of these tensions over the shaping of European space and the construction of European identities are two not unrelated processes: those of education and warfare (Coulby, 1996). Education, to cobble a phrase, might be seen as warfare by other means. It is in schools and universities that the cultural and epistemological underpinnings of national identity and nationalism are produced and reproduced. These institutions have become of pre-eminent importance in many areas as the significance of religious institutions and of the family has been diminished (Althusser, 1972). The curricula of schools and universities represent the particular selections from human knowledge made by the epistemological establishment in each state. Within these selections, too, the two oppositional trends towards fracture and unity can clearly be seen.

In one sense curricular convergence between states in Europe was one of the consequences of the Enlightenment programme. European thought came to recognize and thus to teach only one form of mathematics, only one science and medicine. More precariously schools and universities attempted to define a common international (that is European) culture and philosophy in terms of a canon of texts, scores, artefacts, buildings, etc. To maintain the connection between education and warfare, here is Ezra Pound's depiction of the influence of the European canon on the First World War:

> There died a myriad,
> And of the best, among them,
> For an old bitch gone in the teeth,
> For a botched civilisation,
>
> Charm, smiling at the good mouth,
> Quick eyes gone under earth's lid,
>
> For two gross of broken statues,
> For a few thousand battered books.
>   (*Hugh Selwyn Mauberley*)

The trend towards curricular convergence continues today in at least two ways: as foreign language teaching becomes centred on less languages; and as the Commission of the European Union takes on the role of progenitor of a common European culture. The picture on foreign languages is not quite as universal as Anglophones and the British Council might wish. Certainly English has replaced Russian as the first foreign language in, say, Romanian-speaking schools in Romania and Latvian-speaking schools in Latvia, though not of course in Magyar-speaking schools in Cluj or Russian-speaking schools in Riga. But in other parts of

Central and Eastern Europe the universalistic aspirations of English may not prove as attractive as the trading realities of German. There is also the pressure on foreign language decisions exerted by resurgent nationalisms which is referred to later in this chapter. So although there is some convergence this by no means represents the universal spread of English as a second language. In the unlikely event of the European Union being able to agree on one official language this would inevitably lead to further convergence both within the Union and outwith. This would put pressure on the learning of other large languages and on small national languages.

Following the Maastricht Treaty the Commission has been able to involve itself in all areas of education, not just vocational and higher. Through funding new schemes such as COMMENIUS and through initiatives such as the 1996 White Paper (European Commission, 1996) it is attempting to give a steer to the education policies of member states, and indeed, via the TEMPUS programme, those of non-members. While these initiatives show a proper concern for education to play a part in reducing what the White Paper refers to as marginalization, it is important to notice that post-Maastricht the Commission has placed increased emphasis on the teaching at school and university level of the European theme. The Commission's European theme is the latest politicization of the Enlightenment's common European culture (Sultana, 1994, 1995). It is an attempt to bring together those various and conflicting European identities; indeed to replace them with a universalistic European identity. A common cultural canon, a shared view of history (this is all nonsense, of course), a commitment to West European multilingualism and a belief in the European destiny and in the institutions of the Union as the best way to promote this through a progressive process of widening and deepening: these are some of the characteristics of the European theme as advocated in the White Paper and in the SOCRATES and COMMENIUS documentation.

It is by no means accepted, however, that Europeanization of the curriculum will necessarily lead to less conflicting identities or politics. The European theme or dimension too readily conflates the continent with the Union. The culture, history and science of Eastern Europe are all too readily neglected. The Islamic presence in Europe is ignored or regretted. Furthermore, a careful reading of European documentation over the last ten years seems to indicate a shift away from internationalism (Coulby, 1996). The European theme is being espoused not as part of some wider international movement but more as an assertion of Western European triumphalism. There are indeed sinister parallels between Europeanization in one part of the continent and the previous attempt at Sovietization, which was actually Russification in disguise (Haarmann, 1995; Khazanov, 1995), in another. In the unlikely event of the emergence of a pan-European identity there would be the possibility that this was also formed on a wider nationalism which saw itself as defined against and in conflict with the east and the wider world so tangibly represented by the African, Asian and Latin American presence readily identifiable in the large cities of the Union.

The attraction of Europeanization of education and of the European theme, of course, is that they may serve to reduce those smaller nationalisms, and associated racisms, which remain prevalent in the curricular systems of states in both the West and the East. Against the chauvinism of the state-enforced school curriculum in England and Wales, Greece or Romania, the European theme might seem like a desirable element of internationalization and balance. It is these state curricular systems which are under threat also from the second of my two trends, that towards fracture.

Again languages provide a good starting point and Finland is a progressive example. From the early years of this century Finland has regarded itself as a bilingual state. All Finns learn Swedish in schools and all Swedes learn Finnish. The asymmetrical bilingualism of Latvia, Wales, Catalonia, Transylvania or Alto Adige is thus avoided. Giving recognition and status to the Sami languages in Finland has been a more difficult process. But within many European Union countries and in Hungary there is an increasing recognition of non-state languages and an incorporation of them into educational institutions. Magyar and German schools have survived in Romania; Friesian language teaching in the Netherlands; Welsh schools are increasing in popularity and Catalan is now a language of instruction to university level. There are still many examples of states enforcing one dominant language through educational institutions, in Slovenia, Croatia, Greece and Estonia for example, but patterns of enhanced diversity are gradually solidifying in terms of both the language of instruction and of the first and second foreign languages. This tendency to fracture is a force against the universalistic spread of English and/or German as a first foreign language. While the Finns have become excellent English speakers, the ability to operate in three languages, despite the White Paper's exhortations, is something of a rarity. The trend to learn a national and a state language runs counter to that which advocates a state and a European language.

A similar tension can then be seen in terms of the cultural content of the school and university curriculum. The history and literature taught in Scotland is significantly different from that taught in England; that in

Catalonia different from Castile. Latvian schools and universities are in the process of rediscovering, discovering or, if necessary inventing, literary and artistic traditions to complement the newly dominant Latvian language (Lieven, 1993). Also in Latvia, and to a lesser extent in Denmark, folk music and folk dance take a much more prominent place in the curriculum at all levels than they do in the Netherlands, say, or France. The large powerful states, as part of their modernist attempt to identify themselves with nations, continue to insist on the necessity of schools and universities to emphasize the integrity and general superiority of English or French culture, tradition and heritage, to take the two most obvious culprits. Thus both the nationalism of states and the nationalism that struggles against states serve to resist the homogenization represented by the European theme with its handful of great men and its history of a large, happy family.

THE KNOWLEDGE ECONOMY AND CURRICULAR CONTROL

So far this chapter has treated school and university curricula as knowledge systems which can play an important part in the shaping of identities and in the production and reproduction of cultural and political practices. But curricular systems are increasingly important as economic entities. The new international division of labour, driven by transnational corporations, is progressively shifting extraction and manufacturing industries to Latin America and particularly Asia. Within Europe itself these activities are in the process of being moved in an easterly direction. Western Europe is increasingly centring its economic activities in the tertiary sector of banking, insurance and finance and beyond this in education and research. Europe is moving towards being a knowledge economy. Knowledge has become one of the most important items of international exchange (Castells, 1989; Coulby and Jones, 1995) and it is in the production, organization, storage, retrieval, evaluation, analysis and reproduction of knowledge that Western European states consider that, for economic reasons, they need to excel.

It is schools, universities and research institutions, in the main, on which Europe relies to maintain its privileged position within the world economy and international division of labour. Knowledge about the manufacture and deployment of arms and armament systems (to maintain the connection between education and warfare); pharmaceutical and medical discoveries; the development of information and communications systems; the design of fabrics, fashion and footwear which is subsequently manufactured in sweatshops in the Philippines or Thailand; the design and construction of specialist extraction and manufacturing machines and components; the postgraduate education in medicine, arts or management of élites from Africa, Latin America and Asia; the production, presentation and codification of European culture as part of the explosion in the leisure and tourism industries: all these activities are increasingly based on knowledge which is produced and reproduced in schools and universities. As the pace of knowledge change in Europe has speeded up, experts increasingly need to keep in touch with these institutions so that their skills can be updated and increased or even completely revised. Such renewal is fundamental to the West European economy and parallels the stress on lifelong learning which appears in the Commission's White Paper.

One of the consequences of the enhanced economic importance of knowledge in Europe has been a dramatic expansion of educational provision. Within the European Union countries this has been manifested in a range of policies: the lengthening of the compulsory years of schooling; provision of pre-school education; an increase in the number of pupils studying beyond the point at which they can legally enter the workforce; a dramatic expansion in the number of people seeking university education and obtaining graduate status; an expansion in Masters and Doctoral level study; an increased and enhanced provision of updating courses, refresher courses and retraining courses; the growth of distance and open learning and credit accumulation arrangements (all the latter much favoured by the Commission); the mushrooming of inspection and quality apparatuses at all levels of education. In curricular terms the economic importance of knowledge might itself lead to greater homogenization as manifested by the importance of English language journals in medicine, science and technology or by the progressive advance of Microsoft information storage, handling and communication systems within the educational, commercial and industrial institutions of both East and West Europe. Certainly there has been a widespread attempt to stress vocational relevance in educational provision at all levels in many European countries.

It is against the background of the growth of the knowledge economy, as well as against that of the tensions between unity and fracture, that political conflicts over the control of the school and university curriculum arise. To simplify this conflict it may be seen as being between local, state and European levels. State here implies governmental; local implies provincial, the German *Länder*, say, or one of the Italian regions. Before proceeding to examine these three loci of control it is necessary, perhaps, to make explicit one of the assumptions of this chapter which has so far been implicit. The diversity of the nations of Europe has already been exemplified but the cultural heterogeneity of Europe goes beyond this. Post-war migration into the large cities of the European Union and Switzerland has resulted in highly diverse urban populations. There are significant Islamic groups in the major cities of France (mainly from the Magrheb), the Netherlands, Belgium, Germany (mainly from Anatolia) and the United Kingdom (mainly from the Indian subcontinent and East Africa). London can claim to have over two hundred languages spoken on its streets and it has institutions for all the world's large religions and many of the small ones. In urban as well as national terms, then, Europe is a highly heterogeneous, indeed an international continent. The implicit assumption of this chapter is that this heterogeneity is one of Europe's most important cultural and economic assets and that the role of educational institutions ought to be to preserve it, to enhance it, and to make pupils and students aware of its richness, its value and its fragility. It is against this now explicit criterion that the chapter concludes by examining the three levels of curriculum control.

In terms of *international*, European control, the educational policies of the European Union and the movements in, and away from, the direction of language convergence have already been analysed as has the impact of the knowledge economy. The other remaining forces which exert international control on European curricular systems are international commodity marketing and international (usually meaning American) media and popular culture. In terms of commodities the most important are probably computers and their related programs and communications facilities. Excel, Netscape and WordPerfect, or their equivalents, are found in schools and universities across Europe. Less obviously, some textbooks and journals manage to make an international impact – texts in the field of foreign language teaching for instance.

It is hard to see ways in which the *baccalaureate* or the *abitur*, for instance, have been vastly penetrated by the influence of Disney. But the impact of international media and popular culture is not inconsiderable. The sports taught and played in schools are subject to fashionable fluctuation: football, as a component of education, is only a recent phenomenon in some parts of Europe and the rise in the popularity of basketball indicates the American influence. BBC and some American broadcasts of educational and special interest programmes are used in many different subjects at all levels in many countries.

The internationalization of the curricula of European states is obviously desirable not least with regard to the facilitation of cultural heterogeneity. On the other hand internationalization could lead to the uniform imposition of computing technologies, texts and television programmes in a way which might stifle the growth of more local productions, particularly in the east and south of the continent. It could lead to the homogenized European theme which conceals the full extent of the continent, its wider international role and the richness of its local cultures.

It is at the level of the *state* that conflict concerning the control of school and university curricula is at the most strident and visible. State imposed, centralized, compulsory curricular systems have never been more popular as governments try to use educational institutions to legitimate a version of human knowledge most congruent with their own retention of power. They have been newly introduced in England and Wales and renewed in, for example, Ireland, Norway, Romania, Latvia and France.

These curriculum systems tend to devalue the contributions of those nations with which the state does not identify itself. They tend to emphasize the achievements of inhabitants of the particular state and portray its history as one of benevolent progress. They stress integration into a heritage and tradition, in the United Kingdom through religious education as well as other subjects, rather than a commitment to understanding the human and cultural diversity which actually characterizes the country. National curricular systems tend to be nationalist curricular systems.

Commensurate with this centralization, *local* control of the curriculum would appear to be on the decline. This is not quite the case. The breakup of the Soviet superstate has resulted in control passing to much smaller centres with the resultant rapid implementation of curricular policies to reverse Russification. Federalization in Spain has led to new local curricular control and autonomy at all levels. Even in the United Kingdom, Scotland continues to withstand the National Curriculum imposed on England and Wales.

In one way local control of the curriculum could be seen as a postmodern nightmare, with each ever-smaller locality determining for itself what is knowledge and culture and then propagating it through its educational institutions without regard to either the economic needs of the state or any compatibility with neighbouring localities. But without some local control, those cultures and languages which do not have access to the apparatus of state power are likely to die out in the face of centralized curricular systems.

Schools and universities teach children and young people that their state or, rarely, their superstate is the best, that its government is legitimate, that its contribution to world history, science and culture is grossly disproportionate to its size, that its land and its landscapes are sacred, that because the state is a nation only nationals are true citizens and others are out-siders. The extent to which such messages are stressed will obviously vary from state to state, depending on the previous history. The Norwegian curriculum stresses internationalism (Royal Ministry of Church, Education and Research, 1994), that of Serbia stresses heroic resistance to centuries-long atrocities by neighbouring states (Pesic, 1994). But centrally controlled curriculum systems in Europe tend towards the production and reproduction of nationalism as a political force and as a component of identity. To this extent they teach, at the very least, an habituation towards, and in more extreme cases a glorification of, warfare. Educational institutions teach the importance of warfare in the power of the state, the celebration of warfare in epic poetry, the science and technology necessary to the development of warfare, the skills of obedience and compliance necessary to participation in warfare. The preservation of peace as well as of European cultural heterogeneity depends on a reversal of some of these curricular policies.

REFERENCES

Althusser, L., 'Ideology and the Ideological State Apparatus', in Cosin, B. R. (ed.), *Education: Structure and Society* (Harmondsworth, Penguin, 1972), pp. 247–80.
Appadurai, A., 'Disjuncture and Difference in the Global Cultural Economy', in Featherstone, M. (ed.), *Global Culture: Nationalism, Globalisation and Modernity. A Theory, Culture and Society Special Issue* (London, Sage, 1990), pp. 295–310.
Castells, M., *The Informational City: Information Technology, Economic Restructuring and the Urban–Regional Process* (Oxford, Blackwell, 1989).
Coulby, D., 'European Culture: Unity and Fractures', in Winther-Jensen, T. (ed.), *Challenges to European Education: Cultural Values, National Identities and Global Responsibilities* (Frankfurt am Main, Peter Lang, 1996), pp. 241–52.
Coulby, D., 'European Curricula, Xenophobia and Warfare', *Comparative Education*, Vol. 33, No. 1, 1997, pp. 29–42.
Coulby, D. and Jones, C., *Postmodernity and European Education Systems: Centralist Knowledge and Cultural Diversity* (Stoke-on-Trent, Trentham, 1995).
Coulby, D. and Jones, C., 'Postmodernity, Education and European Identities', in Cowen, R. (ed.), *Comparative Education and Post-modernity: Comparative Education Special Number (18). Comparative Education*, Vol. 32, No. 2, 1996, pp. 171–84.
European Commission, 'White Paper: Teaching and Learning: Towards the Learning Society' (Brussels, European Commission, 1996).
Haarmann, H., 'Multilingualism and Ideology: the Historical Experiment of Soviet Language Politics', *European Journal of Intercultural Studies*, Vol. 5, No. 3, 1995, pp. 6–17.

Khazanov, A. K., *After the USSR: Ethnicity, Nationalism and Politics in the Commonwealth of Independent States* (Madison, University of Wisconsin Press, 1995).

Lieven A., *The Baltic Revolution: Estonia, Latvia, Lithuania and the Path to Independence* (New Haven, Yale University Press, 1993).

Pesic, V., 'Bellicose Virtues in Elementary School Readers', in Rosandic, R. and Pesic, V. (eds), *Warfare, Patriotism, Patriarchy: the Analysis of Elementary School Textbooks* (Belgrade, Centre for Anti-War Action MOST, 1994), pp. 59–80.

Royal Ministry of Church, Education and Research, *Core Curriculum for Primary, Secondary and Adult Education in Norway* (Oslo, Royal Ministry of Church, Education and Research, 1994).

Sultana, R. G., 'Conceptualising Teachers' Work in a Uniting Europe', *Compare*, Vol. 24, No. 2, 1994, pp. 171–82.

Sultana, R. G., 'A Uniting Europe, a Dividing Education? Supranationalism, Euro-Centrism and the Curriculum', *International Studies in Sociology of Education*, Vol. 5, 1995, pp. 115–44.

13 Transnational Affinities in the European Context: the Case of Contemporary French Youth Cultures
Chris Warne

The possible existence of a European cultural identity has come increasingly to the forefront of political and academic debate in recent times. The very term itself is evidently open to question, and is used in different contexts to mean rather different things. Indeed, if we only look at the official pronouncements of the European Union since the early 1970s, it is possible to track an evolving notion of 'European identity'. Bram Boxhoorn (1996) discerns two principal strands in this evolution: first, the concept of an 'external European identity', that occurs in the context of statements on a common European foreign or defence policy; the second, more fluid, notion of 'internal identity', first began to appear in the 1970s, in response to perceived deficiencies in the integration process, and was accompanied by talk of bringing Europe 'closer to its citizens'. In the 1980s, this policy of developing a positive image of European identity continued with the introduction of the symbols of national identity (flag, anthem, ceremonial). However, in the post-Cold War era, and the difficulties post-Maastricht of establishing a clear consensus on the exact degree of integration desirable within the union, references to European identity have taken on a much more modest form. More apparent are ideas of a 'European family of cultures', or that citizens of the European Union should be free to evolve feelings of a 'double belonging' at both national and European level. While this more modest approach is evidently more appropriate to the post-Cold War era, when the conflation of a group of merely *Western* European states with grandiose ideas of European-wide identity becomes unsustainable, such concepts of a 'double belonging' are equally problematic.

Because notions of belonging to a European culture are necessarily vague, the effect is rather to encourage a reinforcement of what is perceived to be more concrete, that is traditional notions of national identity, a necessarily introspective dynamic that in its turn produces yet narrower definitions of European identity. As Pieterse (1991) has noted, the culture of the European Union that is:

> reproduced in textbooks, declarations and media programmes, continues to be the culture of Imperial Europe ...; its self image, its dominant culture, is still that of an Old World ... Certain key experiences are missing from this European culture: the experience of decolonization, of migrations, post-imperial ('we are here because you were there') and otherwise, and of globalization.

(quoted in Morley, 1997, p. 9)

Debates over personal, social and national identity have also taken centre stage in recent times in France, and the introspective dynamic noted above is clearly in evidence. Whether in discussions on the Schengen agreement on the relaxation of border controls within the Union, or in negotiations for the GATT treaties on world trade, French governments have often set a tone which reveals the view that French identity and culture are at risk from external threat, and, accordingly, need to be defended. Meanwhile, the extreme right-wing National Front under the leadership of Jean-Marie Le Pen continues to make inroads into the French political mainstream, and there is little doubt that its discourse on national identity, shot through as it is with notions of a 'Christian' Europe, and of the polarized opposition between French 'insider' and immigrant 'outsider', has had a decisive impact on both the terms of the debate on national identity, and on its direction.

It is interesting therefore that at the same time, and frequently from the same areas in which the National Front is making such headway (that is, France's outer-city housing estates), certain social groupings are generating forms of youth culture based on rap, ragga and dance music, that are marked too by this preoccupation with articulating identity. They have as a common feature a certain loosening of identification with and affinity for what many would consider to be classic definitions of French national culture, a loosening which stems from the very acknowledgement of decolonization, of migration and of globalization that is missing from 'official' European Union notions of European identity. Consequently, they are marked by what until relatively recently would have been considered an unusually international and eclectic mix of affiliations, imagined socialities and cultural histories.

While wishing to avoid the simplistic assumption that the emergence of these cultures marks the dawning of a new age of global consciousness among France's youth (these are the articulations of specific, limited local groupings, and cannot be read as magically expressing the views of a mythically constructed 'new generation'), it is of interest to examine specific reasons for their emergence in the French context, not least because if these cultures do not as yet provide complete answers to the question of 'Why Europe?', and what European identity is, then in my view, they are at least beginning to pose the right questions. Indeed, it is precisely because these cultures are touching on such central issues of concern to the French nation that activities frequently dismissed by social commentators as having only superficial importance in the 'real' business of European politics (music, nocturnal leisure/pleasure-seeking), have recently been provoking a very political reaction in France. The sentencing of two rappers from the group Suprême NTM to six months (suspended) in prison, accompanied by a heavy fine, for defamatory comments made against the police during a concert organized by the anti-racist organization SOS-Racisme at Scyne-sur-Mer in the south of France during July 1995,[1] and the pressure successfully applied by the National Front controlled municipality at Toulon to prevent the group's appearance at a section of the annual Châteauvallon dance festival devoted to hip-hop culture in July 1996, has been accompanied by the continuing severe restrictions imposed by departmental and municipal prefects throughout France on raves and dance parties (Fontaine and Fontana, 1996, pp. 74–6).

In order to understand this very political aspect of these cultural forms, I shall set out the general sociological context for their emergence. I shall then examine their specific parameters by taking the work of three specific practitioners, one drawn from the ragga scene of south-west France, a second drawn from the hip-hop scene in Marseille, and a third taken from the Paris club and dance music scene: in particular, I will concentrate on how an imagined social and geographical space is constituted by each as a focus for local and global affinity. Finally, I will conclude with some comments on how these imagined, transnational spaces relate to the question of European identity.

In order to understand why changing social affinities have been a central feature of certain cultural forms emerging among sections of French youth, some pointers can be found in the local socio-economic environment in which young French people are moving. While seeking to make generalizations about 'youth' as a social category, it is important to be aware of the criticisms that have been made of the term (Bourdieu, 1984). Evidently, definitions of 'youth' depend on a variety of biological, institutional and cultural time frames in the process of social maturation. The term is frequently used in contexts that serve to position social groups in a state of dependency, and lay them open to the possibilities of institutional discipline and regulation.

Finally, when used indiscriminately so as to homogenize individuals having little in common except that they fall into the same chronologically determined age category, the definition 'youth' glosses over real discrepancies between those from different social classes, different local milieux and of different gender in terms of opportunity, available cultural capital and potential social trajectory.

However, since Bourdieu dismissed the possibility of generalizing meaningfully about contemporary society when starting from the category of youth, other French sociologists (Galland, 1991, 1993; Chamboredon, 1985) have tracked the changing parameters of social maturation in post-industrial society, that have as a principal consequence extended the period of insertion into the worlds of work, domestic autonomy and social independence. This prolonged experience is common to young people of both genders drawn from differing social backgrounds and from different parts of France, and leads both to talk of a new social age group covering those in the age range 15–25 and even beyond. Neither, however, explore in more than a very generalized fashion the cultural practices of this new social age group, nor the impact that they might have on society at large.

In contrast, the activist and social commentator Saïd Bouamama, from his position 'on the ground', has begun to explore the relationship of this group to long-standing notions of French national identity and citizenship (Bouamama, 1993; Bouamama et al., 1994). His concern is with the challenge of establishing plural notions of French citizenship for the post-national, post-colonial era. He begins by outlining the features common to the group, which as a whole is experiencing profound modifications to the make-up of Western societies: changes in the structure and availability of work, changes in the apparently solid definitions of social class, changes in moral and cultural values, changes in the fixity or otherwise of national and international, cultural and economic boundaries.

This social age group is, then, the first to emerge into this changing world, which accounts for a certain homogeneity of youth. How individuals respond to this situation, however, will differ, depending as it does on the different social milieu that they start from, on the different cultural capital available to them, and on the different possible social trajectories. This would account for the heterogeneity of youth. This new social age group is in fact, consciously and unconsciously, contributing to this profound process of change in Western societies, from which nothing of certainty has yet emerged.

The importance of this notion of a new social age group, with important features of homogeneity, but which is also strikingly heterogeneous in its cultural and social outlook, is that it enables us to situate the cultural forms under consideration within a wider process: a severe questioning of prevailing concepts of French identity and nationhood. Hitherto, notions of French national culture have depended to a large extent on adopting a position, whether antagonistic or favourable, towards the Republican tradition that is deemed to have developed from the Revolution of 1789, and in particular from the Declaration of the Rights of Man in the same year. While the youth cultures under consideration may reflect features of the Republican tradition (a concern for individual rights, for freedom of expression), or sometimes announce hostility to its out-workings (a denunciation of the distant, paternalistic and bureaucratic state), the relationship is on the whole much less direct, and cues are taken from other cultural traditions.

For Bouamama, this reflects a crisis in traditional concepts of Frenchness, formerly based on clear-cut definitions of nationality, citizenship and identity, but which are today proving insufficient for the task of creating a cohesive and united society out of the varied ethnic and national groupings residing on French soil. Thus, it is not simply the descendants of France's immigrant populations who find themselves positioned as the 'other', the outsider to the national tradition:

> The problem posed by the nationalistic impulse is closely linked to that of identity. It has, at its heart, a confusion of the concepts of nationality, of citizenship and of identity. Under this model, the French person is not only that bearing an abstractly defined French nationality. The mechanisms of exclusion and suspicion which affect foreigners will touch *all* those who by their behaviour, affirm a different identity. Once again, taking into account the dispersal of identity which affects the young and in particular those young French people born of immigrants, they will be automatically suspected of being incapable of fulfiling the role of citizen. Regardless of his nationality, any young person overtly adopting the identity of a sub-culture (funk, Punk, rasta, etc.) will tend to be perceived as unprepared for citizenship. The combined logics of nationalism, of identity and of supposed ability come together to give the model its force.
>
> (Bouamama, 1993, p. 118; my translation)

In a general sense, the quest for new social identities represented by these cultural forms should be placed in a wider context of contemporary uncertainty. In a more particular sense, it means that the forms of popular culture currently being created by young people who find themselves positioned on the margins of French society, constitute a direct challenge, by their very existence, to previously dominant notions of French citizenship and nationality.

So why should the emergence of a new social age group prove so disruptive to the continuity of France's national traditions? The particular factors that account for the development of this new social age category show why this is the case. Taken as a whole, changes in the area of education (its extension to a greater number, the extension of the period actually spent being educated, the consequent devaluation through proliferation of the educational qualification), settling into working life (the gradual disappearance of the 'first-time, once-for-all, job-for-life' to be replaced by the establishing of a professional identity in stages), and the establishing of an independent domestic unit (the rise in cohabitation, the tendency to remain longer with the family unit of origin) are experienced as a series of staged moves from adolescence to adulthood, with the concomitant possibility that each of these moves may take the individual further away from the culture and outlooks of their social milieu or class of origin. This will certainly be the case where the choices and paths pursued by their parents are in fact still available to young people moving into the transitionary phase. Several factors, among which the decline of France's industrial base is perhaps the most important, have contributed to a state of affairs where this is generally not the case. Social *déclassement*, the loosening of ties of loyalty to one's class of origin, is thus a reality affecting young people from a broad range of social backgrounds.

While these are processes that affect young people across the social spectrum, it is obvious that while *déclassement* may represent increased social mobility and widening horizons for some, for others it is experienced as crisis and as a narrowing of the possibilities for social advancement.

This is particularly the case for those who grow up in areas of social exclusion, which in France have predominately developed in the housing developments and estates of the 1960s in the new towns and peripheries of the larger cities. Thus, the physical location of *la banlieue* on the city's outskirts, at its periphery, has come to symbolize the centripetal growth of a society of haves at the centre, with little or no contact with the have-nots who remain invisible at the margins. The extent and depth of social exclusion in contemporary France can be illustrated very clearly. According to official statistics, of France's total population, some three million live in more than 500 areas described as being 'in difficulties'. These areas contain the highest proportion of council-run housing, the oldest housing stock, a higher than average proportion of the population under 20 years old, a greater concentration of inhabitants of ethnic minority origin and rates of unemployment at near twice the national average, which for young males in the 20–24 age range can be as high as 25 per cent (Geindre, 1993).

Such developments have in some areas led to a profound sense of alienation from the political processes that ostensibly seem responsible, a sense most keenly felt by young people from the working classes, growing up in these areas of social exclusion and who are also having to live with the collapse of support provided by traditional working-class cohesion and solidarity based on the common experience of the (now) disappearing industrial workplace. This is why the question of identity seems primordial for significant sections of the young in French society, and also explains why such concerns unite young people of French parentage with those of ethnic origin, whose own experience of a sense of *déclassement*, is rendered more acute by the sense that they are doubly distanced: from their parent's culture, in which they are unable to participate meaningfully, and from the culture of the host nation, which as yet seems incapable of working out a response that both allows cultural difference and ensures national unity. As stated above, debates on French identity have at the national level been dominated by the National Front, with its mono-cultural conceptions of 'Frenchness'.

Consequently, belief in the possibility of a multicultural France, which was at the heart of the anti-racist movements of the 1980s and key to the emergence of a 'mouvement des Beurs' in the same period,[2] and which was apparently reinforced by socialist cultural policy at the time with its emphasis on encouraging plurality and difference, seems to be waning for lack of clear national advocacy (Bouamama et al., 1994, pp. 95–105). The latter years of the Mitterand era saw a move away from pluralistic positions on cultural policy outlined by figures like Jean-Pierre Colin, with his enthusiastic embracing of eclectic youth cultures (Rigby, 1991, pp. 180–5).

The failure to fulfil this promise, with the wider failure of the Socialist government of the early 1990s to renegotiate North–South relations (exemplified for many activists by its stance on the Gulf War) provoked profound disillusionment with the political process not only among militants of the 1980s movements, but more especially among the 'next generation' of young descendants of immigrants living in the *banlieues*, disillusionment only compounded by the return of the right to power in 1992 and yet to be fundamentally addressed by the politics of the returning Socialist government of 1997. However, such disillusionment with traditional militant politics among France's marginalized youth has contributed to a situation where such affiliations have now been superseded by other cultural formers of political and social world-views, among which music is far from insignificant. Younger participants in the associative movements emerging from France's marginalized outer-city suburbs over the last decade frequently express empathy with the experience of the African diaspora, and with the musical traditions in America and the Caribbean that have emerged from it (soul, funk, hip-hop, reggae). This empathy extends to the civil rights struggles of the black Atlantic and the East/ South (Bouamama et al., 1994, pp. 108, 158–9; Leclercq, 1989, pp. 287–9). Cultures built on popular music thus cannot be seen in isolation in France, but as part of a continuum of marginalized cultural practices as a young, ethnically diverse but socially excluded sector of the population embark on the process of articulating identities for the 'post' era. It is this sense of having little to inherit from the immediate past, of having to start from scratch in terms of finding one's place in society that has contributed in my view to the emergence in France of significant youth cultural forms which have at their heart this very matter of identity, of belonging and yet being distinct, of seeking recognition from outside, while remaining autonomous. Furthermore, it accounts for their emergence very particularly in those areas that suffer the most in terms of social exclusion.

Space precludes the provision of a detailed history of the three 'scenes' under consideration (the rap scene in Marseille, the ragga network of south-west France and the Parisian dance music scene).[3] Each has in common a steady development away from the spotlight of media attention, and outside of the central commercial circuits sustained by French subsidiaries of the 'big six' companies that dominate the multinational music industry (Virgin, BMG, EMI, PolyGram, Sony and Warner Music). Consequently, each has expanded to a large extent by creating its own networks of promotion and distribution: independent record labels for the release of auto-produced cassettes, 12" singles or compact discs; fanzines and newsletters; club nights which encourage joining a membership scheme or mailing list. A second feature common to what at first sight might appear very diverse sites of musical production is that each scene has at its core a direct relationship to the musical traditions that have sprung from what Paul Gilroy (1993) calls the Black Atlantic (hip-hop, reggae, club music (house, techno)), traditions that run in parallel to those of rock music, which emerged from the same sources. In fact in France, a distinction between the rock music tradition (perceived by practitioners as a culture now thoroughly absorbed by the ethnic majority 'mainstream' or 'establishment'[4]) and the 'funkier' forms of music cited above, is perhaps more sharply drawn than elsewhere in Europe.

This relationship to the music of the Black Atlantic expresses itself in several important ways. First, there is a foregrounding of references to earlier traditions of music from the African diaspora (blues, jazz, gospel, soul, r'n'b), with practitioners from each of the three scenes expressing their debt to these traditions through the use of musical samples, through direct 'name-checking' in tribute to acknowledged heroes from the past, or through the acknowledgement in interviews of the formative role played by such music in the development of group style and taste. Second, there is an embracing of new digital technologies (the sampler, synthesizer or sequencer), which is central in the production of the music itself. The effects of the use of such technologies are multiple: they enable a 'cut and paste' approach to assembling musical sequences, characterized by a sustained steady-state tonality that is markedly different from the linear sense of progressive tension and release more common to the verse-chorus-verse structures of the pop and traditional song. Furthermore, the manipulation of samples opens up a potentially unlimited, hugely eclectic range of sources that can be drawn on to feed into the musical collage. Finally, the speed with which these technologies can be mastered obviates the need to serve long apprenticeships in musicianship, a feature of most other musical traditions, and renders these three musical scenes singularly egalitarian.

Egalitarianism is also a mark of a third common feature: each scene has as its physical and symbolic centre the collective social celebration (jam, sound system, rave and so on) for which the music is primarily designed. In other words, each scene produces music whose overriding purpose is to be danced to, and danced to with a crowd. On the one hand, this locally-based crowd plays a key role in providing potential competition for the name performers, and this tends to undermine, if not entirely dissolve, the hierarchies of star and audience. On the other, the centrality accorded to rhythm highlights a fourth feature common to the musical output of the scenes under consideration. These are what Sarah Thornton (1995) has called disc cultures, where the previously prevalent hierarchy of preference for the live over the recorded performance is inverted – the musician or band is supplanted by the DJ or selector, who assembles the recorded performance into new, unprecedented 'live' sequences via seamless mixing, or with the more extravagant techniques of cutting, scratching and backspin. A 'good' DJ or selector is one who succeeds in capturing the mood of the gathering, who manages to 'carry the crowd' through the musical choices on offer. In so doing, he or she begins to express the identity of that social collective, with its own particular shared past (that is, certain records, phrases or samples have a localized significance in the history of the gathering). This identity may then be expressed in turn in recorded music produced by individuals or groups whose taste and style has been decisively formed by their participation in the local scene. Such expression of local identities and common experience is the motivation for the final feature shared by each of the youth cultures in question. Within each set of musical practices, a central importance is accorded to the establishing of a highly idiosyncratic and personalized collective mythology, within which particular locations play a vital role in metonymically representing certain features of the culture that are deemed to be decisive. The fact that these physical sites extend far beyond the boundaries of localized experience, and even beyond national boundaries, is indicative that each of these cultures is expressive of transnational affinities: the need to have physically visited these sites is in fact irrelevant. Their importance is symbolic or imaginative, and they form the markers of an imaginatively constituted transnational space, which in its expansiveness and range is frequently in marked contrast both to the physical space actually available to or occupied by the scene in question, and to traditional notions of national culture and identity.

In order to see in more detail how these imagined spaces function, and in what ways they are expressive of transnational affinity, I will look in turn at how groups of practitioners from each scene stake out their imagined social spaces, and how transnational loyalties are sustained through their musical practice. The first group, Massilia Sound System, hail from Marseille (more specifically the Belle de Mai quarter of the city, centrally located, but traditionally working class), and have been prime movers in the creation of a ragga scene in south-west France, a network that has established connections in Italy, and which is associated with groups like the Fabulous Troubadours from Toulouse, the Black Lions from Vitrolles, and Hypnotik Gang, also from Marseille. Three specific cities form the parameters of Massilia's imagined social space: Genoa in Italy (from contacts established with the ragga scene there), Marseille (as the group's birthplace and local setting) and Kingston, Jamaica (as the birthplace of reggae and ragga music, and of the sound system which has become its chief mode of articulation). These three cities are linked by a cultural *Linha Imaginot*[5] 'qui ne passe pas par Paris' ('which avoids Paris'). Starting in the mid-1980s by organizing concerts and sound system events, Massilia Sound System established their own record label, Roker Promocion, in 1990.[6] More recently they created an 'anti-fan' club, the *Chourmo*, which attempts to encourage its members to overcome passivity by emulating Massilia in the fact that they 'got up and did something'. The club currently counts about 400 members, drawn from across the region, with young people of French parentage predominant. The key to the expression of transnational affinity comes in that, for Massilia, ragga is a global phenomenon, but which is simultaneously a vehicle for expressing a local identity and regional culture. This is most noticeable in the use in their toasts of occitan and patois,[7] the unofficial languages of southern France, a use explained by two members of the group, when questioned about the apparent contradiction in mixing the 'modernism' of the imported cultures of rap and ragga, and the 'archaism' of provincial and regional cultures:

Tatou: That's not a contradiction… So why do these words that we don't understand that well, against a music from the other side of the world, why do they affect us?… In the end we realized that rap and ragga are music for folklore. Music that is rooted, and which speaks to people. The Jamaicans tell a story that happens at the end of their street, and that is of interest to the rest of the world. They know how to talk about their culture, their island. We wanted to do the same thing with our Provençal and occitan culture.
Telerama: Your discourse of occitan reggae crossed with the 70-year-old philosopher Félix Castan, the enemy of centralism, reeks of the 1970s and regionalist movements!
Jali: Regionalist? We have wiped that word from our vocabulary. Those bearded militants with their independence theories were mistaken. They held the people as guilty, treated them as victims or as the alienated. We're not only interested in keeping occitan for the occitans. On the contrary, we think that you need to have occitan culture, which has been denied throughout history, to understand French culture.[8]

This concern to redress the balance of history, to reassert the right of speech for dominated, peripheral cultures is frequently expressed using humour as a weapon. One of their tactics has been to create a fake political party, a scam sustained for a couple of years. The PIIM (Parti Indépendantiste Internationaliste Marseillais) is an affectionate pastiche of French regionalist and separatist movements of the 1970s, whose ideas they have to an extent adopted via the Fabulous Troubadours at Toulouse, who introduced them to the philosopher of decentralization, Félix Castan. In press interviews and conversation, Massilia constantly refute the notion that such assertion of occitan identity is necessarily exclusive, inward-looking or inimical to links with other local cultures. Instead, they honour popular traditions of Provençal independence and strong-mindedness, as seen in the fake political party's theme song.[9] It expresses a desire to participate in a revolution encompassing the 'quartiers du monde entier' ('the localities of the whole world'), incorporating a recurrent idea that it is up to marginalized communities to find their own identity, using whatever tools available to turn the tables on the powerful. For Massilia, ragga music is one such tool. The *Chourmo* is another (the name comes from the occitan for galley slave). The Fabulous Troubadours organize banquets to encourage rediscovery of the local social space through participation in an outdoor meal. The sense is of perpetuating traditions of popular festival for which Marseille and the south were once renowned, of being proud of one's local past and traditions, but open minded enough to combine them with newer traditions and outlooks that come from elsewhere, especially if analogies can be drawn in terms of a common response to exclusion, hardship and lack of acknowledgement from the host society.

This concern to seek respect for previously discarded histories marks the second group under consideration, and who spring from the hip-hop end of the rap/ragga spectrum in France. The rap group IAM also originate from Marseille: their 1994 album *Ombre est lumière* and a single taken from it ('Le Mia') sold significantly at national level, gained them recognition at the 1995 national music awards and to an extent has seen them cast in the role of saviours of the *chanson française* (traditional popular song). Its members of West African, North African and Italian origin reflect the fact that in Marseille, the constituency for rap music is more diverse than that for ragga, cutting across boundaries set by the separation into ethnic communities for which Marseille (uniquely in France) is supposedly renowned. IAM reiterate an attachment to Marseille and the locality of their upbringing. In contrast to this specific rootedness, they self-consciously create semi-mythical tropes in constituting identities that differentiate them from (implicit) notions of Frenchness. All members of the group adopt pseudonyms. However, these names of themselves do not bear a single, delineated identity, but are adopted and discarded at will, according to the demands of the situation. Their multiplicity conveys dynamic, not static notions of identity. Indeed, for IAM, apart from the double reference to a divine supreme being in the group's name (the group's logo has been designed to read as *Allah* in Arabic when inverted), it can also be considered as a polyvalent abbreviation: Imperial Asiatic Men, *Invasion Arrivant de Mars, Indépendantistes Autonomes Marseillais…* For IAM, identity originates chiefly in the African nation, now deemed worldwide in scope (the Black Atlantic).

Unlike American rap groups who stress the Zulu character of this nation, IAM incorporate their North African origins, featuring Egyptian hieroglyphics in their artwork. Once again, three sites serve as markers for this transnational space of identity: Marseille (as their city of origin), New York (as the city which witnessed the emergence of rap and hip-hop culture in the 1970s) and North Africa (particularly Egypt) as the (black) source of Western civilization. The group members' pseudonyms reflect this concern: the rapper Akhénaton, the DJ Khéops (both named after Egyptian pharaohs), the sound engineer Imhotep (named after an Egyptian architect of the pyramids). They have also constructed a mythology whereby Marseille was once an Egyptian peninsular, before becoming detached and floating across to France.

Unlike Massilia, traditional religious identities are not rejected – indeed syncretistic references recur, to Allah, Egyptian deities and Chinese philosophies (the group's second rapper Shurik'n'Chang-ti, takes his name from a martial arts weapon). It should be noted that such affiliation with Islam (chiefly through the conversion of one group member Philippe Fragione alias Chill/Akhénaton) marks the group out from other French groups on the rap scene, but this cannot be compared to the black separatism of the American Nation of Islam and its leader Louis Farakhan, which has its advocates in the American rap scene (for example, the group Public Enemy). IAM repeatedly and specifically reject Farakhan's nationalistic version of Islam in interviews,[10] but this should not overlook the fact that such expression of loyalty to an Islamic inheritance is not always well received by some social commentators on the left, whose secular model of integration would look for a situation where the descendants of immigrants would express other loyalties in priority.

Thus, the building of new mythology has political consequences, seen in songs like 'IAM concept' from the 1991 album *De la Planète Mars*, which denounces the falsification inherent in Western portrayals of the African as the Primitive, and reverses the premises, portraying Africa and its culture as the civilizers of the world before it was visited by the barbarities of colonialism. The title track from the same album reverses the discourse of Jean-Marie Le Pen's National Front, with its talk of immigrant invasion. Instead, it is Marseille, with its provincial traditions of language and culture and its historic links with the Mediterranean, that has been subject to invasion and subjugation by the rest of France, and in particular by hordes led by '*un blond haineux et stupide à la fois*' ('a blond man, full of hatred and stupidity'), who have established a kingdom of the blind where the one-eyed man is king (Le Pen has a glass eye).

In a similar fashion to Massilia Sound System, the restrictions imposed by growing up in a marginalized and peripheral sector of society (Marseille as France's periphery, the northern quarters as the city's own periphery) are circumvented by the creation of an expansive social space that escapes the restrictions of the local. This space then serves as a platform from which the prevailing balance of power can be challenged. This challenge is being acted out by IAM in a very concrete fashion: they have created their own record label and production company to encourage and develop other rap groups and artists from Marseille. Members of the group continue to run regular workshops for young people from deprived areas of the city in poetry writing or in the use of technology for music making. In interviews connected with the release of a new album in early 1997 (*L'école du micro d'argent*), the group remained positive in their commitment to a politics of plurality and diversity, despite the advance of the National Front in their very locality.

While such an overt concern with current politics in France is not such a marked feature of the third scene under consideration, the connections that the Paris club music network maintains with the global networks of dance culture suggest a *de facto* opposition to restrictive definitions of national culture and affinity. Indeed, one of the major players on the scene, the DJ Laurent Garnier, has expressed how travel to America and Japan has reinforced his sense of being European, particularly in relation to the feel of the European city (Push, 1997, p. 60). While representing only part of the spectrum of club and dance music in France, the Paris house and techno scene, centred on club nights such as 'Wake up!' at the Rex club, and record labels such as BPM and F-Communications, has in the mid-1990s seen the emergence of musicians and DJs (Motorbass, Daft Punk, Dimitri from Paris, Garnier himself) who have become well established as recognized artists outside of France.

One such practitioner is the Parisian DJ/musician Ludovic Navarre, who has released since 1991 a series of EPs on the label F-Communications under the moniker St Germain. The music he produces for the club scene covers most of its various genres and guises (house, dub, trip-hop, ambient) and is predominantly instrumental. However, what transpires throughout his output is a fascination for America and its culture, but not necessarily that of Coca Cola, Disney and McDonald's. Instead, Navarre is clearly concerned to explore the traditions and cultures of black America, jazz and blues music, the civil rights movement. Consequently, there is a less specifically stated attachment to particular locations that produce the music, though both Chicago (as the site where house music was invented) and Detroit (the home of techno) figure prominently as reference points. Similarly, attachments to Paris are evident in his choice of alias, and in the name of his 1996 album *Boulevard*. Samples (both musically and lyrically) draw principally from the musical traditions of the Black Atlantic (reggae, soul, jazz, funk, blues). To this writer's knowledge, he was one of the first club musicians to incorporate samples from Delta blues men into club music, taking snatches of a lyric to form a rhythmic loop, or opening tracks with samples of blues singers introducing their songs to a live audience.

His 1996 album already mentioned presented a blend of technology and live instrumentation, provided by collaboration with musicians from the Paris jazz scene, which seems to act as an overt statement of his 'connection' with that musical tradition. The track 'Deep in it' has a long talk-over from Navarre himself acknowledging his debt to the creators and DJs of the deep house sound of Detroit, Chicago and New York, as well as name-checking European DJs responsible for keeping the tradition alive. In his use of samples, Navarre also announces an affinity with the American civil rights tradition – for the track 'Easy to remember', against a lengthy sample from a valedictory speech to Malcolm X, describing his life and work, Navarre composes a start stop jazz-house rhythm. Other lyrical samples are more allusive: the track 'My mama said' gets its title from the looped use of a sampled blues singer wailing 'I remember what my mama said', as if to assert the importance of remembrance, of linking into a long running tradition, but one which is able to provide the raw materials for creative and artistic evolution into the future.

Yet other samples indicate a predilection for the more melancholy aspects of the blues – short stabs of tales of woe, of hardship, of difficulty faced and survived. With regard to constituted space, the location is evidently less clearly delineated than with the practitioners previously considered – instead, a symbolic cultural landscape is created, that stems from a certain version, a certain idea of an America that has much to teach those willing to listen. Such a space derives from a stance of openness to other cultural traditions, a desire to absorb the ideas generated in other places and other times. There is a resolute determination to participate in the cross-currents of global popular culture.

While it would be misguided to read the cultures that have emerged from sections of French youth over the past decade as a barometer of social opinion, or as reliable indicators of widespread attitudes held by young people with regard to national and European identity, they do indicate that for significant sectors of young French society, subjectivities prevail which are distinguished by markers taken from a cultural space that transcends that of the European geo-political sphere. Far from contributing to a sense of unattached homogeneity, these markers have been instrumental in revivifying local attachments and have led some to rediscover aspects of that locality that seemed to have been 'levelled out' by the processes of modernization. As a consequence, I believe key questions are raised concerning the possibility of a commonly-held culture that would in some way give depth to the institutions of European integration. Through the deliberate expression of transnational affinities via the constitution of an imagined social space, with its interlinking networks of cultural exchange and cross-current, each of the artists considered is in fact posing a key question for the future development of culture within the European area, whether the label 'European' is attached to it or not. For the ragga group Massilia Sound System and their *Linha Imaginot* linking the cultures of southern Europe with those of the Caribbean, the question revolves around whether Europe can find a meaningful place outside of the museum for those regional cultures and languages that 'lost out' in the processes of nation-building and centralization. For the rap group IAM and their North African triangle that reaches to New York, the question centres on the kind of historical and cultural affinities that parts of Europe have with areas beyond the physical continent, particularly in the common heritage of the Mediterranean. This question reaches its focus through the issue of whether a Europe of Christian tradition can find more than grudging accommodation for the cultural heritage of Islam. Finally, in his celebration of a certain conception of America, Ludovic Navarre is facing the question, and it is one that has faced France in particular for most of this century, of whether Europe can develop a relationship with North American culture that neither demonizes it nor uncritically celebrates it. Thus, in their imaginative constitution of transnational affinity, these groups are at least asking the right questions of any culture that would call itself European.

NOTES

1. Two accounts of this judgement, and of the subsequent response from ministers, intellectuals and politicians, illustrate perfectly the polarized nature of the debate on culture and identity in contemporary France. Brézet (1996) from the right, expresses his approval of the judgement, framed with an account of attacks by young 'immigrants' on off-duty female police officers, while Dupuy (1996) from the left (as editor of the national daily *Libération*) denounces the case as a clear attack on the freedom of artistic expression in France.
2. The term 'beur' was coined from the 'verlan' or back-slang for 'Arabe', and was generally claimed by young people of ethnic parentage (not necessarily North African), but born in France. Its subsequent overuse, particularly in the media, has led some more recently to reject the term as being racially overdetermined. In its original use, the term clearly aimed to designate plurality of cultural identity and affinity.
3. For a brief history of the development of rap and ragga in France, see Warne, 1997, pp. 143–5 and Cachin, 1996, pp. 66–79. For more detail on the nature of hip-hop culture in France (including on the related practices of graffiti art, tagging and dance), see Bazin, 1995 and Lapassade and Rousselot, 1990. Desse et al., 1993, Louis and Prinaz, 1990 and Dufresne, 1991 contain interviews with participants in the movement. The history of dance music in France has yet to be written, but information can be gleaned

from interviews with French DJs and musicians in such specialist music magazines as *Mixmag, DJ magazine* and *Muzik* for example: see Mellor, 1993, Push, 1997 and Petridis, 1997.

4. For example, see comments by Shurik'n and Chill, members of the group IAM, in interview with Guerreiro (1990). This form of distinction is most clearly demonstrated in the output of independent radio stations such as the Paris-based Radio Nova, and in that of music magazines such as *L'Affiche*, which devotes itself to coverage of 'new music' ('les musiques nouvelles'). In both cases, rock music is marked by a complete absence.

5. This phrase from the occitan language is best translated as 'a line of creative imagination'. There is a humorous reference to the Maginot line, a defensive wall of fortifications built on France's Eastern frontier in the inter-war period. (Occitan, the language of the medieval troubadours, was, with the regional variations of patois and Provençale, formerly the language of southern France.)

6. Massilia Sound System have released three albums on this label: *Parla patois* (1992), *Chourmo!* (1993) and *Commando Fada* (1996).

7. Toast/toasting is the name given to the rhythmic speech patterns intoned by the sound-system DJ against a pulsing musical background of bass, drums and other sound effects. Initially a way of 'geeing up' the dance hall crowd, these toasts soon developed into full-length narratives. For a detailed history of the development of the Jamaican sound-system, see Hebdige, 1987, pp. 82–9.

8. Leclère, T., 'Entretien: Massilia Sound System – Aïoli, rap et foot', in *Télérama*, No. 2337, 26 octobre 1994, pp. 24–5.

9. 'PIIM. part 2', track 13, *Parla patois* (1992).

10. See for example Dufresne, 1991, pp. 151–2.

REFERENCES

Bazin, H., *La culture hip-hop* (Paris, Desclée de Brouwer, 1995).

Bouamama, S., *De la galère à la citoyenneté: les jeunes, la cité, la société* (Paris, Desclée de Brouwer, 1993).

Bouamama, S., Djerdoubi, Mokhtar and Sad-Saoud, Hadjila, *Contribution à la mémoire des banlieues* (Paris, Editions du Volga, 1994).

Bourdieu, P., 'La jeunesse n'est qu'un mot', in *Questions de sociologie* (Paris, Minuit, 1984), pp. 143–54.

Boxhoorn, B., 'European Identity and the Process of European Unification: Compatible Notions?', in Wintle, M. (ed.), *Culture and Identity in Europe. Perceptions of Divergence and Unity in Past and Present* (Aldershot, Avebury, 1996), pp. 133–45.

Brézet, A., 'Les rappeurs de la haine', *Le Spectacle du Monde*, No. 417, décembre 1996, pp. 24–30.

Cachin, O., *L'offensive rap* (Paris, Gallimard, 1996).

Chamboredon, J-C., 'Adolescence et post-adolescence: la "juvénisation". Remarques sur les transformations récentes des limites de la définition sociale de la jeunesse', in Alléon, A. M., Morvan, O. and Lebovici, S. (eds), *Adolescence terminée, adolescence interminable* (Paris, PUF, 1985), pp. 13–28.

Desse, Massot, F. and Millet, F., *Freestyle* (Paris, Massot and Millet, 1993).

Dufresne, D., *Yo! révolution rap* (Paris, Ramsay, 1991).

Dupuy, G., 'Editorial: Casser du miroir', *Libération*, 16–17 novembre 1996, p. 2.

Fontaine, A. and Fontana, C., *Raver* (Paris, Anthropos, 1996).

Galland, O., *Sociologie de la jeunesse: l'entrée dans la vie* (Paris, A. Colin, 1991).

Galland, O., 'La jeunesse en France, un nouvel âge de la vie', in Galland, O. and Cavalli, A. (eds), *L'Allongement de la jeunesse* (Poitiers, Actes Sud, 1993), pp. 19–39.

Geindre, F. (coordinator), 'Villes, Démocratie, Solidarité: le prix d'une politique' (Rapport préparatoire au XIe plan) (Paris, La Documentation Française, 1993).

Gilroy, P., *The Black Atlantic: Modernity and Double Consciousness* (London, Verso, 1993).

Guerreiro, J., 'Rap like an Egyptian: Rap'n'Marseille', *Rock & Folk*, No. 280, décembre 1990, pp. 60–5.

Hebdige, D., *Cut'n'Mix: Culture, Identity and Caribbean Music* (London, Comedia/Routledge, 1987).

Lapassade, G. and Rousselot, P., *Le rap ou le fureur de dire* (Paris, Loris Talmart, 1990).

Leclercq, R-J., 'Nature des revendications et des enjeux culturels portés par les minorités actives issues de l'immigration maghrébine en France pour la période 1978–1987', in Lorreyte, B. (ed.), *Les politiques d'intégration des jeunes issus de l'immigration* (Paris, CIEMI/L'Harmattan, 1989), pp. 284–92.

Louis, P. and Prinaz, L., *Skinheads, Taggers, Zulus and Co* (Paris, La Table Ronde, 1990).

Mellor, C., 'Wake up: Paris – French House Music Comes of Age', *DJ magazine*, No. 95, 12–25 August 1993, pp. 12–13.

Morley, D., 'The End of EurAm Man', *Paragraph*, Vol. 20, No. 1, March 1997, pp. 8–27.

Petridis, A., 'Da Funk Mob', *Mixmag*, Vol. 2, No. 70, March 1997, pp. 106–11.

Push, 'Taking the Plunge: Will the Real Laurent Garnier Please Stand Up?', *Muzik*, No. 23, April 1997, pp. 58–60.

Rigby, B., *Popular Culture in Modern France* (London and New York, Routledge, 1991).

Thornton, S., *Club Cultures: Music, Media and Subcultural Capital* (Cambridge, Polity Press, 1995).

Warne, C., 'Articulating Identity from the Margins: "le mouv" and the Rise of Hip-hop and Ragga in France', in Perry, S. and Cross, M. (eds), *Voices of France: Social, Political and Cultural Identity* (London, Cassell, 1997), pp. 141–54.

14 Russia's Identity Crisis: its Effects on the Schools and the Young

Stephen Webber

Educationalists tend to overstate the extent of the influence that the school has on societal development. Nevertheless, this influence is, of course, considerable, and it can be increased further still during a period of societal transformation. In the case of post-Soviet Russia, for instance, one might reasonably expect that the school will have a major role to play in inculcating the values deemed necessary for the transition to a democracy. It is somewhat surprising, therefore, that in the extensive literature produced in English on the process of transition in Russia, the issue of education has consistently received little mention. Instead, the emphasis has been placed on the study of events in the political arena, the analysis of the state of the Russian economy, or on the more visible signs of the social crises which the country is suffering from, such as the increase in organized crime and the spread of poverty and destitution. Moreover, the lack of attention afforded to educational matters in Western studies parallels, to some extent, a similar lack of interest towards educational issues within Russian society itself, as the politicians and the mass media also concentrate on the more immediate, headline-grabbing events, while the average Russian citizen, following the long Soviet tradition, often prefers to retreat into her or his micro-world of family, friends and colleagues, and pays relatively little attention to the possible long-term consequences that developments in the schools might hold for the future of Russia.

Within the school system, considerable efforts are being made, in fact, to effect change in virtually all aspects of the learning process, with the aim, according to the architects of the ambitious reform programme, of rendering the school suitable for the needs of a democracy. This process is being conducted, however, in the absence of a strong societal mandate, and, indeed, in the context of an identity crisis in Russia itself, as the country struggles to come to terms with the legacy of the past, and the need to define some kind of path for its future. The schools may be able to help shape that path in the years to come – in the meantime, can they survive the storms of transition and the consequences of neglect? In this chapter, following a short critical review of the programme for school reform, I aim to provide a brief summary of the current state of the school–society relationship in the 'new' Russia, evaluating first the extent to which society can be said to be taking an interest in education, then going on to look at two 'attempts' on the life of the school, and the response which society made to these events.

THE AIMS OF REFORM: TOWARDS THE FUTURE OR AGAINST THE PAST?

After the dissolution of the USSR in 1991, the Russian Ministry of Education lost little time in introducing legislation to reform the Soviet school system which they had inherited, with a Law on Education passed in July 1992.[1] The main points of the programme can be summarized thus:

- decentralization
- democratization (introducing greater openness and accountability)
- diversification (greater variety of educational establishments, providing greater 'choice' to parents and pupils in the selection of schools)
- humanization (establishing democratic patterns of interpersonal behaviour in the schools, emphasizing the adoption of democratic, humane values)
- humanitirization (placing greater emphasis on the teaching of humanities subjects).

This agenda received a sympathetic reception, on the whole, from both Russian and foreign analysts, impressed by the programme's commitment to the promotion of democracy and the adoption of educational values which appeared to be familiar to those found in Western systems.[2] Indeed, despite the fundamental changes which this reform programme demands of the schools, its aims have been adopted positively, for the most part, by the teaching community itself. To some extent the natural conservatism that teachers often display when faced with reform has been offset by the fact that the *perception* of the demands of change in the schools has been somewhat less than the *aims* of change laid down in the programme. As I argue elsewhere,[3] this is perhaps fortunate, as the capacity of the system to meet those demands is, at present at least, inadequate (see Figure 14.1).

While implementation of new curricula and the introduction of innovation in teaching methods have begun to take place, therefore, such processes are often influenced heavily by the traditions of the Soviet school, allowing the existing staff to draw on their experience of working

> ### a) declared aims > system capacity
>
> ### cf.
>
> ### b) perceived aims ≃ or = (perception of) individual capacity

Figure 14.1 Dichotomy between declared and perceived aims in relation to the actual and perceived capacity of the system and individual schools and teachers to respond to those aims

in the old system. If the wholesale break with such traditions that is promoted by certain educationalists, and practised in certain so-called 'alternative' schools,[4] had been forced on the teaching profession too quickly, as seemed possible in the early days of the educational 'revolution' pursued by Russia's first Minister of Education, Eduard Dneprov,[5] I would suggest that many in the profession would have felt alienated from the reforms, and bitter that the system they had helped to maintain was under threat of being 'dismembered', as one headteacher described it.[6] The pace of implementation seen in the schools may not meet the rather optimistic expectations of some in the reform camp, having been slowed by the inertia of the old system, and by the enormous material problems faced by the schools.[7] However, such 'delays' can be seen to have had at least some positive value, in allowing the system time to adjust to the demands of reform, and enabling the schools to make a more reasoned and informed evaluation of the nature of the changes being proposed. Although many problems remain (such as the need to ensure system-wide cohesion during a process of rapid devolution), I feel that it is possible to speak of early signs of 'settling down' in the process of change, as the ideas of reform are internalized and adapted to suit the realistic capabilities of the schools and the regions.

Nevertheless, while a process of adaptation and, in some ways, 'watering-down' of the reform goals has taken place in the course of implementation, there is still cause for concern with regard to certain key premises which were put forward as justification for the introduction of elements of the reform programme, and whose full implications have yet to be properly debated in Russia, both within the teaching profession and by society at large. The weakness of the reform agenda, as it was originally conceived, lay in the remedial, backward-looking stance implicit in a number of policies which appear, on the surface, to represent rather forward-looking, constructive proposals. It was devised by educationalists and educational psychologists who tended to be scathing in their criticism of the Soviet system, berating it for its inefficiency and poor standards, and attacking it as a symbol of the 'communist' system. To a degree such criticism was justified. The conservatism of the old system had rendered it inflexible and unable to respond to the demands for change in curriculum content and teaching methods. Further, while the 'communist' nature of the curriculum and pastoral work had, by the late 1980s, become increasingly ineffective in bringing up pupils according to the declared ideological principles, such matters clearly required attention if the school was to conform to the needs of a democratic, pluralist society.

In their desire to eradicate the vestiges of communist ideology from the classroom, however, the reformers proved to be rather over-zealous, and misguided in their analysis of the extent of the 'problem'. In common with a similar tendency observed in Russian society at large, the perceived legacy of the Soviet era, as seen by the reform camp, appeared to be exaggerated, and the policies proposed to deal with it, accordingly, went rather too far in rejecting the traditions of the past. In support of calls for the need to 'humanize' the school, for instance, Dneprov (1992, p. 4) labelled the Soviet school a 'prison-like institution'. While teacher–pupil relations do, indeed, tend to be relatively formal and strict in the Russian school, and while this may lead observers from Anglo-Saxon countries to see a need for 'improvements' in this matter, the Russian approach may not appear so alien to educationalists and pupils from, say, the German or French systems. There is a need for 'humanization', but the claims of some that the Soviet school had played a key part in the maintenance of the spirit of totalitarianism in Soviet society were somewhat simplistic.

In this and in other matters, the reform camp showed an inability to 'decontextualize' the Soviet school, to strip away its ideological façade and remove it from its Soviet setting, and thus to examine its work objectively. The issue of 'upbringing' work (*vospitanie*, roughly the equivalent of Personal and Social Education in the English system), for instance, has been neglected for much of the post-Soviet period, as it was felt necessary to abandon the approaches employed in the Soviet period, while ignoring the need to replace the vacuum that the removal of the old programmes would leave. In another area of the reforms, the enthusiasm of the Ministry of Education for the setting up of 'alternative' schools, and the introduction of differentiation and selection of pupils, stems from a reaction against the perceived 'levelling' of pupils which was said to have taken place under the Soviet system, in which all students were supposed to follow a common curriculum, with no variation allowed, ostensibly to cater for children of different ability ranges. Consequently, so the criticism went, all pupils suffered as a result of this levelling to cater for the 'average' student, with, it was argued, the more able pupils most heavily handicapped.

Again, although it is true that the lack of differentiation did inhibit the teacher in catering for all of the pupils, school programmes were, for the most part, rather academic in their orientation, geared towards the preparation of the more able students for entrance to further and higher education. It could therefore be said that the below-average ability pupils were those who fared worse, as they received comparatively less attention according to the old curricula. In the current of reform in the post-Soviet era, however, it was fashionable, at least in the early 1990s, for the educational debate to focus on the need of the supposedly disadvantaged more able pupils, with a particularly active discussion taking place on the requirements of so-called 'gifted' children (Belova, 1994).

Such tendencies in the sphere of education have run parallel, in many ways, to patterns of development observed in Russian society as a whole in recent years, where, for instance, the perceived values of the Soviet era have come increasingly to be rejected by certain sections of the population, while a lack of clarity remains with regard to the type of values that might form the basis of the 'new' Russia. The school does not exist in isolation from its society, of course, but reflects it, and in the current context of social upheaval, the school inevitably suffers from this uncertainty. Although the inertia of the old system may act as a stabilizing factor for a time, the Russian school is in urgent need of support and protection to help it pass through the immediate problems of transition, together with guidance from its society as to the nature of its task in helping to shape the future of Russia. Are these needs being met?

THE SOCIETY–SCHOOL RELATIONSHIP: LESSONS TO BE LEARNED?

The Need for a Vision

The importance of a vision to guide reform has been highlighted frequently in studies of educational change.[8] Alongside the setting of educational goals it is also essential that some kind of discussion be conducted on the desired outcomes that the changes will have in societal terms. This is not to say that there may not be considerable disagreement, even elements of conflict between groups within a society over the course that educational development should take, but that such debate will, in countries which possess effective civil societies, be conducted within the boundaries of social stability.

In the case of the 'new' Russia, as I have noted above, it is extremely difficult to talk with any confidence of a firm consensus within society with regard to the direction in which the population believes the country should proceed. Rigby (1995, p. 217) summarizes succinctly the very varied choices:

> Does Russia need a period of conservative or transformative authoritarianism? If not, should it be a presidential or parliamentary democracy? Should it essentially be a unitary state, a federation, or a confederation? How much freedom is consonant with social and political peace? Should as much 'socialism' as possible be retained? ... Should market reforms go the 'shock therapy' Polish road, the authoritarian Chinese road, or some other? ... All this suggests a near chaos defying analysis.

The traditions of democratic elections and a market economy are slowly being established in Russia, yet the shelling of the White House (the parliament building) to solve the executive–legislature rift in 1993 provides just one of many reminders that such traditions are still weak, while the ongoing and, in some ways, worsening economic and social crises facing the country indicate that Russia still faces many decades of painful transition and reconstruction. It is against this backdrop that the schools must try to adjust to the realities of the post-Soviet era. As I demonstrate below, they must do so with only limited support from Russia's weak civil society.

Society's Neglect: the Implications for the School of a Weak Civil Society

A society's role with regard to its schools should encompass a number of functions, including:

- *Demand*: the expression of what the needs of the individual and society are and their implications for the work of the school.
- *Monitoring*: the task of overseeing developments in the schools (a control–support function).
- *Support*: the provision of material and other support to the school, to enable it to perform the tasks assigned to it.
- *Safety net*: the guarantee that the collective efforts of the disparate bodies which make up civil society will serve to protect the interests of the school system, of the teaching force, pupils, parents and others,

for instance through attempting to influence government policy (in elections, through lobbying, strikes, publicity, etc).

In no country are these functions performed completely effectively; indeed, the capacity of civil society to manage these tasks is often limited by the nature of the system, by the relative power of government policy, and so on. While deep divisions can be seen to exist in British society over the nature of educational values, however, civil society can be seen to be performing its role more or less effectively. In Russia, the picture is rather different.

TOWARDS A COMPREHENSIVE DEBATE

The root of the problem in the school–society relationship centres on the inadequate nature of the debate on education in Russia, which, as I have suggested, tends to be overshadowed by other events. Progress has, nevertheless, been made away from what I term the 'hidden' debate of the Soviet era to the current situation of 'shallow' debate (see Figure 14.2). The next stage of development should be towards a state of 'open' or 'comprehensive' debate, in which the system and society (or groups and individuals within them, including political parties) have a clearer impression of the aims and desired outcomes of the process of education. While the attainment of this open debate offers a number of advantages over the current situation, though, it also holds certain potentially negative consequences.

'Hidden' Debate

The Soviet state promoted, officially, a unitary philosophy of education based on 'communist' principles, and appeared to guard jealously its right to preserve this monopoly. Such restrictions certainly stifled discussion of educational matters, while the 'official' line dominated any discussion which did take place, thus exerting a powerful influence on the views held by teachers, parents and others, who were able to hear only one approach

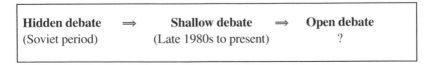

Hidden debate ⟹ **Shallow debate** ⟹ **Open debate**
(Soviet period) (Late 1980s to present) ?

Figure 14.2 The debate on education: from Soviet to Russian school systems

promulgated. However, human nature withstood all Soviet efforts to mould it to conform to one image, and although the centre dominated, it did not hold a monopoly over educational philosophy. Instead, there existed a situation of 'hidden' debate, in which Soviet citizens, as in so many other aspects of their lives, learned to give the appearance of following the official line, while, in fact, pursuing a more personal agenda; Soviet teachers, pupils and parents were inclined to adapt the explicitly declared aims of the curriculum to suit their own needs, as far as this was possible. To some extent, of course, they may not even have realized that they were not adhering to the true course promoted by the centre, for the centre itself did not adhere to it. While elements of 'communist' education were included in the system, the education provided in the schools, at least from the 1930s on, resembled more closely, in many ways, that provided in the pre-revolutionary Tsarist school, and the academically-orientated models of the French lycée, the German gymnasium and the English grammar school. A hidden societal debate was, therefore, an integral part of the Soviet system, even if this fact was not acknowledged by the state.

'Shallow' Debate

This debate developed considerably from the mid-1980s onwards, as the work of the 'Teacher Innovators' (a group of reform-minded educationalists) was publicized and a modest public discussion took place on the perceived problems of the Soviet school. With the arrival of the reform camp at the Russian Ministry of Education, and the open exhortations to the system to diversify, and for regions, schools and teachers to take responsibility for their own actions, the tempo of opening up the philosophical base of the system appeared to gain further momentum. With the presence now, in 1998, of alternative schools, of variety in textbook choice (when textbooks can be obtained), and with the guarantee that anyone is able to put forward their own views on educational issues without fear of retribution, this might be seen as evidence of the development of a more 'open' form of debate, in which the system is supported by a wide cross-section of educational beliefs and aims. Nevertheless, despite such evidence, I would contest that the current scenario is better described as a 'shallow' debate, for a number of reasons that concern both the internal state of the system and, significantly, the school's relationship with its society.

For many schools and teachers, as I argued above, the perception of the aims of reforms represents a diluted version of the agenda, thus allowing the schools to suppose that their capacity to implement these changes is adequate to the task (a factor which is strengthened by the tendency, often noted in school systems, for schools to overestimate their capacity to tackle change). As a result, many schools and teachers may think they are pursuing the course of change set down by the ministry, therefore, but the majority, in fact, is engaged in a lip-service approach to change, in which only a certain amount of innovation is actually taking place. This dilution of the reform agenda may have led to some positive outcomes in the short term, watering down some of the more radical (and potentially damaging) aspects of the reforms, enabling some in the system to make a more reasoned judgement on the relative merits of the policies and developing a more practical approach to dealing with the demands of change. Yet the variety of interpretation of the reform aims which exists in the system, and the degree to which confusion and the lack of clarity still remain, are issues which, if left unaddressed, will serve in the long term both to act as a brake on the reforms and to hinder the development of the system as a whole. Similarly, the eclectic nature of the reform programme put forward by the centre, combined with the vagueness of some of its policies, has undoubtedly contributed to reducing the potential for opposition to and alienation from the change process thus far, establishing a degree of consensus on reform in the educational community. The limitations of the debate on change, however, means that this is what we can call a 'false' consensus, whose ability to keep the system together is likely to prove only temporary. Perhaps such shortcomings would be solved in the transition to a more 'open' form of debate?

'Open' Debate: Prospects and Dangers

The transition to an open debate will require the involvement of society and societal institutions (including the political parties) in order to ensure that the discussion of education and the identification of educational values takes place in this wider arena, rather than being confined to the educational sphere alone. The end result of this process, if it proceeds smoothly, should be the provision of a more solid foundation for the future development of the school system, which will have a more precise understanding of the nature of the tasks set before it by society, while the latter, in turn, will possess a clearer idea of what it needs from the schools, and what its own responsibilities are to the school system.

These, however, are long-term goals. In the short term, the development of an open debate is likely to be a difficult affair, for the level of commitment shown by Russian society towards the school system, and thus its potential to contribute to this debate, remains extremely limited. As a result, patterns of open pluralism are set to appear in a fragmented fashion and, as the psychological framework of Russian society continues to pass through its difficult transformation, the function of checks and balances that is served by a healthy civil society will operate only imperfectly. Accordingly, some elements of the open debate which may later become positive features of the system, may now exert a negative, damaging influence, owing to the weakness of other, less developed elements. This may lead to the development of a greater degree of conflict in the Russian educational debate, as the interests of particular groups and classes, still poorly defined in Russia, begin to emerge in a more explicit fashion. The emergence of a healthy civil society, which could take responsibility for the functions outlined above, however, is still some way off, as the following summary shows.[9]

POLITICIANS AND EDUCATION

The major Russian political parties profess to having some kind of platform on education, although it is rather difficult to discern the exact nature of their policies, owing to the lack of attention paid to educational issues within the parties themselves. For the most part, however, the debate on education in political circles has suffered from the same drawbacks as the general debate on education, namely a lack of interest from potential participants, and an inadequate development of the philosophical framework for the debate, which has meant that apathy and neglect have remained beneath a superficial veneer of glib, general statements on the need for a strong education system, which differ little in their content from party to party, and which do not imply a real commitment from the parties to pursue such aims with any real vigour.[10]

THE MASS MEDIA

The mass media do provide a limited amount of coverage of educational issues, while the major national newspapers maintain educational correspondents. However, the mass media are, of course, driven by major news stories, and there has been no shortage of crises, political and economic scandals, international disputes or crime stories to fill their pages in recent years. Any discussion of educational matters is, therefore, restricted.

COMMERCE AND INDUSTRY

For the most part, the world of commerce and industry is engrossed in what it, perhaps justifiably, sees as the more immediate problems of mere survival in the harsh economic climate of the 'new' Russia, and the level of direct support offered to, or interest shown in, educational matters is somewhat limited.

RELIGIOUS ORGANIZATIONS

The Orthodox Church has shown considerable interest in the schools, although the Ministry of Education has consistently held to the line that the state school must remain secular, arguing – understandably – that in a country with as diverse an ethnic mix as Russia, and with the amount of instability and potential for inter-ethnic tension that is present, any attempt to allow the Orthodox Church or any other religious group to have a strong influence in the running of the schools would entail serious risks.

THE GENERAL PUBLIC

Research studies and opinion poll surveys appear to indicate that the general public, in common with the elements of civil society referred to above, also does not pay very much attention to this question, in comparison with that which it gives to other issues of more immediate concern.[11] An interest is likely to be seen principally among parents whose children are currently attending school, thus establishing direct personal involvement. Such active involvement is more likely to be noted among white-collar, middle-class parents, with some parents now supporting their children's school in material terms, for instance through acting as a financial sponsor. The extent of parental involvement across the school system, however, despite an increased emphasis on the need to encourage such links, is still relatively small. Furthermore, any participation which does occur is almost invariably restricted to the school which those parents' children attend, with few if any attempts made by parents to organize themselves on a wider basis, for example by forming a lobbying group to voice the concerns of parents at the national or regional levels.

THE TEACHERS' TRADE UNION

The successor to the old Soviet educationalists' trade union, the *Profsoyuz rabotnikov narodnogo obrazovaniya i nauki* is still, for all intents and purposes, the only union representing teachers' interests across the Russian

Federation. While it does take a position on the course of reform in the schools, its chief preoccupation has been and remains that of trying to protect its members' material position. For all its efforts, however, the union's voice remains weak in comparison with other professional groups. The miners, for instance, frequently threaten to strike, and often do so, confident in the strength of the economic leverage that such action brings to bear on the government – teachers' strikes, in comparison, have little impact.

THE SCHOOL LEFT TO ITS OWN DEVICES?

From this brief résumé of the nature of civil society's stance (or lack of one) on education, it is clear that the functions referred to in the introduction to this chapter are only partially being performed by Russian society. With regard to the monitoring function, some positive and negative consequences can be observed in the lack of interest which society has paid to developments in the school system. While no school system can lead a separate existence from that of its society, the Russian system, in recent years, has enjoyed, or endured, a degree of autonomy from society, a situation which has placed a great deal of responsibility on the schools, the administrators and the policy-makers. In some cases, certain schools, or even regions, have adopted a rather irresponsible attitude which has ignored the need to keep in mind the interests of systemic cohesion. On the whole, however, the inertia of the old system, and the professionalism of the teaching force, have prevented widespread fragmentation. Meanwhile, at the national level, the policy-makers have also been given a good deal of autonomy in the development of the reform agenda and the subsequent supervision of the process of implementation.

In the absence of any clear mandate from society, or interest in the way in which the educational establishment is looking after the schools, one might conclude that it is fortunate that a path towards a 'democratic' system was chosen, almost independently, one might say, by the reform camp led by Dneprov, notwithstanding the lack of clarity which surrounded their plans. Nevertheless, the lack of societal scrutiny allowed, as I have suggested, certain internal contradictions to be included in the reform programme, the effect of which would soon become apparent, as I will relate in the following sections. The emergence of these problems – which one Russian contact, not without justification, I feel, described as 'attempts on the life of the school' – would prove a severe test for society's safety net.

SELECTION, REJECTION AND THE 43RD ARTICLE AFFAIR

Beneath the veil of uniformity in the Soviet education system, the selection of pupils was widely practised. For example, the school would have a key influence in the decision on which children would stay to study in the senior classes, and which would go on to a technical college (*Professionalno-tekhnicheskoe uchilishche – PTU*), the latter seen as very much a second-best option by many. Meanwhile, in some cases, specialized language schools (*spetsshkoly*) were turned into 'élite' schools catering for the offspring of the more influential sections of Soviet society. In the late 1980s a greater amount of selection was introduced as a result of both top–down and bottom–up initiatives, with the appearance of the first non-state and state-maintained alternative schools. The possibility of moving away from a comprehensive school arrangement, in which the school had to cater for all children in its 'catchment area', to one in which at least part of the school's pupil cohort passed through a selection procedure, was endorsed in Article 16 of the 1992 Law on Education, and quickly proved popular with a large number of establishments.[12] However, selection of some pupils (as a rule, naturally, the more able or those with wealthier parents) inevitably meant that other children were being rejected by those schools. It seemed that the presence of average and below-average ability pupils was no longer required in some schools, and the phenomenon of the *otsev*, or the removal of pupils, gathered pace. In most cases, the selection process took place after completion of basic secondary education in the 9th grade (age 15), and before entrance to the senior grades (10th and 11th grades, ages 15–17), although the practice soon began to be applied to entrance to other grades, even to the 1st grade itself (age 6). The problem for those pupils who found that they were unable to gain access to the school, but who wished nonetheless to continue their education, was that the possibilities for doing so were also quickly contracting. As Frolova noted in late 1993 (p. 18), while the Law on Education declared the right of every child to receive education:

> The reality of the fate of a thousand ninth-graders in one town [Novosibirsk] is that they are not to be 'honoured' with a place in the tenth form. Vocational colleges [PTU] are closing one after another. The number of *tekhnikums* [technical colleges] was already pretty small anyway. Evening schools find themselves in an ever worsening situation, since they have been labelled as having 'no prospects'.

In some schools, where a more humane and sensible approach was adopted, and where it was realized that any short-term gains for an individual teacher or school would be offset by the problems they entailed for the pupils and for society at large, a degree of protection was granted to pupils. Indeed, it should be pointed out that not all schools decided to adopt a selective stance. Nevertheless, across the country an increasing number of pupils were to find that the door to continued schooling had been closed.

The problems of youth did not stem only from the problem of rejection, of course. The material hardships from which an increasing number of families suffer have led a considerable number of children to neglect their schooling in order to engage in money-making activities on the streets, either to supplement their family's income, or because they find more interest and pleasure in such work than sitting in a classroom.[13] Meanwhile, there is a growing problem of 'social orphans', children who, for one reason or another, have been forced to fend for themselves, enjoying little or no support from family or social service structures. The end result is that a growing number of children of, ostensibly, school age are to be found instead outside of the school's walls (Slobodchikova, 1994), with a disturbing proportion of these children falling into a cycle of crime and destitution. While the *otsev* may not be the principal cause of such problems, the practice of selection and rejection clearly contributed to their development.

THE 43rd ARTICLE: BACKGROUND

The pattern of selection and rejection, therefore, was already established before the 43rd Article affair occurred. The importance of this affair lies in the message which it sent to the schools, parents, pupils and society on the degree of protection that the state saw fit to extend to the young, and also in the manner in which it was played out, leading eventually to a rather inconclusive dénouement.

The article itself was part of the Russian constitution (*Konstitutsiya*, 1995, p. 17) which was prepared to be submitted to the newly-elected Duma (parliament), following the October 1993 executive–legislature confrontation. It stated that henceforth, the upper age limit for free education would, effectively, be 15, i.e. to the end of basic secondary education, a drop of two years from the existing level, which was supposed to have guaranteed free complete secondary or preliminary vocational education. It was unclear what the implications were for higher and secondary specialized education, which had also, traditionally, been provided free of charge, yet the effect on the school system, and on its pupils, appeared to be serious indeed, putting a rubber stamp on the practice of selection and rejection, and opening the way for schools to charge fees, should they wish, for any education provided beyond the age of 15, while also endorsing the principle of the *otsev* in general.

REACTIONS TO THE PROBLEM

The 'Establishment'

The 43rd Article affair served to emphasize the relative weakness of the Ministry of Education within the government. The Minister of Education, Evgenii Tkachenko, did take a stance of opposition to the article, but his ability to influence colleagues in other ministries, or indeed the political élite in general, appeared to be limited, and he was subjected to a growing amount of criticism in the pedagogical press:

> Honestly and openly the minister admits that he saw it [the 43rd Article] in its final form and that no one had asked him for his agreement to such an article. In this case...everything becomes clear: both the weakness of the ministry's position within the government, and the fact that it [the ministry] itself openly pronounces its modesty, its unwillingness to debate, to argue.
>
> (Molodtsova, 1994)

The Teaching Force, Parents and Society at Large

Coverage in the mass media was not extensive, although it did increase steadily as the numbers of children affected by the rejectionist tendency grew. Nevertheless, the matter does not seem to have aroused a great deal of interest among the general public, apart from those who were directly concerned because their child was affected, this state of affairs highlighting once more the inadequacies of the monitoring and safety-net functions referred to earlier. With regard to the teaching force itself, a mixed reaction was observed. The pedagogical press and journals did, on the whole, conduct a vigorous campaign against the article throughout the first half of 1994,[14] receiving the support of a good number of educationalists. Alongside such opposition, however, at least some educationalists supported the notion of giving preferential treatment to the more able pupils, regardless of the consequences for those not so fortunate. The most worrying aspect of the reaction of the teaching force and the rest of society, however, was the extent of apathy towards, and ignorance of, the affair.

Among teachers whom I interviewed during this period the level of awareness of the 43rd Article and its implications was disturbingly low. While some were knowledgeable about the matter, and expressed concern over it, others stated that they had not even heard of the article. Indeed, some told me that I must be mistaken, for such an article would not have been allowed to appear in the Constitution; others noted that it did not have any significance anyway, because what is decided at the level of the government and the Parliament in Russia has no bearing on what happens in the country. Perhaps such views are not without some justification, yet concentrating on one's own micro-environment to this extent, and thus ignoring (even denying) what happens at the centre, must be seen as a dangerous phenomenon – whatever view teachers take on such issues as the 43rd Article, it is surely important that they do have an opinion on events which concern them directly as professionals.

TOWARDS A RESOLUTION?

Eventually, notwithstanding the apathy of a certain proportion of the teaching force and of much of the population, the combined efforts of *Uchitelskaya gazeta* (the teachers' newspaper), the more active representatives of the Ministry of Education and others achieved apparent success when President Yeltsin issued a decree which effectively annulled the offending article.[15] However, despite the evident sense of relief present among some in the system, the fact that a presidential decree had been made on the matter did not necessarily mean that the practice of rejection was curtailed. By the summer of 1994, it was reported (Mamedova, 1994) that over the previous two years some 1 700 000 children of school age had not attended school, while disturbing accounts were made (Orlov, 1994) that an ever-increasing number of children below the age of 14 were being excluded from their schools. Although both federal and regional authorities have tried to enforce measures which oblige schools to educate pupils in their catchment area of school age, the practice continues, surreptitiously, to this day, adding to the ever-growing number of children who find themselves, for whatever reason, outside the school walls (in late 1996, the number stood at some 2 500 000).[16]

At the same time, there have been signs that the safety net of society is beginning to be more effective, with the public prosecution service trying to address the problems of delinquency among children, identifying schools acting illegally in rejecting pupils, and bringing sanctions to bear against these establishments (Kekhlerov, 1994). Further, an increasing amount of concern has been expressed with regard to the immediate social consequences of the *otsev* and the reduction of educational provision. The link between rejection and the subsequent involvement of the juveniles in criminal activity has been stressed (Kolysko, 1994), for instance, and the need to provide social protection for such children highlighted. Attempts to implement programmes to provide this cover, however, have been hampered by a shortage of resources. Meanwhile, apart from the immediate consequences felt by those children who continue to find that there is no place for them, apparently, in the education system, and who have, consequently, to adapt to life outside school and try to survive on the limited vocational and academic knowledge and skills they have received, and apart from the associated social problems which accompany the phenomenon of the *otsev*, there are, of course, long-term implications for Russian society as a whole. Before I turn to these, however, we need to review the second 'attempt' on the school's life.

THE PRIVATIZATION ('DESTATIZATION') OF THE SCHOOLS?

The need to take the state out of education had been voiced by Dneprov in the late 1980s, who termed the desired process *razgosudarstvlenie* ('destatization'). The impulse at that time came mainly, it seemed, from a desire to attack the perceived legacy of the Soviet era, and reduce significantly, even remove, what was portrayed as the malign and all-pervading influence of the state in the sphere of education. By the mid-1990s, however, the idea had been adopted by some in the Russian government as part of their overall strategy for economic reform. Accordingly the State Committee for Property (*Goskomimushchestvo*), which was overseeing the privatization drive in Russian industry, decided that the principle of privatization could be applied to the education system as well, and a bill 'On Destatization and Demonopolization in the Sphere of Education' was duly introduced in the autumn of 1994.[17] The aims of the law, as explained by its authors, were to extend the principle of choice in education, allowing parents to select a school through the use of a voucher scheme, and thus render the school system more suitable to the perceived needs of post-Soviet Russian society.

The main fear expressed by Russian contacts whom I interviewed during this period revolved around the expectation that this Law would be used as a means of simply 'selling off' the education system to the highest bidder, regardless of whether the buyer was able to show a strong commitment to maintaining that purchase as an educational establishment, rather than using it for other, more commercially-orientated purposes. As one headteacher put it:

> We are not talking about the acquisition of a factory, its premises and its equipment. We are talking about schools, kindergartens, colleges, we are talking about the lives and the futures of the children who are supposed to study in those places. The death of the Soviet Union does not mean that a profit can be made on everything we have inherited.[18]

Perhaps it was because the educational community had become more aware of what was going on at the centre after the 43rd Article affair, or perhaps an attack on the principle of state education was seen as more serious than the extension of the idea of selection, but the reaction of educationalists towards the publication of this bill was much more audible and determined than had been the case with the 43rd Article. A counter-attack was launched with a bill 'On the Maintenance of the Status of State and Municipal Educational Establishments and a Moratorium on their Privatization' ('O sokhranenii statusa gosudarstvennykh i munitsipalnykh obrazovatelnykh uchrezhdenii i moratorii na ikh privatizatsii'), which was passed by the state Duma at the third reading. Again, however, as with the question of selection, the matter was not finally resolved. Despite a promise by Yeltsin not to privatize the school system, he later overturned the bill opposing the privatization scheme, and preparations seemed to be under way for another attempt by *Goskomimushchestvo* to push their law through. The matter of *razgosudarstvlenie*, then, while less visible during the remainder of 1995 and throughout 1996, has continued to simmer beneath the surface of the debate on education, and is likely to re-emerge in the future.

THE IMPLICATIONS: WHAT NEXT?

As I have shown in the preceding pages, civil society in Russia today has proved itself unable to perform adequately the functions that the school system requires of it, thus allowing such developments as the mass rejection of pupils and the attempt to privatize the schools to occur. What can we conclude from such episodes? We might use these developments to highlight the presence of a degree of social conflict in Russian education. The *razgosudarstvlenie* episode, for instance, was portrayed by Lyubov Rozhkova, then chair of the Duma committee on science, education and culture, as 'An attempt by certain social forces to carry out the privatization of the sphere of education' (Molodtsova, 1995). Perhaps the privatization attempt was, indeed, an example of overt conflict, or perhaps it stemmed more from a short-sighted desire to save the government some money, or perhaps it was primarily a Dneprovian onslaught on the legacy of the past, or a combination of all these factors. In the case of the 43rd Article, and indeed all developments in the school–society relationship of the past few years, it is difficult to identify with confidence any particular trend, as potential divisions and clashes of interest are obscured beneath a variety of layers of confusion, lack of clarity, ill-informed discussion and apparent consensus. Of most concern, however, is the fact that such processes have been allowed to develop in the absence of an effective debate in society. The short-term thinking of politicians and the apathy of the general public leave the school without the protection of an adequate safety net, which is so essential in the period of transition.

The potential consequences for the future of Russian society, then, are worrying. Can a country really survive if it educates an élite alone? Can the transition to the free-market economy, and the revitalization of industry and agriculture be achieved if children are denied the opportunity to receive general and vocational education, even of a basic level? Can we really be optimistic about the democratization of Russian society, when that same society is rejecting thousands of children, leaving them to fend for themselves, having decided that they are not of a sufficiently high calibre to warrant remaining in the schools? Can these children really be expected subsequently to be able to develop qualities of tolerance, understanding, respect for others and for property, not to mention expand their knowledge base, when they have been alienated by society, made to feel that they are outsiders? (Kuminova, 1996). Such issues are being addressed, or at least studied, by some sociologists, administrators, teachers, the police, politicians and others in Russia (Aleshenok et al., 1995). On the whole, however, Russia is not paying enough attention to its children – and, therefore, to its future.

NOTES

1. 'Zakon Rossiiskoi Federatsii ob obrazovanii': see *Uchitelskaya gazeta*, 4 August 1992, pp. 10–15.
2. See, for example, de Groof, 1993.
3. This chapter draws on research conducted for my, as yet unpublished, PhD thesis 'All Change? School, Reform and Society in Russia, 1991–1996', in

which I examine the course of change at all levels within the school system.

4. Under the policy of diversification of educational establishments, the Russian system now includes a bewildering array of state, semi-state and private schools, offering a diverse range of approaches to education. The term 'alternative' school was originally coined in the late 1980s to refer to schools which had incorporated methods which differed from the standard Soviet model of schooling, and tends now to be used rather indiscriminately to describe schools which claim to have introduced 'change'. An 'alternative' school may, for example, resemble a classical gymnasium or lycée (*gimnaziia* or *litsei*), or may be based on the approaches of Montessori or Steiner.

5. Dneprov was Minister of Education of the Russian Federation from 1990 to 1992. A former researcher at the Academy of Pedagogical Sciences of the USSR, from 1988 to 1990 he led a group of reform-minded educationalists in the so-called '*Ad Hoc* Research Group "School"' ('*Vremennyi Nauchno-Issledovatelskii Kollektiv-SHKOLA*', or VNIK), which conducted research on contemporary problems of education and produced a range of proposals for the radical reform of the Soviet school system. An outspoken character, he adopted an aggressive stance in forcing his ideas through, against the opposition of the conservative educational establishment. His account of this early period of reform is found in Eklof and Dneprov, 1993.

6. Interview with the author, April 1993.

7. The Soviet education system traditionally suffered from underfunding, receiving finances under the so-called 'leftover principle' (*ostatochnyi printsip*), allocated resources according to what remained after the powerful industrial and military sectors had taken their share. In the post-Soviet era such problems have intensified (see, for example, 'Dengi, dengi. Nichego, krome deneg', in *Uchitelskaya gazeta*, 6 June 1995, pp. 16–17). The funding crisis has caused severe problems in all aspects of the school's work, from repair of buildings to the purchase of teaching materials and the payment of staff salaries.

8. For discussions of the question of 'vision' in educational change, see: Fullan, 1993 and Louis and Miles, 1990.

9. See Rose, 1994, for an account of the nature of Russian society in transition.

10. See 'Vybiraem dostoinykh. Ne agitiruem ni za kogo', in *Uchitelskaya gazeta*, 30 November 1993, pp. 12–13.

11. See, for example, *Ekonomicheskie i sotsialnye peremeny: Monitoring obshchestvennogo mneniya*, 1993–7.

12. See, for example, Prelovskaya, 1996.

13. For an account of a sociological survey of the lifestyle and attitudes of Russian youth of the 1990s, which includes an analysis of these problems, see Tsymbalenko and Shcheglova, 1996.

14. See, for example, 'Kuda podatsya "15-letnim kapitanam?"', in *Vechernyaya srednyaya shkola*, No. 1, 1994, p. 3.

15. '"O garantiyakh prav grazhdan Rossiiskoi Federatsii na poluchenie obrazovaniya"' (Ukaz Prezidenta Rossiiskoi Federatsii), 1994, in *Sobranie zakonodatelstva Rossiiskoi Federatsii*, No. 11.

16. Information supplied by an official of the Ministry of General and Professional Education, November 1996.

17. 'Zakon Rossiiskoi Federatsii "O razgosudarstvlenii i demonopolizatsii v obrazovatelnoi sfere"', in *Uchitelskaya gazeta*, 13 September 1994, pp. 14–16. For a summary of the bill in English, see Sutherland 1995.
18. Conversation with the author, April 1995.

REFERENCES

Aleshenok, S., Chuprov V. and Zubok, Yu., 'Will it be Possible to Integrate Young People in a Society Undergoing Transformation?', *Prospects*, Vol. 25, No. 3, 1995, pp. 439–49.

Belova, E., 'Odarennyi rebenok na poroge shkoly', *Semya i shkola*, No. 3, 1994, pp. 10–13.

De Groof, J. (ed.), *Comments on the Law on Education of the Russian Federation* (Leuven, 1993).

'Dengi, dengi. Nichego, krome deneg', *Uchitelskaya gazeta*, 6 June 1995, pp. 16–17.

Dneprov, E., *Reform of Education in Russia and State Policy in the Educational System* (Moscow, Ministry of Education, 1992).

Eklof, B. and Dneprov, E. (eds), *Democracy in the Russian School: the Reform Movement in Education since 1984* (Boulder, CO, Westview Press, 1993).

Ekonomicheskie i sotsialnye peremeny: Monitoring obshchestvennogo mneniya, 1993–7.

Frolova, G., 'Nesostoiavshiesya?', *Uchitelskaya gazeta*, 9 November 1993, p. 18.

Fullan, M., *Change Forces* (London, Falmer Press, 1993).

Kekhlerov, F., 'Zakon na storone rebenka', *Pervoe sentyabrya*, 25 June 1994, p. 1.

Kolysko, T., 'V desyatom ty uchitsya ne budesh', *Rossiiskie vesti*, 14 July 1994, p. 8.

Konstitutsiya Rossiiskoi Federatsii (Moscow, 1995).

'Kuda podatsya "15-letnim kapitanam?"', *Vechernyaya srednyaya shkola*, No. 1, 1994, p. 3.

Kuminova, N., 'Kto pomozhet autsaideru?', *Narodnoe obrazovanie*, No. 3, 1996, pp. 67–71.

Louis, K. and Miles, M., *Improving the Urban High School: What Works and Why* (New York, Teachers' College Press, 1990).

Mamedova, T., 'V shkolakh prokhodit "chistka" neugodnykh uchashchikhsya', *Rossiiskie vesti*, 30 June 1994, p. 4.

Molodtsova, V., 'A v ostalnom, prekrasnaya markiza, vse khorosho', *Uchitelskaya gazeta*, 11 January 1994, p. 4.

Molodtsova, V., 'Znakomo li pravitelstvo s Pasterom?', *Uchitelskaya gazeta*, 11 May 1995, p. 24.

'O garantiyakh prav grazhdan Rossiiskoi Federatsii na poluchenie obrazovaniya' (Ukaz Prezidenta Rossiiskoi Federatsii), 1994, *Sobranie zakonodatelstva Rossiiskoi Federatsii*, No. 11.

Orlov, D., 'Molodezh predostavlena sama sebe', *Rossiiskie vesti*, 1 July 1994, p. 2.

Prelovskaya, I., 'Kto vybiraet?', *Semya i shkola*, No. 4, 1996, pp. 2–4.

Rigby, T., 'Russia in Search of its Future', in Saikal, A. and Maley, W. (eds), *Russia in Search of its Future* (Cambridge, Cambridge University Press, 1995), pp. 207–25.

Rose, R., *Getting by without Government: Everyday Life in a Stressful Society* (Glasgow, Centre for the Study of Public Policy, 1994).

Slobodchikova, G., 'Podrostka nelzya ostavit na ulitse', *Pervoe sentyabrya*, 2 July 1994, p. 1.

Sutherland, J., 'The Law on Denationalization and Demonopolization in the Educational Sphere: a Summary', *Education in Russia, the Independent States and Eastern Europe*, Vol. 13, No. 2, 1995, pp. 92–4.

Tsymbalenko, S. and Shcheglova, S., 'Kakie oni, podrostki devianostykh?', *Vospitanie shkolnikov*, No. 1, 1996, pp. 2–5.

'Vybiraem dostoinykh. Ne agitiruem ni za kogo', *Uchitelskaya gazeta*, 30 November 1993, pp. 12–13.

Webber, S., 'All Change? School, Reform and Society in Russia, 1991–1996' (Unpublished PhD thesis, University of Birmingham, 1997).

'Zakon Rossiiskoi Federatsii "O razgosudarstvlenii i demonopolizatsii v obrazovatelnoi sfere" ', *Uchitelskaya gazeta*, 13 September 1994, pp. 14–16.

'Zakon Rossiiskoi Federatsii ob obrazovanii', *Uchitelskaya gazeta*, 4 August 1992, pp. 10–15.

Index